T0198007

Get the eBook FREE!

(PDF, ePub, Kindle, and liveBook all included)

We believe that once you buy a book from us, you should be able to read it in any format we have available. To get electronic versions of this book at no additional cost to you, purchase and then register this book at the Manning website.

Go to https://www.manning.com/freebook and follow the instructions to complete your pBook registration.

That's it!
Thanks from Manning!

Praise for the First Edition

From the first edition of *Machine Learning with TensorFlow*:

An excellent book about TensorFlow, with many examples to get hands-on experience.
—Mikaël Dautrey, founder and infrastructure consultant, Isitix

A good way to quickly learn TensorFlow!
—David Krief, data scientist, Altansia

A great guide to machine learning. It helped launch my third career!
—William Wheeler, Java, Scala, Akka and Python developer, TekSystems

Great introduction to machine learning with TensorFlow.
—Hamish Dickson, backend developer, DriveTribe

The book helped me jumpstart TensorFlow and work effectively with it.
—Ursin Stauss, software developer, Swiss Post

Machine Learning
with TensorFlow

SECOND EDITION

CHRIS MATTMANN
FOREWORD BY SCOTT PENBERTHY

MANNING
Shelter Island

For online information and ordering of this and other Manning books, please visit
www.manning.com. The publisher offers discounts on this book when ordered in quantity.
For more information, please contact

> Special Sales Department
> Manning Publications Co.
> 20 Baldwin Road
> PO Box 761
> Shelter Island, NY 11964
> Email: orders@manning.com

Manning Publications Co.   Development editor: Toni Arritola
20 Baldwin Road   Technical development editor: Al Krinker
PO Box 761   Review editor: Aleksandar Dragosavljević
Shelter Island, NY 11964   Project editor: Lori Weidert
     Copy editor: Keir Simpson
     Proofreader: Keri Hales
     Technical proofreader: Bhagvan Kommadi
     Typesetter: Gordan Salinovic
     Cover designer: Marija Tudor

ISBN 9781617297717
Printed in the United States of America

To my wife, Lisa,
and to CJ, Heath, and Hailey

brief contents

contents

foreword

It's been two years since the publication of the first edition of *Machine Learning with TensorFlow*. Two years is a *long* time in the field of artificial intelligence.

Today, we are fascinated by a human-language model with more than 80 billion artificial neurons that have learned more than 170 billion parameters. The cost of training such a model is measured in millions of dollars. Lex Fridman of MIT projected that with the improvements in computing and algorithm design, we'll soon train a model the size of the human brain for less than a few thousand dollars. Just think—in our near-term future, we'll train an AI model with the raw capacity of the human brain for less than the cost of a Peloton stationary bike.

Writing a book to capture this fast-moving technology is fraught with risk. By the time Chris wrote a few chapters, researchers likely produced newer, more elegant approaches to solving the same problems. Yet there are perhaps only 10,000 people today who understand AI deeply. You want to jump in, learn, and start using AI in your work. What is one to do?

Buy this book—even if you have the first edition. Pay special attention to seven new chapters that walk you through fundamental techniques in AI:

- Chapter 6, "Sentiment classification: Large movie-review dataset"
- Chapter 8, "Inferring user activity from Android accelerometer data"
- Chapter 10, "Part-of-speech tagging and word-sense disambiguation"
- Chapter 12, "Applying autoencoders: The CIFAR-10 image dataset"
- Chapter 15, "Building a real-world CNN: VGG-Face and VGG-Face Lite"

- Chapter 17, "LSTMs and automatic speech recognition"
- Chapter 18, "Sequence-to-sequence models for chatbots"

Chris helps you learn how machines see, hear, speak, write, and feel within our world. He shows how machines can instantly spot that speck of dust on a windshield, much as human eyes do, with autoencoders.

The modeling techniques, which Chris describes with frustratingly delicious, hands-on detail, will persist through time. They're fundamental to framing a problem as tensors in, tensors out, flowing through a graph. Framing a problem correctly is far more important than describing the individual details of how it is solved. Expect those details to change and improve rapidly.

Armed with an appreciation of AI modeling, you'll be well-prepared to enjoy the rapid, exponential journey forward in artificial intelligence. Welcome to our world! Jump in, have some fun, crank those GPUs, and do your part to assist humanity in solving intelligence. Reimagine our world with smart machines—then make it so with TensorFlow.

Chris, thanks for taking the time to be our guide, peppered with that godawful dad humor that I just love.

SCOTT PENBERTHY, DIRECTOR OF APPLIED AI AT GOOGLE
PALO ALTO, CALIFORNIA
AUGUST 2020

It was about 15 months ago to this day that I sat down with my freshly-minted copy of the first edition of this book, opened it, and dived right in. I currently manage the Artificial Intelligence, Analytics and Innovative Development Division at NASA's Jet Propulsion Laboratory in beautiful Pasadena, California. At the time, however, I was the deputy chief technology officer (CTO) for IT, with a strong background in data science, information retrieval, and software, but only a surface knowledge of the hot topic called machine learning. I had dabbled with it, but never dived deep, as they say. Knowing Manning and its coverage of topics with practicality, in-depth examples, and most of all *humor* (I desperately seek it in *everything*; humor makes things better), I had a good feeling about the book. At the time, it had been almost a full year since I'd had the time to read a technical book, let alone sit down and try the code and exercises.

I decided that with this book, I would have to run the code, pull out pencil and paper, and draw matrices, and write things down—you know, *learn* what I was reading instead of *reading* but not learning. Whoo, boy, this book was a doozy. It was humorous—probably the easiest introduction to machine learning that I had read—and I actually understood it. I remember remarking to my wife one night, "This is why all the billionaire CEOs like [Elon] Musk are afraid of AI." I could see its application to a variety of formats, such as text, sound, vision, and speech. And it uses this amazing framework called TensorFlow that I had been hearing so much about.

There was one problem, though. The first edition of the book had a habit of throwing out a bullet point at the end of the chapter—something to the effect of "Well, you've just covered AI or ML topic X; you could try building a model for X like this state-of-the-art one and test it." I was curious and willing to devote the time. About nine weeks later, I had trained and rebuilt the Visual Geometry Group's (VGG) Face seminal model and found a whole bunch of improvements and rebuilt the dataset that no longer existed. I had written code to take Android cell phone data and infer the user's activity, such as running or walking. I had built a robust sentiment classifier that would have scored in the top 100 results on Kaggle during the Bag of Popcorn Movie Challenge (since closed).

Ultimately, I had built enough code, notes, and material for a second edition of this book. I collected the data, wrote Jupyter notebooks and documented them, and fixed the bugs in the code; even in the two years between Nishant Shukla's first edition of the book and this one, TensorFlow had made around 20 releases in the 1.x branch, and the 2.x version was about to land (as it did while I wrote this book).

All the code, examples, bug fixes, data downloading, ancillary software library installations, and Dockerization are what you get in this book. Don't think of it as *yet another* TensorFlow book; I could have easily called it *Machine Learning with TensorFlow and Friends, 2nd Edition: NumPy, SciPy, Matplotlib, Jupyter, Pandas, Tika, SKLearn, TQDM, and More.* You need all these elements to do data science and machine learning. To be clear, this book isn't only about TensorFlow; it's a book about machine learning and how to do it: how to clean data, build a model and train it, and (most importantly) how to evaluate it.

I hope you enjoy machine learning as much as I do now and will forever. This journey hasn't been easy, including being caught in a global pandemic while writing, but I've never been more optimistic, as I've seen the light and power of what artificial intelligence and machine learning can do. I hope that you will too, after reading this book!

acknowledgments

I'd be remiss without thanking Nishant Shukla, who wrote the first edition of this book. His clever, witty discussion was an inspiration to undertake the journey that led me to create this book.

I would like to sincerely thank my acquisitions editor, Michael Stephens, for believing in my book proposal and sticking with my insistence, passion, and vision for the work. The book is better for your strong feedback and critiques. Thanks to Marjan Bace, the publisher of Manning, for greenlighting the book idea and giving this author another shot 10 years after his first book.

Toni Arritola, my development editor, has been my biggest cheerleader and strongest advocate for ensuring that the book is a success. Her belief in me, the vision, and the process, and our trust in each other, made this book an amazing one. Toni's challenges to my AI and data science jargon and her strength in editing and reformulating my 50,000-feet concepts into practical solutions and problem solving make machine learning with TensorFlow a consumable treat, regardless of your knowledge of coding, AI, or ML. Thanks for her calmness, wisdom, and heart.

Thank you to my technical development editor, Al Krinker, for his technical editing and suggestions that no doubt improved the book.

To all the reviewers: Alain Couniot, Alain Lompo, Ariel Gamino, Bhagvan Kommadi, David Jacobs, Dinesh Ghanta, Edward Hartley, Eriks Zelenka, Francisco José Lacueva, Hilde Van Gysel, Jeon Kang, Johnny L. Hopkins, Ken W. Alger, Lawrence Nderu, Marius Kreis, Michael Bright, Teresa Fontanella de Santis, Vishwesh Ravi Shrimali, and Vittal Damaraju—your suggestions helped make this a better book. In addition, I would like to thank the anonymous reviewers who provided valuable feedback and suggestions, and encouraged me to strive for a better installation, which led to the comprehensive Docker install and branch in the repository and to better organization of the code overall.

I would like to thank Candace Gillhoolley for organizing what seemed like dozens of podcasts, promotions, and connections in promoting the book and getting the word out.

Thanks to my colleagues and teammates in the industry for spending their own time reading some early drafts of the book chapters and providing critical feedback. I especially would like to thank Philip Southam for believing in me and doing the early work on Docker installs, and Rob Royce for working the TensorFlow2 branch and being interested in the code. I also deeply thank Zhao Zhang for helping to flesh out the CNN chapter ideas and Thamme Gowda for providing pointers and discussions.

Finally, I thank my amazing wife, Lisa Mattmann, who nearly a decade later let me do what I promised her I wouldn't do again after my last book (and before that, my PhD dissertation). I have a terrible track record on staying away from writing, but this time was different, in that after nearly 20 years together, she knows me and knows that writing is my passion. Thank you, honey.

I dedicate this book to my children. My eldest son, Christian John (CJ) Mattmann, demonstrated interest in the sentiment analysis chapter and text processing. He's a chip off the old block, if you will. I hope that, someday, he'll have the gumption to run the code and perform his own even-better sentiment analysis and ML. I suspect that he will. Thanks to Heath and Hailey Mattmann for understanding when Daddy was up late at night finishing the book and working through chapters and coding. This one's for you!

about this book

To get the most benefit from this book, you'll want to approach it as two parts: a sprinkle of math and theory, followed by practical applications with Python, TensorFlow, and friends. When I reference uses of machine-learning techniques such as regression or classification in particular domains and cite example datasets or problems, think about how you can use those data and/or problem domains to test the new machine learning you are using. That's what I did as a reader of the first edition, poring over the chapters and then applying the "what ifs" and pointers to datasets to create new chapters for this edition, based on the notebooks I made and the work I did.

The whole process took weeks or months to complete for each chapter. I've captured all the updates in the second edition. As you progress through the early parts of the book, you will see that the order of chapters remains similar to that of the first edition. After regression, however, there is now a chapter on applying regression to the suggested 311 service exercises from the first edition. Likewise, the second edition has a full chapter on using classification to perform sentiment analysis on the Netflix movie reviews data.

Throughout the rest of the book, you will explore topics including unsupervised clustering, hidden Markov models (HMMs), autoencoders, deep reinforcement learning, convolutional neural networks (CNNs), and CNN classifiers. I've also added a chapter on taking positional data from Android phones and inferring what type of activity the user was doing, as well as a chapter on re-creating the VGG-Face facial identification CNN model. To perform some of the later exercises, you will want access to a GPU, either locally on your laptop or via some cloud access at Google, Amazon, or one of the big providers. I'll help you along the way.

Please be sure to post any questions, comments, or suggestions you have about the book in the liveBook Discussion Forum (https://livebook.manning.com/book/machine-learning-with-tensorflow-second-edition/discussion). Your feedback is important in keeping the book up-to-date and ensuring that it's the best book possible. I look forward to helping you in your machine-learning odyssey!

How this book is organized: A roadmap

This book is divided into three parts.

Part 1, "Your machine-learning rig," explains the general theory of machine learning and gives some motivation for its massive uptick and use in today's world, grounding the discussion in one of the most widely used frameworks for implementing machine learning: TensorFlow.

- Chapter 1 introduces machine learning and explains it as teaching a computer to classify, predict, aggregate, and identify based on input images, text, sound, and other formats.
- Chapter 2 covers TensorFlow essentials and introduces the reader to the TensorFlow framework; the concept of tensors; graph-based execution; and the process of creating, training, and saving models.

Part 2, "Core learning algorithms," gives you your machine-learning toolbox: regression for learning continuous value prediction or classification for discrete categorical prediction and inference. The chapters in this part are paired; one chapter focuses on a tool and general theory, and the following chapter provides a detailed example problem involving data cleaning, preparation, training, inference, and evaluation. Techniques taught include regression, classification, unsupervised clustering, and HMMs. All these techniques are explainable in that you can explain the steps of the machine-learning process and use math and statistics directly to evaluate their value.

- Chapter 3 covers regression, which is a modeling problem involving continuous input and a possibly discrete or continuous output.
- Chapter 4 applies regression to real-world call center data from New York City's 311 service, which provides help to citizens. You will collect a dataset of weekly call volumes and use regression to predict with high accuracy the number of calls expected per week.
- Chapter 5 covers classification, which is a modeling problem that takes as input discrete or continuous data and outputs single or multiple categorical class labels.
- Chapter 6 uses classification on Netflix and IMDb movie-review data to build a movie sentiment classifier based on reviews that identify a movie as positive or negative.

- Chapter 7 demonstrates unsupervised clustering, showing automatic grouping of input data into discrete categories without labels.
- Chapter 8 applies automatic clustering to input Android phone positional data to show you how to infer user activity based on phone accelerometer positional data.
- Chapter 9 eases you into the topic of HMMs and shows how indirect evidence can lead to explainable decisions.
- Chapter 10 applies HMMs to text input to disambiguate classification of parts of speech in text when it's hard to tell whether *engineer* is a noun or a verb. (When isn't it, right?)

The final part of the book covers the neural network paradigm that is sweeping the community: helping cars to drive automatically, physicians to diagnose cancer, and phones to use biometrics like your face to decide whether you can log in. A neural network is a particular machine-learning model inspired by the human brain and its structure as a graph of neurons that fire based on input, emitting predictions, confidence, beliefs, structure, and shapes. Neurons map nicely to the concept of *tensors*, which are nodes in a graph that allow information such as scalar values, matrices, and vectors to *flow* through them, be manipulated, transformed, and so on—hence, Google's framework name *TensorFlow*. This part of the book covers autoencoders for compressing and representing input using hidden layers, CNNs for automatically classifying objects and faces in images, and recurrent neural networks (RNNs) for time-series data or speech data converted to text. Part 3 also covers the seq2seq RNN architecture, which can be used to associate input text and statements with responses from an intelligent digital assistant such as a chatbot. The last chapter in the book applies neural networks to evaluating the utility of a robot folding cloth based on input video and images.

- Chapter 11 covers autoencoders, which take input data and compact it into a much smaller representation by using hidden layers in a neural network.
- Chapter 12 explores several types of autoencoders, including stacked and denoising autoencoders, and demonstrates how the network learns a compact representation of images from the CIFAR-10 dataset.
- Chapter 13 introduces the reader to a different kind of network: a deep reinforcement learning network, which learns an optimal policy for investing in a stock portfolio.
- Chapter 14 is all about CNN, a neural architecture inspired by the visual cortex. CNNs use several convolutional filters to develop a compact representation of input images and their higher- and lower-order features.
- Chapter 15 teaches you how to build two real-world CNNs: one for the CIFAR-10 dataset for object recognition and another for a facial recognition system called VGG-Face.

- Chapter 16 covers the RNN paradigm for time-series data and represents the decisions of neural networks over time, not only in a particular instance.
- Chapter 17 shows you how to build a real-world RNN model type called long short-term memory (LSTM) for automatic speech to text recognition, rebuilding the deep-speech model architecture made famous by Baidu.
- Chapter 18 reuses RNNs and demonstrates the seq2seq architecture, which can be used to build an intelligent chatbot that responds to user chat with realistic responses trained on previous questions and answers.
- Chapter 19 rounds out the book by exploring the utility landscape, using neural architectures to create image embeddings from videos of cloth-folding and then use those embeddings to infer the utility of each step of the task over time.

About the code

This book contains many examples of source code, both in numbered listings and inline with normal text. In both cases, source code is formatted in a `fixed-width font like this` to separate it from ordinary text. Sometimes code is also **in bold** to highlight code that has changed from previous steps in the chapter, such as when a new feature adds to an existing line of code.

In many cases, the original source code has been reformatted; we've added line breaks and reworked indentation to accommodate the available page space in the book. In rare cases, even this was not enough, and listings include line-continuation markers (➥). Additionally, comments in the source code have often been removed from the listings when the code is described in the text. Code annotations accompany many of the listings, highlighting important concepts.

Many graphics in this book include color, which can be viewed in the e-book versions. To get your free e-book in PDF, ePub, or Kindle format, go to http://mng.bz/JxPo to register your print book.

The code for the book is organized by chapter as a series of Jupyter notebooks. The associated Docker container that you can pull from Docker Hub or build yourself will automatically install Python 3 and Python 2.7 and TensorFlow 1.15 and 1.14, respectively, so that you can run all the examples in the book. Listings in the book are clearly delineated and numbered; they map to the chapters and listing-numbered .ipynb files in the GitHub repo at http://mng.bz/MoJn, and from the Manning website at https://www.manning.com/books/machine-learning-with-tensorflow-second-edition.

The Docker file automatically downloads and installs third-party libraries (the *and friends* part of *TensorFlow and friends*, as referenced through the book) and the necessary datasets from a remote Dropbox link that you need to run all the code. You may also run the download scripts for libraries and data outside the Docker container if you installed locally in your own Python environments.

The author will be happy to receive reported issues in the code on GitHub and even happier to receive pull requests for any issues you discover. There is also an active effort to port the listings in the book to TensorFlow2. You can find the current work in the tensorflow2 branch at https://github.com/chrismattmann/MLwithTensorFlow2ed/tree/tensorflow2.

liveBook discussion forum

Purchase of *Machine Learning with TensorFlow* includes free access to a private web forum run by Manning Publications where you can make comments about the book, ask technical questions, and receive help from the author and from other users. To access the forum, go to https://livebook.manning.com/book/machine-learning-with-tensorflow-second-edition/discussion. You can also learn more about Manning's forums and the rules of conduct at https://livebook.manning.com/#!/discussion.

Manning's commitment to our readers is to provide a venue where a meaningful dialogue between individual readers and between readers and the author can take place. It is not a commitment to any specific amount of participation on the part of the author, whose contribution to the forum remains voluntary (and unpaid). We suggest you try asking the author some challenging questions lest his interest stray! The forum and the archives of previous discussions will be accessible from the publisher's website as long as the book is in print.

about the author

CHRIS MATTMANN is division manager of the Artificial Intelligence, Analytics and Innovative Development Organization at NASA's Jet Propulsion Lab, where he has been recognized as JPL's first principal scientist in the area of data science. Chris has applied TensorFlow to challenges he's faced at NASA, including building an implementation of Google's Show & Tell algorithm for image captioning using TensorFlow. He contributes to open source projects as a former director of the Apache Software Foundation and teaches graduate courses in content detection and analysis, as well as search engines and information retrieval, at the University of Southern California.

about the cover illustration

The figure on the cover of *Machine Learning with TensorFlow* is captioned "Man from the island Pag, Dalmatia, Croatia." The illustration is taken from the reproduction, published in 2006, of a nineteenth-century collection of costumes and ethnographic descriptions titled *Dalmatia* by Professor Frane Carrara (1812–1854), an archaeologist and historian, and the first director of the Museum of Antiquity in Split, Croatia. The illustrations were obtained from a helpful librarian at the Ethnographic Museum (formerly the Museum of Antiquity), itself situated in the Roman core of the medieval center of Split, in the ruins of Emperor Diocletian's retirement palace from around AD 304. The book includes finely-colored illustrations of figures from different regions of Dalmatia, accompanied by descriptions of the costumes and of everyday life. Dress codes have changed since the nineteenth century, and the diversity by region, so rich at the time, has faded away. It is now hard to tell apart the inhabitants of different continents, let alone different towns or regions. Perhaps we have traded cultural diversity for a more varied personal life—certainly for a more varied and fast-paced technological life.

At a time when it's hard to tell one computer book from another, Manning celebrates the inventiveness and initiative of the computer business with book covers based on the rich diversity of regional life of two centuries ago, brought back to life by illustrations from collections such as this one.

Part 1

Your machine-learning rig

The first rule of machine learning is seeing its use in everyday life. From deciding which car is better based on features rather than pictures of it, to deciding based on pictures whether a robot is folding clothes correctly, to learning to hear by modeling the auditory function of the brain to turn sound waves into text representations your brain can understand, machine learning is everywhere!

To do machine learning, you need data—many times, lots of it, but not all the time. That data is often not prepared the right way and needs to be cleaned up. You'll also need some suppositions or hypotheses about that data that you'd like to test and evaluate. Speaking of which, you also need tools to evaluate how well your machine learning is making predictions, or grouping things, or ranking and rating things. All these components are part of your machine-learning rig, which you will use to take in input data and answer questions about that data in meaningful ways that you can evaluate.

The first part of the book focuses on the components of the machine-learning rig, showing how Google's TensorFlow framework, along with a set of associated machine-learning tools and utilities in the Python programming language, can help you apply and use the machine-learning rig for the real-world problems that you'll explore in the remainder of the book.

1

A machine-learning
odyssey

This chapter covers

- Machine-learning fundamentals
- Data representation, features, and vector norms
- Why TensorFlow?

Have you ever wondered whether there are limits to what computer programs can solve? Nowadays, computers appear to do a lot more than unravel mathematical equations. In the past half-century, programming has become the ultimate tool for automating tasks and saving time. But how much can we automate, and how do we go about doing so?

Can a computer observe a photograph and say, "Aha—I see a lovely couple walking over a bridge under an umbrella in the rain"? Can software make medical decisions as accurately as trained professionals can? Can software make better predictions about stock market performance than humans could? The achievements of the past decade hint that the answer to all these questions is a resounding yes and that the implementations appear to have a common strategy.

Recent theoretical advances coupled with newly available technologies have enabled anyone with access to a computer to attempt their own approach to solving these incredibly hard problems. (Okay, not just anyone, but that's why you're reading this book, right?)

A programmer no longer needs to know the intricate details of a problem to solve it. Consider converting speech to text. A traditional approach may involve understanding the biological structure of human vocal cords to decipher utterances by using many hand-designed, domain-specific, ungeneralizable pieces of code. Nowadays, it's possible to write code that looks at many examples and figures out how to solve the problem, given enough time and examples.

Take another example: identifying the sentiment of text in a book or a tweet as positive or negative. Or you may want to identify the text even more granularly, such as text that implies the writer's likes or loves, things that they hate or is angry or sad about. Past approaches to performing this task were limited to scanning the text in question, looking for harsh words such as *ugly*, *stupid*, and *miserable* to indicate anger or sadness, or punctuation such as exclamation marks, which could mean happy or angry but not exactly in-between.

Algorithms learn from data, similar to the way that humans learn from experience. Humans learn by reading books, observing situations, studying in school, exchanging conversations, and browsing websites, among other means. How can a machine possibly develop a brain capable of learning? There's no definitive answer, but world-class researchers have developed intelligent programs from different angles. Among the implementations, scholars have noticed recurring patterns in solving these kinds of problems that led to a standardized field that we today label *machine learning* (ML).

As the study of ML has matured, the tools for performing machine learning have become more standardized, robust, high-performing, and scalable. This is where TensorFlow comes in. This software library has an intuitive interface that lets programmers dive into using complex ML ideas.

Keeping up with the versions: TensorFlow 2 and beyond

This book is standardized on two versions of TensorFlow from the 1.x series. Version 1.15, which is the latest release in the 1.x series, works well with Python 3. In chapters 7 and 19, you'll read about a few examples that require Python 2; for that reason, TensorFlow 1.14 is required.

Also, a complete port of the listings and code that address TensorFlow 2 was released while this book was under development. (See the appendix for the details.) You'll notice that 85–90% of the code for the listings that work in TensorFlow 2 is the same. The main reason is that the data cleaning, gathering, preparation, and evaluation code is fully reusable because it uses accompanying ML libraries like Scikit and Matplotlib.

The TensorFlow 2 version of the listings incorporates new features, including *always eager* execution and updated package names for the optimizers and training. The new listings work well in Python 3; I welcome your feedback on them if you give them a try. You can find the TensorFlow 2 listing code at https://github.com/chrismattmann/MLwithTensorFlow2ed/tree/master/TFv2.

Chapter 2 presents the ins and outs of this library, and every chapter thereafter explains how to use TensorFlow for the various ML applications.

1.1 Machine-learning fundamentals

Have you ever tried to explain to someone how to swim? Describing the rhythmic joint movements and fluid patterns is overwhelming in its complexity. Similarly, some software problems are too complicated for us to easily wrap our minds around. For this task, machine learning may be the tool to use.

Full speed ahead!

Machine learning is a relatively young technology, so imagine that you're a geometer in Euclid's era, paving the way to a newly discovered field. Or consider yourself to be a physicist during the time of Newton, possibly pondering something equivalent to general relativity for the field of machine learning.

Handcrafting carefully tuned algorithms to get the job done was once the only way of building software. From a simplistic point of view, traditional programming assumes a deterministic output for each input. Machine learning, on the other hand, can solve a class of problems for which the input-output correspondences aren't well understood.

Machine learning is characterized by software that learns from previous experiences. Such a computer program improves performance as more and more examples are available. The hope is that if you throw enough data at this machinery, it'll learn patterns and produce intelligent results for newly-fed input.

Trusting and explaining machine-learning output

Pattern detection is a trait that's no longer unique to humans. The explosive growth of computer clock speed and memory led to an unusual situation: computers can now be used to make predictions, catch anomalies, rank items, and label images automatically. This new set of tools provides intelligent answers to ill-defined problems, but at the subtle cost of trust. Would you trust a computer algorithm to dispense vital medical advice such as whether to perform heart surgery or, more important, to explain *why* it gave you such vital medical advice?

There's no place for mediocre machine-learning solutions. Human trust is too fragile, and our algorithms must be robust against doubt. Follow along closely and carefully in this chapter.

Another name for machine learning is *inductive learning*, because the code is trying to infer structure from data alone. The process is like going on vacation in a foreign country and reading a local fashion magazine to figure out how to dress. You can develop an idea of the culture from images of people wearing local articles of clothing. You're learning *inductively*.

You may never have used such an approach when programming, because inductive learning isn't always necessary. Consider the task of determining whether the sum of two arbitrary numbers is even or odd. Sure, you can imagine training a machine-learning algorithm with millions of training examples (outlined in figure 1.1), but you certainly know that this approach would be overkill. A more direct approach can easily do the trick.

The sum of two odd numbers is always an even number. Convince yourself: take any two odd numbers, add them, and check whether the sum is an even number. Here's how you can prove that fact directly:

- For any integer n, the formula $2n + 1$ produces an odd number. Moreover, any odd number can be written as $2n + 1$ for some value n. The number 3 can be written as $2(1) + 1$. And the number 5 can be written as $2(2) + 1$.

- Suppose that we have two odd numbers, $2n + 1$ and $2m + 1$, where n and m are integers. Adding two odd numbers yields $(2n + 1) + (2m + 1) = 2n + 2m + 2 = 2(n + m + 1)$. This number is even because 2 times anything is even.

Input		Output
$x_1 = (2, 2)$	→	$y_1 = $ Even
$x_2 = (3, 2)$	→	$y_2 = $ Odd
$x_3 = (2, 3)$	→	$y_3 = $ Odd
$x_4 = (3, 3)$	→	$y_4 = $ Even
...		...

Figure 1.1   Each pair of integers, when summed, results in an even or odd number. The input and output correspondences listed are called the *ground-truth dataset*.

Likewise, we see that the sum of two even numbers is an even number: $2m + 2n = 2(m + n)$. Last, we also deduce that the sum of an even with an odd is an odd number: $2m + (2n + 1) = 2(m + n) + 1$. Figure 1.2 presents this logic more clearly.

That's it! With absolutely no use of machine learning, you can solve this task on any pair of integers someone throws at you. Directly applying mathematical rules can solve this problem. But in ML algorithms, we can treat the inner logic as a *black box*, meaning that the logic happening inside may not be obvious to interpret, as depicted in figure 1.3.

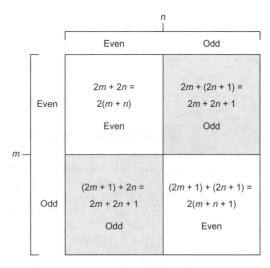

Figure 1.2   The inner logic behind how the output response corresponds to the input pairs

Figure 1.3 An ML approach to solving problems can be thought of as tuning the parameters of a black box until it produces satisfactory results.

1.1.1 Parameters

Sometimes, the best way to devise an algorithm that transforms an input to its corresponding output is too complicated. If the input is a series of numbers representing a grayscale image, for example, you can imagine the difficulty of writing an algorithm to label every object in the image. Machine learning comes in handy when the inner workings aren't well understood. It provides us a toolkit for writing software without defining every detail of the algorithm. The programmer can leave some values undecided and let the machine-learning system figure out the best values by itself.

The undecided values are called *parameters*, and the description is referred to as the *model*. Your job is to write an algorithm that observes existing examples to figure out how to best tune parameters to achieve the best model. Wow, that's a mouthful! But don't worry; this concept will be a recurring motif.

> **Machine learning might solve a problem without much insight**
>
> By mastering the art of inductive problem solving, we wield a double-edged sword. Although ML algorithms may perform well when solving specific tasks, tracing the steps of deduction to understand why a result is produced may not be as clear. An elaborate machine-learning system learns thousands of parameters, but untangling the meaning behind each parameter sometimes isn't the prime directive. With that in mind, I assure you that there's a world of magic to unfold.
>
> **Exercise 1.1**
>
> Suppose that you've collected three months' worth of stock market prices. You'd like to predict future trends to outsmart the system for monetary gains. Without using ML, how would you go about solving this problem? (As you'll see in chapter 13, this problem becomes approachable with ML techniques.)
>
> **Answer**
>
> Believe it or not, hard-designed rules are a common way to define stock market trading strategies. An algorithm as simple as "If the price drops 5%, buy some stocks" are often used. Notice that no machine learning is involved—only traditional logic.
>
> **Exercise 1.2**
>
> The National Aeronautics and Space Administration (NASA) launches satellites into space, and the satellites collect data that we call *telemetry*. Sometimes, anomalies in the collected data indicates that something was wrong with the instrument or the conditions under which the data was collected. For simplification, assume that telemetry data is a time-based sequence of numbers. To detect an anomaly today, most approaches use simple thresholds, or max or min values for those numbers, to trigger alarms. What's a better way to trigger alarms and detect anomalies, using ML?

(continued)

Answer

You could record a series of nominal NASA telemetry data at each time step—say, 5 seconds. Then take the data values, and whenever they trigger an alarm, record 1 (anomaly); otherwise, record 0 (normal). Congrats—you've built a ground-truth dataset that you can feed into any one of the predictive models you'll learn about later in this book, such as regression, or classification. You could even build a deep learning model. See, isn't machine learning fun?

1.1.2   *Learning and inference*

Suppose that you're trying to bake desserts in an oven. If you're new to the kitchen, it can take days to come up with both the right combination and perfect ratio of ingredients to make something that tastes great. By recording a recipe, you can remember how to repeat a dessert.

Machine learning shares the idea of recipes. Typically, we examine an algorithm in two stages: *learning* and *inference*. The objective of the learning stage is to describe the data, which is called the *feature vector*, and summarize it in a *model*. The model is our recipe. In effect, the model is a program with a couple of open interpretations, and the data helps disambiguate it.

> **NOTE**   A *feature vector* is a practical simplification of data. You can think of it as a sufficient summary of real-world objects in a list of attributes. The learning and inference steps rely on the feature vector instead of the data directly.

Similar to the way that recipes can be shared and used by other people, the learned model is reused by other software. The learning stage is the most time-consuming. Running an algorithm may take hours, if not days or weeks, to converge into a useful model, as you will see when you begin to build your own in chapter 3. Figure 1.4 outlines the learning pipeline.

The inference stage uses the model to make intelligent remarks about never-before-seen data. This stage is like using a recipe you found online. The process of inference typically takes orders of magnitude less time than learning; inference can be

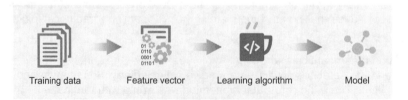

Training data   Feature vector   Learning algorithm   Model

Figure 1.4   The learning approach generally follows a structured recipe. First, the dataset needs to be transformed into a representation—most often, a list of features—that the learning algorithm can use. Then the learning algorithm chooses a model and efficiently searches for the model's parameters.

Figure 1.5 **The inference approach generally uses a model that has already been learned or given. After converting data into a usable representation, such as a feature vector, this approach uses the model to produce intended output.**

fast enough to work on real-time data. Inference is all about testing the model on new data and observing performance in the process, as shown in figure 1.5.

1.2   *Data representation and features*

Data is a first-class citizen of machine learning. Computers are nothing more than sophisticated calculators, so the data we feed our machine-learning systems must be mathematical objects such as scalars, vectors, matrices, and graphs.

The basic theme in all forms of representation is *features*, which are observable properties of an object:

- *Vectors* have a flat and simple structure, and are the typical embodiments of data in most real-world machine-learning applications. A *scalar* is a single element in the vector. Vectors have two attributes: a natural number representing the dimension of the vector, and a type (such as real numbers, integers, and so on). Examples of 2D vectors of integers are (1, 2) and (–6, 0); similarly, a scalar could be 1 or the character *a*. Examples of 3D vectors of real numbers are (1.1, 2.0, 3.9) and (Π, $\Pi/2$, $\Pi/3$). You get the idea: a collection of numbers of the same type. In a program that uses machine learning, a vector measures a property of the data, such as color, density, loudness, or proximity—anything you can describe with a series of numbers, one for each thing being measured.

- Moreover, a vector of vectors is a *matrix*. If each feature vector describes the features of one object in your dataset, the matrix describes all the objects; each item in the outer vector is a node that's a list of features of one object.

- Graphs, on the other hand, are more expressive. A *graph* is a collection of objects (*nodes*) that can be linked with *edges* to represent a network. A graphical structure enables representing relationships between objects, such as in a friendship network or a navigation route of a subway system. Consequently, they're tremendously harder to manage in machine-learning applications. In this book, our input data will rarely involve a graphical structure.

Feature vectors are practical simplifications of real-world data, which can be too complicated to deal with. Instead of attending to every little detail of a data item, using a feature vector is a practical simplification. A car in the real world, for example, is much more than the text used to describe it. A car salesman is trying to sell you the car, not the intangible words spoken or written. Those words are abstract concepts, similar to the way that feature vectors are summaries of the data.

The following scenario explains this concept further. When you're in the market for a new car, keeping tabs on every minor detail of different makes and models is essential. After all, if you're about to spend thousands of dollars, you may as well do so diligently. You'd likely record a list of the features of each car and compare these features. This ordered list of features is the feature vector.

When shopping for cars, you might find comparing mileage to be more lucrative than comparing something less relevant to your interest, such as weight. The number of features to track also must be right—not too few, or you'll lose information you care about, and not too many, or they'll be unwieldy and time consuming to keep track of. This tremendous effort to select both the number of measurements and which measurements to compare is called *feature engineering* or *feature selection*. Depending on which features you examine, the performance of your system can fluctuate dramatically. Selecting the right features to track can make up for a weak learning algorithm.

When training a model to detect cars in an image, for example, you'll gain an enormous performance and speed improvement if you first convert the image to grayscale. By providing some of your own bias when preprocessing the data, you end up helping the algorithm, because it won't need to learn that colors don't matter when detecting cars. The algorithm can instead focus on identifying shapes and textures, which will lead to much faster learning than trying to process colors as well.

The general rule of thumb in ML is that more data produces better results. But the same isn't always true of having more features. Perhaps counterintuitively, if the number of features you're tracking is too high, performance may suffer. Populating the space of all data with representative samples requires exponentially more data as the dimension of the feature vector increases. As a result, feature engineering, as depicted in figure 1.6, is one of the most significant problems in ML.

Curse of dimensionality

To model real-world data accurately, we clearly need more than one or two data points. But how much data depends on a variety of things, including the number of dimensions in the feature vector. Adding too many features causes the number of data points required to describe the space to increase exponentially. That's why we can't design a 1,000,000-dimension feature vector to exhaust all possible factors and then expect the algorithm to learn a model. This phenomenon is called the *curse of dimensionality*.

You may not appreciate this fact right away, but something consequential happens when you decide which features are worth observing. For centuries, philosophers have pondered the meaning of *identity*; you may not immediately realize that you've come up with a definition of *identity* through your choice of specific features.

Figure 1.6 Feature engineering is the process of selecting relevant features for the task.

Imagine writing a machine-learning system to detect faces in an image. Suppose that one of the necessary features for something to be a face is the presence of two eyes. Implicitly, a face is now defined as something with eyes. Do you realize the kind of trouble that this definition can get you into? If a photo of a person shows them blinking, your detector won't find a face, because it can't find two eyes. The algorithm would fail to detect a face when a person is blinking. The definition of a face was inaccurate to begin with, and it's apparent from the poor detection results.

Nowadays, especially with the tremendous speed at which capabilities like smart vehicles and autonomous drones are evolving, identity bias, or simply bias, in ML is becoming a big concern, because these capabilities can cause loss of human life if they screw up. Consider a smart vehicle that has never seen a person in a wheelchair because the training data never included those examples, so the smart car does not stop when the wheelchair enters the crosswalk. What if the training data for a company's drone delivering your package never saw a female wearing a hat before, and all other training instances with things that look like hats were places to land? The hat—and, more important, the person—may be in grave danger!

The identity of an object is decomposed into the features from which it's composed. If the features you're tracking for one car match the corresponding features of another car, they may as well be indistinguishable from your perspective. You'd need to add another feature to the system to tell the cars apart; otherwise, you'll think they're the same item (like the drone landing on the poor lady's hat). When handcrafting features, you must take great care not to fall into this philosophical predicament of identity.

Exercise 1.3

Suppose that you're teaching a robot how to fold clothes. The perception system sees a shirt lying on a table, as shown in the following figure. You'd like to represent the shirt as a vector of features so that you can compare it with different clothes. Decide which features are most useful to track. (Hint: What types of words do retailers use to describe their clothing online?)

A robot is trying to fold a shirt. What are good features of the shirt to track?

Answer

The width, height, x-symmetry score, y-symmetry score, and flatness are good features to observe when folding clothes. Color, cloth texture, and material are mostly irrelevant.

Exercise 1.4

Now, instead of detecting clothes, you ambitiously decide to detect arbitrary objects; the following figure shows some examples. What are some salient features that can easily differentiate objects?

Here are images of three objects: a lamp, a pair of pants, and a dog. What are some good features that you should record to compare and differentiate objects?

Answer

Observing brightness and reflection may help differentiate the lamp from the other two objects. The shape of pants often follows a predictable template, so shape would be another good feature to track. Finally, texture may be a salient feature for differentiating the picture of a dog from the other two classes.

Feature engineering is a refreshingly philosophical pursuit. For those who enjoy thought-provoking escapades into the meaning of self, I invite you to meditate on feature selection, because it's still an open problem. Fortunately for the rest of you, to alleviate extensive debates, recent advances have made it possible to automatically determine which features to track. You'll be able to try this process yourself in chapter 7.

Now consider the problem of a doctor looking at a set of N 244 × 244 (width × height) squamous-cell images like the ones shown in figure 1.7 and trying to determine whether they indicate the presence of cancer. Some images definitely indicate cancer; others do not. The doctor may have a set of historical patient images that he could examine and learn from over time, so that when he sees new images, he develops his own representation model of what cancer looks like.

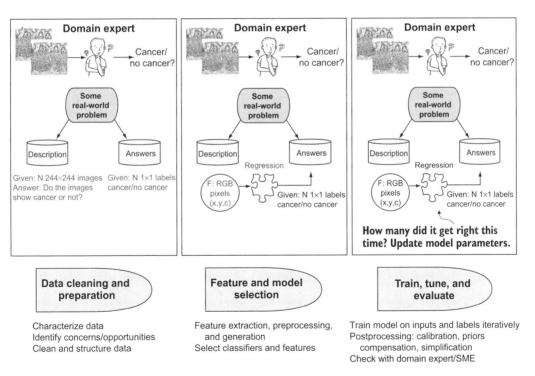

Figure 1.7   The machine-learning process. From left to right, doctors try to determine whether images representing biopsies of cells indicate cancer in their patients.

Feature vectors are used in both learning and inference

The interplay between learning and inference provides a complete picture of a machine-learning system, as shown in the following figure. The first step is representing real-world data in a feature vector. We can represent images by a vector of numbers corresponding to pixel intensities, for example. (We'll explore how to represent images in greater detail in future chapters.) We can show our learning algorithm the ground-truth labels (such as Bird or Dog) along with each feature vector. With enough data, the algorithm generates a learned model. We can use this model on other real-world data to uncover previously unknown labels.

Feature vectors are a representation of real-world data used by both the learning and inference components of machine learning. The input to the algorithm isn't the real-world image directly, but its feature vector.

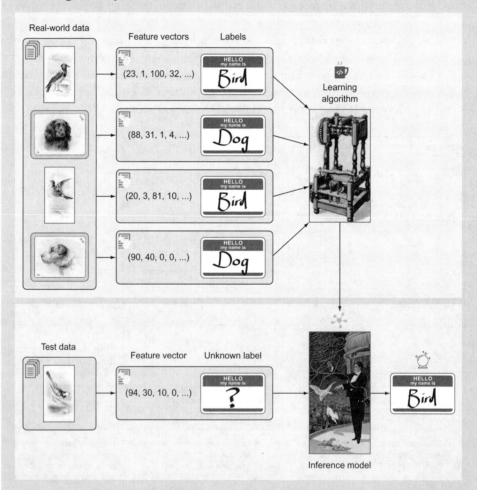

Feature vectors are representations of real-world data used by both the learning and inference components of machine learning. The input to the algorithm isn't the real-world image directly, but its feature vector.

In machine learning, we are trying to emulate this model building process. First, we take N input squamous cancer cell 244×244 images from the historical patient data and prepare the problem by lining up the images with their associated labels (cancer or no cancer). We call this stage the data cleaning and preparation stage of machine learning. What follows is the process of identifying important features. Features include the image pixel intensities, or early value for each x, y, and c, or (244, 244, 3), for the image's height, width, and three-channel red/green/blue (RGB) color. The model creates the mapping between those feature values and the desired label output: cancer or no cancer.

1.3 Distance metrics

If you have feature vectors of cars you may want to buy, you can figure out which two cars are most similar by defining a distance function on the feature vectors. Comparing similarities between objects is an essential component of machine learning. Feature vectors allow us to represent objects so that we may compare them in a variety of ways. A standard approach is to use the *Euclidian distance*, which is the geometric interpretation you may find most intuitive when thinking about points in space.

Suppose that we have two feature vectors, $x = (x_1, x_2, \ldots, x_n)$ and $y = (y_1, y_2, \ldots, y_n)$. The Euclidian distance $\|x - y\|$ is calculated with the following equation, which scholars call the *L2 norm*:

$$\sqrt{(x_1 + y_1)^2 + (x_2 - y_2)^2 + \ldots + (x_n - y_n)^2}$$

The Euclidian distance between $(0, 1)$ and $(1, 0)$ is

$$\|(0, 1) - (1, 0)\|$$

$$\|(-(1, 1))\|$$

$$\sqrt{(-1)^2 + 1^2}$$

$$= \sqrt{2} = 1.414\ldots$$

That function is only one of many possible distance functions, however. The L0, L1, and L-infinity norms also exist. All these norms are valid ways to measure distance. Here they are in more detail:

- The *L0 norm* counts the total nonzero elements of a vector. The distance between the origin $(0, 0)$ and vector $(0, 5)$ is 1, for example, because there's only one nonzero element. The L0 distance between $(1, 1)$ and $(2, 2)$ is 2, because neither dimension matches up. Imagine that the first and second dimensions represent username and password, respectively. If the L0 distance between a login attempt and the true credentials is 0, the login is successful. If the distance is 1, either the username or password is incorrect, but not both. Finally, if the distance is 2, neither username nor password is found in the database.

- The *L1 norm*, shown in figure 1.8, is defined as $\sum x_n$. The distance between two vectors under the L1 norm is also referred to as the *Manhattan distance*. Imagine living in a downtown area like Manhattan, where the streets form a grid. The shortest distance from one intersection to another is along the blocks. Similarly, the L1 distance between two vectors is along the orthogonal directions. The distance between (0, 1) and (1, 0) under the L1 norm is 2. Computing the L1 distance between two vectors is the sum of absolute differences at each dimension, which is a useful measure of similarity.

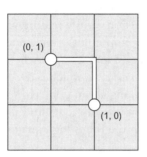

Figure 1.8   The L1 distance is called the *Manhattan distance* (also the *taxicab metric*) because it resembles the route of a car in a gridlike neighborhood such as Manhattan. If a car is traveling from point (0, 1) to point (1, 0), the shortest route requires a length of 2 units.

- The *L2 norm*, shown in figure 1.9, is the Euclidian length of a vector, $\left(\sum (x_n)^2\right)^{1/2}$. It's the most direct route you can possibly take on a geometric plane to get from one point to another. For the mathematically inclined, this norm implements the least-squares estimation as predicted by the Gauss-Markov theorem. For the rest of you, it's the shortest distance between two points in space.

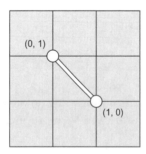

Figure 1.9   The L2 norm between points (0, 1) and (1, 0) is the length of a single straight-line segment between both points.

- The *L-N norm* generalizes this pattern, resulting in $\left(\sum |x_n|^N\right)^{1/N}$. We rarely use finite norms above L2, but it's here for completeness.
- The *L-infinity norm* is $\left(\sum |x_n|^\infty\right)^{1/\infty}$. More naturally, it's the largest magnitude among each element. If the vector is (–1, –2, –3), the L-infinity norm is 3. If a feature vector represents costs of various items, minimizing the L-infinity norm of the vector is an attempt to reduce the cost of the most expensive item.

When do I use a metric other than the L2 norm in the real world?

Let's say you're working for a search-engine startup trying to compete with Google. Your boss assigns you the task of using machine learning to personalize the search results for each user.

A good goal might be that users shouldn't see five or more incorrect search results per month. A year's worth of user data is a 12-dimensional vector (each month of the year is a dimension), indicating the number of incorrect results shown per month. You're trying to satisfy the condition that the L-infinity norm of this vector must be less than 5.

Suppose instead that your boss changes the requirements, saying that fewer than five erroneous search results are allowed for the entire year. In this case, you're trying to achieve an L1 norm below 5, because the sum of all errors in the entire space should be less than 5.

Now your boss changes the requirements again: the number of months with erroneous search results should be fewer than 5. In that case, you're trying to achieve an L0 norm less than 5, because the number of months with a nonzero error should be fewer than 5.

1.4 Types of learning

Now that you can compare feature vectors, you have the tools necessary to use data for practical algorithms. Machine learning is often split into three perspectives: supervised learning, unsupervised learning, and reinforcement learning. An emerging new area is meta-learning, sometimes called *AutoML*. The following sections examine all four types.

1.4.1 Supervised learning

By definition, a supervisor is someone higher up in the chain of command. When we're in doubt, our supervisor dictates what to do. Likewise, *supervised learning* is all about learning from examples laid out by a supervisor (such as a teacher).

A supervised machine-learning system needs labeled data to develop a useful understanding, which we call its *model*. Given many photographs of people and their recorded corresponding ethnicities, for example, we can train a model to classify the ethnicity of a never-before-seen person in an arbitrary photograph. Simply put, a model is a function that assigns a label to data by using a collection of previous examples, called a *training dataset*, as reference.

A convenient way to talk about models is through mathematical notation. Let x be an instance of data, such as a feature vector. The label associated with x is $f(x)$, often referred to as the *ground truth* of x. Usually, we use the variable $y = f(x)$ because it's quicker to write. In the example of classifying the ethnicity of a person through a photograph, x can be a 100-dimensional vector of various relevant features, and y is one of a couple of values to represent the various ethnicities. Because y is discrete with few values, the model is called a *classifier*. If y can result in many values, and the values have a natural ordering, the model is called a *regressor*.

Let's denote a model's prediction of x as $g(x)$. Sometimes, you can tweak a model to change its performance dramatically. Models have parameters that can be tuned by a human or automatically. We use the vector to represent the parameters. Putting it all together, $g(x|)$ more completely represents the model, read "g of x given."

> **NOTE** Models may also have *hyperparameters*, which are extra ad-hoc properties of a model. The term *hyper* in *hyperparameter* may seem a bit strange at first. A better name could be *metaparameter*, because the parameter is akin to metadata about the model.

The success of a model's prediction $g(x|)$ depends on how well it agrees with the ground truth y. We need a way to measure the distance between these two vectors. The L2 norm may be used to measure how close two vectors lie, for example. The distance between the ground truth and the prediction is called the *cost*.

The essence of a supervised machine-learning algorithm is to figure out the parameters of a model that result in the least *cost*. Mathematically put, we're looking for a θ^* (pronounced *theta star*) that minimizes the cost among all data points $x \in X$. One way of formalizing this optimization problem is the following equation:

$$\theta^* = \text{argmin}_\theta \, Cost(\theta|X)$$

where

$$Cost(\theta|X) = \sum_{x \in X} \|g(x|\theta) - f(x)\|$$

Clearly, brute-forcing every possible combination of x (also known as a *parameter space*) will eventually find the optimal solution, but at an unacceptable run time. A major area of research in machine learning is about writing algorithms that efficiently search this parameter space. Some of the early algorithms include *gradient descent, simulated annealing*, and *genetic algorithms*. TensorFlow automatically takes care of the low-level implementation details of these algorithms, so I won't get into them in too much detail.

After the parameters are learned one way or another, you can finally evaluate the model to figure out how well the system captured patterns from the data. A rule of thumb is to not evaluate your model on the same data you used to train it, because you already know it works for the training data; you need to tell whether the model works for data that *wasn't* part of the training set, to make sure your model is general-purpose and not *biased* to the data used to train it. Use the majority of the data for training and the remainder for testing. If you have 100 labeled data points, for example, randomly select 70 of them to train a model and reserve the other 30 to test it, creating a 70-30 split.

Why split the data?

If the 70-30 split seems odd to you, think about it this way. Suppose that your physics teacher gives you a practice exam and tells you that the real exam will be no different. You might as well memorize the answers and earn a perfect score without understanding the concepts. Similarly, if you test your model on the training dataset, you're not doing yourself any favors. You risk a false sense of security, because the model may merely be memorizing the results. Now, where's the intelligence in that?

Instead of using the 70-30 split, machine-learning practitioners typically divide their datasets 60-20-20. Training consumes 60% of the dataset, and testing uses 20%, leaving the other 20% for *validation*, which is explained in chapter 2.

1.4.2 Unsupervised learning

Unsupervised learning is about modeling data that comes without corresponding labels or responses. The fact that we can make any conclusions at all on raw data feels like magic. With enough data, it may be possible to find patterns and structure. Two of the most powerful tools that machine-learning practitioners use to learn from data alone are clustering and dimensionality reduction.

Clustering is the process of splitting the data into individual buckets of similar items. In a sense, clustering is like classifying data without knowing any corresponding labels. When organizing your books on three shelves, for example, you likely place similar genres together, or maybe you group them by the authors' last names. You might have a Stephen King section, another for textbooks, and a third for anything else. You don't care that all the books are separated by the same feature, only that each book has something unique that allows you to organize it into one of several roughly equal, easily identifiable groups. One of the most popular clustering algorithms is *k-means*, which is a specific instance of a more powerful technique called the *E-M algorithm.*

Dimensionality reduction is about manipulating the data to view it from a much simpler perspective—the ML equivalent of the phrase "Keep it simple, stupid." By getting rid of redundant features, for example, we can explain the same data in a lower-dimensional space and see which features matter. This simplification also helps in data visualization or preprocessing for performance efficiency. One of the earliest algorithms is *principle component analysis* (PCA), and a newer one is *autoencoders*, which are covered in chapter 7.

1.4.3 Reinforcement learning

Supervised and unsupervised learning seem to suggest that the existence of a teacher is all or nothing. But in one well-studied branch of machine learning, the environment acts as a teacher, providing hints as opposed to definite answers. The learning system receives feedback on its actions, with no concrete promise that it's progressing in the right direction, which might be to solve a maze or accomplish an explicit goal.

Exploration vs. exploitation: The heart of reinforcement learning

Imagine playing a video game that you've never seen before. You click buttons on a controller and discover that a particular combination of strokes gradually increases your score. Brilliant! Now you repeatedly exploit this finding in the hope of beating the high score. In the back of your mind, however, you wonder whether you're missing out on a better combination of button clicks. Should you exploit your current best strategy or risk exploring new options?

Unlike supervised learning, in which training data is conveniently labeled by a "teacher," *reinforcement learning* trains on information gathered by observing how the environment reacts to actions. Reinforcement learning is a type of machine learning that interacts with the environment to learn which combination of actions yields the most favorable results. Because we're already anthropomorphizing algorithms by using the words *environment* and *action*, scholars typically refer to the system as an autonomous *agent*. Therefore, this type of machine learning naturally manifests itself in the domain of robotics.

To reason about agents in the environment, we introduce two new concepts: states and actions. The status of the world frozen at a particular time is called a state. An agent may perform one of many actions to change the current state. To drive an agent to perform actions, each state yields a corresponding reward. An agent eventually discovers the expected total reward of each state, called the *value* of a state.

Like any other machine-learning system, performance improves with more data. In this case, the data is a history of experiences. In reinforcement learning, we don't know the final cost or reward of a series of actions until that series is executed. These situations render traditional supervised learning ineffective, because we don't know exactly which action in the history of action sequences is to blame for ending up in a low-value state. The only information an agent knows for certain is the cost of a series of actions that it has already taken, which is incomplete. The agent's goal is to find a sequence of actions that maximizes rewards. If you're more interested in this subject, you may want to check out another topical book in the Manning Publications family: *Grokking Deep Reinforcement Learning*, by Miguel Morales (Manning, 2020; https://www.manning.com/books/grokking-deep-reinforcement-learning).

1.4.4   *Meta-learning*

Relatively recently, a new area of machine learning called meta-learning has emerged. The idea is simple. Data scientists and ML experts spend a tremendous amount of time executing the steps of ML, as shown in figure 1.7. What if those steps—defining and representing the problem, choosing a model, testing the model, and evaluating the model—could themselves be automated? Instead of being limited to exploring only one or a small group of models, why not have the program itself try all the models?

Many businesses separate the roles of the domain expert (refer to the doctor in figure 1.7), the data scientist (the person modeling the data and potentially extracting or choosing features that are important, such as the image RGB pixels), and the ML engineer (responsible for tuning, testing, and deploying the model), as shown in figure 1.10a. As you'll remember from earlier in the chapter, these roles interact in three basic areas: data cleaning and prep, which both the domain expert and data scientist may help with; feature and model selection, mainly a data-scientist job with a little help from the ML engineer; and then train, test, and evaluate, mostly the job of the ML engineer with a little help from the data scientist. We've added a new wrinkle: taking our model and deploying it, which is what happens in the real world and is something that brings its own set of challenges. This scenario is one reason why you are reading the second edition of this book; it's covered in chapter 2, where I discuss deploying and using TensorFlow.

What if instead of having data scientists and ML engineers pick models, train, evaluate, and tune them, we could have the system automatically search over the space of possible models, and try them all? This approach overcomes limiting your overall ML experience to a small number of possible solutions wherein you'll likely choose the first one that performs reasonably. But what if the system could figure out which models are best and how to tune the models automatically? That's precisely what you see in figure 1.10b: the process of meta-learning, or AutoML.

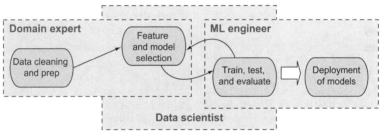

a. Traditional machine-learning pipeline and process (left to right)
and the role of domain experts, data scientists, and ML engineers

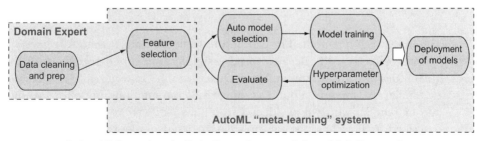

b. AutoML "meta-learning" pipeline and process (left to right). Now you have
automatic decisions on ML from the system and limited domain-expert feedback.

Figure 1.10 Traditional ML and its evolution to meta-learning, in which the system does its own model selection, training, tuning, and evaluation to pick the best ML model among many candidates

Data scientists, you're canceled!

Today's cancel culture lends itself nicely to the concept of meta-learning, whose roots grew from the idea that data science itself—the process of creating and experimenting with many types of ML pipelines, including data cleaning, model building, and testing—can be automated. An associated Defense Advanced Research Projects Agency (DARPA) program, Data Driven Discovery of Models (D3M), had the purported goal of doing away with data scientists and instead automating their activities. Although the results of that DARPA program and the field of meta-learning thus far are promising, we're not quite ready to fully cancel data scientists . . . yet. Don't worry; you're safe!

Exercise 1.5

Would you use supervised, unsupervised, reinforcement, or meta-learning to solve the following problems? (a) Find the best ML algorithm that takes baseball statistics and predicts whether a player will make the Hall of Fame. (b) Organize various fruits in three baskets based on no other information. (c) Predict the weather based on sensor data. (d) Learn to play chess well after many trial-and-error attempts.

Answer

(a) Meta-learning; (b) Unsupervised; (c) Supervised; (d) Reinforcement.

1.5   *TensorFlow*

Google open-sourced its machine-learning framework, TensorFlow, in late 2015 under the Apache 2.0 license. Before that, it was used proprietarily by Google in speech recognition, Search, Photos, and Gmail, among other applications.

A bit of history

A former scalable distributed training and learning system called DistBelief is the primary influence on TensorFlow's current implementation. Have you ever written a messy piece of code and wished you could start over? That's the dynamic between DistBelief and TensorFlow. TensorFlow is not the first system Google open-sourced based on an internal project. Google's famous Map-Reduce system and Google File System (GFS) are the basis of modern Apache data processing, web-crawling, and big data systems including Hadoop, Nutch, and Spark. Additionally, Google's bigTable system is where the Apache Hbase project came from.

The library is implemented in C++ and has a convenient Python API, as well as a less-appreciated C++ API. Because of the simpler dependencies, TensorFlow can be quickly deployed to various architectures.

Similar to Theano—a popular numerical computation library for Python that you may be familiar with (http://deeplearning.net/software/theano)—computations are described as flowcharts, separating design from implementation. With little to no hassle, this dichotomy allows the same design to be implemented on mobile devices as well as large-scale training systems with thousands of processors. The single system spans a broad range of platforms. TensorFlow also plays nicely with a variety of newer, similarly-developed ML libraries, including Keras (TensorFlow 2.0 is fully integrated with Keras), along with libraries such as PyTorch (https://pytorch.org), originally developed by Facebook, and richer application programming interfaces for ML such as Fast.Ai. You can use many toolkits to do ML, but you're reading a book about TensorFlow, right? Let's focus on it!

One of the fanciest properties of TensorFlow is its *automatic differentiation* capabilities. You can experiment with new networks without having to redefine many key calculations.

> **NOTE** Automatic differentiation makes it much easier to implement *backpropagation*, which is a computationally-heavy calculation used in a branch of machine learning called *neural networks*. TensorFlow hides the nitty-gritty details of backpropagation so you can focus on the bigger picture. Chapter 11 covers an introduction to neural networks with TensorFlow.

All the mathematics is abstracted away and unfolded under the hood. Using Tensor-Flow is like using WolframAlpha for a calculus problem set.

Another feature of this library is its interactive visualization environment, called *TensorBoard*. This tool shows a flowchart of the way data transforms, displays summary logs over time, and traces performance. Figure 1.11 shows what TensorBoard looks like; chapter 2 covers using it.

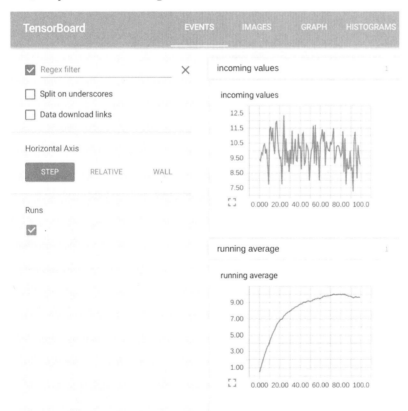

Figure 1.11 Example of TensorBoard in action

Prototyping in TensorFlow is much faster than in Theano (code initiates in a matter of seconds as opposed to minutes) because many of the operations come precompiled. It becomes easy to debug code due to subgraph execution; an entire segment of computation can be reused without recalculation.

Because TensorFlow isn't only about neural networks, it also has out-of-the-box matrix computation and manipulation tools. Most libraries, such as PyTorch, Fast.Ai, and Caffe, are designed solely for deep neural networks, but TensorFlow is more flexible as well as scalable.

The library is well-documented and officially supported by Google. Machine learning is a sophisticated topic, so having an exceptionally reputable company behind TensorFlow is comforting.

1.6   *Overview of future chapters*

Chapter 2 demonstrates how to use various components of TensorFlow (see figure 1.12). Chapters 3–10 show how to implement classic machine-learning algorithms in TensorFlow, and chapters 11–19 cover algorithms based on neural networks. The algorithms solve a wide variety of problems, such as prediction, classification, clustering, dimensionality reduction, and planning.

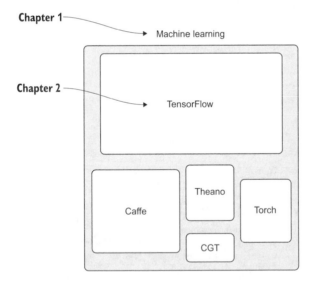

Figure 1.12   **This chapter introduces fundamental machine-learning concepts, and chapter 2 begins your journey in TensorFlow. Other tools can apply machine-learning algorithms (such as Caffe, Theano, and Torch), but you'll see in chapter 2 why TensorFlow is the way to go.**

Many algorithms can solve the same real-world problem, and many real-world problems can be solved by the same algorithm. Table 1.1 covers the ones laid out in this book.

Table 1.1 Many real-world problems can be solved by using the corresponding algorithm found in its respective chapter.

Real-world problem	Algorithm	Chapter(s)
Predicting trends, fitting a curve to data points, describing relationships between variables	Linear regression	3, 4
Classifying data into two categories, finding the best way to split a dataset	Logistic regression	5, 6
Classifying data into multiple categories	Softmax regression	5, 6
Revealing hidden causes of observations, finding the most likely hidden reason for a series of outcomes	Hidden Markov model (Viterbi)	9, 10
Clustering data into a fixed number of categories, automatically partitioning data points into separate classes	k-means	7, 8
Clustering data into arbitrary categories, visualizing high-dimensional data in a lower-dimensional embedding	Self-organizing map	7, 8
Reducing dimensionality of data, learning latent variables responsible for high-dimensional data	Autoencoder	11, 12
Planning actions in an environment using neural networks (reinforcement learning)	Q-policy neural network	13
Classifying data using supervised neural networks	Perceptron	14, 15
Classifying real-world images using supervised neural networks	Convolution neural network	14, 15
Producing patterns that match observations using neural networks	Recurrent neural network	16, 17
Predicting natural-language responses to natural-language queries	Seq2seq model	18
Ranking items by learning their utility	Ranking	19

TIP If you're interested in the intricate architecture details of TensorFlow, the best available source is the official documentation at https://www.tensorflow.org/tutorials/customization/basics. This book sprints ahead and uses TensorFlow without slowing down for the breadth of low-level performance tuning. If you're interested in cloud services, you may want to consider Google's solution for professional-grade scale and speed (https://cloud.google.com/products/ai).

Summary

- TensorFlow has become the tool of choice among professionals and researchers for implementing machine-learning solutions.
- Machine learning uses examples to develop an expert system that can make useful statements about new inputs.

- A key property of ML is that performance tends to improve with more training data.
- Over the years, scholars have crafted three major archetypes that most problems fit: supervised learning, unsupervised learning, and reinforcement learning. Meta-learning is a new area of ML that focuses on exploring the entire space of models, solutions, and tuning tricks automatically.
- After a real-world problem is formulated in a machine-learning perspective, several algorithms become available. Of the many software libraries and frameworks that can accomplish an implementation, we chose TensorFlow as our silver bullet. Developed by Google and supported by its flourishing community, TensorFlow gives us a way to implement industry-standard code easily.

TensorFlow essentials

Before implementing machine-learning algorithms, let's get familiar with how to use TensorFlow. You're going to get your hands dirty writing simple code right away! This chapter covers some essential advantages of TensorFlow to convince you that it's the machine-learning library of choice. Before you continue, follow the procedures in the appendix for step-by-step installation instructions, then return here.

As a thought experiment, let's see what happens when we use Python code without a handy computing library. It'll be like using a new smartphone without installing any additional apps. The functionality will be there, but you'd be much more productive if you had the right tools.

Suppose you're a private business owner tracking the flow of sales for your products. Your inventory consists of 100 items, and you represent each item's price in a vector called `prices`. Another 100-dimensional vector called `amounts` represents the inventory count of each item. You can write the chunk of Python code shown in listing 2.1 to calculate the revenue of selling all products. Keep in mind that this code doesn't import any libraries.

Listing 2.1 Computing the inner product of two vectors without using a library

```
revenue = 0
for price, amount in zip(prices, amounts):
    revenue += price * amount
```

That's too much code to calculate the inner product of two vectors (also known as the *dot product*). Imagine how much code would be required for something more complicated, such as solving linear equations or computing the distance between two vectors, if you still lacked TensorFlow and its friends, like the Numerical Python (NumPy) library.

When installing the TensorFlow library, you also install a well-known, robust Python library called NumPy, which facilitates mathematical manipulation in Python. Using Python without its libraries (NumPy and TensorFlow) is like using a camera without an autofocus mode; sure, you gain more flexibility, but you can easily make careless mistakes. (For the record, we have nothing against photographers who micromanage aperture, shutter, and ISO—the so-called "manual" knobs used to prepare your camera to take an image.) It's easy to make mistakes in machine learning, so let's keep our camera on autofocus and use TensorFlow to help automate tedious software development.

The following code snippet shows how to write the same inner product concisely using NumPy:

```
import numpy as np
revenue = np.dot(prices, amounts)
```

Python is a succinct language. Fortunately for you, this book doesn't have pages and pages of cryptic code. On the other hand, the brevity of the Python language also implies that a lot is happening behind each line of code, which you should study carefully as you follow along in this chapter. You will find that this is a core theme for TensorFlow, something that it balances elegantly as an add-on library to Python. TensorFlow hides enough of the complexity (like autofocus) but also allows you to turn those magical configurable knobs when you want to get your hands dirty.

Machine-learning algorithms require many mathematical operations. Often, an algorithm boils down to a composition of simple functions iterated until convergence. Sure, you may use any standard programming language to perform these computations, but the secret to both manageable and high-performing code is the use of a well-written library, such as TensorFlow (which officially supports Python, C++, JavaScript, Go, and Swift).

> **TIP**   Detailed documentation about various functions for the APIs is available at https://www.tensorflow.org/api_docs.

The skills you'll learn in this chapter are geared toward using TensorFlow for computations, because machine learning relies on mathematical formulations. After going through the examples and code listings, you'll be able to use TensorFlow for arbitrary tasks, such as computing statistics on big data, and to use TensorFlow friends like NumPy and Matplotlib (for visualization) to understand why your machine-learning algorithms are making those decisions and provide explainable results. The focus here is entirely on how to use TensorFlow as opposed to general machine learning, which we will get into in later chapters. That sounds like a gentle start, right?

Later in this chapter, you'll use flagship TensorFlow features that are essential for machine learning. These features include representation of computation as a data-flow graph, separation of design and execution, partial subgraph computation, and autodifferentiation. Without further ado, let's write our first TensorFlow code!

2.1 *Ensuring that TensorFlow works*

First, you should ensure that everything is working correctly. Check the oil level in your car, repair the blown fuse in your basement, and ensure that your credit balance is zero. I'm kidding; we're talking about TensorFlow.

Create a new file called test.py for your first piece of code. Import TensorFlow by running the following script:

```
import tensorflow as tf
```

Having technical difficulty?

An error commonly occurs at this step if you installed the GPU version and the library fails to search for CUDA drivers. Remember that if you compiled the library with CUDA, you need to update your environment variables with the path to CUDA. Check the CUDA instructions on TensorFlow. (See https://www.tensorflow.org/install/gpu for further information.)

This single import prepares TensorFlow to do your bidding. If the Python interpreter doesn't complain, you're ready to start using TensorFlow.

Sticking with TensorFlow conventions

The TensorFlow library is usually imported with the `tf` alias. Generally, qualifying TensorFlow with `tf` is a good idea because it keeps you consistent with other developers and open source TensorFlow projects. You may use another alias (or no alias), of course, but then successfully reusing other people's snippets of TensorFlow code in your own projects will be an involved process. The same is true of NumPy as `np`, and Matplotlib as `plt`, which you will see used as conventions throughout the book.

2.2   *Representing tensors*

Now that you know how to import TensorFlow into a Python source file, let's start using it! As discussed in chapter 1, a convenient way to describe an object in the real world is to list its properties or features. You can describe a car, for example, by its color, model, engine type, mileage, and so on. An ordered list of features is called a *feature vector*, and that's exactly what you'll represent in `TensorFlow` code.

Feature vectors are among the most useful devices in machine learning because of their simplicity; they're lists of numbers. Each data item typically consists of a feature vector, and a good dataset has hundreds, if not thousands, of feature vectors. No doubt you'll often deal with more than one vector at a time. A matrix concisely represents a list of vectors, in which each column of a matrix is a feature vector.

The syntax to represent matrices in TensorFlow is a vector of vectors, all of the same length. Figure 2.1 is an example of a matrix with two rows and three columns, such as $[[1, 2, 3], [4, 5, 6]]$. Notice that this vector contains two elements and that each element corresponds to a row of the matrix.

We access an element in a matrix by specifying its row and column indices. The first row and first column indicate the first top-left element, for example. Sometimes, it's convenient to use more than two indices, such as when referencing a pixel in a color image not only by its row and column, but also by its red/green/blue channel. A *tensor* is a generalization of a matrix that specifies an element by an arbitrary number of indices.

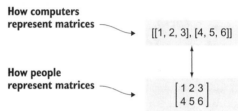

Figure 2.1   The matrix in the bottom half of the diagram is a visualization from its compact code notation in the top half of the diagram. This form of notation is a common paradigm in scientific computing libraries.

Example of a tensor

Suppose that an elementary school enforces assigned seating for all its students. You're the principal, and you're terrible with names. Luckily, each classroom has a grid of seats, and you can easily nickname a student by their row and column index.

The school has multiple classrooms, so you can't simply say, "Good morning 4,10! Keep up the good work." You need to also specify the classroom: "Hi, 4,10 from classroom 2." Unlike a matrix, which needs only two indices to specify an element, the students in this school need three numbers. They're all part of a rank-3 tensor.

The syntax for tensors is even more nested vectors. As shown in figure 2.2, a $2 \times 3 \times 2$ tensor is $[[[1, 2], [3, 4], [5, 6]], [[7, 8], [9, 10], [11, 12]]]$, which can be thought of as two matrices, each of size 3×2. Consequently, we say that this tensor has a *rank* of 3. In general, the rank of a tensor is the number of indices required to specify an element. Machine-learning algorithms in TensorFlow act on tensors, so it's important to understand how to use them.

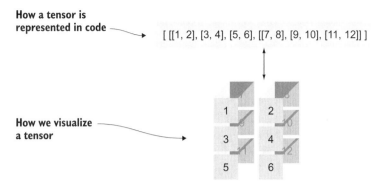

How a tensor is represented in code → [[[1, 2], [3, 4], [5, 6], [[7, 8], [9, 10], [11, 12]]]

How we visualize a tensor →

Figure 2.2　You can think of this tensor as being multiple matrices stacked on top of one another. To specify an element, you must indicate the row and column, as well as which matrix is being accessed. Therefore, the rank of this tensor is 3.

It's easy to get lost in the many ways to represent a tensor. Intuitively, three lines of code in listing 2.2 are trying to represent the same 2×2 matrix. This matrix represents two feature vectors of two dimensions each. It could, for example, represent two people's ratings of two movies. Each person, indexed by the row of the matrix, assigns a number to describe their review of the movie, indexed by the column. Run the code to see how to generate a matrix in TensorFlow.

Listing 2.2　Different ways to represent tensors

```
import tensorflow as tf          You'll use NumPy
import numpy as np               matrices in TensorFlow.

m1 = [[1.0, 2.0],
      [3.0, 4.0]]

m2 = np.array([[1.0, 2.0],
               [3.0, 4.0]], dtype=np.float32)      Defines a 2 × 2
                                                    matrix in three ways
m3 = tf.constant([[1.0, 2.0],
                  [3.0, 4.0]])

print(type(m1))      Prints the type
print(type(m2))      for each matrix
print(type(m3))

t1 = tf.convert_to_tensor(m1, dtype=tf.float32)     Creates tensor objects
t2 = tf.convert_to_tensor(m2, dtype=tf.float32)     from the various types
t3 = tf.convert_to_tensor(m3, dtype=tf.float32)

print(type(t1))      Notice that the types
print(type(t2))      will be the same now.
print(type(t3))
```

The first variable (m1) is a list, the second variable (m2) is an `ndarray` from the NumPy library, and the last variable (m3) is TensorFlow's constant `Tensor` object, which you initialize by using `tf.constant`. None of the three ways to specify a matrix is necessarily better than any another, but each way does give you a raw set of list values (m1), a typed NumPy object (m2), or an initialized data flow operation: a tensor (m3).

All operators in TensorFlow, such as `negative`, are designed to operate on tensor objects. A convenient function you can sprinkle anywhere to make sure that you're dealing with tensors as opposed to the other types is `tf.convert_to_tensor(...)`. Most functions in the TensorFlow library already perform this function (redundantly), even if you forget to do so. Using `tf.convert_to_tensor(...)` is optional, but we show it here because it helps demystify the implicit type system being handled across the library and overall as part of the Python programming language. Listing 2.3 outputs the following three times:

```
<class 'tensorflow.python.framework.ops.Tensor'>
```

> **TIP** To make copying and pasting easier, you can find the code listings on the book's GitHub site: https://github.com/chrismattmann/MLwithTensorFlow2ed. You will also find a fully functional Docker image that you can use with all the data, and code and libraries to run the examples in the book. Install it, using `docker pull chrismattmann/mltf2`, and see the appendix for more details.

Let's take another look at defining tensors in code. After importing the TensorFlow library, you can use the `tf.constant` operator as follows. Listing 2.3 shows a couple of tensors of various dimensions.

Listing 2.3 Creating tensors

```
import tensorflow as tf

m1 = tf.constant([[1., 2.]])          Defines a 2 × 1
                                      matrix of rank 2

m2 = tf.constant([[1],
                  [2]])               Defines a 1 × 2
                                      matrix of rank 2
m3 = tf.constant([ [[1,2],
                   [3,4],
                   [5,6]],
                  [[7,8],
                   [9,10],
                   [11,12]] ])        Defines a rank-3 tensor

print(m1)          Try printing
print(m2)          the tensors.
print(m3)
```

Running listing 2.3 produces the following output:

```
Tensor( "Const:0",
        shape=TensorShape([Dimension(1), Dimension(2)]),
        dtype=float32 )
Tensor( "Const_1:0",
        shape=TensorShape([Dimension(2), Dimension(1)]),
        dtype=int32 )
Tensor( "Const_2:0",
        shape=TensorShape([Dimension(2), Dimension(3), Dimension(2)]),
        dtype=int32 )
```

As you can see from the output, each tensor is represented by the aptly named `Tensor` object. Each `Tensor` object has a unique label (`name`), a dimension (`shape`) to define its structure, and a data type (`dtype`) to specify the kind of values you'll manipulate. Because you didn't explicitly provide a name, the library automatically generated the names: `Const:0`, `Const_1:0`, and `Const_2:0`.

> **Tensor types**
>
> Notice that each element of `m1` ends with a decimal point. The decimal point tells Python that the data type of the elements isn't an integer, but a float. You can pass in explicit `dtype` values. Much like NumPy arrays, tensors take on a data type that specifies the kind of values you'll manipulate in that tensor.

TensorFlow also comes with a few convenient constructors for some simple tensors. The constructor `tf.zeros(shape)`, for example, creates a tensor with all values initialized at 0 of a specific shape, such as `[2, 3]` or `[1, 2]`. Similarly, `tf.ones(shape)` creates a tensor of a specific shape with all values initialized to 1 at the same time. The `shape` argument is a one-dimensional (1D) tensor of type `int32` (a list of integers) describing the dimensions of the tensor.

> **Exercise 2.1**
>
> How would you initialize a 500 × 500 tensor with all elements equaling 0.5?
>
> **Answer**
> ```
> tf.ones([500,500]) * 0.5
> ```

2.3 Creating operators

Now that you have a few starting tensors ready to be used, you can apply more interesting operators, such as addition and multiplication. Consider each row of a matrix representing the transaction of money to (positive value) and from (negative value) another person. Negating the matrix is a way to represent the transaction history of the other person's flow of money. Let's start simple and run a negation op (short for *operation*) on the m1 tensor from listing 2.3. Negating a matrix turns the positive numbers into negative numbers of the same magnitude, and vice versa.

Negation is one of the simplest operations. As shown in listing 2.4, negation takes only one tensor as input and produces a tensor with every element negated. Try running the code. If you master defining negation, you can generalize that skill for use in all other TensorFlow operations.

> **NOTE** *Defining* an operation, such as negation, is different from *running* it. So far, you've *defined* how operations should behave. In section 2.4, you'll *evaluate* (or *run*) them to compute their values.

Listing 2.4 Using the negation operator

```
import tensorflow as tf

x = tf.constant([[1, 2]])          ⟵——— Defines an arbitrary tensor
negMatrix = tf.negative(x)         ⟵——— Negates the tensor
print(negMatrix)                   ⟵——— Prints the object
```

Listing 2.4 generates the following output:

```
Tensor("Neg:0", shape=TensorShape([Dimension(1), Dimension(2)]), dtype=int32)
```

Notice that the output isn't `[[-1, -2]]` because you're printing the definition of the negation op, not the actual evaluation of the op. The printed output shows that the negation op is a `Tensor` class with a name, shape, and data type. The name was assigned automatically, but you could've provided it explicitly as well when using the `tf.negative` op in listing 2.4. Similarly, the shape and data type were inferred from the `[[1, 2]]` that you passed in.

Useful TensorFlow operators

The official documentation at https://github.com/tensorflow/docs/tree/r1.15/site/en/api_docs/python/tf/math carefully lays out all available math ops. Specific examples of commonly used operators include the following:

`tf.add(x, y)`—Adds two tensors of the same type, $x + y$

`tf.subtract(x, y)`—Subtracts tensors of the same type, $x - y$

`tf.multiply(x, y)`—Multiplies two tensors elementwise

`tf.pow(x, y)`—Takes the elementwise x to the power of y

`tf.exp(x)`—Equivalent to $pow(e, x)$, where e is Euler's number (2.718 …)

`tf.sqrt(x)`—Equivalent to $pow(x, 0.5)$

`tf.div(x, y)`—Takes the elementwise division of x and y

tf.truediv(x, y)—Same as tf.div, but casts the arguments as a float

tf.floordiv(x, y)—Same as truediv, but rounds down the final answer into an integer

tf.mod(x, y)—Takes the elementwise remainder from division

Exercise 2.2

Use the TensorFlow operators you've learned so far to produce the Gaussian distribution (also known as the normal distribution). See figure 2.3 for a hint. For reference, you can find the probability density of the normal distribution online: https://en.wikipedia.org/wiki/Normal_distribution.

Answer

Most mathematical expressions—such as ×, –, +, and so on—are shortcuts for their TensorFlow equivalents, used for brevity. The Gaussian function includes many operations, so it's cleaner to use shorthand notations as follows:

```
from math import pi
mean = 0.0
sigma = 1.0
(tf.exp(tf.negative(tf.pow(x - mean, 2.0) /
           (2.0 * tf.pow(sigma, 2.0) ))) *
 (1.0 / (sigma * tf.sqrt(2.0 * pi) )))
```

2.4 *Executing operators within sessions*

A *session* is an environment of a software system that describes how the lines of code should run. In TensorFlow, a session sets up how the hardware devices (such as CPU and GPU) talk to one another. That way, you can design your machine-learning algorithm without worrying about micromanaging the hardware on which it runs. Later, you can configure the session to change its behavior without changing a line of the machine-learning code.

To execute an operation and retrieve its calculated value, TensorFlow requires a session. Only a registered session may fill the values of a Tensor object. To do so, you must create a session class by using tf.Session() and tell it to run an operator, as shown in listing 2.5. The result will be a value you can use for further computations later.

Listing 2.5 Using a session

```
import tensorflow as tf              Defines an arbitrary matrix

x = tf.constant([[1., 2.]])          Runs the negation
neg_op = tf.negative(x)              operator on it

with tf.Session() as sess:           Starts a session to be
    result = sess.run(negMatrix)     able to run operations
print(result)
                                     Tells the session to
         Prints the resulting matrix  evaluate negMatrix
```

Congratulations! You've written your first full TensorFlow code. Although all that this code does is negate a matrix to produce `[[-1, -2]]`, the core overhead and framework are the same as everything else in TensorFlow. A session not only configures *where* your code will be computed on your machine, but also crafts *how* the computation will be laid out to parallelize computation.

Code performance seems a bit slow

You may have noticed that running your code took a few seconds more than you expected. It may appear to be unnatural that TensorFlow takes seconds to negate a small matrix. But substantial preprocessing occurs to optimize the library for larger, more complicated computations.

Every `Tensor` object has an `eval()` function to evaluate the mathematical operations that define its value. But the `eval()` function requires defining a session object for the library to understand how to best use the underlying hardware. In listing 2.5, we used `sess.run(...)`, which is equivalent to invoking the `Tensor`'s `eval()` function in the context of the session.

When you're running TensorFlow code through an interactive environment (for debugging or presentation purposes or when using Jupyter, as described later in the chapter), it's often easier to create the session in interactive mode, in which the session is implicitly part of any call to `eval()`. That way, the session variable doesn't need to be passed around throughout the code, making it easier to focus on the relevant parts of the algorithm, as shown in listing 2.6.

Listing 2.6   Using the interactive session mode

```
import tensorflow as tf
sess = tf.InteractiveSession()        ⟵── Starts an interactive session so the sess
                                           variable no longer needs to be passed around

x = tf.constant([[1., 2.]])           │  Defines an arbitrary
negMatrix = tf.negative(x)            │  matrix and negates it

result = negMatrix.eval()        ⟵─┐
print(result)          ⟵─┐          │  You can evaluate negMatrix now
                         │          │  without explicitly specifying a session.
┌─▷ sess.close()    Prints the
│                   negated matrix
Remember to close the session to free resources.
```

2.5   *Understanding code as a graph*

Consider a doctor who predicts the expected weight of a newborn to be 7.5 pounds. You'd like to figure out how that prediction differs from the actual measured weight. Being an overly analytical engineer, you design a function to describe the likelihood of all possible weights of the newborn. A weight of 8 pounds is more likely than 10 pounds, for example.

You can choose to use the Gaussian (otherwise known as normal) probability distribution function. This function takes a number as input and outputs a non-negative number describing the probability of observing the input. This function shows up all the time in machine learning and is easy to define in TensorFlow. It uses multiplication, division, negation, and a couple of other fundamental operators.

Think of every operator as being a node in a graph. Whenever you see a plus symbol (+) or any mathematical concept, picture it as one of many nodes. The edges between these nodes represent the composition of mathematical functions. Specifically, the `negative` operator we've been studying is a node, and the incoming/outgoing edges of this node are how the `Tensor` transforms. A tensor flows through the graph, which is why this library is called TensorFlow.

Here's a thought: every operator is a strongly typed function that takes input tensors of a dimension and produces output of the same dimension. Figure 2.3 is an example of how the Gaussian function can be designed with TensorFlow. The function is represented as a graph in which operators are nodes and edges represent interactions between nodes. This graph as a whole represents a complicated mathematical function (specifically, the Gaussian function). Small segments of the graph represent simple mathematical concepts, such as negation and doubling.

TensorFlow algorithms are easy to visualize. They can be described simply by flowcharts. The technical (and more correct) term for such a flowchart is a *dataflow graph*. Every arrow in a dataflow graph is called an *edge*. In addition, every state of the dataflow graph is called a *node*. The purpose of the session is to interpret your Python code

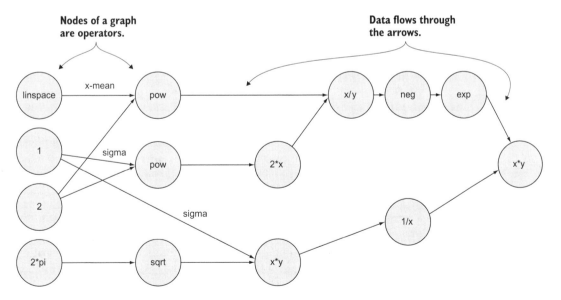

Figure 2.3 The graph represents the operations needed to produce a Gaussian distribution. The links between the nodes represent how data flows from one operation to the next. The operations themselves are simple; the complexity arises from the way they intertwine.

into a dataflow graph and then associate the computation of each node of the graph to the CPU or GPU.

2.5.1 *Setting session configurations*

You can also pass options to `tf.Session`. TensorFlow automatically determines the best way to assign a GPU or CPU device to an operation, for example, depending on what's available. You can pass an additional option, `log_device_placement=True`, when creating a session. Listing 2.7 shows you exactly where on your hardware the computations are evoked.

> ### Listing 2.7 Logging a session

```
import tensorflow as tf

x = tf.constant([[1., 2.]])       Defines a matrix       Starts the session with a
negMatrix = tf.negative(x)        and negates it         special config passed into the
                                                         constructor to enable logging

with tf.Session(config=tf.ConfigProto(log_device_placement=True)) as sess:
    options = tf.RunOptions(output_partition_graphs=True)
    metadata = tf.RunMetadata()
    result = sess.run(negMatrix,options=options, run_metadata=metadata)
                                                         Evaluates negMatrix
print(result)    ◁──── Prints the resulting value

print(metadata.partition_graphs)    ◁──── Prints the resulting graph
```

This code outputs info about which CPU/GPU devices are used in the session for each operation. Running listing 2.7 results in traces of output like the following to show which device was used to run the negation op:

```
Neg: /job:localhost/replica:0/task:0/cpu:0
```

Sessions are essential in TensorFlow code. You need to call a session to "run" the math. Figure 2.4 maps out how the components on TensorFlow interact with the machine-learning pipeline. A session not only runs a graph operation, but also can take place-holders, variables, and constants as input. We've used constants so far, but in later sections, we'll start using variables and placeholders. Here's a quick overview of these three types of values:

- *Placeholder*—A value that's unassigned but will be initialized by the session wher-ever it's run. Typically, placeholders are the input and output of your model.
- *Variable*—A value that can change, such as parameters of a machine-learning model. Variables must be initialized by the session before they're used.
- *Constant*—A value that doesn't change, such as a hyperparameter or setting.

The entire pipeline for machine learning with TensorFlow follows the flow of figure 2.4. Most of the code in TensorFlow consists of setting up the graph and session. After you design a graph and hook up the session to execute it, your code is ready to use.

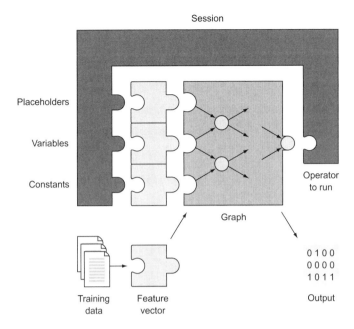

Figure 2.4 **The session dictates how the hardware will be used to process the graph most efficiently. When the session starts, it assigns the CPU and GPU devices to each of the nodes. After processing, the session outputs data in a usable format, such as a NumPy array. A session optionally may be fed placeholders, variables, and constants.**

2.6 *Writing code in Jupyter*

Because TensorFlow is primarily a Python library, you should make full use of Python's interpreter. *Jupyter* is a mature environment for exercising the interactive nature of the language. It's a web application that displays computation elegantly so that you can share annotated interactive algorithms with others to teach a technique or demonstrate code. Jupyter also easily integrates with visualization libraries like Python's Matplotlib and can be used to share elegant data stories about your algorithm, to evaluate its accuracy, and to present results.

You can share your Jupyter notebooks with other people to exchange ideas, and you can download their notebooks to learn about their code. See the appendix to get started installing the Jupyter Notebook application.

From a new terminal, change the directory to the location where you want to practice TensorFlow code, and start a notebook server:

```
$ cd ~/MyTensorFlowStuff
$ jupyter notebook
```

Running this command should launch a new browser window with the Jupyter notebook's dashboard. If no window opens automatically, you can navigate to http://localhost:8888 from any browser. You'll see a web page similar to the one in figure 2.5.

TIP The `jupyter notebook` command didn't work? Make sure that your `PYTHONPATH` environment variable includes the path to the `jupyter` script created when you installed the library. Also, this book uses both Python 3.7 (recommended) and Python 2.7 examples (due to the BregmanToolkit, which you'll read about in chapter 7). For this reason, you will want to install Jupyter with Python kernels enabled. For more information, see https://ipython .readthedocs.io/en/stable/install/kernel_install.html.

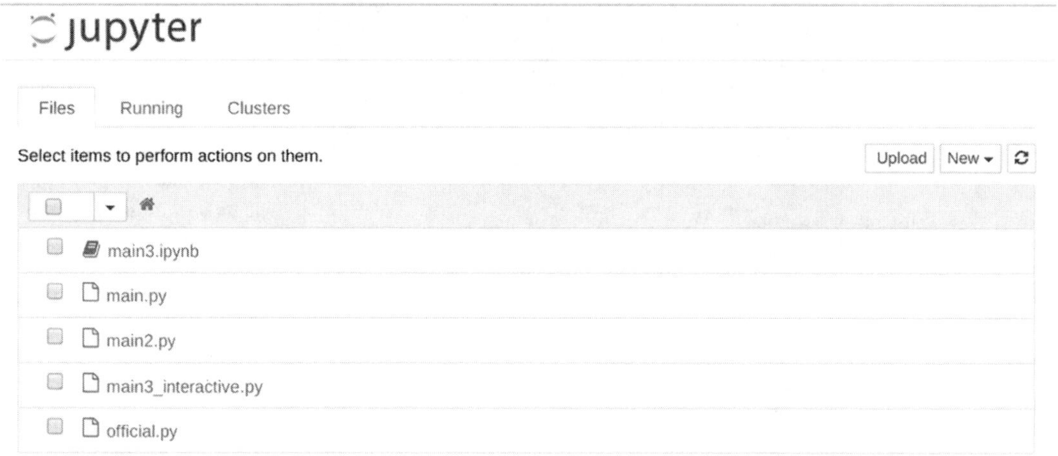

Figure 2.5   Running the Jupyter notebook will launch an interactive notebook on http://localhost:8888.

Create a new notebook by clicking the New drop-down menu at top right; then choose Notebooks > Python 3. The new Python3 kernel is enabled and is the only option by default because Python 2 was deprecated as of January 1, 2020. This command creates a new file called Untitled.ipynb, which you can start editing immediately through the browser interface. You can change the name of the notebook by clicking the current Untitled name and typing something more memorable, such as TensorFlow Example Notebook. The convention you use when you look at the listing code is simply titling the notebook Listing <Chapter Number>.<Number>.ipynb (for example, Listing 2.8.ipynb), but you can pick whatever you want. Organization—who'd have thought that was useful?

Everything in the Jupyter notebook is an independent chunk of code or text called a *cell*. Cells help divide a long block of code into manageable pieces of code snippets and documentation. You can run cells individually or choose to run everything at the same time, in order. There are three common ways to evaluate cells:

- Pressing Shift-Enter in a cell executes the cell and highlights the cell below it.
- Pressing Ctrl-Enter maintains the cursor in the current cell after executing it.
- Pressing Alt-Enter executes the cell and inserts a new empty cell directly below it.

You can change the cell type by clicking the drop-down menu in the toolbar, as shown in figure 2.6. Alternatively, you can press Esc to leave edit mode, use the arrow keys to highlight a cell, and press Y (for code mode) or M (for markdown mode).

Figure 2.6   The drop-down menu changes the type of cell in the notebook. The Code cell is for Python code, whereas the Markdown code is for text descriptions.

Finally, you can create a Jupyter notebook that elegantly demonstrates TensorFlow code by interlacing code and text cells as shown in figure 2.7.

Exercise 2.3

If you look closely at figure 2.7, you'll notice that it uses `tf.neg` instead of `tf.negative`. That's strange. Could you explain why we might have done that?

Answer

You should be aware that the TensorFlow library changed naming conventions, and you may run into these artifacts when following old TensorFlow tutorials online.

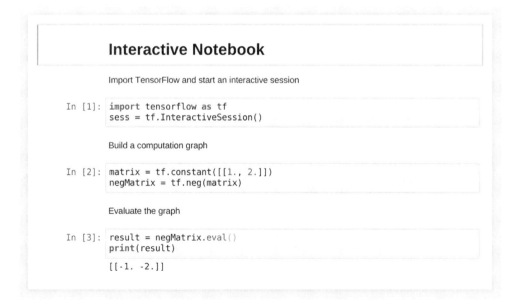

Figure 2.7   An interactive Python notebook presents both code and comments grouped for readability.

One mistake people often make when using Jupyter, though, is relying too much on it for some of the more complex machine learning that you can do with TensorFlow. Jupyter makes interacting with Python code and TensorFlow a pleasure, but it is no substitute for long-running training that you need to code up and then "fire and forget" for hours, days, or even weeks. In those situations, we recommend taking your notebook; using Jupyter's `save as Python file` functionality (available from the File menu); and then running the saved Python file from the command line, using the Python interpreter, in a `tmux` *or* `screen`. These command-line utilities let your current interactive session keep running while you log off and allow you to come back and check the status of your command later, placing you back in the session as though you never left. These tools are UNIX tools, but through Cygwin and virtual machines, they also work in Windows. As you will learn in later chapters, especially when performing distributed, multi-GPU training elegantly with TensorFlow's session API, you will be stuck if your code exists only in a Jupyter notebook. The notebook environment binds you to a particular run time, may be shut down unintentionally (especially on a supercomputer), or may freeze or lock up after days, because Jupyter can eat up a bunch of memory if you let it run for a while.

> **TIP**   Visit the Juptyer home screen periodically, look for notebooks that are running (green) that no longer need to be, select those notebooks, and then click the Shutdown button near the top to free memory. Your email, web browsing, and other activities will thank you!

2.7   *Using variables*

Using TensorFlow constants is a good start, but most interesting applications require data to change. A neuroscientist may be interested in detecting neural activity from sensor measurements, for example. A spike in neural activity could be a Boolean variable that changes over time. To capture this activity in TensorFlow, you can use the `Variable` class to represent a node whose value changes over time.

Example of using a variable object in machine learning

Finding the equation of a line that best fits many points is a classic machine-learning problem that's discussed in greater detail in chapter 3. The algorithm starts with an initial guess, which is an equation characterized by a few numbers (such as the slope or y-intercept). Over time, the algorithm generates increasingly better guesses for these numbers, which are also called *parameters*.

So far, we've been manipulating only constants. Programs with only constants aren't that interesting for real-world applications, though, so TensorFlow allows richer tools such as variables, which are containers for values that may change over time. A machine-learning algorithm updates the parameters of a model until it finds the optimal value for each variable. In the world of machine learning, it's common for parameters to fluctuate until eventually settling down, making variables an excellent data structure for them.

The code in listing 2.8 is a simple TensorFlow program that demonstrates how to use variables. It updates a variable whenever sequential data abruptly increases in value. Think about recording measurements of a neuron's activity over time. This piece of code can detect when the neuron's activity suddenly spikes. The algorithm is an over-simplification for didactic purposes, of course.

Start with importing TensorFlow. TensorFlow allows you to declare a session by using `tf.InteractiveSession()`. When you've declared an interactive session, TensorFlow functions don't require the session attribute that they would otherwise, which makes coding in Jupyter notebooks easier.

Listing 2.8 Using a variable

Starts the session in interactive mode so you won't need to pass around sess

```
import tensorflow as tf
sess = tf.InteractiveSession()


raw_data = [1., 2., 8., -1., 0., 5.5, 6., 13]
spike = tf.Variable(False)
spike.initializer.run()


for i in range(1, len(raw_data)):
    if raw_data[i] - raw_data[i-1] > 5:
        updater = tf.assign(spike, True)
        updater.eval()
    else:
        tf.assign(spike, False).eval()
    print("Spike", spike.eval())

sess.close()
```

Let's say you have some raw data like this.

Creates a Boolean variable called spike to detect a sudden increase in a series of numbers

Because all variables must be initialized, initialize the variable by calling run() on its initializer.

Loops through the data (skipping the first element) and updates the spike variable when a significant increase occurs

To update a variable, assign it a new value, using tf.assign(<var name>, <new value>). Evaluate it to see the change.

Remember to close the session after it'll no longer be used.

The expected output of listing 2.8 is a list of spike values over time:

```
('Spike', False)
('Spike', True)
('Spike', False)
('Spike', False)
('Spike', True)
('Spike', False)
('Spike', True)
```

2.8 Saving and loading variables

Imagine writing a monolithic block of code, of which you'd like to individually test a tiny segment. In complicated machine-learning situations, saving and loading data at known checkpoints makes debugging code much easier. TensorFlow provides an elegant interface to save and load variable values to disk; let's see how to use it for that purpose.

You'll revamp the code that you created in listing 2.8 to save the spike data to disk so that you can load it elsewhere. You'll change the spike variable from a simple Boolean to a vector of Booleans that captures the history of spikes (listing 2.9). Notice that you'll explicitly name the variables so that they can be loaded later with the same names. Naming a variable is optional but highly encouraged for organizing your code. Later in the book, particularly in chapters 14 and 15, you will also use the `tf.identity` function to name the variable so that you can reference it when restoring a saved model graph.

Try running this code to see the results.

Listing 2.9   Saving variables

```
import tensorflow as tf                              Imports TensorFlow and        Let's say you have a
sess = tf.InteractiveSession()                       enables interactive sessions  series of data like this.


raw_data = [1., 2., 8., -1., 0., 5.5, 6., 13]                                      Defines a Boolean
spikes = tf.Variable([False] * len(raw_data), name='spikes')                       vector called spikes
spikes.initializer.run()        Don't forget to initialize the variable.           to locate a sudden
                                                                                   spike in raw data

saver = tf.train.Saver()                             The saver op will enable saving and restoring variables.
                                                     If no dictionary is passed into the constructor, it saves
    for i in range(1, len(raw_data)):                all variables in the current program.
        if raw_data[i] - raw_data[i-1] > 5:
Loop through the   spikes_val = spikes.eval()
data and update    spikes_val[i] = True                              Updates the value of spikes by
the spikes variable  updater = tf.assign(spikes, spikes_val)          using the tf.assign function
when a significant  updater.eval()
increase occurs.                         Don't forget to evaluate the updater;
                                         otherwise, spikes won't be updated.

    save_path = saver.save(sess, "spikes.ckpt")
    print("spikes data saved in file: %s" % save_path)         Saves the variable to disk

                                                               Prints the relative file path
                                                               of the saved variables
    sess.close()
```

You'll notice that a couple of files are generated—one of them being spikes.ckpt—in the same directory as your source code. This file is a compactly stored binary file, so you can't easily modify it with a text editor. To retrieve this data, you can use the restore function from the saver op, as demonstrated in listing 2.10.

Listing 2.10   Loading variables

```
import tensorflow as tf                   Creates a variable of
sess = tf.InteractiveSession()            the same size and name
                                          as the saved data         You no longer need to initialize
                                                                    this variable because it'll be
                                                                    loaded directly.
spikes = tf.Variable([False]*8, name='spikes')
spikes.initializer.run()
saver = tf.train.Saver()

                           Creates the saver op to restore saved data
```

```
saver.restore(sess, "./spikes.ckpt")     ◁─────  Restores data from
print(spikes.eval())   ◁───                       the spikes.ckpt file
                           Prints the
                           loaded data
sess.close()
```

The expected output of listing 2.10 is a Python list of the spikes in your data that looks like the following. The first message is simply TensorFlow telling you that it is loading the model graph and associated parameters (later in the book, we will refer to these as *weights*) from the checkpoint file spikes.ckpt:

```
INFO:tensorflow:Restoring parameters from ./spikes.ckpt
[False False   True False False   True False   True]
```

2.9 Visualizing data using TensorBoard

In machine learning, the most time-consuming part isn't programming; it's waiting for code to finish running unless you use early stopping or see overfitting and want to terminate your model training process. A famous dataset called ImageNet, for example, contains more than 14 million images prepared to be used in a machine-learning context. *Sometimes, it can take days or weeks to finish training an algorithm using a large dataset.* TensorFlow's handy dashboard, TensorBoard, affords you a quick peek at the way values are changing in each node of the graph, giving you some idea of how your code is performing.

Let's see how to visualize variable trends over time in a real-world example. In this section, you'll implement a moving-average algorithm in TensorFlow; then you'll carefully track the variables you care about for visualization in TensorBoard.

> **Wondering why there is a second edition of this book?**
>
> One key reason why this book exists is the preceding italicized text (*Sometimes, it can take days or weeks to finish training an algorithm using a large dataset*). Prepare for that experience in this book. Later in the book, I will be re-creating some famous (read: *big*) models, including the VGG-Face model for facial identification, and generating a sentiment analysis model using all the Netflix review data in natural-language processing. Prepare in this case for TensorFlow to run overnight on your laptop or for it to take days on the supercomputer that you have access to. Don't worry; I'm here to guide you along the way and be your emotional support!

2.9.1 Implementing a moving average

In this section, you'll use TensorBoard to visualize how data changes. Suppose that you're interested in calculating the average stock price of a company. Typically, computing the average is a matter of adding all the values and dividing by the total: mean $= (x_1 + x_2 + \ldots + x_n) / n$. When the total number of values is unknown, you can use a technique called *exponential averaging* to estimate the average value of an unknown number of data points. The exponential average algorithm calculates the current estimated average as a function of the previous estimated average and the current value.

More succinctly, $Avg_t = f(Avg_{t-1}, x_t) = (1 - \alpha)\ Avg_{t-1} + \alpha\ x_t$. Alpha ($\alpha$) is a parameter that will be tuned, representing how strongly recent values should be biased in the calculation of the average. The higher the value of α, the more dramatically the calculated average will differ from the previously estimated average. Figure 2.8 (shown after listing 2.15 later in this chapter) shows how TensorBoard visualizes the values and corresponding running average over time.

When you code this moving average, it's a good idea to think about the main piece of computation that takes place in each iteration. In this case, each iteration will compute $Avg_t = (1 - \alpha)\ Avg_{t-1} + \alpha\ x_t$. As a result, you can design a TensorFlow operator (listing 2.11) that does exactly as the formula says. To run this code, you'll eventually have to define `alpha`, `curr_value`, and `prev_avg`.

Listing 2.11   Defining the average update operator

```
update_avg = alpha * curr_value + (1 - alpha) * prev_avg
```

> alpha is a tf.constant, curr_value is a
> placeholder, and prev_avg is a variable.

You'll define the undefined variables later. The reason you're writing code in such a backward way is that defining the interface first forces you to implement the peripheral setup code to satisfy the interface. Skipping ahead, let's jump right to the session part to see how your algorithm should behave. Listing 2.12 sets up the primary loop and calls the `update_avg` operator on each iteration. Running the `update_avg` operator depends on the `curr_value`, which is fed via the `feed_dict` argument.

Listing 2.12   Running iterations of the exponential average algorithm

```
raw_data = np.random.normal(10, 1, 100)

with tf.Session() as sess:
    for i in range(len(raw_data)):
        curr_avg = sess.run(update_avg, feed_dict={curr_value:raw_data[i]})
        sess.run(tf.assign(prev_avg, curr_avg))
```

Great. The general picture is clear, and all that's left to do is write out the undefined variables. Let's fill in the gaps and implement a working piece of TensorFlow code. Copy listing 2.13 so that you can run it.

Listing 2.13 Filling in missing code to complete the exponential average algorithm

Creates a vector of 100 numbers with a mean of 10 and standard deviation of 1

```
import tensorflow as tf
import numpy as np
                                          Defines alpha as a constant
raw_data = np.random.normal(10, 1, 100)
                                          A placeholder is like a variable, but
alpha = tf.constant(0.05)             ◁   the value is injected from the session.
curr_value = tf.placeholder(tf.float32) ◁
prev_avg = tf.Variable(0.)                          ◁      Initializes the previous
update_avg = alpha * curr_value + (1 - alpha) * prev_avg   average to zero

init = tf.global_variables_initializer()

with tf.Session() as sess:                  Loops through the data one
    sess.run(init)                          by one to update the average
    for i in range(len(raw_data)):    ◁
        curr_avg = sess.run(update_avg, feed_dict={curr_value: raw_data[i]})
        sess.run(tf.assign(prev_avg, curr_avg))
        print(raw_data[i], curr_avg)
```

2.9.2   *Visualizing the moving average*

Now that you have a working implementation of a moving-average algorithm, let's visualize the results by using TensorBoard. Visualization with TensorBoard is usually a two-step process:

1 Pick out which nodes you care about measuring by annotating them with a *summary op.*
2 Call add_summary on them to queue up data to be written to disk.

Suppose that you have an img placeholder and a cost op, as shown in listing 2.14. You can annotate them (by giving each a name such as img or cost) so that they're capable of being visualized in TensorBoard. You'll do something similar with your moving-average example.

Listing 2.14 Annotating with a summary op

```
img = tf.placeholder(tf.float32, [None, None, None, 3])
cost = tf.reduce_sum(...)

my_img_summary = tf.summary.image("img", img)
my_cost_summary = tf.summary.scalar("cost", cost)
```

More generally, to communicate with TensorBoard, you must use a summary op, which produces serialized strings used by a SummaryWriter to save updates to a directory. Every time you call the add_summary method from SummaryWriter, TensorFlow saves data to disk for TensorBoard to use.

WARNING   Be careful not to call the add_summary function too often! Although doing so will produce higher-resolution visualizations of your variables, it'll be at the cost of more computation and slightly slower learning.

Run the following command to make a directory called logs in the same folder as this source code:

```
$ mkdir logs
```

Run TensorBoard with the location of the logs directory passed in as an argument:

```
$ tensorboard --logdir=./logs
```

Open a browser, and navigate to http://localhost:6006, which is the default URL for TensorBoard. Listing 2.15 shows how to hook up the SummaryWriter to your code. Run it, and refresh TensorBoard to see the visualizations.

Listing 2.15   Writing summaries to view in TensorBoard

```
import tensorflow as tf
import numpy as np

raw_data = np.random.normal(10, 1, 100)

alpha = tf.constant(0.05)                                    Creates a summary node
curr_value = tf.placeholder(tf.float32)                         for the averages
prev_avg = tf.Variable(0.)
update_avg = alpha * curr_value + (1 - alpha) * prev_avg                 Creates a
                                                                        summary node
avg_hist = tf.summary.scalar("running_average", update_avg)   ◁──      for the values
value_hist = tf.summary.scalar("incoming_values", curr_value)  ◁──
merged = tf.summary.merge_all()                       ◁──
writer = tf.summary.FileWriter("./logs")   ◁──        Merges the summaries to make
init = tf.global_variables_initializer()             them easier to run at the same time

with tf.Session() as sess:                     Passes in the logs directory's
    sess.run(init)                             location to the writer
    sess.add_graph(sess.graph)          ◁──
    for i in range(len(raw_data)):                        Optional, but allows
        summary_str, curr_avg = sess.run([merged, update_avg],   you to visualize the
            ➥ feed_dict={curr_value: raw_data[i]})         computation graph
        sess.run(tf.assign(prev_avg, curr_avg))            in TensorBoard
        print(raw_data[i], curr_avg)
        writer.add_summary(summary_str, i)     ◁──── Adds the summary to the writer
```

Runs the merged op and the update_avg op at the same time

TIP   You may need to ensure that the TensorFlow session has ended before starting TensorBoard. If you rerun listing 2.15, you'll need to remember to clear the logs directory.

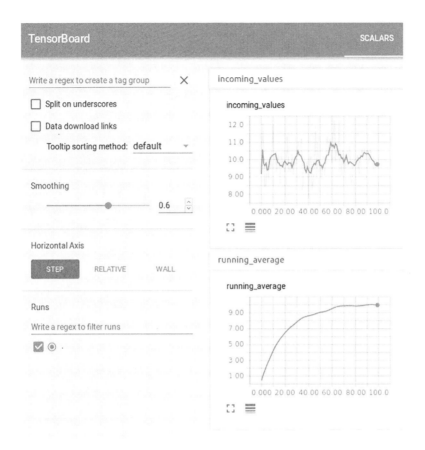

Figure 2.8   The summary display in TensorBoard created in listing 2.15. TensorBoard provides a user-friendly interface to visualize data produced in TensorFlow.

2.10   *Putting it all together: The TensorFlow system architecture and API*

I have not delved into everything that TensorFlow can do—the rest of the book is for those topics—but I have illustrated its core components and the interfaces between them. The collection of these components and interfaces makes up the TensorFlow architecture, shown in figure 2.9.

The TensorFlow 2 version of the listings incorporates new features, including *always eager* execution and updated package names for the optimizers and training. The new listings work well in Python 3; I welcome your feedback on them if you give them a try. You can find the TensorFlow 2 listing code at https://github.com/chrismattmann/MLwithTensorFlow2ed/tree/master/TFv2.

One reasons why it's so hard to pick a version of the framework to depend on and go with it is that software changes so quickly. The author of this book found that out when trying to run some listings from the first edition. Though the concepts and

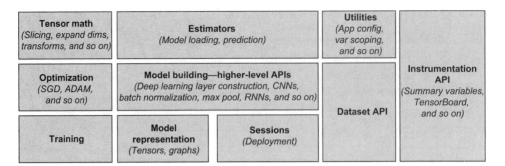

Figure 2.9   The TensorFlow system architecture and API. We've spent a lot of time on sessions, instrumentations, model representation, and training thus far. The later portions of the book progressively explore math, complex models for facial recognition called convolution neural networks (CNNs), optimization, and the rest of the system.

Keeping up with the versions: TF2 and beyond

This book is standardized on two versions of TensorFlow from the 1.x series. Version 1.15, which is the latest release in the 1.x series, works well with Python 3. In chapters 7 and 19, you'll read about a few examples that require Python 2; for that reason, TensorFlow 1.14 is required.

Also, a complete port of the listings and code that address TensorFlow 2 was released while this book was under development. (See the appendix for all the details.) You'll notice that 85–90% of the code for the listings that work in TensorFlow 2 is the same. The main reason is that the data cleaning, gathering, preparation, and evaluation code is fully reusable because it uses accompanying ML libraries like Scikit and Matplotlib.

architecture and system itself remained the same and are close to what would actually run, even in two years, TensorFlow changed a great deal, with more than 20 versions released since TensorFlow 1.0 and the current 1.15.2 version—notably, the last 1.x release. Parts of these changes had to do with breaking changes in the 1.x version of the system, but other parts had to do with a more fundamental architectural understanding gained by performing some of the suggested examples at the end of each chapter, stumbling, and then realizing that TensorFlow has code and interfaces to tackle the problem. As Scott Penberthy, head of applied AI at Google and TensorFlow guru, states in the foreword, chasing TensorFlow versions isn't the point; the details, architecture, cleaning steps, processing, and evaluation techniques will withstand the test of time while the great software engineers improve the scaffolding around tensors.

Today, TensorFlow 2.0 is attracting a lot of attention, but rather than chase the latest version, which has some fundamental (breaking) changes from the 1.x version, I want to deliver a core understanding that will last beyond (breaking) changes and enshrine the fundamentals of machine learning and concepts that make TensorFlow so special, independent of the version. This edition of the book exists largely due to many sleepless nights stumbling through machine-learning concepts (such as model building, estimation, and tensor math) that are core elements of the TensorFlow architecture.

Some of those concepts are shown in figure 2.9. We've spent a lot of time in this chapter discussing the power of sessions, how to represent tensors and graphs, and how to train a model, save it to disk, and restore it. But I haven't covered how to perform a prediction, how to build even more complex graphs (such as regression, classification, CNNs, and RNNs), and how to run TensorFlow on gigabytes and terabytes of data. Those tasks are all possible with TensorFlow because Google and the developers spent so much time thinking through all the challenges you will face doing machine learning at scale.

Each of those challenges is a gray box in the TensorFlow architecture, meaning that it is a component with easy-to-use programming language APIs *and* has plenty of documentation and support. When something doesn't make sense, that's what I'm here for. All the gray boxes will be addressed in the rest of the book. How's that for customer service?

Summary

- You should start thinking of mathematical algorithms in terms of a flowchart of computation. When you consider nodes to be operations and edges to be data flow, writing TensorFlow code becomes trivial. After you define your graph, you evaluate it under a session, and you have your result.

- No doubt there's more to TensorFlow than representing computations as a graph. As you'll see in the coming chapters, some of the built-in functions are tailored to the field of machine learning. In fact, TensorFlow has some of the best support for CNNs, a popular type of model for processing images (with promising results in audio and text as well).

- TensorBoard provides an easy way to visualize the way data changes in Tensor-Flow code, as well as troubleshoot bugs by inspecting trends in data.

- TensorFlow works wonderfully with the Jupyter Notebook application, which is an elegant interactive medium for sharing and documenting Python code.

- The book is standardized on TensorFlow 1.15 and 1.14 for Python 3 and 2, respectively, and I'm committed to showing you the power of the architecture by discussing all the components and interfaces in the system. There's an effort to port the code examples in the book to TensorFlow 2 in a branch of the book's GitHub code repo. Where possible, the book maps concepts in a way that is resilient to API-level changes. See the appendix for details.

Part 2

Core learning algorithms

Learning boils down to looking at past data and predicting its future values in a meaningful way. When the data is continuous, like stock prices or call volumes in a call center, we call that *prediction regression*. If we're predicting specific discrete classes of things like whether an image is a dog or a bird or a cat, we call that *prediction classification*. Classification doesn't work only on images; you can classify all sorts of things, like text, including deciding whether the text has a positive or negative sentiment.

Sometimes, you simply want natural patterns to emerge in the data that allow you to group it, such as cluster data with related properties (such as all the coughing sounds in a big tranche of audio files) or even cell phone data that gives some hints about what types of activities its owner was doing—walking, talking, and the like.

You can't always observe the direct cause of events, which makes it challenging to predict everything. Take the weather. Even with our advanced modeling capabilities, it's a 50/50 bet whether a day will be rainy, sunny, or cloudy. The reason is that sometimes, rain, sun, or clouds is the observed output, but the real causality is hidden and not directly observable. We call models that can predict outcomes based on hidden causality *Markov models*. These models are a fantastic explainable technique that can be part of your machine-learning rig, for weather and for all sorts of other things, such as automatically reading tons of text from books and then disambiguating whether a word is a noun or an adjective.

These techniques are your core learning techniques. In this part of the book, you'll learn how to deploy and apply these techniques by using TensorFlow and other machine-learning utilities and how to evaluate how well they are doing.

Linear regression and beyond

This chapter covers

- Fitting a line to data points
- Fitting arbitrary curves to data points
- Testing performance of regression algorithms
- Applying regression to real-world data

Remember science courses back in high school? It might have been a while ago, or who knows—maybe you're in high school now, starting your journey in machine learning early. Either way, whether you took biology, chemistry, or physics, a common technique to analyze data is plotting how changing one variable affects another.

Imagine plotting the correlation between rainfall frequency and agriculture production. You may observe that an increase in rainfall produces an increase in agriculture production rate. Fitting a line to these data points enables you to make predictions about the production rate under different rain conditions: a little less rain, a little more rain, and so on. If you discover the underlying function from a few data points, that learned function empowers you to make predictions about the values of unseen data.

Regression is the study of how to best fit a curve to summarize your data and is one of the most powerful, best-studied types of supervised-learning algorithms. In regression, we try to understand the data points by discovering the curve that might have generated them. In doing so, we seek an explanation for why the given data is scattered the way it is. The best-fit curve gives us a model for explaining how the dataset might have been produced.

This chapter shows you how to formulate a real-world problem to use regression. As you'll see, TensorFlow is the right tool, delivering some of the most powerful predictors.

3.1   *Formal notation*

If you have a hammer, every problem looks like a nail. This chapter demonstrates the first major machine-learning tool, regression, and formally defines it by using precise mathematical symbols. Learning regression first is a great idea, because many of the skills you'll develop will carry over to other types of problems in future chapters. By the end of this chapter, regression will become the "hammer" in your box of machine-learning tools.

Let's say you have data about how much money people spent on bottles of beer. Alice spent $4 on 2 bottles, Bob spent $6 on 3 bottles, and Clair spent $8 on 4 bottles. You want to find an equation that describes how the number of bottles affects the total cost. If the linear equation $y = 2x$ describes the cost of buying a particular number of bottles, for example, you can find out how much each bottle of beer costs.

When a line appears to fit some data points well, you might claim that your linear model performs well. But you could have tried many possible slopes instead of choosing the value 2. The choice of slope is the *parameter*, and the equation containing the parameter is the *model*. Speaking in machine-learning terms, the equation of the best-fit curve comes from learning the parameters of a model.

As another example, the equation $y = 3x$ is also a line, except with a steeper slope. You can replace that coefficient with any real number (let's call it w), and the equation will still produce a line: $y = wx$. Figure 3.1 shows how changing the parameter w affects the model. The set of all equations you can generate this way is denoted as $M = \{y = wx \mid w \in \mathbb{R}\}$, which is read "all equations $y = wx$ such that w is a real number."

M is a set of all possible models. Choosing a value for w generates a candidate model $M(w) : y = wx$. The regression algorithms that you'll write in TensorFlow will iteratively converge to progressively better values for the model's parameter w. An optimal parameter, which we'll call w^* (pronounced w *star*), is the best-fit equation $M(w^*) : y = w^*x$. *Best-fit* implies that the model produces the least error or difference from its prediction and the actual value, often called the *ground truth*. We'll talk more about this throughout the chapter.

In the most general sense, a regression algorithm tries to design a function, which we'll call *f*, that maps an input to an output. The function's domain is a real-valued vector $\mathbb{R}^d$, and its range is the set of real numbers $\mathbb{R}$.

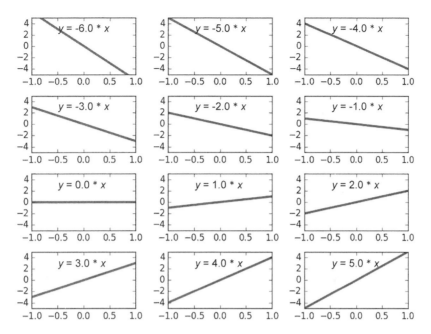

Figure 3.1   Different values of the parameter *w* result in different linear equations. The set of all these linear equations is what constitutes the linear model *M*.

NOTE   Regression can also be posed with multiple outputs, as opposed to one real number. In that case, we call it *multivariate regression.*

The input of the function could be continuous or discrete. But the output must be continuous, as demonstrated in figure 3.2.

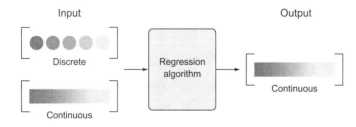

Figure 3.2   A regression algorithm is meant to produce continuous output. The input is allowed to be discrete or continuous. This distinction is important because discrete-valued outputs are handled better by classification, which is discussed in chapters 5 and 6.

NOTE   Regression predicts continuous outputs, but sometimes, that's overkill. Sometimes, we want to predict a discrete output, such as 0 or 1, and nothing in between. Classification is a technique better suited for such tasks, and it's discussed in chapter 5.

We'd like to discover a function *f* that agrees well with the given data points, which are essentially input/output pairs. Unfortunately, the number of possible functions is infinite, so we'll have no luck trying them one by one. Having too many options available to choose among is usually a bad idea. It behooves us to tighten the scope of all the functions we want to deal with. If we look at only straight lines to fit a set of data points, for example, the search becomes much easier.

Exercise 3.1

How many possible functions exist that map 10 integers to 10 integers? Let $f(x)$ be a function that can take numbers 0 through 9 and produce numbers 0 through 9. One example is the identity function that mimics its input—for example, $f(0) = 0$, $f(1) = 1$, and so on. How many other functions exist?

Answer

$10^{10} = 10,000,000,000$

3.1.1   *How do you know the regression algorithm is working?*

Let's say you're trying to sell a housing-market-predictor algorithm to a real estate firm. The algorithm predicts housing prices given properties such as the number of bedrooms and lot size. Real estate companies can easily make millions with such information, but they need some proof that the algorithm works before buying it from you.

To measure the success of the learning algorithm, you'll need to understand two important concepts:

- *Variance* indicates how sensitive a prediction is to the training set that was used. Ideally, how you choose the training set shouldn't matter, meaning that a lower variance is desired.

- *Bias* indicates the strength of assumptions made about the training dataset. Making too many assumptions might make the model unable to generalize, so you should prefer low bias as well.

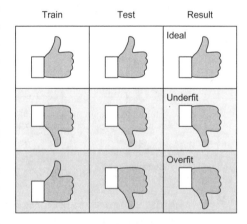

If a model is too flexible, it may accidentally memorize the training data instead of resolving useful patterns. You can imagine a curvy function passing through every point of a dataset, appearing to produce no error. If that happens, we say that the learning algorithm *overfits* the data. In this case, the best-fit curve will agree with the training data well, but it may perform abysmally when evaluated on the testing data (see figure 3.3).

At the other end of the spectrum, a not-so-flexible model may generalize better to

Figure 3.3   Ideally, the best-fit curve fits well on both the training data and the test data. If we witness it fitting poorly with the test data and the training data, there's a chance that our model is underfitting. On the other hand, if it performs poorly on the test data but well on the training data, we know that the model is overfitting.

Transfer learning and overfitting

One of the big overfitting challenges today arises from the process of *transfer learning*: taking knowledge that a model learns in one domain and applying that knowledge to another. Amazingly, this process works extremely well for computer vision, speech recognition, and other domains. But many transfer learning models suffer from overfitting issues. As an example, consider the famous MNIST *(Modified National Institute of Standards and Technology)* dataset and problem for recognition of black-and-white digits for the numbers 1 through 10. The learned model from MNIST can be applied to other non-black-and-white digits (such as street signs), but not without fine-tuning, because even the best MNIST model usually exhibits some overfitting.

unseen testing data but score relatively low on the training data. That situation is called *underfitting*. A too-flexible model has high variance and low bias, whereas a too-strict model has low variance and high bias. Ideally, you want a model with both low-variance error and low-bias error. That way, the model both generalizes to unseen data and captures the regularities of the data. See figure 3.4 for examples of a model underfitting and overfitting data points in 2D.

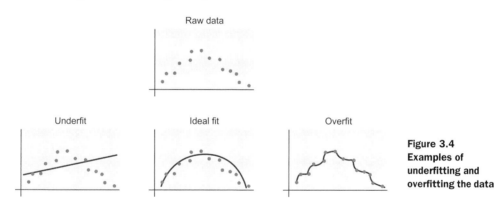

Figure 3.4 Examples of underfitting and overfitting the data

Concretely, the *variance* of a model is a measure of how badly the responses fluctuate, and the *bias* is a measure of how badly the response is offset from the ground truth, as discussed earlier in this chapter. You want your model to achieve accurate (low-bias) as well as reproducible (low-variance) results.

Exercise 3.2

Let's say that your model is $M(w) : y = wx$. How many possible functions can you generate if the values of the weight parameter w must be integers between 0 and 9 (inclusive)?

Answer

Only 10: $\{y = 0, y = x, y = 2x, \ldots, y = 9x\}$

In summary, measuring how well your model does on the training data isn't a great indicator of its generalizability. Instead, you should evaluate your model on a separate batch of testing data. You might find out that your model performs well on the data you trained it with but terribly on the test data, in which case your model is likely overfitting the training data. If the testing error is around the same as the training error, and both errors are similar, your model may be fitting well or (if that error is high) underfitting.

This is why, to measure success in machine learning, you partition the dataset into two groups: a training dataset and a testing dataset. The model is learned using the training dataset, and performance is evaluated on the testing dataset. (Section 3.2 describes how to evaluate performance.) Of the many possible weight parameters you can generate, the goal is to find the one that best fits the data. You measure best fit by defining a cost function, which is discussed in greater detail in section 3.2. The cost function can also drive you to split your test data into even another parameter that tunes the cost and an evaluation dataset (which is the true unseen data). We'll explain more in the ensuing sections.

3.2   *Linear regression*

Let's start by creating fake data for a leap into the heart of linear regression. Create a Python source file called regression.py, and follow along with listing 3.1 to initialize data. The code will produce output similar to figure 3.5.

Listing 3.1   Visualizing raw input

Imports NumPy to help generate initial raw data

Uses Matplotlib to visualize the data

```
import numpy as np
import matplotlib.pyplot as plt
```

The input values are 101 evenly spaced numbers between –1 and 1.

```
x_train = np.linspace(-1, 1, 101)
y_train = 2 * x_train + np.random.randn(*x_train.shape) * 0.33
```

The output values are proportional to the input, but with added noise.

```
plt.scatter(x_train, y_train)
plt.show()
```

Uses Matplotlib's function to generate a scatter plot of the data

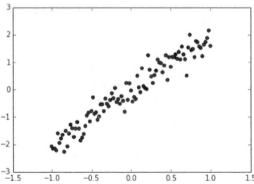

Figure 3.5   Scatter plot of *y = x +* (noise)

Now that you have some data points available, you can try fitting a line. At the very least, you need to provide TensorFlow with a score for each candidate parameter it tries. This score assignment is commonly called a *cost function*. The higher the cost, the worse the model parameter will be. If the best-fit line is $y = 2x$, a parameter choice of 2.01 should have low cost, but the choice of -1 should have higher cost.

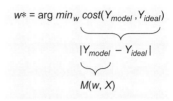

$$w* = \arg \min_w cost(Y_{model}, Y_{ideal})$$

$$|Y_{model} - Y_{ideal}|$$

$$M(w, X)$$

Figure 3.6 Whichever parameter *w* minimizes, the cost is optimal. Cost is defined as the norm of the error between the ideal value with the model response. Finally, the response value is calculated from the function in the model set.

After you define the situation as a cost-minimization problem, as denoted in figure 3.6, TensorFlow takes care of the inner workings, trying to update the parameters in an efficient way to eventually reach the best possible value. Each step of looping through all your data to update the parameters is called an *epoch*.

In this example, you define *cost* by the sum of errors. The error in predicting x is often calculated by the squared difference between the actual value $f(x)$ and the predicted value $M(w, x)$. Therefore, the cost is the sum of the squared differences between the actual and predicted values, as shown in figure 3.7.

Figure 3.7 The cost is the norm of the pointwise difference between the model response and the true value.

Update your previous code to look like listing 3.2. This code defines the cost function and asks TensorFlow to run an optimizer to find the optimal solution for the model parameters.

Listing 3.2 Solving linear regression

```
import tensorflow as tf
import numpy as np
import matplotlib.pyplot as plt
```
Imports TensorFlow for the learning algorithm. You'll need NumPy to set up the initial data, and you'll use Matplotlib to visualize your data.

```
learning_rate = 0.01
training_epochs = 100
```
Defines constants used by the learning algorithm. These constants are called hyperparameters.

```
x_train = np.linspace(-1, 1, 101)
y_train = 2 * x_train + np.random.randn(*x_train.shape) * 0.33
```
Sets up fake data that you'll use to find a best-fit line

```
X = tf.placeholder(tf.float32)
Y = tf.placeholder(tf.float32)
```
Sets up the input and output nodes as placeholders because the value will be injected by x_train and y_train

```
def model(X, w):          <——— Defines the model as y = w*X
    return tf.multiply(X, w)

w = tf.Variable(0.0, name="weights")   <——— Sets up the weights variable

y_model = model(X, w)          | Defines the              Defines the operation that will
cost = tf.square(Y-y_model)    | cost function            be called on each iteration of
                                                          the learning algorithm
train_op = tf.train.GradientDescentOptimizer(learning_rate).minimize(cost)   <——|

sess = tf.Session()                    | Sets up a session and      Loops through the
init = tf.global_variables_initializer()| initializes all variables  dataset multiple
sess.run(init)                                                        times per specified
                                                                     number of epochs

for epoch in range(training_epochs):           <——
    for (x, y) in zip(x_train, y_train):       <——
        sess.run(train_op, feed_dict={X: x, Y: y})   <——          Loops through each
                                                                  item in the dataset
                        | Obtains the final
w_val = sess.run(w)     | parameter value                         Updates the model
                                                                  parameter(s) to try
sess.close()                              | Closes the session    to minimize the cost
plt.scatter(x_train, y_train)   <——— Plots the original data      function
y_learned = x_train*w_val
plt.plot(x_train, y_learned, 'r')   | Plots the
plt.show()                          | best-fit line
```

As figure 3.8 shows, you've just solved linear regression by using TensorFlow! Conveniently, the rest of the topics in regression are minor modifications of listing 3.2. The entire pipeline involves updating model parameters using TensorFlow, as summarized in figure 3.9.

You've learned how to implement a simple regression model in TensorFlow. Making further improvements is a simple matter of enhancing the model with the right medley of variance and bias, as discussed earlier. The linear regression model you've designed so far is burdened with a strong bias; it expresses only a limited set of functions, such as linear functions. In section 3.3, you'll try a more flexible model. You'll notice that only the TensorFlow graph needs to be rewired; everything else (such as preprocessing, training, and evaluation) stays the same.

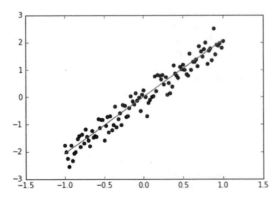

Figure 3.8   Linear regression estimate shown by running listing 3.2

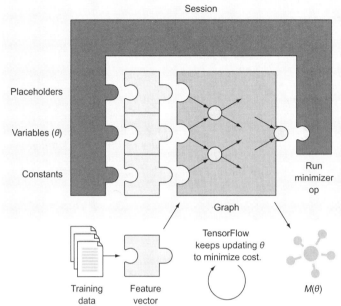

Learning algorithm in TensorFlow

Figure 3.9   The learning algorithm updates the model's parameters to minimize the given cost function.

3.3   *Polynomial model*

Linear models may be an intuitive first guess, but real-world correlations are rarely so simple. The trajectory of a missile through space, for example, is curved relative to the observer on Earth. Wi-Fi signal strength degrades with an inverse square law. The change in height of a flower over its lifetime certainly isn't linear.

When data points appear to form smooth curves rather than straight lines, you need to change your regression model from a straight line to something else. One such approach is to use a polynomial model. A *polynomial* is a generalization of a linear function. The *nth* degree polynomial looks like the following:

$$f(x) = w_n\, x^n + \ldots + w_1\, x + w_0$$

NOTE   When $n = 1$, a polynomial is simply a linear equation $f(x) = w_1\, x + w_0$.

Consider the scatter plot in figure 3.10, showing the input on the x-axis and the output on the y-axis. As you can tell, a straight line is insufficient to describe all the data. A polynomial function is a more flexible generalization of a linear function.

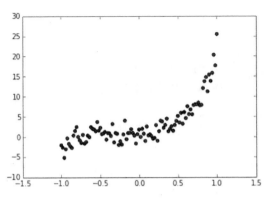

Figure 3.10   Data points like these aren't suitable for a linear model.

Let's try to fit a polynomial to this kind of data. Create a new file called polynomial.py, and follow along with listing 3.3.

Listing 3.3   Using a polynomial model

```
import tensorflow as tf
import numpy as np
import matplotlib.pyplot as plt
```
Imports the relevant libraries and initializes the hyperparameters

```
learning_rate = 0.01
training_epochs = 40

trX = np.linspace(-1, 1, 101)
```
Sets up fake raw input data

```
num_coeffs = 6
trY_coeffs = [1, 2, 3, 4, 5, 6]
trY = 0
for i in range(num_coeffs):
    trY += trY_coeffs[i] * np.power(trX, i)
```
Sets up raw output data based on a fifth-degree polynomial

```
trY += np.random.randn(*trX.shape) * 1.5
```
◁——— Adds noise

```
plt.scatter(trX, trY)
plt.show()
```
Shows a scatter plot of the raw data

```
X = tf.placeholder(tf.float32)
Y = tf.placeholder(tf.float32)
```
Defines the nodes to hold values for input/output pairs

```
def model(X, w):
    terms = []
    for i in range(num_coeffs):
        term = tf.multiply(w[i], tf.pow(X, i))
        terms.append(term)
    return tf.add_n(terms)
```
Defines your polynomial model

```
w = tf.Variable([0.] * num_coeffs, name="parameters")
y_model = model(X, w)
```
Sets up the parameter vector to all zeros

Defines the cost function as before

```
cost = (tf.pow(Y-y_model, 2))
train_op = tf.train.GradientDescentOptimizer(learning_rate).minimize(cost)
```

```
sess = tf.Session()
init = tf.global_variables_initializer()
sess.run(init)

Jr epoch in range(training_epochs):
    for (x, y) in zip(trX, trY):
        sess.run(train_op, feed_dict={X: x, Y: y})

w_val = sess.run(w)
print(w_val)

sess.close()

plt.scatter(trX, trY)
trY2 = 0
for i in range(num_coeffs):
    trY2 += w_val[i] * np.power(trX, i)

plt.plot(trX, trY2, 'r')
plt.show()
```

Sets up the session and runs the learning algorithm as before

Closes the session when done

Plots the result

The final output of this code is a fifth-degree polynomial that fits the data, as shown in figure 3.11.

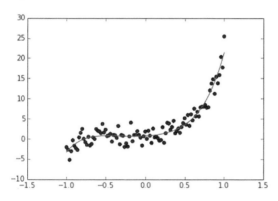

Figure 3.11 The best-fit curve aligns smoothly with the nonlinear data.

3.4   *Regularization*

Don't be fooled by the wonderful flexibility of polynomials, as shown in section 3.3. Just because higher-order polynomials are extensions of lower ones doesn't mean that you should always prefer the more flexible model.

In the real world, raw data rarely forms a smooth curve mimicking a polynomial. Suppose that you're plotting house prices over time. The data likely will contain fluctuations. The goal of regression is to represent the complexity in a simple mathematical equation. If your model is too flexible, the model may be overcomplicating its interpretation of the input.

Take, for example, the data presented in figure 3.12. You try to fit an eighth-degree polynomial into points that appear to follow the equation $y = x^2$. This process fails miserably, as the algorithm tries its best to update the nine coefficients of the polynomial.

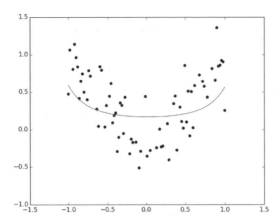

Figure 3.12   When the model is too flexible, a best-fit curve can look awkwardly complicated or unintuitive. We need to use regularization to improve the fit so that the learned model performs well against test data.

Regularization is a technique to structure the parameters in a form you prefer, often to solve the problem of overfitting (see figure 3.13). In this case, you anticipate the learned coefficients to be 0 everywhere except for the second term, thus producing the curve $y = x^2$. The regression algorithm may produce curves that score well but look strangely overcomplicated.

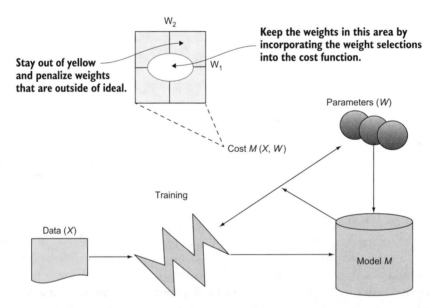

Figure 3.13   An overview of regularization. The modeling process takes data (X) as input and tries to learn the model parameters (W) that minimize the cost function or distance between the model predictions and the ground truth. The top yellow quadrant shows a 2D model parameter space for picking weights for simplicity. Regularization ensures that the training algorithm does not select weights in the less-than-ideal (yellow) areas, but stays inside the white circle of ideal weight values.

To influence the learning algorithm to produce a smaller coefficient vector (let's call it w), you add that penalty to the loss term. To control how significantly you want to weigh the penalty term, you multiply the penalty by a constant non-negative number, λ, as follows:

$$Cost(X, Y) = Loss(X, Y) + \lambda$$

If λ is set to 0, regularization isn't in play. As you set λ to larger and larger values, parameters with larger norms will be heavily penalized. The choice of norm varies case by case, but parameters are typically measured by their L1 or L2 norm. Simply put, regularization reduces some of the flexibility of the otherwise easily tangled model.

To figure out which value of the regularization parameter λ performs best, you must split your dataset into two disjointed sets. About 70% of the randomly chosen input/output pairs will consist of the training dataset; the remaining 30% will be used for testing. You'll use the function provided in listing 3.4 for splitting the dataset.

Listing 3.4 Splitting the dataset into testing and training sets

**Takes the input and output dataset
as well as the desired split ratio**

```
def split_dataset(x_dataset, y_dataset, ratio):
    arr = np.arange(x_dataset.size)
    np.random.shuffle(arr)                                    Shuffles a list of numbers
    num_train = int(ratio * x_dataset.size)
    x_train = x_dataset[arr[0:num_train]]                     Uses the shuffled list
    x_test = x_dataset[arr[num_train:x_dataset.size]]         to split the x_dataset
    y_train = y_dataset[arr[0:num_train]]
    y_test = y_dataset[arr[num_train:x_dataset.size]]         Likewise, splits the y_dataset
    return x_train, x_test, y_train, y_test                   Returns the split x and y datasets
```

Calculates the number of training examples points to `num_train = int(ratio * x_dataset.size)`

Exercise 3.3

A Python library called SK-learn supports many useful data-preprocessing algorithms. You can call a function in SK-learn to do exactly what listing 3.4 achieves. Can you find this function in the library's documentation? (Hint: See http://mng.bz/7Grm.)

Answer

It's called `sklearn.model_selection.train_test_split`.

With this handy tool, you can begin testing which value of performs best on your data. Open a new Python file, and follow along with listing 3.5.

Listing 3.5   Evaluating regularization parameters

```
import tensorflow as tf
import numpy as np
import matplotlib.pyplot as plt          Imports the relevant
                                         libraries and initializes
learning_rate = 0.001                    the hyperparameters
training_epochs = 1000
reg_lambda = 0.

x_dataset = np.linspace(-1, 1, 100)

num_coeffs = 9
y_dataset_params = [0.] * num_coeffs
y_dataset_params[2] = 1                          Creates a fake
y_dataset = 0                                     dataset, y = x²
for i in range(num_coeffs):
    y_dataset += y_dataset_params[i] * np.power(x_dataset, i)
y_dataset += np.random.randn(*x_dataset.shape) * 0.3

(x_train, x_test, y_train, y_test) = split_dataset(x_dataset, y_dataset, 0.7)

X = tf.placeholder(tf.float32)
Y = tf.placeholder(tf.float32)
                                              Splits the dataset into
def model(X, w):                              70% training and 30%
    terms = []                                testing, using listing 3.4
    for i in range(num_coeffs):
        term = tf.multiply(w[i], tf.pow(X, i))    Sets up the input/output
        terms.append(term)                        placeholders
    return tf.add_n(terms)

w = tf.Variable([0.] * num_coeffs, name="parameters")
y_model = model(X, w)                                  Defines your model
cost = tf.div(tf.add(tf.reduce_sum(tf.square(Y-y_model)),
                tf.multiply(reg_lambda, tf.reduce_sum(tf.square(w)))),
            2*x_train.size)
train_op = tf.train.GradientDescentOptimizer(learning_rate).minimize(cost)

sess = tf.Session()                                      Defines the
init = tf.global_variables_initializer()  Sets up the     regularized
sess.run(init)                            session         cost function

for reg_lambda in np.linspace(0,1,100):
    for epoch in range(training_epochs):
        sess.run(train_op, feed_dict={X: x_train, Y: y_train})    Tries various
    final_cost = sess.run(cost, feed_dict={X: x_test, Y:y_test})  regularization
    print('reg lambda', reg_lambda)                               parameters
    print('final cost', final_cost)

sess.close()     ◁──── Closes the session
```

If you plot the corresponding output per each regularization parameter from listing 3.5, you can see how the curve changes as λ increases. When λ is 0, the algorithm favors using the higher-order terms to fit the data. As you start penalizing parameters with a high L2 norm, the cost decreases, indicating that you're recovering from overfitting, as shown in figure 3.14.

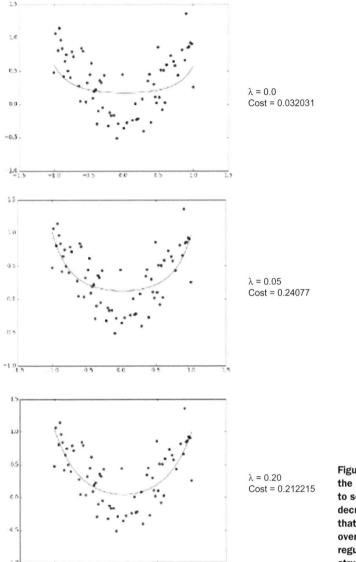

λ = 0.0
Cost = 0.032031

λ = 0.05
Cost = 0.24077

λ = 0.20
Cost = 0.212215

**Figure 3.14   As you increase
the regularization parameter
to some extent, the cost
decreases. This result implies
that the model was originally
overfitting the data and that
regularization helped add
structure.**

TensorFlow library support for regularization

TensorFlow is a fully capable library for supporting machine learning, and even though
the focus in this section is on how to implement regularization yourself, the library
provides its own functions for computing L2 regularization. You can use the function
`tf.nn.l2_loss(weights)` to produce equivalent results by adding the regularization
loss to your cost function for each of your weights.

3.5 *Application of linear regression*

Running linear regression on fake data is like buying a new car and never driving it. This awesome machinery begs to manifest itself in the real world! Fortunately, many datasets are available online to test your newfound knowledge of regression:

- The University of Massachusetts Amherst supplies small datasets of various types at https://scholarworks.umass.edu/data.
- Kaggle provides all types of large-scale data for machine-learning competitions at https://www.kaggle.com/datasets.
- Data.gov (https://catalog.data.gov) is an open data initiative by the US government that contains many interesting and practical datasets.

A good number of datasets contain dates. You can find a dataset of all phone calls to the 311 nonemergency line in Los Angeles, California, for example, at https://www .dropbox.com/s/naw774olqkve7sc/311.csv?dl=0. A good feature to track could be the frequency of calls per day, week, or month. For convenience, listing 3.6 allows you to obtain a weekly frequency count of data items.

Listing 3.6   Parsing raw CSV datasets

```
import csv          ◁──── For reading CSV files easily
import time          ◁───┐
                          └── For using useful date functions
def read(filename, date_idx, date_parse, year, bucket=7):

    days_in_year = 365

    freq = {}                                        ◁──┐ Sets up initial frequency map
    for period in range(0, int(days_in_year / bucket)):
        freq[period] = 0

    with open(filename, 'rb') as csvfile:   ◁───┐
        csvreader = csv.reader(csvfile)          │ Reads data and aggregates
        csvreader.next()                         │ count per period
        for row in csvreader:
            if row[date_idx] == '':
                continue
            t = time.strptime(row[date_idx], date_parse)
            if t.tm_year == year and t.tm_yday < (days_in_year-1):
                freq[int(t.tm_yday / bucket)] += 1

    return freq
                                              ┌── Obtains a weekly frequency
freq = read('311.csv', 0, '%m/%d/%Y', 2014   ◁─┘  count of 311 phone calls in 2014
```

This code gives you the training data for linear regression. The `freq` variable is a dictionary that maps a period (such as a week) to a frequency count. A year has 52 weeks, so you'll have 52 data points if you leave `bucket=7` as is.

Now that you have data points, you have exactly the input and output necessary to fit a regression model by using the techniques covered in this chapter. More practically, you can use the learned model to interpolate or extrapolate frequency counts.

Summary

- Regression is a type of supervised machine learning for predicting continuous-valued output.
- By defining a set of models, you greatly reduce the search space of possible functions. Moreover, TensorFlow takes advantage of the differentiable property of the functions by running its efficient gradient-descent optimizers to learn the parameters.
- You can easily modify linear regression to learn polynomials and other, more complicated curves.
- To avoid overfitting your data, regularize the cost function by penalizing larger-valued parameters.
- If the output of the function isn't continuous, use a classification algorithm instead (see chapter 4).
- TensorFlow enables you to solve linear-regression machine-learning problems effectively and efficiently, and hence to make useful predictions about important matters such as agricultural production, heart conditions, and housing prices.

Using regression for call-center volume prediction

This chapter covers

- Applying linear regression to real-world data
- Cleaning data to fit curves and models you have not seen before
- Using Gaussian distributions and predicting points along them
- Evaluating how well your linear regression predicts the expected values

Armed with the power of regression-based prediction and TensorFlow, you can get started working on real-world problems involving more of the steps in the machine-learning process, such as data cleaning, fitting models to unseen data, and identifying models that aren't necessarily an easy-to-spot best-fit line or a polynomial curve. In chapter 3, I showed you how to use regression when you control all steps of the machine-learning process, from using NumPy to generate fake data points that

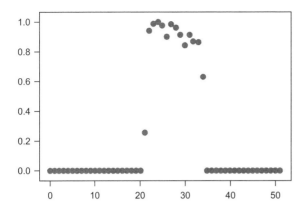

Figure 4.1 A set of data points corresponding to weeks of the year on the x-axis (0–51) and normalized call volume (number of calls in a particular week/max calls for all weeks)

nicely fit a linear function (a line) or a polynomial function (a curve). But what happens in real life, when the data points don't fit one of the patterns you've seen before, such as the set of points shown in figure 4.1? Take a close look at figure 4.1. Is a linear regression model a good predictor here?

Figure 4.2 gives you two best-fit lines, using a linear regression model for the call data, and it seems to be wildly off. Can you imagine the errors between the predicted and actual values in the middle or the tail end of the graphs on the left and right sides of figure 4.2? Polynomial models would be equally abysmal because the data does not neatly fit a curve and both increases and decreases in y-value at seemingly random moments along the x-axis. Convince yourself by drawing a second- or third-order polynomial. Can you get it to fit the data? If you can't, it's likely that a computer program will have similar difficulty. In situations like this one, it's perfectly normal to ask yourself these questions:

- Can regression still help me predict the next set of points?
- What regression models exist besides lines and polynomial curves?
- Because real-life data traditionally doesn't come in the form of nice (x, y) points that are easy to plot and model with things like regression, how do I prepare the data so that it cleanly fits a particular model or find models that better fit messy data?

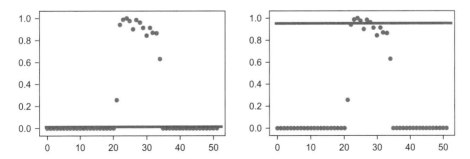

Figure 4.2 Two linear best-fit models for the data points shown in figure 4.1

In chapter 3 and throughout the book, sometimes for illustration I generate fake data such as the output from the NumPy `np.random.normal` function, but it cannot be overstated that real data rarely looks this way.

> **NOTE** I know that several authors are writing books on the subject of data cleaning for machine learning. Although the gory details are beyond the scope of this book, I won't hide data cleaning steps from you; you'll get experience using techniques that make this process easier with TensorFlow.

Another question that arises in applying regression to real-world problems is how you evaluate the accuracy of your predictions by computing the bias, or the difference between the predicted values of the model and the actual values. The lines generated by the regression model in figure 4.2 seem to be off, but you can make stronger statements by quantitatively measuring and evaluating the error between your model predictions and the ground truth. TensorFlow provides easy-to-use constructs with its data flow graph to compute error in a few lines of code. Matplotlib similarly furnishes capabilities that let you visually inspect and evaluate the model error with a few lines of code.

Linear regression is a good predictor in many real-world problems, so it's hard to choose one. In general, problems that are temporal in nature provide a natural ordering of data on the x-axis for historical data training and a future state (such as N hours or weeks in the future) that forms a good prediction target on which to test regression. So choosing a problem that involves time as a dependent variable lends itself quite nicely to regression models.

Lots of time-based datasets exist for machine learning, and many open data challenges that use them are available for free on Kaggle (https://www.kaggle.com), a widely-used open machine-learning platform. Kaggle provides datasets, documentation, shareable code, and a platform for executing machine learning, including first-class support for TensorFlow-based notebooks and code. Kaggle has a large number of temporal datasets to try regression machine-learning models on, such as the real-estate price challenge (http://mng.bz/6Ady) and the New York City (NYC) 311 open dataset (http://mng.bz/1gPX). The NYC 311 dataset is interesting because it is time-based, requires some cleaning, and does not cleanly fit a line or polynomial-curve regression model.

New York City's Open Data platform
The city of New York has an Open Data initiative that provides easy application programming interfaces (APIs) to download data for machine learning and other uses. You can access the Open Data portal at http://opendata.cityofnewyork.us.

New York City's 311 data is a set of information collected for each call made by a resident to the city's customer call center requesting information about city and other government non-emergency services, such as waste disposal, code enforcement, and building maintenance. It's probably not hard to imagine that customer call centers like this one get a lot of calls each day, because they help people get to the information they need in a timely fashion. But how many calls does the call center get in a week? How about in a year? Are there particular months or weeks when the call center can expect to get more or fewer calls?

Imagine that you are responsible for staffing at this type of service, especially during the holidays. Should you have more or fewer customer service agents manning the phone lines? Do spikes in calls correspond to seasons? Should you allow for extra seasonal employees, or will the full-time employees be enough? Regression and Tensor-Flow can help you find answers to these questions.

4.1   *What is 311?*

311 is a national service in the United States and in Canada that provides information about non-emergency municipal services. The service allows you to report that the trash collectors did not arrive to take your garbage or to find out how to get leaves and shrubs removed from the common area in front of your residence. The volume of calls to 311 vary, but in large cities and municipalities, it can range from thousands to tens of thousands of calls per month.

One key question that these call centers and their associated information services must deal with is how many calls will come in a particular month. This information may help the service plan staffing levels during holiday periods or decide how much storage and computing for their resource and services directories will cost. Also, it may help 311 advocate and provide information on the number of people it expects to serve in any given year, which would help justify continued support for critical services.

The first 311

The first 311 service opened its doors in Baltimore, Maryland, in 1996. The two main goals of the service were to develop a closer connection between the government and its citizens, and to create a customer relationship management (CRM) capability to ensure better service to the community. The CRM function today lends itself to the types of data-driven predictions that we'll explore in this chapter.

Being able to predict call volume in any given month would be an extremely useful capability for any 311 service. You could perform this prediction by looking at a year's worth of calls and their associated dates and times, and then rolling those calls up on a weekly basis to construct a set of points in which the x value is the week number (1–52, or 365 days divided by 7 days in a week) and the y value is the count of calls in that particular week. Then you would do the following:

- Plot the number of calls on the y-axis and the week number (1–52) on the x-axis.
- Examine the trend to see whether it resembles a line, a curve, or something else.

- Select and train a regression model that best fits the data points (week number and number of calls).
- Evaluate how well your model performs by calculating and visualizing its errors.
- Use your new model to predict how many calls 311 can expect in any given week, season, and year.

This prediction seems like something that a linear regression model and TensorFlow could help you make, and that's precisely what you are going to work on in this chapter.

4.2 Cleaning the data for regression

First, download this data—a set of phone calls from the summer of 2014 from the New York City 311 service—from http://mng.bz/P16w. Kaggle has other 311 datasets, but you'll use this particular data due to its interesting properties. The calls are formatted as a comma-separated values (CSV) file that has several interesting features, including the following:

- A unique call identifier showing the date when the call was created
- The location and ZIP code of the reported incident or information request
- The specific action that the agent on the call took to resolve the issue
- What borough (such as the Bronx or Queens) the call was made from
- The status of the call

This dataset contains lot of useful information for machine learning, but for purposes of this exercise, you care only about the call-creation date. Create a new file named 311.py. Then write a function to read each line in the CSV file, detect the week number, and sum the call counts by week.

Your code will need to deal with some messiness in this data file. First, you aggregate individual calls, sometimes hundreds in a single day, into a seven-day or weekly bin, as identified by the `bucket` variable in listing 4.1. The `freq` (short for frequency) variable holds the value of calls per week and per year. If the 311 CSV contains more than a year's worth of data (as other 311 CSVs that you can find on Kaggle do), gin up your code to allow for selection by year of calls to train on. The result of the code in listing 4.1 is a `freq` dictionary whose values are the number of calls indexed by year and by week number via the `period` variable. The `t.tm_year` variable holds the parsed year resulting from passing the call-creation-time value (indexed in the CSV as `date_idx`, an integer defining the column number where the date field is located) and the `date_parse` format string to Python's `time` library's `strptime` (or string parse time) function. The `date_parse` format string is a pattern defining the way the date appears as text in the CSV so that Python knows how to convert it to a datetime representation.

Listing 4.1   Reading and aggregating the call count by week from the 311 CSV

```
def read(filename, date_idx, date_parse, year=None, bucket=7):
    days_in_year = 365

    freq = {}
    if year != None:
        for period in range(0, int(days_in_year / bucket)):
            freq[period] = 0

    with open(filename, 'r') as csvfile:
        csvreader = csv.reader(csvfile)
        next(csvreader)
        for row in csvreader:
            if row[date_idx] == '':
                continue

            t = time.strptime(row[date_idx], date_parse)
            if year == None:
                if not t.tm_year in freq:
                    freq[t.tm_year] = {}
                    for period in range(0, int(days_in_year / bucket)):
                        freq[t.tm_year][period] = 0

                if t.tm_yday < (days_in_year - 1):
                    freq[t.tm_year][int(t.tm_yday / bucket)] += 1
            else:
                if t.tm_year == year and t.tm_yday < (days_in_year-1):
                    freq[int(t.tm_yday / bucket)] += 1

    return freq
```

7 days in a week and 365 days in a year yields 52 weeks.

If the year is specified, select only calls for that year.

If the year column is not present in the call data, skip the row.

Initialize the (year, week) cell value to 0 if the CSV file contains more than a year of data.

For each row, add 1 call to the (year, week) or (week) indexed cell previous count (starts at 0).

Most of the code in listing 4.1 handles real-world data not generated by some NumPy call that generates random (x, y) data points along a normal distribution—a theme in the book. Machine learning expects clean data to perform all its black magic, and real-world data is not clean. Take a random set of 311 CSV files from NYC's Open Data portal (https://data.cityofnewyork.us/browse?q=311), and you will find a lot of variance. Some files have calls from multiple years, so your code needs to handle that situation; some files have missing rows, or missing year and date values for a particular cell, and your code still needs to hold up. Writing resilient data-cleaning code is one of the fundamental principles of machine learning, so writing this code will be the first step in many examples in this book.

Call the `read` function defined in listing 4.1, and you will get back a Python dictionary indexed by (year, week number) or simply by (week number), depending on whether you passed in the year as the last functional argument. Call the function in your 311.py code. The function takes as input the column index (1 for the second column, indexed by 0) and then a string that looks like

```
freq = read('311.csv', 1, '%m/%d/%Y %H:%M:%S %p', 2014)
```

Tell the function that the date field is in index 1 (or the second column based on a 0 index), that your dates are formatted as strings that look like `'month/day/year hour:minutes:seconds AM/PM'` or `'12/10/2014 00:00:30 AM'` (corresponding to December 10, 2014 at 30 seconds past midnight), and that you would like to obtain only dates from 2014 from the CSV.

You can print the values from the frequency buckets if you are using Jupyter by inspecting the `freq` dictionary. The result is a 52-week (indexed from 0, so 0–51) histogram with call counts per week. As you can tell from the output, the data is clustered from week 22 to week 35, which is May 26 to August 25, 2014:

```
freq
{0: 0,
 1: 0,
 2: 0,
 3: 0,
 4: 0,
 5: 0,
 6: 0,
 7: 0,
 8: 0,
 9: 0,
 10: 0,
 11: 0,
 12: 0,
 13: 0,
 14: 0,
 15: 0,
 16: 0,
 17: 0,
 18: 0,
 19: 0,
 20: 0,
 21: 10889,
 22: 40240,
 23: 42125,
 24: 42673,
 25: 41721,
 26: 38446,
 27: 41915,
 28: 41008,
 29: 39011,
 30: 36069,
 31: 38821,
 32: 37050,
 33: 36967,
 34: 26834,
 35: 0,
 36: 0,
 37: 0,
 38: 0,
 39: 0,
 40: 0,
```

```
41: 0,
42: 0,
43: 0,
44: 0,
45: 0,
46: 0,
47: 0,
48: 0,
49: 0,
50: 0,
51: 0}
```

The International Standards Organization (ISO) body, which defines standards for computer code, data, and software, publishes the frequently used ISO-8601 standard for representing dates and times as strings. Python's `time` and `iso8601` libraries implement this standard, which includes a specification of week numbers associated with dates and times for weeks starting on Mondays (https://www.epochconverter .com/weeknumbers), which seems to be a useful representation for the 311 data. Though other week-number representations are available, most of them have a different starting day for the week, such as Sunday.

By translating time-based dates to week numbers on the x-axis, you have an integer value representing time that can be easily ordered and visualized. This value goes along with your call-frequency y-axis values that the regression function will predict.

Converting week numbers to dates

Much of the time-based data that you will deal with is sometimes better represented by a week number. Dealing with an integer from 1 to 52 is a lot better than the string value `'Wednesday, September 5, 2014'`, for example. The EpochConverter website can easily tell you the week number for a year and date. To see the list of days mapped to week numbers for 2014 output from listing 4.1, visit https://www.epochconverter .com/weeks/2014.

You can get the same information in plain Python by using the `datetime` library:

```
import datetime
datetime.date(2010, 6, 16).isocalendar()[1]
```

This code outputs 24 because June 16, 2010, was the 24th week of that year.

You're welcome!

Open a Jupyter notebook, and paste listing 4.2 into it to visualize the binned histogram of call frequencies per week from your `freq` dictionary (returned from the `read` function) and to generate figure 4.3, which is the distribution of points discussed at the beginning of the chapter. By examining the point distribution, you can decide on a model for your regression predictor to code in TensorFlow. Listing 4.2 sets up your input training values as weeks 1–52 and your prediction output as the number of calls expected in that week. The X_train variable holds an array of the keys of the frequency dictionary (the integers 0–51, for 52 weeks), and the Y_train variable holds the number of 311 calls per week. nY_train holds the normalized Y values (divided by maxY) between 0 and 1. I explain why later in the chapter, but the preview is that it eases learning during the training process. The final lines of code use Matplotlib to create a scatter plot of the (week number, call frequency) points.

Listing 4.2 Visualizing and setting up the input data

Defines the input training data X as the week numbers, which are the keys of the python freq dictionary

Defines the input training data Y as the number of calls corresponding to the specific week

```
X_train = np.asarray(list(freq.keys()))
Y_train = np.asarray(list(freq.values()))
print("Num samples", str(len(X_train)))
maxY = np.max(Y_train)
nY_train = Y_train / np.max(Y_train)

plt.scatter(X_train, nY_train)
plt.show()
```

Normalizes the number of calls to values between 0 and 1 to ease learning

Plots the data to learn

The output of listing 4.2 is shown in figure 4.3. It's quite dissimilar from the lines and curves we tried to fit a model for in chapter 3. Remember that I said that real-world data isn't always pretty? Intuitively, the data tells us that for most of the first two quarters of the year, there were no calls; a large spike in spring extended through the summer; and in the fall and winter, there were no calls. Perhaps summer is a season when many people in New York use 311, at least in 2014. More likely, the data is only a subset of the available *actual* information, but let's still see whether we can make a good model of it.

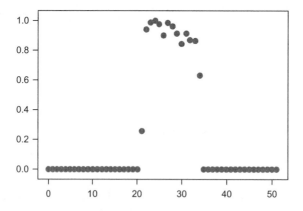

Figure 4.3   **A plot of call-frequency counts on the y-axis compared with weeks of the year (0–51) on the x-axis. Activity swells in the May 2014 timeframe and tapers in late August 2014.**

If you have ever looked at the distribution of scores on a test, one common model for describing the sorted score distribution from 0 to 100 is a curve or a bell curve. As it turns out, we'll be teaching our TensorFlow predictor to emulate that type of model in the remainder of the chapter.

4.3 *What's in a bell curve? Predicting Gaussian distributions*

A bell or normal curve is a common term to describe data that we say fits a normal distribution. The largest Y values of the data occur in the middle or statistically the mean X value of the distribution of points, and the smaller Y values occur on the early and tail X values of the distribution. We also call this a *Gaussian* distribution after the famous German mathematician Carl Friedrich Gauss, who was responsible for the Gaussian function that describes the normal distribution.

We can use the NumPy method `np.random.normal` to generate random points sampled from the normal distribution in Python. The following equation shows the Gaussian function that underlies this distribution:

$$e^{\frac{(-(x-\mu)^2)}{2\sigma^2}}$$

The equation includes the parameters μ (pronounced *mu*) and σ (pronounced *sigma*), where mu is the mean and sigma is the standard deviation of the distribution, respectively. Mu and sigma are the parameters of the model, and as you have seen, TensorFlow will learn the appropriate values for these parameters as part of training a model.

To convince yourself that you can use these parameters to generate bell curves, you can type the code snippet in listing 4.3 into a file named gaussian.py and then run it to produce the plot that follows it. The code in listing 4.3 produces the bell curve visualizations shown in figure 4.4. Note that I selected values of mu between –1 and 2. You should see center points of the curve in figure 4.4, as well as standard deviations (sigma) between 1 and 3, so the width of the curves should correspond to those values inclusively. The code plots 120 linearly-spaced points with X values between –3 and 3 and Y values between 0 and 1 that fit the normal distribution according to mu and sigma, and the output should look like figure 4.4.

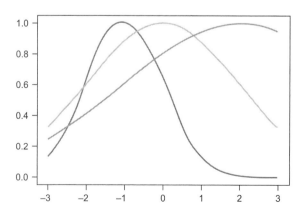

Figure 4.4 Three bell curves with means between –1 and –2 (their center points should be near those points) and with standard deviations between 1 and 3. Curves are generated from 120 points generated with linear distribution between –3 and 3.

Listing 4.3   Producing some Gaussian distributions and visualizing them

Implement the Gaussian curve with mu and sigma.

```
def gaussian(x, mu, sig):
    return np.exp(-np.power(x - mu, 2.) / (2 * np.power(sig, 2.)))
x_values = np.linspace(-3, 3, 120)          ◁────────────┐
for mu, sig in [(-1, 1), (0, 2), (2, 3)]:                 Randomly pick 120 linearly spaced
    plt.plot(x_values, gaussian(x_values, mu, sig))       samples of X between –3 and 3.

plt.show()
```

4.4   Training your call prediction regressor

Now you are ready to use TensorFlow to fit your NYC 311 data to this model. It's probably clear by looking at the curves that they seem to comport naturally with the 311 data, especially if TensorFlow can figure out the values of mu that put the center point of the curve near spring and summer and that have a fairly large call volume, as well as the sigma value that approximates the best standard deviation.

Listing 4.4 sets up the TensorFlow training session, associated hyperparameters, learning rate, and number of training epochs. I'm using a fairly large step for learning rate so that TensorFlow can appropriately scan the values of mu and sig by taking big-enough steps before settling down. The number of epochs—5,000—gives the algorithm enough training steps to settle on optimal values. In local testing on my laptop, these hyperparameters arrived at strong accuracy (99%) and took less than a minute. But I could have chosen other hyperparameters, such as a learning rate of 0.5, and given the training process more steps (epochs). Part of the fun of machine learning is hyperparameter training, which is more art than science, though techniques such as meta-learning and algorithms such as HyperOpt may ease this process in the future. A full discussion of hyperparameter tuning is beyond the scope of this chapter, but an online search should yields thousands of relevant introductions.

When the hyperparameters are set up, define the placeholders X and Y, which will be used for the input week number and associated number of calls (normalized), respectively. Earlier, I mentioned normalizing the Y values and creating the nY_train variable in listing 4.2 to ease learning. The reason is that the model Gaussian function that we are attempting to learn has Y values only between 0 and 1 due to the exponent *e*. The model function defines the Gaussian model to learn, with the associated variables mu and sig initialized arbitrarily to 1. The cost function is defined as the L2 norm, and the training uses Gradient descent. After training your regressor for 5,000 epochs, the final steps in listing 4.4 print the learned values for mu and sig.

Listing 4.4   Setting up and training the TensorFlow model for your Gaussian curve

```
learning_rate = 1.5      ◁──── Sets the learning rate for each epoch
training_epochs = 5000        ◁────┐
                                    Trains for 5,000 epochs

X = tf.placeholder(tf.float32)      Sets up the input (X) and
Y = tf.placeholder(tf.float32)      the values to predict (Y)
```

```
def model(X, mu, sig):
    return tf.exp(tf.div(tf.negative(tf.pow(tf.subtract(X, mu), 2.)),
    ➥ tf.multiply(2., tf.pow(sig, 2.)))))

mu = tf.Variable(1., name="mu")
sig = tf.Variable(1., name="sig")
y_model = model(X, mu, sig)

cost = tf.square(Y-y_model)
train_op = tf.train.GradientDescentOptimizer(learning_rate).minimize(cost)

sess = tf.Session()
init = tf.global_variables_initializer()
sess.run(init)

for epoch in range(training_epochs):
    for(x, y) in zip(X_train, nY_train):
        sess.run(train_op, feed_dict={X:x, Y:y})

mu_val = sess.run(mu)
sig_val = sess.run(sig)
print(mu_val)
print(sig_val)
sess.close()
```

Defines the learned parameters mu and sig for the model

Creates the model based on the TensorFlow graph

Defines the cost function as the L2 norm and sets up the training operation

Initializes the TensorFlow session

Performs the training and learns the values for mu and sig

Prints the learned values for mu and

Closes the session

The output of listing 4.4 should look similar to the following, which corresponds to the learned values for mu and sig:

```
27.23236
4.9030166
```

When you finish printing the values and saving them in the local variables mu_val and sig_val, don't forget to close your TensorFlow session so that you can free the resources it was using for its 5,000 iterations of training. You can take care of this task by invoking sess.close().

> **TIP** Listing 4.4 shows you how to build the call-center volume prediction algorithm with TensorFlow 1.x. In case you were wondering how the algorithm would look in TensorFlow 2.x, jump to the appendix, where I've discussed and reworked the model for you in TensorFlow 2.x-speak. There are some minor differences, but they're worth checking out. The other data cleaning and preparation code that you've seen thus far stays the same, as do the validation and error calculation that you're about to see.

4.5 *Visualizing the results and plotting the error*

How well did your linear regression do at predicting the 311 call frequencies per week? Take the mu and sigma values from mu_val and sig_val, and use them to plot the learned model in listing 4.5 and figure 4.5. Matplotlib takes care of the initial scatter plot of week number (x-axis) by frequency of calls normalized (y-axis). Then you

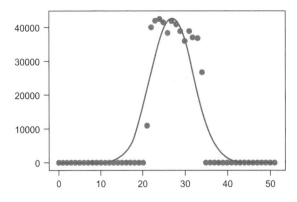

Figure 4.5   The learned TensorFlow model (shown in red) that predicts call volume per week of the year (0–51) for weeks 1–52 (indexed at 0). The actual call data volume per week is shown in blue.

take the learned parameters for mu_val and sig_val and plug them into a one-line unfolding of the model equation from listing 4.4. The reason to do this instead of reusing the model function and passing in mu_val and sig_val as arguments is that when TensorFlow learns the optimal parameter values, you don't need to set up a TensorFlow graph again or pass a session to it to evaluate the model values. Instead, you can use NumPy and its analogous functions such as np.exp (exponent) and np.power. These functions are equivalent to TensorFlow's same-named functions, except that NumPy doesn't require a TensorFlow session and its associated resources to evaluate the value at each point. trY2 has the resulting learned call-frequency predictions; because they were normalized to values between 0 and 1 to learn the Gaussian function, you have to multiply the learned values by maxY to discern the actual unnormalized call-frequency predictions per week. The result is plotted in red alongside the original training data, and the prediction for the number of calls in an arbitrary week is printed and compared with the original training data value to test the model.

Listing 4.5   Visualizing the learned model

Plots the training data points of week number (X) by number of calls (Y) as blue scatter points

```
plt.scatter(X_train, Y_train)
trY2 = maxY * (np.exp(-np.power(X_train - mu_val, 2.) / (2 *
    np.power(sig_val, 2.))))
plt.plot(X_train, trY2, 'r')
plt.show()
print("Prediction of week 35", trY2[33])
print("Actual week 35", Y_train[33])
```

Fits the Gaussian function model with the learned mu and sig parameters

Plots the learned model in red

The results of listing 4.5 should be similar to the following:

```
Prediction of week 35 21363.278811768592
Actual week 35 36967
```

Although it may seem crazy that your model predicted a call volume that was ~15,000 calls off the actual value, remember the discussion of bias and variance in chapter 3. You aren't looking for a model that is insanely overfitted to the data and contorts every which way to ensure that it crosses through every point. Those models exhibit high bias and low variance, and as such, they are overfitted to the training data. Instead, you want models that show low bias and low variance and that perform well on unseen data.

Provided with new unseen calls, so long as NYC 311 populations seem to be seasonally based in spring and summer, your model is well fitted and will perform well. It can even handle distribution shift (shift in call volumes among seasons) as long as the input is within the standard deviation and/or a particular center mean corresponds to the largest number of calls. You can update your model and have it learn new `mu` and `sig` values; then you're all set.

You may have one question about this discussion, though. You are evaluating your model's performance by talking about how far off the predictions are from the actual values. You can use some tools that you've already seen—Jupyter and Matplotlib—to measure the error quantitatively. Run listing 4.6 to compute the error, average error, and accuracy of your model and then visualize the model as shown in figure 4.6. The `error` variable is defined as the square root of the squared difference between the predicted data and the training data (which, as you may recall from chapter 1, is the L2 norm). This error variable yields a distance for every predicted call frequency by week from training data and is best visualized as a bar graph. The `avg_error` is computed as the variance between each predicted point in `trY2` compared with `Y_train` divided by the total number of weeks to get the average error in predicted calls per week. The overall accuracy of the algorithm is 1 (the average error in call predictions per week divided by the maximum calls per week). The result is stored in the `acc` variable and printed at the end of the listing.

Listing 4.6 Computing the error and visualizing it

Error is the square root of the squared difference between the model's predicted value and the actual value.

Computes the overall average error (number of calls difference per week) by using Map Reduce to sum the differences and divide by total weeks

```
error = np.power(np.power(trY2 - Y_train, 2), 0.5)
plt.bar(X_train, error)
plt.show()
```

Shows the error as a histogram of errors at each week value

```
avg_error = functools.reduce(lambda a,b: a+b, (trY2-Y_train))
avg_error = np.abs(avg_error) / len(X_train)
print("Average Error", avg_error)
acc = 1. - (avg_error / maxY)
print("Accuracy", acc)
```

Computes the accuracy by subtracting the average error divided by the max number of calls across the whole dataset from 1

The resulting plot, showing the errors per week in phone-call prediction, also resembles the prediction curve.

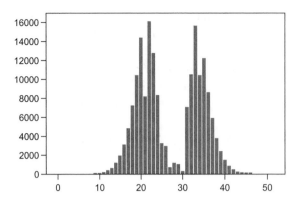

Figure 4.6   **Visualizing the error in number of calls predicted per week. The model performs quite well in the weeks that have high call volume.**

Though it may seem that the overall error is high—and it is at the tails of the distribution—overall, the average error is only 205 calls per week of variance due to the model's spot-on predictions when it matters most: during high-call-volume weeks. You can see the model's average error and accuracy (99%) in the output of listing 4.6:

```
Average Error 205.4554733031897
Accuracy 0.9951853520187662
```

You learned about regularization and training test splits in chapter 3. I cover them briefly in section 4.6.

4.6   *Regularization and training test splits*

The concept of regularization is probably best described in figure 4.7. During training, a machine-learning model (M), given some input data (X) for the cost function, the training process explores the space for the parameters (W) that should minimize the difference between the model response (predictions) and the actual training input values (X). This cost is captured in the function M(X, W). The challenge is that during training and parameter exploration, the algorithm sometimes picks locally optimal though globally poor parameter values for W. Regularization can influence this choice by penalizing larger values of W for weights and trying to keep the weight exploration to the optimal area denoted in figure 4.7 (the white circular region with the red outline).

You should consider using regularization when models underfit or overfit your input data or when the weight exploration process during training needs some help with penalizing the higher or yellow spaces of the parameter space W. Your new Gaussian bell-curve model for 311 demonstrates suitably high accuracy, though it has errors on the tail ends of the call-volume distribution. Would regularization help get rid of these errors?

It may be counterintuitive, but the answer is no, due to four concepts: the hyperparameters to our training process, the learning rate, the number of training steps

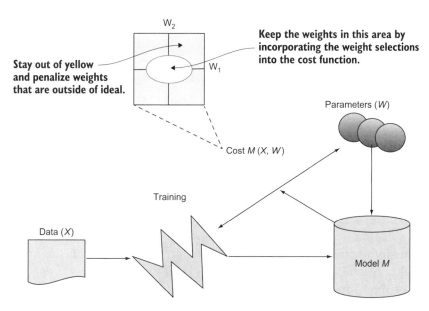

Figure 4.7 Reviewing the concept of regularization. Input data (X) provided during training is fitted to a model (M) through the training process of learning the parameters (W) by measuring the predictions of those parameters against a cost function M(X, W). During the training process, you want the exploration of the parameter space W (top left) to zero in on the white area and stay out of the yellow. Regularization enables this result.

(epochs), and the initial values of mu and sig from listing 4.4. I've copied them here for your convenience:

```
learning_rate = 1.5
training_epochs = 5000
mu = tf.Variable(1., name="mu")
sig = tf.Variable(1., name="sig")
```

These are the hyperparameters and learned parameters of the model. The initial values matter significantly and were not picked out of thin air. Knowing the optimal values for mu and sig (~27 and ~4.9, respectively) would have been great ahead of time, but you didn't have that knowledge. Instead, you set them to default values (1 for each) and allowed the learning rate 1.5 to control the steps of exploration. Set the learning-rate value too low (such as 0.1 or 0.001), and the algorithm could require hundreds of thousands of training epochs and still never achieve an optimal value for the learned parameters. Set the learning rate beyond 1.5 (say, 3.5.) and the algorithm will skip the optimal values in a particular training step.

TIP Despite not knowing mu (mean) and sigma (standard deviation) ahead of time, you can eyeball the data and derive them partially. Near week 27 is the peak or mean of the distribution. As for the standard deviation, eyeballing it as ~5 is hard but not impossible. Standard deviation is a measure of the spread of numbers in each unit from the mean. Low standard deviation means that the tails of the distribution are close to the mean. Being able to use your eyeballs to explore the inputs and expected values and tune the initial model parameters will save you lots of time and epochs later.

Regularization isn't needed in this particular case because intuitively, you explored your training data, visualized it, and normalized the call frequencies to values between 0 and 1 to ease learning, and because your model fits the data and is not over- or underfitted. Penalizing the parameter exploration step would have a net negative effect in this case, possibly preventing you from fitting the model more precisely.

Additionally, given the sparsity of the data—something you found out only by visualizing and performing the exploratory data analysis process—splitting the data into train/test isn't tenable because you will lose too much information for your model. Suppose that your split at 70/30 removed anything other than the tails of the distribution. The information loss could make your regression see not a bell curve, but lines or small polynomial curves, and learn the wrong model—or, worse, learn the right model of the wrong data, such as the graphs in figure 4.2. Train/test splits do not make sense here.

Rejoice! You've trained a real-world regressor that has 99% accuracy on the available data and reasonable error. You've helped 311 develop a seasonally accurate predictor for its call volume, helped it predict how many call agents it will need to answer the phones, and justified its value to the community by how many calls it takes each week. Was this task something that you thought machine learning and TensorFlow could help you with? They could, and they did.

In chapter 5, we delve into developing powerful predictive capabilities on discrete outputs by constructing classifiers with TensorFlow. Onward!

Summary

- Applying linear regression in TensorFlow to lines and polynomials assumes that all data is clean and neatly fits lines and points. This chapter shows you real-world data that doesn't look like what you saw in chapter 3 and explains how to use TensorFlow to fit the model.
- Visualizing your input data points helps you select a model to fit for regression—in this case, the Gaussian model.
- Learning how to evaluate your bias and error by using visualization is a key part of using TensorFlow and tuning your machine-learning model.
- Looking at regularization on this model doesn't help fit the data better. Use regularization when the training step is producing parameters that are too far outside the bounds of your learning step.

A gentle introduction to classification

5

This chapter covers

- Writing formal notation
- Using logistic regression
- Working with a confusion matrix
- Understanding multiclass classification

Imagine an advertisement agency collecting information about user interactions to decide what type of ad to show. That's not uncommon. Google, Twitter, Facebook, and other big tech giants that rely on ads have creepy-good personal profiles of their users to help deliver personalized ads. A user who's recently searched for gaming keyboards or graphics cards is probably more likely to click ads about the latest and greatest video games.

Delivering an advertisement specially crafted to each person may be difficult, so grouping users into categories is a common technique. A user may be categorized as a gamer to receive relevant video game–related ads, for example.

Machine learning is the go-to tool for accomplishing such a task. At the most fundamental level, machine-learning practitioners want to build a tool to help them understand data. Labeling data items as belonging in separate categories is an excellent way to characterize data for specific needs.

Chapter 4 dealt with regression, which is about fitting a curve to data. As you recall, the best-fit curve is a function that takes as input a data item and assigns it a number drawn from a continuous distribution. Creating a machine-learning model that instead assigns discrete labels to its inputs is called *classification*. Classification is a supervised learning algorithm for dealing with discrete output. (Each discrete value is called a *class*.) The input is typically a feature vector, and the output is a class. If there are only two class labels (True/False, On/Off, Yes/No), we call this learning algorithm a *binary classifier*; otherwise, it's called a *multiclass classifier*.

There are many types of classifiers, but this chapter focuses on the ones outlined in table 5.1. Each has advantages and disadvantages, which we'll delve into deeper after we start implementing each one in TensorFlow.

Linear regression is the easiest type to implement because we did most of the hard work in chapters 3 and 4, but as you'll see, it's a terrible classifier. A much better classifier is the logistic regression algorithm. As the name suggests, it uses logarithmic properties to define a better cost function. Finally, softmax regression is a direct approach to solving multiclass classification. It's a natural generalization of logistic regression and is called softmax regression because a function called softmax is applied as the last step.

Table 5.1   Classifiers

Type	Pros	Cons
Linear regression	Simple to implement	Not guaranteed to work Supports only binary labels
Logistic regression	Highly accurate Flexible ways to regularize model for custom adjustment Model responses are measures of probability. Easy-to-update model with new data	Supports only binary labels
Softmax regression	Supports multiclass classification Model responses are measures of probability.	More complicated to implement

5.1   *Formal notation*

In mathematical notation, a classifier is a function $y = f(x)$, where x is the input data item and y is the output category (figure 5.1). Adopting from traditional scientific literature, we often refer to the input vector x as the *independent variable* and the output y as the *dependent variable*.

Formally, a category label is restricted to a range of possible values. You can think of two-valued labels as being like Boolean variables in Python. When the input features have only a fixed set of possible values, you need to ensure that your model can

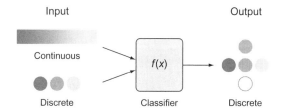

Figure 5.1 **A classifier produces discrete outputs but may take either continuous or discrete inputs.**

understand how to handle those values. Because the functions in a model typically deal with continuous real numbers, you need to preprocess the dataset to account for discrete variables, which are either ordinal or nominal (figure 5.2).

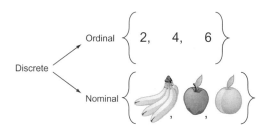

Figure 5.2 **There are two types of discrete sets: those with values that can be ordered (ordinal) and those with values that can't be ordered (nominal).**

Values of an ordinal type, as the name suggests, can be ordered. The values in a set of even numbers from 1 to 10 are ordinal, for example, because integers can be compared with one another. On the other hand, an element from a set of fruits {banana, apple, orange} might not come with a natural ordering. We call values from such a set *nominal* because they can be described by only their names.

A simple approach to representing nominal variables in a dataset is to assign a number to each label. The set {banana, apple, orange} could instead be processed as {0, 1, 2}. But some classification models may have a strong bias about how the data behaves. Linear regression, for example, would interpret our apple as being midway between a banana and an orange, which makes no natural sense.

A simple workaround to represent nominal categories of a dependent variable is to add dummy variables for each value of the nominal variable. In this example, the fruit variable would be removed and replaced by three separate variables: banana, apple, and orange. Each variable holds a value of 0 or 1 (figure 5.3), depending on whether the category for that fruit holds true. This process is often referred to as *one-hot encoding*.

As in linear regression from chapters 3 and 4, the learning algorithm must traverse the possible functions supported by the underlying model, called M. In linear regression, the model was parameterized by w. So the function y = M(w) can be tried to measure its cost. In the end, we choose a value of w with the least cost. The only difference between regression and classification is that the output is no longer a continuous spectrum, but a discrete set of class labels.

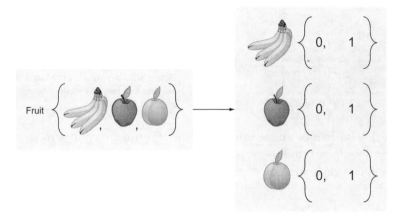

Figure 5.3   If the values of a variable are nominal, they may need to be preprocessed. One solution is to treat each nominal value as a Boolean variable, as shown on the right; banana, apple, and orange are three newly added variables, each having a value of 0 or 1. The original fruit variable is removed.

Exercise 5.1
Is it a better idea to treat each of the following as a regression or classification task?

(a) Predicting stock prices

(b) Deciding which stocks you should buy, sell, or hold

(c) Rating the quality of a computer on a 1–10 scale

Answers

(a) Regression

(b) Classification

(c) Either

Because the input/output types for regression are even more general than those of classification, nothing prevents you from running a linear regression algorithm on a classification task. In fact, that's exactly what you'll do in section 5.3.

Before you begin implementing TensorFlow code, however, it's important to gauge the strength of a classifier. Section 5.2 covers state-of-the-art approaches for measuring a classifier's success.

5.2   *Measuring performance*

Before you begin writing classification algorithms, you should be able to check the success of your results. This section covers essential techniques for measuring performance in classification problems.

5.2.1 Accuracy

Do you remember those multiple-choice exams in high school or college? Classification problems in machine learning are similar. Given a statement, your job is to classify it as one of the given multiple-choice "answers." If you have only two choices, as in a true-or-false exam, we call it a *binary classifier*. In a graded exam in school, the typical way to measure your score is to count the number of correct answers and divide that number by the total number of questions.

Machine learning adopts the same scoring strategy and calls it *accuracy*. Accuracy is measured by the following formula:

$$accuracy = \frac{\#correct}{\#total}$$

This formula provides a crude summary of performance, which may be sufficient if you're worried only about the overall correctness of the algorithm. But the accuracy measure doesn't reveal a breakdown of correct and incorrect results for each label.

To account for this limitation, a confusion matrix provides a more detailed report on a classifier's success. A useful way to describe how well a classifier performs is to inspect the way it performs on each of the classes.

Consider a binary classifier with positive and negative labels, for example. As shown in figure 5.4, a *confusion matrix* is a table that compares how the predicted responses compare with actual ones. Data items that are correctly predicted as positive are called *true positives* (TP). Those that are incorrectly predicted as positive are called *false positives* (FP). If the algorithm accidentally predicts an element to be negative when in reality it is positive, we call this situation a *false negative* (FN). Finally, when prediction and reality agree that a data item is a negative label, it's called a *true negative* (TN). As you can see, a confusion matrix enables you to see easily how often a model confuses two classes that it's trying to differentiate.

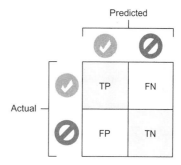

Figure 5.4 You can compare predicted results with actual results by using a matrix of positive (green check mark) and negative (red forbidden) labels.

> **NOTE** Many graphics in this book include color, which can be viewed in the e-book versions. To get your free e-book in PDF, ePub, or Kindle format, go to http://mng.bz/JxPo to register your print book.

5.2.2 Precision and recall

Although the definitions of true positives (TP), false positives (FP), true negatives (TN), and false negatives (FN) are all useful individually, the power comes in the interplay among them.

The ratio of true positives to total positive examples is *precision*—a score of how likely a positive prediction is to be correct. The left column in figure 5.4 is the total number of positive predictions (TP + FP), so the equation for precision is

$$precision = \frac{TP}{TP + FP}$$

The ratio of true positives to all possible positives is *recall*, which measures the ratio of true positives found. It's a score of how many true positives were successfully predicted (that is, recalled). The top row in figure 5.4 is the total number of positives (TP + FN), so the equation for recall is

$$recall = \frac{TP}{TP + FN}$$

Simply put, *precision* is a measure of the predictions the algorithm got right, and *recall* is a measure of the right things the algorithm identified in the final set. If the precision is higher than the recall, the model is better at successfully identifying correct items than not identifying some wrong items, and vice versa.

Here's a quick example. Suppose that you're trying to identify cats in a set of 100 pictures, in which 40 of the pictures are of cats, and 60 are of dogs. When you run your classifier, 10 of the cats are identified as dogs, and 20 of the dogs are identified as cats. Your confusion matrix looks like figure 5.5.

Confusion matrix		Predicted	
		Cat	Dog
	Cat	30 True positives	20 False positives
Actual	Dog	10 False negatives	40 True negatives

Figure 5.5   An example confusion matrix for evaluating the performance of a classification algorithm

You can see the total number of cats on the left side of the prediction column: 30 identified correctly and 10 not, totaling 40.

Exercise 5.2

What are the precision and recall for cats? What's the accuracy of the system?

Answers

For cats, the precision is 30 / (30 + 20) or 3/5, or 60%. The recall is 30 / (30 + 10) or 3/4, or 75%. The accuracy is (30 + 40) / 100, or 70%.

5.2.3   *Receiver operating characteristic curve*

Because binary classifiers are among the most popular tools, many mature techniques exist for measuring their performance, such as the *receiver operating characteristic (ROC) curve*, a plot that lets you compare the trade-offs between false positives and true positives. The x-axis is the measure of false-positive values, and the y-axis is the measure of true-positive values.

A binary classifier reduces its input feature vector to a number and then decides the class based on whether the number is greater than or less than a specified threshold. As you adjust a threshold of the machine-learning classifier, you plot the various values of false-positive and true-positive rates.

A robust way to compare various classifiers is to compare their ROC curves. When two curves don't intersect, one method is certainly better than the other. Good algorithms are far above the baseline. For two choices, they do better than a random choice, or a 50/50 guess. A quantitative way to compare classifiers is to measure the area under the ROC curve. If a model has an area-under-curve (AUC) value higher than 0.9, it's an excellent classifier. A model that randomly guesses the output will have an AUC value of about 0.5. See figure 5.6 for an example.

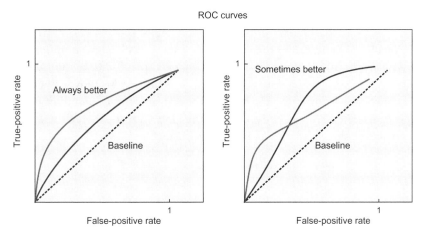

ROC curves

Figure 5.6   **The principled way to compare algorithms is to examine their ROC curves. When the true-positive rate is greater than the false-positive rate in every situation, it's straightforward to declare that one algorithm is dominant in terms of its performance. If the true-positive rate is less than the false-positive rate, the plot dips below the baseline shown by the dotted line.**

Exercise 5.3

How would a 100% correct rate (all true positives, no false positives) look as a point on an ROC curve?

Answers

The point for a 100% correct rate would be located on the positive y-axis of the ROC curve, as shown in figure 5.7.

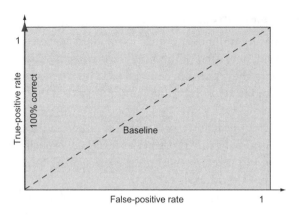

Figure 5.7   A 100% correct classifier with the blue ROC curve alongside the vertical true-positive (y) axis

5.3   *Using linear regression for classification*

One of the simplest ways to implement a classifier is to tweak a linear regression algorithm, as discussed in chapter 3. As a reminder, a linear regression model is a set of functions that look linear: `f(x) = wx`. The function `f(x)` takes continuous real numbers as input and produces continuous real numbers as output. Remember that classification is all about discrete outputs. So one way to force the regression model to produce a two-valued (binary) output is to set values above a certain threshold to a number (such as `1`) and values below that threshold to a different number (such as `0`).

We'll proceed with the following motivating example. Suppose that Alice is an avid chess player, and you have records of her win/loss history. Moreover, each game has a time limit ranging from 1 to 10 minutes. You can plot the outcome of each game as shown in figure 5.8. The x-axis represents the time limit of the game, and the y-axis signifies whether she won (`y = 1`) or lost (`y = 0`).

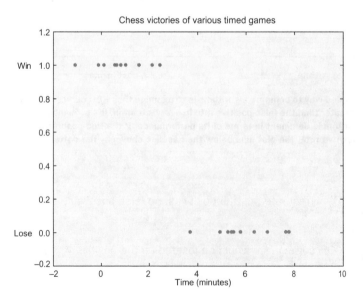

Figure 5.8   A visualization of a binary classification training dataset. The values are divided into two classes: all points where y = 1 and all points where y = 0.

As you see from the data, Alice is a quick thinker: she always wins short games. But she usually loses games that have longer time limits. From the plot, you'd like to predict the critical game time-limit that decides whether she'll win.

You want to challenge her to a game that you're sure of winning. If you choose an obviously long game, such as one that takes 10 minutes, she'll refuse to play. Let's set up the game time to be as short as possible so she'll be willing to play against you while tilting the balance to your advantage.

A linear fit on the data gives you something to work with. Figure 5.9 shows the best-fit line computed by using linear regression from listing 5.1 (appearing later in this section). The value of the line is closer to 1 than it is to 0 for games that Alice will likely win. It appears that if you pick a time corresponding to when the value of the line is less than 0.5 (that is, when Alice is more likely to lose than to win), you have a good chance of winning.

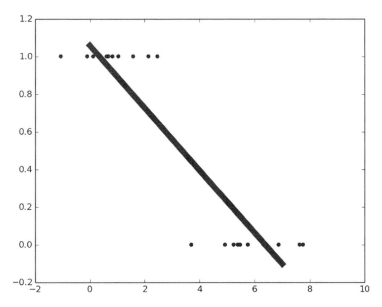

Figure 5.9 The diagonal line is the best-fit line on a classification dataset. Clearly, the line doesn't fit the data well, but it provides an imprecise approach for classifying new data.

The line is trying to fit the data as best as possible. Due to the nature of the training data, the model will respond with values near 1 for positive examples and values near 0 for negative examples. Because you're modeling this data with a line, some input may produce values between 0 and 1. As you may imagine, values too far into one category will result in values greater than 1 or less than 0. You need a way to decide when an item belongs to one category more than another. Typically, you choose the midpoint, 0.5, as a deciding boundary (also called the *threshold*). As you've seen, this procedure uses linear regression to perform classification.

Exercise 5.4

What are the disadvantages of using linear regression as a tool for classification? (See listing 5.4 for a hint.)

Answers

Linear regression is sensitive to outliers in your data, so it isn't an accurate classifier.

Let's write your first classifier! Open a new Python source file, and call it linear.py. Use listing 5.1 to write the code. In the TensorFlow code, you'll need to first define placeholder nodes and then inject values into them from the session.run() statement.

Listing 5.1 Using linear regression for classification

```
import tensorflow as tf
import numpy as np
import matplotlib.pyplot as plt
```
Imports TensorFlow for the core learning algorithm, NumPy for manipulating data, and Matplotlib for visualizing

```
x_label0 = np.random.normal(5, 1, 10)
x_label1 = np.random.normal(2, 1, 10)
xs = np.append(x_label0, x_label1)
labels = [0.] * len(x_label0) + [1.] * len(x_label1)
```
Initializes fake data, 10 instances of each label centered at 5 and 2, with stddev 1, respectively

Initializes the corresponding labels

```
plt.scatter(xs, labels)
```
Plots the data

```
learning_rate = 0.001
training_epochs = 1000
```
Declares the hyperparameters

```
X = tf.placeholder("float")
Y = tf.placeholder("float")
```
Sets up the placeholder nodes for the input/output pairs

```
def model(X, w):
    return tf.add(tf.multiply(w[1], tf.pow(X, 1)),
                  tf.multiply(w[0], tf.pow(X, 0)))
```
Defines a linear y = w1 * x + w0 model

Sets up the parameter variables

```
w = tf.Variable([0., 0.], name="parameters")
y_model = model(X, w)
cost = tf.reduce_sum(tf.square(Y-y_model))
```
Defines a helper variable, because you'll refer to it multiple times

Defines the cost function

```
train_op = tf.train.GradientDescentOptimizer(learning_rate).minimize(cost)
```
Defines the rule to learn the parameters

After designing the TensorFlow graph, see listing 5.2 to find out how to open a new session and execute the graph. train_op updates the model's parameters to better guesses. You run train_op multiple times in a loop because each step iteratively improves the parameter estimate. Listing 5.2 generates a plot similar to figure 5.8.

Listing 5.2 Executing the graph

```
sess = tf.Session()
init = tf.global_variables_initializer()          Opens a new session
sess.run(init)                                     and initializes the
                                                   variables
                                                                          Runs the learning
                                                                          operation multiple
for epoch in range(training_epochs):                                      times
    sess.run(train_op, feed_dict={X: xs, Y: labels})
    current_cost = sess.run(cost, feed_dict={X: xs, Y: labels})
    if epoch % 100 == 0:                                                  Records the cost
        print(epoch, current_cost)                                       computed with
                                                                         the current
                                                                         parameters
w_val = sess.run(w)                     Prints the learned
print('learned parameters', w_val)      parameters

sess.close()    ←——— Closes the session when no longer in use

all_xs = np.linspace(0, 10, 100)
plt.plot(all_xs, all_xs*w_val[1] + w_val[0])       Shows the
plt.show()                                         best-fit line
```

Prints log info while the code runs

To measure success, you can count the number of correct predictions and compute a success rate. In listing 5.3, you add two more nodes to the previous code in linear.py: correct_prediction and accuracy. Then you can print the value of accuracy to see the success rate. The code can be executed right before closing the session.

Listing 5.3 Measuring accuracy

```
When the model's response is greater
than 0.5, it should be a positive label,                     Computes the
and vice versa.                                             percent of success

correct_prediction = tf.equal(Y, tf.to_float(tf.greater(y_model, 0.5)))
accuracy = tf.reduce_mean(tf.to_float(correct_prediction))        ←

print('accuracy', sess.run(accuracy, feed_dict={X: xs, Y: labels}))  ←
print('correct_prediction', predict_val)  ←
          Prints the correct predictions          Prints the success measure
                                                   from provided input
```

The code in listing 5.3 produces the following output:

```
('learned parameters', array([ 1.2816, -0.2171], dtype=float32))
('accuracy', 0.95)
correct_prediction [ True False  True   True   True   True   True   True   True
     True   True   True
  True   True   True   True   True   True   True False]
```

If classification were that easy, this chapter would be over by now. Unfortunately, the linear regression approach fails miserably if you train on more-extreme data, also called *outliers*.

Suppose that Alice lost a game that took 20 minutes. You train the classifier on a dataset that includes this new outlier data point. Listing 5.4 replaces one of the game times with the value of 20. Let's see how introducing an outlier affects the classifier's performance.

Listing 5.4   Linear regression failing miserably for classification

```
x_label0 = np.append(np.random.normal(5, 1, 9), 20)
```

When you rerun the code with these changes, you see a result similar to figure 5.10.

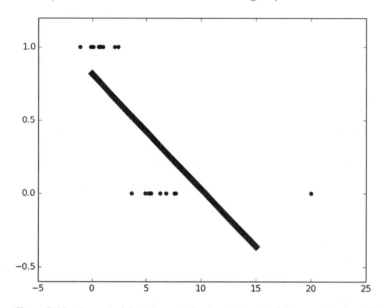

Figure 5.10   A new training element of value 20 greatly influences the best-fit line. The line is too sensitive to outlying data; therefore, linear regression is a sloppy classifier.

The original classifier suggested that you could beat Alice in a three-minute game. She'd probably agree to play such a short game. But the revised classifier, if you stick with the same 0.5 threshold, is suggesting that the shortest game she'll lose is a five-minute game. She'll likely refuse to play such a long game!

5.4   *Using logistic regression*

Logistic regression provides an analytic function with theoretical guarantees on accuracy and performance. It's like linear regression, except that you use a different cost function and slightly transform the model response function.

Let's revisit the linear function shown here:

$$y(x) = wx$$

In linear regression, a line with a nonzero slope may range from negative infinity to infinity. If the only sensible result for classification is 0 or 1, it would be intuitive to fit a function with that property instead. Fortunately, the sigmoid function depicted in figure 5.11 works well because it converges to 0 or 1 quickly.

When x is 0, the sigmoid function results in 0.5. As x increases, the function converges to 1. And as x decreases to negative infinity, the function converges to 0.

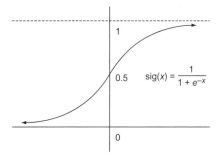

Figure 5.11   A visualization of the sigmoid function

In logistic regression, our model is sig(linear(x)). As it turns out, the best-fit parameters of this function imply a linear separation between the two classes. This separating line is also called a *linear decision boundary*.

5.4.1   Solving 1D logistic regression

The cost function used in logistic regression is a bit different from the one you used in linear regression. Although you could use the same cost function as before, it won't be as fast or guarantee an optimal solution. The sigmoid function is the culprit here, because it causes the cost function to have many "bumps." TensorFlow and most other machine-learning libraries work best with simple cost functions. Scholars have found a neat way to modify the cost function to use sigmoids for logistic regression.

The new cost function between the actual value (y) and model response (h) will be a two-part equation:

$$Cost(y, h) = \begin{cases} -\log(h), & \text{if } y = 1 \\ -\log(1 - h), & \text{if } y = 0 \end{cases}$$

You can condense the two equations into one long equation:

$$Cost(y, h) = -y\log(h) - (1 - y)\log(1 - h)$$

This function has exactly the qualities needed for efficient and optimal learning. Specifically, it's convex, but don't worry too much about what that means. You're trying to minimize the cost: think of cost as an altitude and the cost function as a terrain. You're trying to find the lowest point in the terrain. It's a lot easier to find the lowest point in the terrain if there's no place you can ever go uphill. Such a place is called *convex*. There are no hills.

You can think of this function as being like a ball rolling down a hill. Eventually, the ball will settle to the bottom, which is the *optimal point*. A nonconvex function might have a rugged terrain, making it difficult to predict where a ball will roll. It might not even end up at the lowest point. Your function is convex, so the algorithm will easily figure out how to minimize this cost and "roll the ball downhill."

Convexity is nice, but correctness is also an important criterion when picking a cost function. How do you know this cost function does exactly what you intended it to do?

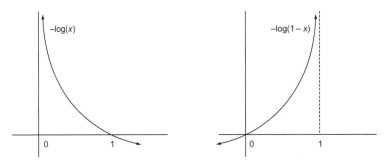

Figure 5.12   Here's a visualization of how the two cost functions penalize values at 0 and 1. Notice that the left function penalizes 0 heavily but has no cost at 1. The right cost function displays the opposite phenomena.

To answer that question most intuitively, take a look at figure 5.12. You use `-log(x)` to compute the cost when you want your desired value to be 1 (notice: `-log(1) = 0`). The algorithm strays away from setting the value to 0, because the cost approaches infinity. Adding these functions together gives a curve that approaches infinity at both 0 and 1, with the negative parts canceling out.

Sure, figures are an informal way to persuade you of the importance of convexity in picking a cost function, but a technical discussion of why the cost function is optimal is beyond the scope of this book. If you're interested in the mathematics, you'll be interested to learn that the cost function is derived from the principle of maximum entropy, which you can look up anywhere online.

See figure 5.13 for a best-fit result from logistic regression on a 1D dataset. The sigmoid curve that you'll generate will provide a better linear decision boundary than that from linear regression.

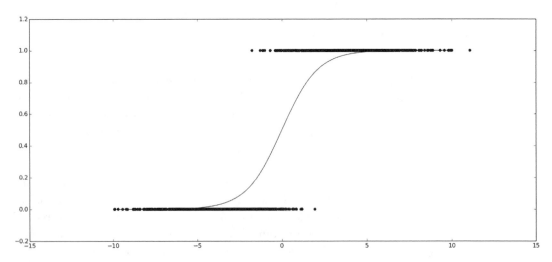

Figure 5.13   Here's a best-fit sigmoid curve for a binary classification dataset. Notice that the curve resides within y = 0 and y = 1. That way, this curve isn't too sensitive to outliers.

You'll start to notice a pattern in the code listings. In simple/typical use of Tensor-Flow, you generate a fake dataset, define placeholders, define variables, define a model, define a cost function on that model (which is often a mean squared error or a mean squared log error), create a `train_op` by using gradient descent, iteratively feed it example data (possibly with a label or output), and finally collect the optimized values. Create a new source file called logistic_1d.py, and copy into it listing 5.5, which generates figure 5.13.

Listing 5.5 Using 1D logistic regression

```
import numpy as np
import tensorflow as tf          ⎤ Imports relevant
import matplotlib.pyplot as plt  ⎦ libraries
learning_rate = 0.01            ⎤ Sets the hyperparameters
training_epochs = 1000          ⎦

def sigmoid(x):                 ⎤ Defines a helper function to
    return 1. / (1. + np.exp(-x))⎦ calculate the sigmoid function

x1 = np.random.normal(-4, 2, 1000)         ⎤ Initializes fake data
x2 = np.random.normal(4, 2, 1000)          ⎦
xs = np.append(x1, x2)                      ⎤ Defines the input/output
ys = np.asarray([0.] * len(x1) + [1.] * len(x2)) ⎦ placeholders

plt.scatter(xs, ys)        ◁——— Visualizes the data

X = tf.placeholder(tf.float32, shape=(None,), name="x")    ⎤ Defines the
Y = tf.placeholder(tf.float32, shape=(None,), name="y")    ⎦ model by using
w = tf.Variable([0., 0.], name="parameter", trainable=True) ◁— TensorFlow's
y_model = tf.sigmoid(w[1] * X + w[0])                       ◁— sigmoid function
cost = tf.reduce_mean(-Y * tf.log(y_model) - (1 - Y) * tf.log(1 - y_model)) ◁—
                                  Defines the cross-entropy loss function
train_op = tf.train.GradientDescentOptimizer(learning_rate).minimize(cost) ◁—
                                        Defines the minimizer to use

with tf.Session() as sess:
    sess.run(tf.global_variables_initializer())   ⎤ Defines a variable to keep
    prev_err = 0                            ◁——— ⎦ track of the previous error
    for epoch in range(training_epochs):    ◁—
        err, _ = sess.run([cost, train_op], {X: xs, Y: ys}) ◁—
        print(epoch, err)                         Computes the cost and
        if abs(prev_err - err) < 0.0001: ◁—       updates the learning
            break                                 parameters
        prev_err = err
    w_val = sess.run(w, {X: xs, Y: ys}) ◁—
                   Obtains the learned parameter value
all_xs = np.linspace(-10, 10, 100)
plt.plot(all_xs, sigmoid((all_xs * w_val[1] + w_val[0])))
plt.show()
```

Defines the parameter node

Opens a session and defines all variables

Updates the previous error value

Iterates until convergence or until the maximum number of epochs is reached

Checks for convergence. If you're changing by < .01% per iteration, you're done.

Plots the learned sigmoid function

And there you have it! If you were playing chess against Alice, you'd now have a binary classifier to decide the threshold indicating when a chess match might result in a win or loss.

> ## Cross-entropy loss in TensorFlow
>
> As shown in listing 5.5, the cross-entropy loss is averaged over each input/output pair by using the `tf.reduce_mean` op. Another handy and more general function is provided by the TensorFlow library, called `tf.nn.softmax_cross_entropy_with_logits`. You can find more about it in the official documentation at http://mng.bz/8mEk.

5.4.2 Solving 2D regression

Now we'll explore how to use logistic regression with multiple independent variables. The number of independent variables corresponds to the number of dimensions. In our case, a 2D logistic regression problem will try to label a pair of independent variables. The concepts you learn in this section extrapolate to arbitrary dimensions.

> **NOTE** Suppose that you're thinking about buying a new phone. The only attributes you care about are (1) operating system, (2) size, and (3) cost. The goal is to decide whether a phone is a worthwhile purchase. In this case, there are three independent variables (the attributes of the phone) and one dependent variable (whether it's worth buying). So we regard this problem as a classification problem in which the input vector is 3D.

Consider the dataset shown in figure 5.14, which represents the crime activity of two gangs in a city. The first dimension is the x-axis, which can be thought of as the latitude, and the second dimension is the y-axis, representing longitude. There's one cluster around (3, 2) and another around (7, 6). Your job is to decide which gang is most likely responsible for a new crime that occurred at location (6, 4).

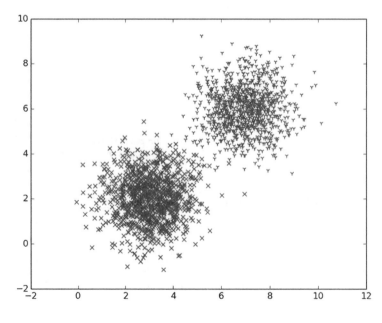

Figure 5.14
The x-axis and y-axis represent the two independent variables. The dependent variable holds two possible labels, represented by the shape and color of the plotted points.

Another way to visualize figure 5.14 is to project the independent variables x=latitude and y=longitude as a 2D plane and then draw the vertical axis as the result of the sigmoid function for the one-hot-encoded categories. You could visualize the function as shown in figure 5.15.

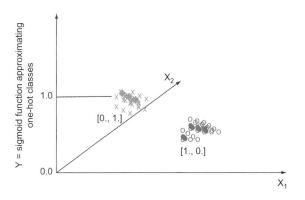

Figure 5.15 Another way to visualize the two independent variables, this time taking into account the dependent variable defined by the sigmoid function, which represents the one-hot-encoded classes for gang 1 (green) and gang 2 (red).

Create a new source file called logistic_2d.py, and follow along with listing 5.6.

Listing 5.6 Setting up data for 2D logistic regression

```
import numpy as np                      Imports relevant
import tensorflow as tf                 libraries
import matplotlib.pyplot as plt

learning_rate = 0.1                 Sets the hyperparameters
training_epochs = 2000
def sigmoid(x):                     Defines a helper sigmoid function
    return 1. / (1. + np.exp(-x))

x1_label1 = np.random.normal(3, 1, 1000)
x2_label1 = np.random.normal(2, 1, 1000)
x1_label2 = np.random.normal(7, 1, 1000)
x2_label2 = np.random.normal(6, 1, 1000)           Initializes
x1s = np.append(x1_label1, x1_label2)              fake data
x2s = np.append(x2_label1, x2_label2)
ys = np.asarray([0.] * len(x1_label1) + [1.] * len(x1_label2))
```

You have two independent variables (x1 and x2). A simple way to model the mapping between the input x's and output M(x) is the following equation, where w is the parameter to be found with TensorFlow:

$$M(x, v) = sig(w_2 x_2 + w_1 x_1 + w_0)$$

In listing 5.7, you'll implement the equation and its corresponding cost function to learn the parameters.

Listing 5.7   Using TensorFlow for multidimensional logistic regression

Defines the input/output
placeholder nodes

Defines the
parameter node

Defines the sigmoid
model, using both
input variables

```
X1 = tf.placeholder(tf.float32, shape=(None,), name="x1")
X2 = tf.placeholder(tf.float32, shape=(None,), name="x2")
Y = tf.placeholder(tf.float32, shape=(None,), name="y")
w = tf.Variable([0., 0., 0.], name="w", trainable=True)
```

Defines the
learning step

```
y_model = tf.sigmoid(w[2] * X2 + w[1] * X1 + w[0])
cost = tf.reduce_mean(-tf.log(y_model * Y + (1 - y_model) * (1 - Y)))
train_op = tf.train.GradientDescentOptimizer(learning_rate).minimize(cost)
```

```
with tf.Session() as sess:
    sess.run(tf.global_variables_initializer())
    prev_err = 0
    for epoch in range(training_epochs):
        err, _ = sess.run([cost, train_op], {X1: x1s, X2: x2s, Y: ys})
        print(epoch, err)
        if abs(prev_err - err) < 0.0001:
            break
        prev_err = err
    w_val = sess.run(w, {X1: x1s, X2: x2s, Y: ys})
```

Creates a new session,
initializes variables, and learns
parameters until convergence

Defines arrays to
hold boundary
points

Obtains the learned parameter
value before closing the session

```
x1_boundary, x2_boundary = [], []
for x1_test in np.linspace(0, 10, 100):
    for x2_test in np.linspace(0, 10, 100):
        z = sigmoid(-x2_test*w_val[2] - x1_test*w_val[1] - w_val[0])
        if abs(z - 0.5) < 0.01:
            x1_boundary.append(x1_test)
            x2_boundary.append(x2_test)
```

Loops through
a window of
points

If the model response is close to
0.5, updates the boundary points

```
plt.scatter(x1_boundary, x2_boundary, c='b', marker='o', s=20)
plt.scatter(x1_label1, x2_label1, c='r', marker='x', s=20)
plt.scatter(x1_label2, x2_label2, c='g', marker='1', s=20)

plt.show()
```

Shows the
boundary line
along with the
data

Figure 5.16 depicts the linear boundary line learned from the training data. A crime
that occurs on this line has an equal chance of being committed by either gang.

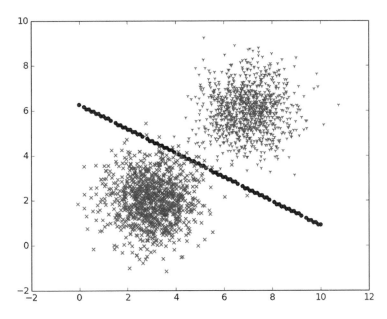

Figure 5.16 The diagonal dotted line represents when the probability between the two decisions is split equally. Confidence in a decision increases as data lies farther from the line.

5.5 *Multiclass classifier*

So far, you've dealt with multidimensional input but not with multivariate output, shown in figure 5.17. Instead of binary labels on the data, what if you have 3, 4, or 100 classes? Logistic regression requires two labels—no more.

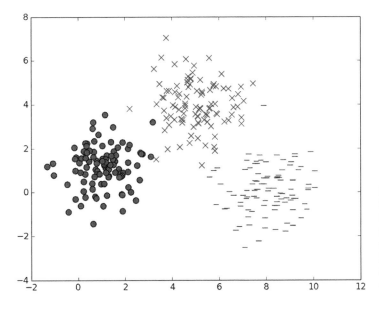

Figure 5.17 The independent variable is 2D, indicated by the x-axis and y-axis. The dependent variable can be one of three labels, shown by the color and shape of the data points.

Image classification, for example, is a popular multivariate classification problem because the goal is to decide the class of an image from a collection of candidates. A photograph may be bucketed into one of hundreds of categories.

To handle more than two labels, you may reuse logistic regression in a clever way (using a one-versus-all or one-versus-one approach) or develop a new approach (softmax regression). We look at each of the approaches in the following sections. The logistic regression approaches require a decent amount of ad hoc engineering, so let's focus on softmax regression.

5.5.1 One-versus-all

First, you train a classifier for each of the labels, as shown in figure 5.18. If there are three labels, you have three classifiers available to use: f1, f2, and f3. To test on new data, you run each of the classifiers to see which one produces the most confident response. Intuitively, you label the new point by the label of the classifier that responded most confidently.

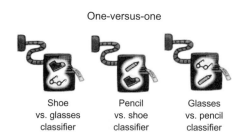

Figure 5.18   One-versus-all is a multiclass classifier approach that requires a detector for each class.

5.5.2 One-versus-one

Then you train a classifier for each pair of labels (see figure 5.19). If there are three labels, that's three unique pairs. But for k number of labels, that's $k(k-1)/2$ pairs of labels. On new data, you run all the classifiers and choose the class with the most wins.

5.5.3 Softmax regression

Softmax regression is named after the traditional max function, which takes a vector and returns the max value. But softmax isn't exactly the max function, because it has the added benefit of being continuous and differentiable. As a result, it has the helpful properties for stochastic gradient descent to work efficiently.

Figure 5.19   In one-versus-one multiclass classification, there's a detector for each pair of classes.

In this type of multiclass classification setup, each class has a confidence (or probability) score for each input vector. The softmax step picks the highest-scoring output.

Open a new file called softmax.py, and follow along with listing 5.8. First, you'll visualize fake data to reproduce figure 5.17 (also reproduced here in figure 5.20).

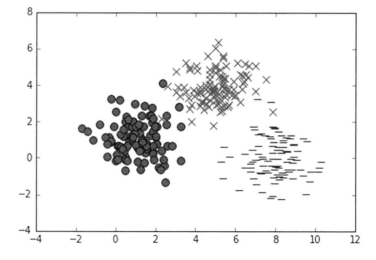

Figure 5.20 2D training data for multi-output classification

Listing 5.8 Visualizing multiclass data

```
import numpy as np                                    Imports NumPy
import matplotlib.pyplot as plt                       and Matplotlib

x1_label0 = np.random.normal(1, 1, (100, 1))          Generates points near (1, 1)
x2_label0 = np.random.normal(1, 1, (100, 1))
x1_label1 = np.random.normal(5, 1, (100, 1))
x2_label1 = np.random.normal(4, 1, (100, 1))          Generates points near (5, 4)
x1_label2 = np.random.normal(8, 1, (100, 1))
x2_label2 = np.random.normal(0, 1, (100, 1))          Generates points near (8, 0)

plt.scatter(x1_label0, x2_label0, c='r', marker='o', s=60)
plt.scatter(x1_label1, x2_label1, c='g', marker='x', s=60)     Visualizes the three
plt.scatter(x1_label2, x2_label2, c='b', marker='_', s=60)     labels on a scatter
plt.show()                                                      plot
```

Next, in listing 5.9, you set up the training and test data to prepare for the softmax regression step. The labels must be represented as a vector in which only one element is 1 and the rest are 0s. This representation is called *one-hot encoding*. If there are three labels, they'd be represented as the following vectors: $[1, 0, 0]$, $[0, 1, 0]$, and $[0, 0, 1]$.

Exercise 5.5

One-hot encoding might appear to be an unnecessary step. Why not have 1D output with values of 1, 2, and 3 representing the three classes?

Answer

Regression may induce a semantic structure in the output. If outputs are similar, regression implies that their inputs were also similar. If you use one dimension, you're implying that labels 2 and 3 are more similar to each other than 1 and 3. You must be careful about making unnecessary or incorrect assumptions, so it's a safe bet to use one-hot encoding.

Listing 5.9 Setting up training and test data for multiclass classification

```
xs_label0 = np.hstack((x1_label0, x2_label0))       Combines all input
xs_label1 = np.hstack((x1_label1, x2_label1))       data into one big
xs_label2 = np.hstack((x1_label2, x2_label2))       matrix
xs = np.vstack((xs_label0, xs_label1, xs_label2))
labels = np.matrix([[1., 0., 0.]] * len(x1_label0) + [[0., 1., 0.]] *
    len(x1_label1) + [[0., 0., 1.]] * len(x1_label2))
                                                    Creates the corresponding
arr = np.arange(xs.shape[0])                        one-hot labels
np.random.shuffle(arr)
xs = xs[arr, :]                     Shuffles the
labels = labels[arr, :]             dataset

test_x1_label0 = np.random.normal(1, 1, (10, 1))            Constructs the test
test_x2_label0 = np.random.normal(1, 1, (10, 1))            dataset and labels
test_x1_label1 = np.random.normal(5, 1, (10, 1))
test_x2_label1 = np.random.normal(4, 1, (10, 1))
test_x1_label2 = np.random.normal(8, 1, (10, 1))
test_x2_label2 = np.random.normal(0, 1, (10, 1))
test_xs_label0 = np.hstack((test_x1_label0, test_x2_label0))
test_xs_label1 = np.hstack((test_x1_label1, test_x2_label1))
test_xs_label2 = np.hstack((test_x1_label2, test_x2_label2))

test_xs = np.vstack((test_xs_label0, test_xs_label1, test_xs_label2))

test_labels = np.matrix([[1., 0., 0.]] * 10 + [[0., 1., 0.]] * 10 + [[0., 0.,
    1.]] * 10)
                                           The shape of the dataset tells you the number
train_size, num_features = xs.shape        of examples and features per example.
```

You see the use of the hstack and vstack methods in listing 5.9, corresponding to horizontal stack and vertical stack, respectively—two functions available from the NumPy library. The hstack function takes arrays and stacks them in sequence horizontally (column-wise), and the vstack function takes arrays and stacks them in sequence vertically (row-wise). As an example, x1_label0 and x2_label0 from listing 5.8 look similar to this when printed:

```
print(x1_label0)
 [[ 1.48175716]
 [ 0.34867807]
 [-0.35358866]
...
 [ 0.77637156]
 [ 0.9731792 ]]

print(x2_label0)
 [[ 2.02688   ]
 [ 2.37936835]
 [ 0.24260849]
 ...
 [ 1.58274368]
 [-1.55880602]]
```

The resulting value of the `xs_label0` variable would look something like this:

```
array([[ 1.48175716,  2.02688   ],
       [ 0.34867807,  2.37936835],
       [-0.35358866,  0.24260849],
       [ 0.60081539, -0.97048316],
       [ 2.61426058,  1.8768225 ],
...
       [ 0.77637156,  1.58274368],
       [ 0.9731792 , -1.55880602]])
```

Finally, in listing 5.10, you use softmax regression. Unlike the sigmoid function in logistic regression, here you use the `softmax` function provided by the TensorFlow library. The `softmax` function is similar to the `max` function, which outputs the maximum value from a list of numbers. It's called *softmax* because it's a "soft" or "smooth" approximation of the `max` function, which is not smooth or continuous (and that's bad). Continuous and smooth functions facilitate learning the correct weights of a neural network by backpropagation.

Exercise 5.6

Which of the following functions is continuous?

```
f(x) = x2
f(x) = min(x, 0)
f(x) = tan(x)
```

Answer

The first two are continuous. The last one, `tan(x)`, has periodic asymptotes, so there are some values for which there are no valid results.

Listing 5.10   Using softmax regression

```
import tensorflow as tf

learning_rate = 0.01          Defines              Defines the
training_epochs = 1000        hyperparameters      input/output
num_labels = 3                                     placeholder
batch_size = 100                                   nodes        Defines the model
                                                                parameters
X = tf.placeholder("float", shape=[None, num_features])
Y = tf.placeholder("float", shape=[None, num_labels])
                                                                Defines an op to
                                                                measure success rate
W = tf.Variable(tf.zeros([num_features, num_labels]))
b = tf.Variable(tf.zeros([num_labels]))                         Sets up the
y_model = tf.nn.softmax(tf.matmul(X, W) + b)    Designs the     learning algorithm
                                                softmax model
cost = -tf.reduce_sum(Y * tf.log(y_model))
train_op = tf.train.GradientDescentOptimizer(learning_rate).minimize(cost)

correct_prediction = tf.equal(tf.argmax(y_model, 1), tf.argmax(Y, 1))
accuracy = tf.reduce_mean(tf.cast(correct_prediction, "float"))
```

Now that you've defined the TensorFlow computation graph, execute it from a session. You'll try a new form of iteratively updating the parameters this time, called *batch learning*. Instead of passing in the data one piece at a time, you'll run the optimizer on batches of data. This technique speeds things but introduces a risk of converging to a local optimum solution instead of the global best. Use listing 5.11 to run the optimizer in batches.

Listing 5.11   Executing the graph

Opens a new session and initializes all variables

Loops only enough times to complete a single pass through the dataset

```
with tf.Session() as sess:
    tf.global_variables_initializer().run()

    for step in range(training_epochs * train_size // batch_size):
        offset = (step * batch_size) % train_size
        batch_xs = xs[offset:(offset + batch_size), :]
        batch_labels = labels[offset:(offset + batch_size)]
        err, _ = sess.run([cost, train_op], feed_dict={X: batch_xs, Y:
            batch_labels})
        print (step, err)

    W_val = sess.run(W)
    print('w', W_val)
    b_val = sess.run(b)
    print('b', b_val)
    print("accuracy", accuracy.eval(feed_dict={X: test_xs, Y:
        test_labels}))
```

Retrieves a subset of the dataset corresponding to the current batch

Prints ongoing results

Runs the optimizer on this batch

Prints the final learned parameters

Prints the success rate

The final output of running the softmax regression algorithm on the dataset is

```
('w', array([[-2.101, -0.021,  2.122],
             [-0.371,  2.229, -1.858]], dtype=float32))
('b', array([10.305, -2.612, -7.693], dtype=float32))
Accuracy 1.0
```

You've learned the weights and biases of the model. You can reuse these learned parameters to infer on test data. A simple way to do so is to save and load the variables by using TensorFlow's Saver object (see https://www.tensorflow.org/guide/saved_model). You can run the model (called y_model in our code) to obtain the model responses on your test data.

5.6   *Application of classification*

Emotion is a difficult concept to operationalize. Happiness, sadness, anger, excitement, and fear are examples of emotions that are subjective. What comes across as exciting to one person might appear sarcastic to another. Text that appears to convey anger to some people might convey fear to others. If humans have so much trouble, what luck can computers have?

At the very least, machine-learning researchers have figured out ways to classify positive and negative sentiments within text. Suppose that you're building an Amazon-like website on which each item has user reviews. You want your intelligent search engine to prefer items with positive reviews. Perhaps the best metric you have available is the average star rating or number of thumbs ups. But what if you have a lot of heavy-text reviews without explicit ratings?

Sentiment analysis can be considered to be a binary classification problem. The input is natural language text, and the output is a binary decision that infers positive or negative sentiment. Following are datasets you can find online to solve this exact problem:

- Large Movie Review Dataset—http://mng.bz/60nj
- Sentiment Labelled Sentences Data Set—http://mng.bz/CzSM
- Twitter Sentiment Analysis Dataset—http://mng.bz/2M4d

The biggest hurdle is to figure out how to represent raw text as an input to a classification algorithm. Throughout this chapter, the input to classification has always been a feature vector. One of the oldest methods of converting raw text into a feature vector is called Bag of Words. You can find a nice tutorial and code implementation for it at http://mng.bz/K8yz.

Summary

- There are many ways to solve classification problems, but logistic regression and softmax regression are two of the most robust in terms of accuracy and performance.
- It's important to preprocess data before running classification. Discrete independent variables can be readjusted into binary variables, for example.
- So far, you've approached classification from the point of view of regression. In later chapters, you'll revisit classification by using neural networks.
- There are various ways to approach multiclass classification. There's no clear answer as to which one you should try first: one-versus-one, one-versus-all, or softmax regression. But the softmax approach is a little more hands-free and allows you to fiddle with hyperparameters.

Sentiment classification: Large movie-review dataset

This chapter covers

- Using text and word frequency (Bag of Words) to represent sentiment
- Building sentiment classifier using logistic regression and with softmax
- Measuring classification accuracy
- Computing ROC curve and measure classifier effectiveness
- Submitting your results to the Kaggle challenge for movie reviews

One of the magic uses of machine learning that impresses everyone nowadays is teaching the computer to learn from text. With social media, SMS text, Facebook Messenger, What's App, Twitter, and other sources generating hundreds of billions of text messages a day, there is no shortage of text to learn from.

TIP Check out this famous infographic demonstrating the abundance of textual data arriving each day from various media platforms: http://mng.bz/yrXq.

Social media companies, phone providers, and app makers are all trying to use the messages you send to make decisions and classify you. Have you ever sent your significant other an SMS text message about the Thai food you ate for lunch and then later saw ads on your social media pop up, recommending new Thai restaurants to visit? Scary as it seems that Big Brother is trying to identify and understand your food habits, online streaming service companies are also using practical applications to try to determine whether you enjoyed their products.

After watching a film, have you ever taken the time to issue a simple review, such as "Wow, that was a great movie! Loved Bill's performance!" or "That movie was grossly inappropriate, was well over three hours long, and after first being disgusted by the gore, I fell asleep because there was no plot!" (Okay, admittedly, I *may* have written that last comment on some online platform.) YouTube is famous for other users coming not only to watch the videos and viral content, but also to engage in the act of reading the comments—looking at the written reviews of content for movies, videos, and other digital media. These reviews are simple in the sense that you can fire and forget a quick sentence or two, get your feelings out there, and move on with your life. Sometimes, the comments are hilarious, or angry, or extremely positive; ultimately, they run the gamut of emotions that online participants could experience while viewing the content.

Those emotions are quite useful to online media service companies. Given an easy way to classify sentiment, the companies could determine whether a particular video of a celebrity generated extreme sadness or extremely positive responses. In turn, if the companies could first classify and then associate those emotions with what you did next—if, after watching a movie, you provided a few sentences of positive commentary and clicked a link to buy more movies starring the lead actor—they'd have the whole cause-and-effect pipeline. The media company could generate more of that content or show you more of the types of content that you are interested in. Doing so may generate increased revenue, such as if your positive reaction led you to purchase something about that celebrity afterward.

You're learning about a methodology for using machine learning to perform classification on input data and, by classifying it, generating some label for that input. Sentiment can be thought of in two ways: first as binary sentiment (such as positive/negative reaction) and then as multiclass sentiment (such as hate, sad, neutral, like, or love). You learned the two following techniques to handle those cases, which you'll try out in this chapter:

- Logistic regression for the binary sentiment
- Softmax regression for multiclass classification

The challenge with the input in this case is that it's text, not some nice input vector of numbers like the randomly generated data points that our trusty NumPy library generated for us in chapter 5. Luckily for you, the text and information retrieval community has developed a technique to handle mapping text to a numerical feature vector—perfect for machine learning. This technique is called the Bag of Words model.

6.1 Using the Bag of Words model

The *Bag of Words* model is a method from natural language processing (NLP) that takes as input text in the form of a sentence and turns it into a feature vector by considering the extracted vocabulary words and the frequency of their occurrences. It's named as such because each word frequency count is like a "bag," with each occurrence of a word being an item in that bag. Bag of Words is a state-of-the-art model that allows you to take a review of a movie and convert it to a feature vector, which you will need to classify its sentiment. Consider the following review snippet text, written about a Michael Jackson movie:

```
With all this stuff going down at the moment with MJ i've started listening
to his music, watching the odd documentary here and there, watched The Wiz
and watched Moonwalker again.
```

The first step in applying the Bag of Words model to process this review is preprocessing the text and extract only the words with actual meaning. Usually, this process involves removing any nonletter characters—such as numbers, annotations such as HTML tags, and punctuation—and strips the text down to its bare words. After that, the approach reduces the remaining words in the subset to those that are nouns, verbs, or adjectives, and takes out articles, conjunctions, and other *stop words*—words that are not distinguishing features of the text itself.

> **NOTE**   Many canned stop-word lists are available. Those used by Python's Natural Language Toolkit (NLTK) are a good starting point; you can find them at https://gist.github.com/sebleier/554280. Stop words are usually language-specific, so you want to make sure whichever list you use suits the language you are processing. Luckily for you, NLTK currently handles stop words from 21 languages. You can read more about it at http://mng.bz/MoPn.

When that step is complete, the Bag of Words model generates a count histogram of the remaining vocabulary words, and that histogram becomes the fingerprint for the input text. Often, the fingerprint is normalized by dividing the counts by the max count, resulting in a feature vector of values between 0 and 1. The whole process is shown in figure 6.1.

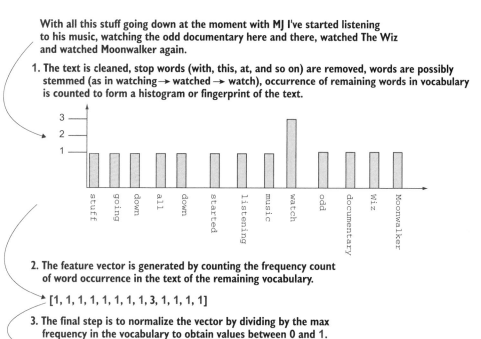

With all this stuff going down at the moment with MJ I've started listening to his music, watching the odd documentary here and there, watched The Wiz and watched Moonwalker again.

1. The text is cleaned, stop words (with, this, at, and so on) are removed, words are possibly stemmed (as in watching → watched → watch), occurrence of remaining words in vocabulary is counted to form a histogram or fingerprint of the text.

2. The feature vector is generated by counting the frequency count of word occurrence in the text of the remaining vocabulary.

[1, 1, 1, 1, 1, 1, 1, 1, 3, 1, 1, 1, 1]

3. The final step is to normalize the vector by dividing by the max frequency in the vocabulary to obtain values between 0 and 1.

[0.33, 0.33, 0.33, 0.33, 0.33, 0.33, 0.33 ,0.33, 1., 0.33, 0.33, 0.33, 0.33]

Figure 6.1 A visual depiction of the Bag of Words model. Text is analyzed and cleaned, and words are counted to form a histogram, which is then normalized to obtain a feature vector representation of the input text.

6.1.1 Applying the Bag of Words model to movie reviews

To get started with the Bag of Words model, you'll need some review text. The Kaggle Bag of Words Meets Bags of Popcorn challenge is an excellent, already-completed competition that looked at 50,000 movie reviews from Internet Movie Database (IMDb.com) to generate a sentiment classification from those movie reviews. You can read more about the challenge at http://mng.bz/aw0B. You will use those reviews in this chapter to build sentiment classifiers.

To get started, grab the labeledTrainData.tsv file from http://mng.bz/ggEE, and save it to your local drive. You'll also want to download the testData.tsv file from http://mng.bz/emWv; you'll use that file later. The files are formatted as tab-separated values (TSV) files, with the columns corresponding to a unique identifier (id), the sentiment (1 for positive or 0 for negative), and the review itself in HTML format, per row.

Let's try our Bag of Words model and create a function to handle creating machine-learning-ready input features from the input labeledTrainData.tsv file. Open a new notebook called sentiment_classifier.ipynb, and create a review_to_words function. The first thing the function does is convert an HTML review from IMDb into review text by calling the Tika Python library. Tika Python is a content analysis library whose main functionalities include file type identification, text and metadata extraction from more than 1,400 formats, and language identification.

> **TIP** A full explanation of Tika is the subject of another Manning book written by me. Seriously, check out *Tika in Action* (https://www.manning.com/books/tika-in-action). Here, you use it to strip all the HTML tags in text, using the `parser` interface and its `from_buffer` method, which takes as input a string buffer and outputs the associated extracted text from the HTML parser.

With the extracted review text in hand, use Python's `re` (for *regular expression*) module to use a common pattern `[^a-zA-z]`, which means start from the beginning of the string (the ^ symbol), scan and identify only uppercase and lowercase letters *a* through *z*, and replace everything else with a whitespace character.

The next step is converting the text all to lowercase. Word-case has meaning for interpreting a sentence or language but little meaning for counting word occurrences independent of the structure. Stop words, including conjunctions and articles, are removed next via Python's NLTK library. The library has support for stop words from 21 languages, so you'll use the ones for English, because you're working with IMDb's English reviews. The final step is joining the remaining words as a string. The output of listing 6.1 is a thinned-down version of the original listing with only the meaningful words and no HTML—in other words, *clean text*. That clean text will be the actual input to the Bag of Words model.

Listing 6.1   Creating features from the input text of the reviews

```
from tika import parser
from nltk.corpus import stopwords
import re

def review_to_words( raw_review ):
    review_text = parser.from_buffer( "<html>" + raw_review + "</html>"
    ⇒ )["content"]
    letters_only = re.sub("[^a-zA-Z]", " ", review_text)
    words = letters_only.lower().split()
    stops = set(stopwords.words("english"))
    meaningful_words = [w for w in words if not w in stops]
    return( " ".join( meaningful_words ))
```

Function converts a raw review to a string of words by using Apache Tika.

Removes nonletters

Converts to lowercase, split into individual words

Removes stop words

Converts stop words to a set, which is much faster than searching list

Joins the words back into one string separated by space

Armed with our function to generate clean review text, you can start running the function over the 25,000 reviews in labeledTrainData.tsv. But first, you need to load those reviews into Python.

6.1.2   Cleaning all the movie reviews

A handy library that loads a TSV into Python efficiently is the Pandas library for creating, manipulating, and saving dataframes. You can think of a dataframe as being a table that is machine-learning-ready. Each column in the table is a feature you can use in machine learning, and the rows are input for training or testing. Pandas provides functions for adding and dropping feature columns, and for augmenting and replacing row values in sophisticated ways. Pandas is the subject of many books (I didn't write them!), and Google provides tens of thousands of results on the subject, but for your purposes here, you can use Pandas to create a machine-learning-ready dataframe from the input TSV file. Then Pandas can help you inspect the number of features, rows, and columns in your input.

   With that dataframe, you run your review-text-cleaning code to generate clean reviews to which you can apply the Bag of Words model. First, call the Pandas `read_csv` function, and tell it that you are reading a TSV file with no header row, with the tab character (\t) as the delimiter, and that you do not want it to quote the feature values. When the train data is loaded, print its shape and column values, demonstrating the ease of using Pandas to inspect your dataframe.

   Because cleaning 25,000 movie reviews can take a while, you will use Python's TQDM helper library to keep track of your progress. TQDM is an extensible progress-bar library that print status to the command line or to a Jupyter notebook. You wrap your iteration step—the `range` function in listing 6.2—as a `tqdm` object. Then every iteration step causes a progress-bar increment to be visible to the user, either via the command line or in a notebook. TQDM is a great way to fire and forget a long-running machine-learning operation and still know that something is going on when you come back to check on it.

   Listing 6.2 prints the training shape `(25000, 3)` corresponding to 25,000 reviews and 3 columns (id, sentiment, and review), and the output `array(['id', 'sentiment', 'review'], dtype=object)` corresponding to those column values. Add the code in listing 6.2 to your sentiment_classifier.ipynb notebook to generate 25,000 clean-text reviews and keep track of the progress.

Listing 6.2   Using Pandas to read the movie reviews and apply your cleaning function

Reads the 25,000 reviews from the input TSV file

```
import pandas as pd
from tqdm import tqdm_notebook as tqdm

train = pd.read_csv("labeledTrainData.tsv", header=0,
                    delimiter="\t", quoting=3)
print(train.shape)
print(train.columns.values)

num_reviews = train["review"].size
```

Prints the shape of the training data and number of values

Gets the number of reviews based on the dataframe column size

```
clean_train_reviews = []                          ◁──────   Initializes an empty list to
                                                            hold the clean reviews
for i in tqdm(range( 0, num_reviews )):
    clean_train_reviews.append( review_to_words( train["review"][i] ) )
```

Loops over each review and
cleans it by using your function

Now that you have the clean reviews, it's time to apply the Bag of Words model. Python's SK-learn library (https://scikit-learn.org) is an extensible machine-learning library that provides a lot of features complementary to TensorFlow. Even though some of the features overlap, I use SK-learn's data cleaning functions quite a bit throughout the book. You don't have to be a purist. SK-learn comes with a fantastic implementation of Bag of Words called `CountVectorizer`, for example; you'll use it in listing 6.3 to apply the Bag of Words model.

First, create the `CountVectorizer` with some initial hyperparameters. These hyperparameters tell SK-learn whether you want it to do any text analysis, such as tokenization, preprocessing, or removal of stop words. I omit it here because you've already written your own text-cleaning function in listing 6.1 and applied it in 6.2 to the input text.

One parameter of note is `max_features`, which controls the size of the learned vocabulary from the text. Choosing a size of 5000 ensures that the TensorFlow model you build has sufficient richness and that the resulting Bag of Words fingerprints for each review can be learned without exploding the amount of RAM on your machine. Obviously, you can play around with this example of parameter tuning later, given a larger machine and more time. A general rule of thumb is that a vocabulary on the order of thousands should provide sufficient learnability for English movies. For news, scientific literature, and other domains, however, you may need to experiment to find an optimal value.

Call `fit_transform` to provide the clean reviews you generated in listing 6.2 and to get back the vectorized Bag of Words, one row per review, with the row contents being the count per vocabulary word per review. Then convert the vector to a NumPy array; print its shape; and ensure that you see (25000,5000), corresponding to 25,000 input rows with 5,000 features per row. Add the code from listing 6.3 to your notebook.

Listing 6.3   Applying the Bag of Words model to obtain your training data

```
from sklearn.feature_extraction.text import CountVectorizer
vectorizer = CountVectorizer(analyzer = "word",    \
                             tokenizer = None,       \
                             preprocessor = None,   \
                             stop_words = None,     \
                             max_features = 5000)

train_data_features = vectorizer.fit_transform(clean_train_reviews)
train_data_features = train_data_features.toarray()
print(train_data_features.shape)
```

Imports the CountVectorizer and
instantiates the Bag of Words model

Fits the model, learns
the vocabulary, and
transforms training
data into vectors

Prints the resultant input
feature shape (25000,5000)

Converts the results
to a NumPy array

6.1.3 *Exploratory data analysis on your Bag of Words*

Doing some exploratory data analysis is always a good thing, and you may want to inspect the values of the vocabulary returned from CountVectorizer to get a feel for what words are present across all the reviews. You'll want to convince yourself that there is something to learn here. What you are looking for is some statistical distribution across the words and associated patterns that the classifier will learn to identify from that distribution. If all the counts are the same in every review, and you can't eyeball a difference between them, the machine-learning algorithm will have the same difficulty.

The great things about SK-learn and CountVectorizer is that they not only provide a one- or two-line API call to create the Bag of Words output, but also allow easy inspection of the result. You can get the vocabulary words learned and print them, count their size by using a quick NumPy sum method to bin by word, and then take a look at the first 100 words and their sums across all reviews. The code to perform these tasks is in listing 6.4.

Listing 6.4 Exploratory data analysis on the returned Bag of Words

```
vocab = vectorizer.get_feature_names()          Gets the learned vocabulary and
print("size %d %s " % (len(vocab), vocab))      prints its size and the learned words

dist = np.sum(train_data_features, axis=0)  ◁── Sums the counts of each vocabulary word

for tag, count in zip(vocab, dist):         Prints the vocabulary word and the number
    print("%d, %s" % (count, tag))          of times it appears in the training set

plt.scatter(vocab[0:99], dist[0:99])        Plots the word count
plt.xticks(vocab[0:99], rotation='vertical')  for the first 100 words
plt.show()
```

Figure 6.2 shows the output set of words printed for the first 100 words in all 25,000 reviews. I could have picked any random set of 100 words from the vocabulary, but to keep the example simple, I picked the first 100. Even in the first 100 words, there appears to be statistical significance in the count of those words across reviews; the

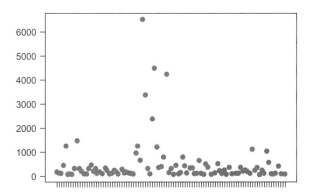

Figure 6.2 Vocabulary counts summed across all 25,000 reviews of the first 100 words in the extracted 5,000-word vocabulary

counts are not all the same, and there is no uniformity. Some words are used more often than others, and there are some obvious outliers, so it looks as though there is a signal for a classifier to learn. You get started building a logistic regression classifier in section 6.2.

6.2 *Building a sentiment classifier using logistic regression*

In chapter 5, when dealing with logistic regression, you identified the dependent and independent variables. In sentiment analysis, your dependent variable is your 5,000D feature vector Bag of Words per review, and you have 25,000 to train on. Your independent variable is the sentiment value: a 1 corresponding to a positive review from IMDb or a 0 corresponding to a user's negative sentiment about the movie.

> ### What about the movie titles?
> Have you noticed that the IMDb data you are using is the review and the sentiment, but no title? Where are the title words? Those words could factor into the sentiment if they contain trigger words that map to the words that moviegoers used in their reviews. But overall, you don't need the titles—only a sentiment (something to learn) and a review.

Try to picture the space of solutions that your classifier will be exploring, given the training data and feature space. You can imagine a vector plane—call it the *ground*—and call the vertical axis the elevation distance from the ground as though you were standing on it and looking up to the sky—the *sentiment*. On the ground plane, you have a vector beginning at the origin from where you are standing and proceeding in every direction corresponding to a particular word from your vocabulary—5,000 axes, if you will—shooting out a distance that corresponds to the count of that particular word that the vector describes. Data points in this plane are the specific counts on each of the word axes, and the y value is whether the collection of counts on each plane for a particular point implies a sentiment of 1 or 0. Your imagining should look similar to figure 6.3.

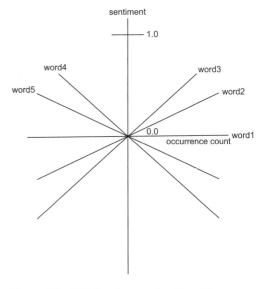

Figure 6.3 Picturing the construction of the classifier by using logistic regression. Your feature space is the count of the words arranged as the plane three-dimensionally, where the value is the occurrence count. The y-axis corresponds to the sentiment result (0 or 1).

Given this construction, we can represent the logistic regression equation that corresponds to this classifier by using the following equations. The goal is to have a linear function with all the dependent variables and their associated weights (1 through 5000) as the parameter to the sigmoid (sig) function, which results in a smooth curve that fluctuates between 0 and 1, corresponding to the sentiment independent variable:

$$M(x, w) = sig(wx + w)$$

$$sentiment = sig(w_1 x_1 + w_2 x_2 + \ldots + w_{5000} x_{5000} + w_0)$$

6.2.1 Setting up the training for your model

You're ready to set up your TensorFlow logistic regression classifier. Begin with an arbitrary learning rate of 0.1 to start, and train for 2,000 epochs (which worked well on my laptop), especially because you will perform early stopping. *Early stopping* is a technique that measures the difference in loss (or error rate) between the previous epoch and the current epoch. If the error rate shifts between epochs by some minor threshold epsilon, the model is said to be stable, and you can break early in your training.

You'll set up your sigmoid function, which is needed for the model as well. As discussed in chapter 5, this function ensures that the backpropagation process used to learn the appropriate model weights during each training step after applying the cost function has a smooth gradient step that fluctuates between 0 and 1. The sigmoid function has precisely those properties.

Create the placeholders in TensorFlow for the Y values that you will learn, the sentiment labels, and your placeholder for the X input 5,000 × 25,000-dimensional feature vector: one Bag of Words vector per movie review and 25,000 movie reviews. In listing 6.5, you use a Python dictionary to store each Bag of Words vector, indexed X0-X4999. The w variable (the weights) is one for each dependent variable X and one constant w added at the end of the linear equation.

The cost function is the same convex cross-entropy loss function used in chapter 5, and you will use gradient descent as your optimizer. The complete code to set up the model is shown in listing 6.5.

Listing 6.5 Setting up the training for the logistic regression sentiment classifier

```
learning_rate = 0.1             Sets up the initial model hyperparameters
training_epochs = 2000          for learning rate and number of epochs
def sigmoid(x):
    return 1. / (1. + np.exp(-x))    ◁——— Sets up the logistic regression model

Y = tf.placeholder(tf.float32, shape=(None,), name="y")
w = tf.Variable([0.] * (len(train_data_features)+1), name="w", trainable=True)

ys = train['sentiment'].values ◁——│ Extracts the labels to learn       Defines TensorFlow
Xs = {}                            │ from the Pandas dataframe           placeholders to
for i in range(train_data_features.shape[1]):                           inject the actual
                                                                        input and label
                                                                        values
```

```
Xs["X"+str(i)] = tf.placeholder(tf.float32, shape=(None,),
    name="x"+str(i))
```

```
linear = w[0]
for i in range(0, train_data_features.shape[1]):      Constructs the
    linear = linear + (w[i+1] * Xs["X"+str(i)])       logistic regression
y_model = tf.sigmoid(linear)                       ◄──── model to learn
```

```
cost = tf.reduce_mean(-tf.log(y_model * Y + (1 - y_model) * (1 - Y)))
train_op = tf.train.GradientDescentOptimizer(learning_rate).minimize(cost)
```

**Defines the cross-entropy cost function and
train operation for each learning step**

After setting up your model, you can perform the training by using TensorFlow. As I
mentioned earlier, you'll perform early stopping to save yourself useless epochs when
the loss function and model response cost settle down.

6.2.2 Performing the training for your model

Create a tf.train.Saver to save the model graph and the trained weights so that you
can reload them later to make classification predictions with your trained model. The
training steps are similar to what you've seen before: you initialize TensorFlow and this
time use TQDM to keep track of and incrementally print the progress in training so
that you have some indicator. Training will possibly take 30 to 45 minutes to train and
will consume gigabytes of memory—at least, it did on my fairly beefy Mac laptop—
so TQDM is a must-have, letting you know how the training process is going.

The training step injects the 5,000-dimensional feature vector into the X placeholder dictionary that you created and the associated sentiment labels into the Y
placeholder variables from TensorFlow. You'll use your convex loss function as the
model cost and compare the value of the cost in the previous epoch with the current
one to determine whether your code should perform early stopping in the training to
save precious cycles. The threshold value of 0.0001 was chosen arbitrarily but could
be a hyperparameter to explore, given additional cycles and time. Listing 6.6 shows
full training process for the logistic regression sentiment classifier.

> **Listing 6.6 Performing the training step for the logistic regression sentiment classifier**

**Creates the saver to capture your model
graph and associated trained weights**

```
└─▷ saver = tf.train.Saver()
    with tf.Session() as sess:
        sess.run(tf.global_variables_initializer())
    ┌─▷ prev_err = 0.                              Provides the 25,000-review,
        for epoch in tqdm(range(training_epochs)):   5,000-dimensional feature
            feed_dict = {}                           vectors and the sentiment
            for i in range(train_data_features.shape[1]):         labels
                feed_dict[Xs["X"+str(i)]] = train_data_features[:, i,
                    None].reshape(len(train_data_features))
            feed_dict[Y] = ys
```

**Captures the
previous loss
function value
to test for early
stopping**

```
      err, _ = sess.run([cost, train_op], feed_dict=feed_dict)
      print(epoch, err)
      if abs(prev_err - err) < 0.0001:
           break
      prev_err = err

    w_val = sess.run(w, feed_dict)
    save_path = saver.save(sess, "./en-netflix-binary-sentiment.ckpt")

print(w_val)
print(np.max(w_val))
```

Obtains the trained weights while the model graph is still loaded →

Tests whether the previous loss value varies from the current loss value by some small threshold and breaks if so

Saves the model graph and associated trained weights

You've trained your first text sentiment classifier by using logistic regression!

Next, I'll show you how to use this sentiment classifier to make predictions on new unseen data. You'll also learn how to evaluate the classifier's accuracy and precision, and get a feel for how well it is performing by running it against the test data from the Kaggle competition and then submitting your results to Kaggle.

6.3 *Making predictions using your sentiment classifier*

Now that you've built your classifier, how do you use it to make predictions? Two key pieces of information are stored when you make that trusty call to `tf.train.Saver` to save your checkpoint file:

- The checkpoint contains the model weights you arrived at—in this case, the weights of the `sigmoid` linear portion corresponding to each vocabulary word in your Bag of Words model.
- The checkpoint contains the model graph and its current state, in case you want to pick up where you left off and continue training its next epochs.

Making predictions is as simple as loading the checkpoint file and applying those weights to the model. As I showed you in chapter 5, there is no need to reuse your TensorFlow version of the `y_model` function from listing 6.5—the `tf.sigmoid` function—because doing so loads the model graph and requires additional resources to prepare TensorFlow to continue training. Instead, you can apply the learned weights to a NumPy version of the model—the inline `sigmoid` function from listing 6.5—because you won't be doing any further training on it.

Seems pretty simple, right? But I left out one major thing that I need to cover first. This will generalize to the rest of the book, in which you perform machine learning, train a model, and use it to make predictions that aid your automated decisions. Consider the steps you performed for your model training:

1 Perform data cleaning of 25,000 movie reviews.
   a Strip HTML.
   b Remove punctuation and consider only `a-zA-Z`.
   c Remove stop words.
2 Apply the Bag of Words model, limiting vocabulary to a 5,000-word feature vector.
3 Use 25,000 vectors of size 5,000 and associated 25,000 labels for sentiment 1, 0 and logistic regression to make a classification model.

Now suppose that you want to use your model to perform predictions on some new text, such as the following two sentences. The first sentence is clearly a negative review, and the second is a positive review:

```
new_neg_review = "Man, this movie really sucked. It was terrible. I could not
    possibly watch this movie again!"
new_pos_review = "I think that this is a fantastic movie, it really "
```

How do you provide these sentences to your model to make sentiment predictions? You need to apply to the prediction process the data-preprocessing steps that you used during training so that you are considering the text the same way that you trained on it. You were training on 5,000-dimensional feature vectors, so you'll need to do the same thing to prepare the input text to make predictions. Additionally, you need to take heed of one more step. The weights that you generated during training were under the auspices of a common shared vocabulary of 5,000 words generated by the CountVectorizer. The unseen input text that you are making predictions on may have a different vocabulary from your trained text vocabulary. In other words, that unseen text may use other words, perhaps more or less, than you trained on. Yet you spent nearly 45 minutes training your logistic-regression sentiment classifier and perhaps even longer preparing the input and labels for that training. Is that work invalidated? Do you have to perform training all over again?

Remember I mentioned earlier that choosing a value of 5000 for the vocabulary size in CountVectorizer allows for sufficient richness, but you may have to tune or explore to get the best fit. So vocabulary size does matter, and what you are predicting with your trained model matters as well. Having 5,000 words in a vocabulary left after preprocessing steps and data cleaning can achieve high accuracy during training and on unseen data—as high as 87% in my training, which you'll reproduce later in the chapter when you use receiver operating characteristic (ROC) curves. But who is to say that 10,000 words wouldn't have achieved even higher accuracy? Not me!

Indeed, using more words in your vocabulary may achieve higher accuracy. The result depends on the data you intend to make predictions on and the generality of that data. It also has a big influence on your overall memory and CPU and GPU requirements for training, because using more features for each input vector will no doubt take more resources. Note that if the vocabulary of your unseen data overlaps sufficiently with the representative vocabulary from your training data, there is no need to increase its size.

> **TIP** Figuring optimal vocabulary size is an exercise best left for a semester-long statistics or NLP graduate course, but suffice it to say that you may want to explore this hyperparameter further. This posting has some nice pointers on vocabulary size: http://mng.bz/pzA8.

To move forward and implement the sentiment-prediction function that this chapter focuses on, you need to figure out the overlap of the vocabulary vector from your new text and its vector with the existing vocabulary words from training. Then you will consider only the counts in your Bag of Words model for prediction for those overlapping terms in the fingerprint. These counts will be compared with those of the new text that you want to predict sentiment on based on your trained model. The entire prediction pipeline and its relationship with the training pipeline are illustrated in figure 6.4.

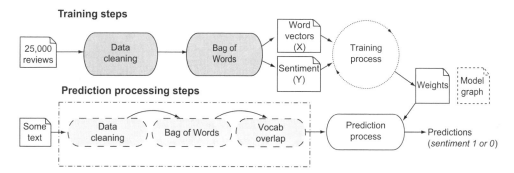

Figure 6.4 Making predictions with machine learning. During training (top), you preprocess the input data by cleaning the text, convert it to a 5,000-dimensional feature vector, and use it to learn sentiment labels (1 or 0) for 25,000 movie reviews. To make predictions with the learned model (right), you need to perform the same data cleaning steps and in addition figure out the overlap of next text and its vocabulary with your trained one.

Let's start writing the `predict` function, which should take the unmodified review text as input, along with the training vocabulary and learned weights from the training process. You need to apply the same data cleaning process, so you clean the text by doing the following:

- Tokenizing it
- Removing punctuation and noncharacters
- Removing stop words
- Rejoining the tokens

Afterward, apply the Bag of Words model again, and generate a function with which you can make sentiment predictions on unseen input text. The function should focus on figuring out the overlap of the new learned vocabulary words from the input with those of the training vocabulary. For each overlapping word, consider the word count; and other elements in the feature vector will be zero. The resultant feature vector should be fed to the sigmoid function for your logistic regression model, using the optimal learned weights. The result—a probability between 0 and 1 of its sentiment—is compared with a threshold value of 0.5 to determine whether the sentiment is 1 or 0. Listing 6.7 shows the `predict` function.

Listing 6.7   Making predictions with the logistic regression sentiment classifier

Takes review text to test, with the training vocabulary, learned weights, and threshold cutoff for a positive or negative prediction as parameters

```
def predict(test_review, vocab, weights, threshold=0.5):

    test_review_c = review_to_words(test_review)

    n_vectorizer = CountVectorizer(analyzer = "word",    \
                            tokenizer = None,      \
                            preprocessor = None,  \
                            stop_words = None,      \
                            max_features = 5000)
    ex_data_features = n_vectorizer.fit_transform([test_review_c])
    ex_data_features = ex_data_features.toarray()
    test_vocab = n_vectorizer.get_feature_names()
    test_vocab_counts = ex_data_features.reshape(ex_data_features.shape[1])

    ind_dict = dict((k, i) for i, k in enumerate(vocab))
    test_ind_dict = dict((k, i) for i, k in enumerate(test_vocab))
    inter = set(ind_dict).intersection(test_vocab)
    indices = [ ind_dict[x] for x in inter ]
    test_indices = [test_ind_dict[x] for x in inter]

    test_feature_vec = np.zeros(train_data_features.shape[1])
    for i in range(len(indices)):
        test_feature_vec[indices[i]] = test_vocab_counts[test_indices[i]]

    test_linear = weights[0]
    for i in range(0, train_data_features.shape[1]):
        test_linear = test_linear + (weights[i+1] * test_feature_vec[i])
    y_test = sigmoid(test_linear)

    return np.greater(y_test, threshold).astype(float)
```

Cleans the review, using the same function you used for training

Creates the test vocabulary and counts

Converts to a NumPy array of vocabulary and counts

Figures out the intersection of the test vocabulary from the review with the actual full vocabulary

All zeros for the 5,000-feature vector except for the overlap indices that we have counts for

If the predicted probability is greater than 0.5, sentiment is 1; otherwise, it is 0.

Applies your logistic regression model with the learned weights

Try the function on the following test reviews, new_neg_review and new_pos_review. The function properly predicts the negative review as a 0 and the positive review as a 1. Cool, right?

```
new_neg_review = "Man, this movie really sucked. It was terrible. I could not
    possibly watch this movie again!"
new_pos_review = "I think that this is a fantastic movie, it really "
predict(new_neg_review, vocab, w_val)
predict(new_pos_review, vocab, w_val)
```

Now that you have a predict function, you can use it to compute a confusion matrix (chapter 3). Creating a confusion matrix of true positives, false positives, true negatives, and false negatives allows you to measure the classifier's ability to predict each class and compute precision and recall. Additionally, you can generate an ROC curve and test how much better your classifier is than the baseline.

6.4 *Measuring the effectiveness of your classifier*

Now that you can predict the sentiment of unseen text with your logistic-regression classifier, a good way to measure its general effectiveness is to test it at scale on lots of unseen text. You used 25,000 IMDb movie reviews to train the classifier, so you'll use the other 25,000 that you held out for testing. When you trained your classifier by using Kaggle's TSV file, you were using a joined version of the raw IMDb review data. You won't always have that benefit; sometimes, you need to preprocess the raw data. To make sure that you can handle both approaches to data preparation and cleaning, use the original raw aclImdb_v1.tar.gz file (http://mng.bz/Ov5R) and prepare it for testing.

Unzip the aclImdb_v1.tar.gz file. You see have a folder structure that looks like this where each entry below is either a file (like README) or a directory (like test and train):

```
README    imdb.vocab    imdbEr.txt    test/    train/
```

Open the test directory. Inside are more files (*.txt and *.feat) and folders (neg and pos):

```
labeledBow.feat      neg/        pos/        urls_neg.txt      urls_pos.txt
```

The folders pos (for *positive*) and neg (for *negative*) hold 12,500 text files containing the movie reviews, each corresponding to unseen positive and negative reviews, so you'll create two variables—only_pos_file_contents and only_neg_file_contents—to correspond to them. Read the reviews into those two variables by using the two loops. Python's built-in os.isfile function makes sure that as the code iterates through and assesses directory listing objects, a test is performed to identify whether the object is a file (not a directory). The os.listdir method lists files in a directory. The code in listing 6.8 loads the test IMDb reviews.

> **Listing 6.8 Loading the test IMDb reviews**

```
from os import listdir
from os.path import isfile, join

pos_test_path = "aclImdb/test/pos/"
neg_test_path = "aclImdb/test/neg/"                      Iterates and identifies
only_pos_files = [f for f in listdir(pos_test_path) if   paths for text files of
    isfile(join(pos_test_path, f))]                      positive and negative
only_neg_files = [f for f in listdir(neg_test_path) if   reviews
    isfile(join(neg_test_path, f))]

only_pos_file_contents = []
for i in range(0, len(only_pos_files)):                  ◁——┐ Reads the positive
    with open(pos_test_path + only_pos_files[i], 'r') as file:    reviews into a list of
        r_data = file.read()                                     12,500 text objects
        only_pos_file_contents.append(r_data)
```

```
only_neg_file_contents = []
for i in range(0, len(only_neg_files)):
    with open(neg_test_path + only_neg_files[i], 'r') as file:
        r_data = file.read()
        only_neg_file_contents.append(r_data)

predictions_test = np.zeros(len(only_pos_file_contents) * 2)
```

Reads the negative reviews into a list of 12,500 text objects

Creates a placeholder for the 25,000 sentiment values

With the test reviews loaded into memory, in `only_pos_file_contents` and `only_neg_file_contents` and with the labels placeholder `predictions_test` variable, you can use the `predict` function to count true and false positives and true and false negatives, and then compute precision and recall for your classifier. Precision is defined as

$$\frac{TP}{TP + FP}$$

and recall is defined as

$$\frac{TP}{TP + FN}$$

The code in listing 6.9 iterates through the positive-sentiment files, invokes your `predict` function, stores the result in the `predictions_test` variable. It follows up by calling the `predict` function on the negative file contents. Because calling the `predict` function can take a few seconds per call, depending on the horsepower on your laptop, you will again use the `tqdm` library to track progress during each iteration loop. The final parts of the listing print the precision and recall of your classifier, and then the sum of true and false positives and true and false negatives. True and false positives and negatives are measured from applying your classifier to the unseen test reviews. Running listing 6.9 outputs `precision 0.859793 recall 0.875200`, which is an exceptional result for your first classifier!

Listing 6.9 Computing the confusion matrix, precision, and recall

```
TP = 0.
TN = 0.
FP = 0.
FN = 0.

for i in tqdm(range(0, len(only_pos_file_contents))):
    sent = predict(only_pos_file_contents[i], vocab, w_val)
    predictions_test[i] = sent
    if sent == 1.:
        TP += 1
    elif sent == 0.:
        FN += 1

for i in tqdm(range(0, len(only_neg_file_contents))):
    sent = predict(only_neg_file_contents[i], vocab, w_val)
```

Initializes count of true and false positives and true and false negatives

Iterates through positive sentiment text files and call predict function, and computes TP and FN

Iterates through negative sentiment text files and call predict function, and computes TN and FP

```
     predictions_test[len(only_neg_file_contents)+i] = sent
     if sent == 0.:
         TN += 1
     elif sent == 1.:
         FP += 1
```

```
precision = (TP) / (TP + FP)
recall = (TP) / (TP + FN)
print("precision %f recall %f" % (precision, recall))
print(TP)
print(TN)
print(FP)
print(FN)
```
Computes and prints precision and recall

Given the generated predictions, you can take the next step: examining the area under the curve (AUC) and creating an ROC curve to determine how much better your classifier is than the baseline. Rather than implementing this process yourself, you can use the roc_curve function from SK-learn and then some Matplotlib to plot the results.

To use the roc_curve function, you need the predictions_test variable from listing 6.9, which is the result of running the predict function on all the true-positive examples and then on the true-negative examples. Then you need a variable that you will call outcomes_test, which is the ground truth. Because the ground truth includes 12,500 positive followed by 12,500 negative sentiment examples, you can create the outcomes_test variable by initializing a call to np.ones—a NumPy function that creates an array of the size-specified (12,500 1s)—and then appending a call to np.zeros—a NumPy function that creates an array of the size specified (12,500 0s).

When those variables are generated, you call the roc_curve function; obtain the true-positive (tpr) and false-positive (fpr) rates; and pass them to the auc function, which gives the AUC stored in the roc_auc variable. The remaining portions of listing 6.10 set up the plot with the baseline classifier in dashed line at 0, 1 on the x-axis to 0, 1 on the y-axis and then your actual results from the classifier, using the tpr and fpr values in a solid line above the dashed line (figure 6.5).

Listing 6.10   Measuring your classifier's performance against the baseline with ROC

Creates an array of labels of 1s (for positive) and 0s (for negative) sized proportional to the number of positive and negative files

Computes false positive rate (fpr), true positive rate (tpr), and area under the curve (roc_auc)

```
from sklearn.metrics import roc_curve, auc

outcome_test = np.ones(len(only_pos_files))
outcome_test = np.append(outcome_test, np.zeros(len(only_neg_files)))

fpr, tpr, thresholds = roc_curve(predictions_test, outcome_test)
roc_auc = auc(fpr, tpr)
```

```
plt.figure()
plt.plot(fpr, tpr, color='darkorange', lw=1, label='ROC curve
    (area = %0.2f)' % roc_auc)
plt.plot([0, 1], [0, 1], color='navy', lw=1, linestyle='--')
plt.xlim([0.0, 1.0])
plt.ylim([0.0, 1.05])
plt.xlabel('False Positive Rate')
plt.ylabel('True Positive Rate')
plt.title('Receiver operating characteristic')
plt.legend(loc="lower right")
plt.show()
```

Initializes Matplotlib and sets up the line style and labels for the baseline ROC and for the classifier results

Creates the legend and plot title

Shows the plot

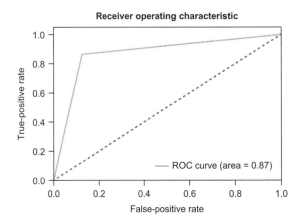

Figure 6.5   **The ROC curve for your logistic regression sentiment classifier. The performance is much better than the baseline, with an ROC curve/AUC of 0.87, or 87%.**

You've assessed the accuracy of your logistic regression classifier, computing its precision, recalling and generating an ROC and AUC curve, and comparing its performance with the baseline, which is quite good (nearly 90%). As I mentioned in chapter 5, any classifier with this type of performance likely will perform well in the wild because it was trained on a balanced dataset and evaluated on unseen data with equal balance.

Another technique discussed in chapter 5 is softmax regression, which has the natural benefit of extending beyond two-class prediction (or binary classification) to N-class prediction. Even though we don't have N>2 classes to train on here, it's worth exploring how you would create a softmax version of your sentiment classifier so that you can get some real experience building it. You can reuse most of the work you've performed in this chapter, so let's get to it!

6.5   *Creating the softmax-regression sentiment classifier*

The benefit of the softmax-regression approach is that it extends classification to prediction of more than two classes. The construction of the classification approach is similar to logistic regression. You have the following equations, in which you take a linear set of dependent variables (the weights, w, that you learn) and run them through the `sigmoid` function, which resolves the value in a smooth curve to `0` or `1` quickly. Recall the logistic regression construction:

$Y = sig(linear)$

$Y = sig(w_1 x_1 + w_2 x_2 + \ldots + w_0)$

With softmax regression, you have a similar construction, wherein you learn weights of size `num_features` × `num_labels`. In this case, the weights correspond to the weights to be multiplied by the dependent variables, similar to logistic regression. You also learn a bias matrix of size `num_labels`, again similar to standard logistic regression. The key difference with softmax regression is that you apply the `softmax` function instead of `sigmoid` to learn the probability distribution over the *N* classes you are trying to predict. The equation for `softmax` is

$Y = WX + B$

Now consider the `softmax` classifier in the context of your sentiment classification problem. You are trying to learn the probability, *Y*, that a set of text implies one of two labels, positive or negative, for each of the 25,000 reviews that you will test on. The set of text for each review is converted to a feature vector of 5,000 dimensions, one for each of the 25,000 reviews (*X*). The weights are associated weights for each of the two classes—positive or negative—to multiply by the 5,000 dependent variables, the associated matrix of which we refer to as *W*. Finally, *B* is the bias for each of the two classes—positive and negative—to add, forming the linear equation used for regression. Figure 6.6 shows this construction.

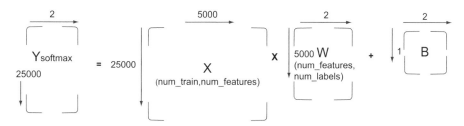

Figure 6.6   The softmax-regression approach. The input X field is 25,000 reviews and a 5,000-dimensional Bag of Words feature vector. The model learns W, which is a matrix of size num features, 5000, by num labels 2, for positive and negative classes.

Given this construction, you can start with some code to put together these matrices and prepare them for your classifier. You'll begin by creating the label matrix ground truth. Each entry in the ground truth needs to be encoded with one-hot encoding (chapter 5). One-hot encoding is the process of generating categorical labels such as `[0, 1]` and `[1,0]` to represent categories A and B—in this case, positive sentiment and negative sentiment. Because softmax regression predicts the particular class according to an ordered matrix, if you would like `1` to correspond to positive and `0` to negative, the column order of that matrix should be that the 0th index represents negative and the 1th index is positive, so your label encoding should be [1,0] for negative sentiment and [0,1] for positive.

You'll reuse the Pandas dataframe from listing 6.2 and use some of the powerful features of the Pandas libraries. Dataframes are like in-memory Python relational tables, so you can query them with SQL-like constructs. To select all the rows in the dataframe in which sentiment is positive (or 1), for example, you can iterate the dataframe by its length and then individually select rows whose value for the sentiment column is 1.0. You'll use this capability to generate your one-hot encoding and then create a NumPy matrix of size 25,000 × 2 out of the result.

Your training input is the output from the CountVectorizer in listing 6.11 converted to a NumPy float matrix of size (25000 × 5000) features. In listing 6.11, you create the input for your softmax-regression sentiment classifier. The output of the listing is the shape of the *X* input xs.shape, or (25000,5000), and the label matrix shape labels.shape, or (25000,2).

Listing 6.11 Creating the input for your softmax-regression classifier

```
lab_mat = []                                      One-hot encodes the positive
for i in range(len(train['sentiment'])):          sentiment examples
    if train['sentiment'][i] == 1.0:      ◁──┐
        lab_mat = lab_mat + [[0., 1.]]            One-hot encodes the negative
    elif train['sentiment'][i] == 0.0:    ◁──     sentiment examples
        lab_mat = lab_mat + [[1., 0.]]

                                                  Converts the label matrix to
                                                  a NumPy matrix for training
labels = np.matrix(lab_mat)               ◁──┘
xs = train_data_features.astype(float)    ◁──┐
train_size, num_features = xs.shape
                                                  Extracts the NumPy array of
print(xs.shape)                                   25000 × 5000 Bag of Words
print(labels.shape)                               vectors for the training reviews
```
Prints the shape of the X input matrix
(25000,5000) and of the label (25000,2) matrix

With the training inputs encoded, the next step before creating your TensorFlow softmax-regression classifier is shuffling the input data. One reason to do this is to prevent the classifier from remembering the order of the inputs and labels, instead learning that the mapping of input Bag of Words vectors to sentiment labels is what matters. You can use NumPy's arange method, which generates a range of number indices with the given shape, to take care of this task.

You can call arange with the size of the number of training samples (xs.shape[0], or 25000) and then use NumPy's random module and its shuffle method np.random.shuffle to randomize those indices. The randomized index array arr can be used to index into the xs and labels array to shuffle them randomly. You can apply code to prevent the classifier from remembering the order of the data from listing 6.12 and use it to set up your training process.

Listing 6.12 Preventing the classifier from remembering the order of the input

Generates an array of indices of size 25,000

Shuffles the indices and stores the result in arr

```
arr = np.arange(xs.shape[0])
np.random.shuffle(arr)
xs = xs[arr, :]
labels = labels[arr, :]
```

Uses the shuffled index array arr to shuffle X and the labels

You're almost ready to code your softmax classifier. The last step before model construction and training is getting your test data ready for accuracy evaluation, which you want to do after training and which you need for your softmax-predict function, which looks a teeny bit different. So that you don't have to run through the whole cleaning process again on your reviews (you took care of that job in listing 6.2), you'll need to create a function that assumes that you already have clean reviews but runs the Bag of Words model against those clean reviews separately to generate the test feature vectors of size 25000 × 5000.

In addition, you need to use the training vocabulary generated for the 25,000 training reviews when testing your softmax classifier on unseen data, so you will prepare the test reviews and labels for evaluation now that you have a trained sentiment classifier. If you employ the `predict` function from listing 6.7, you can separate the call to `review_to_words` at the beginning and then perform the same steps. Listing 6.13 performs this task and generates the test feature vectors for the 25,000 test reviews. You'll use those vectors to measure accuracy after training and to measure the performance of your new softmax classifier shortly thereafter.

Listing 6.13 Preparing test reviews and labels for evaluation after training

Assumption is that the review is clean, so create the test vocabulary and counts.

```
def softmax_feat_vec_from_review(test_review, vocab):
    n_vectorizer = CountVectorizer(analyzer = "word",    \
                                   tokenizer = None,       \
                                   preprocessor = None,    \
                                   stop_words = None,      \
                                   max_features = 5000)

    ex_data_features = n_vectorizer.fit_transform([test_review])
    ex_data_features = ex_data_features.toarray()
    test_vocab = n_vectorizer.get_feature_names()
    test_vocab_counts = ex_data_features.reshape(ex_data_features.shape[1]).

    ind_dict = dict((k, i) for i, k in enumerate(vocab))
    test_ind_dict = dict((k, i) for i, k in enumerate(test_vocab))
    inter = set(ind_dict).intersection(test_vocab)
    indices = [ ind_dict[x] for x in inter ]
    test_indices = [test_ind_dict[x] for x in inter]
```

Figures out the intersection of the test vocabulary from the review with the actual full vocabulary

Runs the CountVectorizer and generates the 25000 × 5000 feature matrix

Gets the vocabulary of the provided test review set for evaluation

```
        test_feature_vec = np.zeros(train_data_features.shape[1])
        for i in range(len(indices)):
            test_feature_vec[indices[i]] = test_vocab_counts[test_indices[i]]


    return test_feature_vec
```

Returns the feature vector for the provided individual review and training vocabulary

All zeros for the 5000 feature vector except for the overlap indices that we have counts for

```
test_reviews = []
clean_test_reviews = []
test_reviews.extend(only_pos_file_contents)
test_reviews.extend(only_neg_file_contents)
```

Creates a new array containing the set of 12,500 positive reviews and then appends text from the 12,500 negative reviews

```
for i in tqdm(range(len(test_reviews))):
    test_review_c = review_to_words(test_reviews[i])
    clean_test_reviews.append(test_review_c)
```

Cleans the text from the test reviews

```
test_xs = np.zeros((len(clean_test_reviews), num_features))
for i in tqdm(range(len(clean_test_reviews))):
    test_xs[i] = softmax_feat_vec_from_review(clean_test_reviews[i], vocab)
```

Creates the (25000,5000) feature vector to evaluate your classifier against

Armed with data to evaluate your classifier, you're ready to begin the training process. As with your earlier TensorFlow training, you'll define hyperparameters first. Arbitrarily train for 1,000 epochs, and use a learning rate of 0.01 with batch size 100. Again, with some experimentation and hyperparameter tuning, you may find better starting values, but the parameters in listing 6.14 are good enough to experiment with. The training process can take up to 30 minutes on your laptop, so you'll employ your friend TQDM again to make sure you are tracking the progress if you can step away from your computer while it learns. After your model is trained, you'll use a tf.train.Saver to save the file, and you'll print the test accuracy, which ends up being 0.81064, or 82%. Not bad!

Listing 6.14 Training the softmax-regression classifier using batch training

Defines the TensorFlow placeholders for input vectors, sentiment labels, weights, and biases

Creates the model using TensorFlow softmax and matrix multiplication **Y = WX+b**

```
learning_rate = 0.01
training_epochs = 1000
num_labels = 2
batch_size = 100
```

Defines the hyperparameters

Defines the log loss cost and train operation, and accounts for when loss is zero preventing NaN issues

```
X = tf.placeholder("float", shape=[None, num_features])
Y = tf.placeholder("float", shape=[None, num_labels])
W = tf.Variable(tf.zeros([num_features, num_labels]))
b = tf.Variable(tf.zeros([num_labels]))
y_model = tf.nn.softmax(tf.matmul(X, W) + b)

cost = -tf.reduce_sum(Y * tf.log(tf.maximum(y_model, 1e-15)))
train_op = tf.train.GradientDescentOptimizer(learning_rate).minimize(cost)
```

```
saver = tf.train.Saver()
with tf.Session() as sess:
    tf.global_variables_initializer().run()
    for step in tqdm(range(training_epochs * train_size // batch_size)):
        offset = (step * batch_size) % train_size
        batch_xs = xs[offset:(offset + batch_size), :]
        batch_labels = labels[offset:(offset + batch_size)]
        err, _ = sess.run([cost, train_op], feed_dict={X: batch_xs, Y:
            batch_labels})
        print (step, err)

    W_val = sess.run(W)
    print('w', W_val)
    b_val = sess.run(b)
    print('b', b_val)
    print("accuracy", accuracy.eval(feed_dict={X: test_xs, Y: test_labels}))
    save_path = saver.save(sess, "./softmax-sentiment.ckpt")
    print("Model saved in path: %s" % save_path)
```

Creates a saver to save the model graph and weights

Trains on a batch of 100 input Bag of Words vectors and sentiment labels

Computes and prints the loss for each batch step of 250,000

Prints learned weights and biases

Prints the accuracy by evaluating against unseen 25,000 reviews and sentiment labels

Saves the softmax-regression model

Besides the accuracy, which is quite decent, you can see that the softmax classifier performed slightly worse than the logistic regression binary classifier. But don't worry; you didn't do any parameter tuning. Still, convince yourself of your classifier's power by generating its ROC curve and computing the AUC to evaluate it. I'll take you through that process next. Before you start on the ROC, though, you'll need one new function to perform predictions.

This function differs only slightly from that shown in listing 6.7, and that subtle difference is one of the key takeaways that you'll use to choose between using logistic regression or softmax regression in your future machine-learning tasks. In listing 6.7, the last step in the predict function used a threshold to determine whether your sigmoid output should be mapped to a 0 or 1. As you'll recall, sigmoid oscillates between 0 and 1 toward its edges. You need to define a threshold—usually, the median, 0.5—to determine whether the points in the middle should fall on the 0 or 1 side. So the output of binary logistic regression is 0 or 1, and what comes with it is a corresponding distance between the actual value and the defined threshold. You could think of that distance as showing confidence in the algorithm's decision to classify the input as 1 or 0.

Softmax logistic regression is a bit different. The output is a matrix of size (num_samples, num_classes) or size (rows, columns). When you give the algorithm one review or row and try to classify the input into two classes or columns, you get a matrix like [[0.02 98.4]]. This matrix indicates the algorithm is 0.02% confident that the input is a negative sentiment (the 0th column) and 98.4% confident that it is positive (the 1th column). For 25,000 reviews, you would get a matrix with 25,000 rows of those two-column confidence values for each class. The softmax output isn't a 0 or a 1, as it is in binary logistic regression. The predict_softmax function needs to take that fact into account and figure out what the maximum value is in the column dimension.

NumPy provides the `np.argmax` function to do precisely that. You provide a NumPy array as the first parameter; the second parameter identifies which dimensional axis to test. The function returns the axis index with the maximum value. For `np.argmax([[0.02 98.4]],1)`, the function would yield `1`. Listing 6.15 is similar to listing 6.7; the only difference is the way you interpret the output with `np.argmax`.

Listing 6.15   Creating the `predict` function for your softmax-regression classifier

Cleans the review

Creates the test vocabulary and counts

```
def predict_softmax(test_review, vocab):
    test_review_c = review_to_words(test_review)

    n_vectorizer = CountVectorizer(analyzer = "word",    \
                                   tokenizer = None,      \
                                   preprocessor = None,   \
                                   stop_words = None,     \
                                   max_features = 5000)
    ex_data_features = n_vectorizer.fit_transform([test_review_c])
    ex_data_features = ex_data_features.toarray()
    test_vocab = n_vectorizer.get_feature_names()
    test_vocab_counts = ex_data_features.reshape(ex_data_features.shape[1])

    ind_dict = dict((k, i) for i, k in enumerate(vocab))
    test_ind_dict = dict((k, i) for i, k in enumerate(test_vocab))
    inter = set(ind_dict).intersection(test_vocab)
    indices = [ ind_dict[x] for x in inter ]
    test_indices = [test_ind_dict[x] for x in inter]

    test_feature_vec = np.zeros(train_data_features.shape[1])
    for i in range(len(indices)):
        test_feature_vec[indices[i]] = test_vocab_counts[test_indices[i]]

    predict = y_model.eval(feed_dict={X: [test_feature_vec], W: W_val,
        b: b_val})
    return np.argmax(predict, 1)
```

Figures out the intersection of the test vocabulary from the review with the actual full vocabulary

Applies the Bag of Words model and generates the vocabulary for the review to test

All zeros for the 5,000-feature vector except for the overlap indices that we have counts for

Makes the prediction and gets the softmax matrix back

The predicted class is 0-axis for negative or 1-axis for positive with np.argmax.

Armed with your new `predict_softmax` function, you can generate the ROC curve to evaluate your classifier, which is similar to listing 6.10. Instead of calling `predict` on each review, you load the saved softmax-regression model; apply its predictions to the entire test review dataset, with the learned weights and biases; and then use `np.argmax` to obtain the set of predictions for all 25,000 reviews at the same time. The output ROC curve follows listing 6.16 and demonstrates 81% accuracy against the test data when your softmax classifier is used. If you've got some extra time and cycles, play around with those hyperparameters; see whether you can tune them to achieve better results than your logistic regression classifier. Isn't baking off your machine-learning algorithms fun?

Listing 6.16 Generating the ROC curve and evaluating your softmax classifier

Loads and restores the softmax-regression model

Predicts the sentiment of all 25,000 reviews at the same time and use np.argmax to generate all sentiments

```
saver = tf.train.Saver()
with tf.Session() as sess:
    saver.restore(sess, save_path)
    print("Model restored.")
    predict_vals = np.argmax(y_model.eval(feed_dict={X: test_xs, W: W_val,
      b: b_val}), 1)

outcome_test = np.argmax(test_labels, 1)      ⟵— Uses np.argmax to obtain
                                                 the testing sentiment levels
predictions_test = predict_vals      ⟵
                                        Sets up the predict sentiments to test

fpr, tpr, thresholds = roc_curve(predictions_test, outcome_test)
roc_auc = auc(fpr, tpr)
```

Creates the ROC curve and AUC, using the resultant false positive rate and true positive rate

```
plt.figure()
plt.plot(fpr, tpr, color='darkorange', lw=1,
   label='ROC curve (area = %0.2f)' % roc_auc)
plt.plot([0, 1], [0, 1], color='navy', lw=1, linestyle='--')
plt.xlim([0.0, 1.0])
plt.ylim([0.0, 1.05])
plt.xlabel('False Positive Rate')
plt.ylabel('True Positive Rate')
plt.title('Receiver operating characteristic')
plt.legend(loc="lower right")
plt.show()
```

Generates the plot for the baseline classifier and your softmax classifier

You can see the result of running listing 6.16 in figure 6.7, which depicts the ROC curve evaluating your classifier. In the spirit of competition, why not submit your results to the original Bag of Words Meets Bags of Popcorn challenge on the machine-learning competition platform, Kaggle? The process is amazingly simple, as I'll show you in section 6.6.

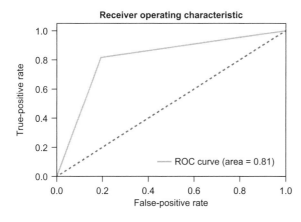

Figure 6.7 The ROC curve and AUC curve for the softmax-regression sentiment classifier, which performs slightly worse than your logistic regression classifier, with 81% accuracy

6.6   *Submitting your results to Kaggle*

The Bag of Words Meets Bags of Popcorn challenge ended some years ago, but Kaggle will still let you upload your machine-learning algorithm to see where it places on the leaderboard. This simple process shows you how well your machine-learning measures up. The Python code with all the work you've already done is fairly trivial.

Call your `predict` function from the original binary logistic-regression sentiment classifier. Because it performed better than the softmax one—87% compared with 81%—you'll want to submit your best work. If you use the original Kaggle test CSV that you loaded in listing 6.2, you can generating the resulting Pandas dataframe test and run your `predict` function over it. Then you can use another great feature of Pandas to add an entire column, mapping it to the associated rows. As long as the new column has the same number of columns, you can use a one-line function to create a new dataframe with the additional column. Given that new dataframe, you can use Pandas's built-in function to output a dataframe to a CSV and obtain your `Bag_of_Words_model.csv` output to upload to Kaggle. The code in listing 6.17 generates that CSV file.

Listing 6.17   Generating a Kaggle submission of your sentiment classification results

**Generates Kaggle submission empty
list and appends reviews one by one**

```
num_reviews = len(test["review"])
result = []
for i in tqdm(range(0, num_reviews)):
    r = predict(test["review"][i], vocab, w_val)      Calls the predict function to
    result.append(r)                                   get a sentiment of 1 or 0

output = pd.DataFrame( data={"id":test["id"], "sentiment":result} )
output.to_csv( "Bag_of_Words_model.csv", index=False, quoting=3 )
```

**Uses Pandas to write the
comma-separated output file**

**Copies the results to a Pandas dataframe
with an id column and a sentiment column**

Now that you've generated the Kaggle submission, you can upload the results CSV file to Kaggle. Assuming that you have already created your account, you can visit https://www.kaggle.com/c/word2vec-nlp-tutorial to make your submission. Use the following instructions, which you can repeat for future Kaggle competitions:

1 Click the blue Join the Competition function.
2 Click the blue Make a Late Submission button.
3 Click the window area, do a file select after you have run listing 6.17 and generated the Bag_of_Words_model.csv file, and then select that file.
4 Click the blue Make Submission button to submit your predictions and see where you stand on the leaderboard.

I told you it was easy, right? You can see the results of making your Kaggle submission in figure 6.8.

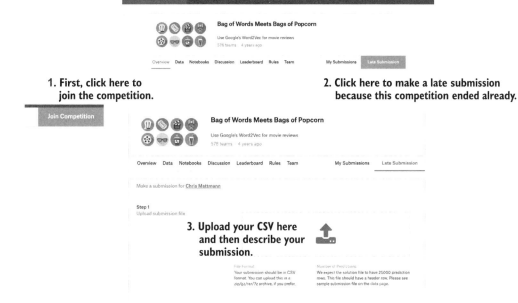

Figure 6.8 Making your Kaggle submission

That's it! You've submitted your results to Kaggle and entered your results for the world of machine-learning experts to see. Those reasonable results should place you squarely in the top middle of the competition. (Too bad it's over.)

You've done excellent work applying logistic regression and softmax regression to text analysis. You'll spend the next few chapters finding out how you can learn from data without labels, using unsupervised approaches.

Summary

- You can transform text into n-dimensional features by creating a vocabulary and counting the occurrence of those words.
- Using text and word frequency, you can apply the famous Bag of Words model from NLP to represent sentiment over a corpus of text reviews of movies from IMDb.
- Using Pandas dataframes, you can use a Python machine-learning library for representing matrices and vectors as in-memory tables to store classifier output and associated text.

- You built a TensorFlow-based sentiment classifier for text-based movie reviews using logistic regression and the associated process. You also built a TensorFlow-based sentiment classifier using logistic regression with softmax. It varies in both the data preparation steps but also in how you interpret the model response.
- Measuring classification accuracy is typically done by identifying and counting true positives, false positives, true negatives, false negatives.
- Computing an ROC curve allows you to measure the effectiveness of both of your trained classifiers and their effectiveness.
- You submitted your results to the Kaggle challenge for Movie Reviews to see how well you scored against other machine-learning researchers trying to automatically predict sentiment from text.

Automatically clustering data 7

This chapter covers

- Performing basic clustering with k-means
- Representing audio
- Segmenting audio
- Clustering with a self-organizing map

Suppose that you have a collection of not-pirated, totally legal MP3s on your hard drive. All your songs are crowded into one massive folder. Perhaps automatically grouping similar songs into categories such as Country, Rap, and Rock would help organize them. This act of assigning an item to a group (such as an MP3 to a playlist) in an unsupervised fashion is called *clustering*.

Chapter 6 assumes that you're given a training dataset of correctly labeled data. Unfortunately, you don't always have that luxury when you collect data in the real world. Suppose that you want to divide a large amount of music into interesting playlists. How could you possibly group songs if you don't have direct access to their metadata?

Spotify, SoundCloud, Google Music, Pandora, and many other music-streaming services try to solve this problem to recommend similar songs to customers. Their approach includes a mixture of various machine-learning techniques, but clustering is often at the heart of the solution.

Clustering is the process of intelligently categorizing the items in your dataset. The overall idea is that two items in the same cluster are "closer" to each other than items that belong to separate clusters. That's the general definition, leaving the interpretation of *closeness* open. Perhaps cheetahs and leopards belong in the same cluster, whereas elephants belong to another cluster, when closeness is measured by the similarity of two species in the hierarchy of biological classification (family, genus, and species).

You can imagine that many clustering algorithms exist. This chapter focuses on two types: *k-means* and *self-organizing map*. These approaches are *unsupervised*, meaning that they fit a model without ground-truth examples.

First, you'll learn how to load audio files into TensorFlow and represent them as feature vectors. Then you'll implement various clustering techniques to solve real-world problems.

7.1   *Traversing files in TensorFlow*

Some common input types in machine-learning algorithms are audio and image files. This shouldn't come as a surprise, because sound recordings and photographs are raw, redundant, often-noisy representations of semantic concepts. Machine learning is a tool to help handle these complications.

These data files have various implementations. An image can be encoded as a PNG or JPEG file, for example, and an audio file can be an MP3 or a WAV. In this chapter, you'll investigate how to read audio files as input to your clustering algorithm so that you automatically group music that sounds similar.

Exercise 7.1

What are the pros and cons of MP3 and WAV? How about PNG versus JPEG?

Answer

MP3 and JPEG significantly compress the data, so such files are easy to store or transmit. But because these files are lossy, WAV and PNG are closer to the original content.

Reading files from disk isn't exactly a machine-learning-specific ability. You can use a variety of Python libraries, such as NumPy or SciPy, to load files into memory, as I have shown you in earlier chapters. Some developers like to treat the data-preprocessing step separately from the machine-learning step. There's no absolute right or wrong way to manage the pipeline, but you will try TensorFlow for both data preprocessing and learning.

TensorFlow provides an operator called `tf.train.match_filenames_once` to list files in a directory. You can pass this information along to the queue operator `tf.train.string_input_producer`. That way, you can access filenames one at a time without loading everything at the same time. Given a filename, you can decode the file to retrieve usable data. Figure 7.1 outlines the process of using the queue.

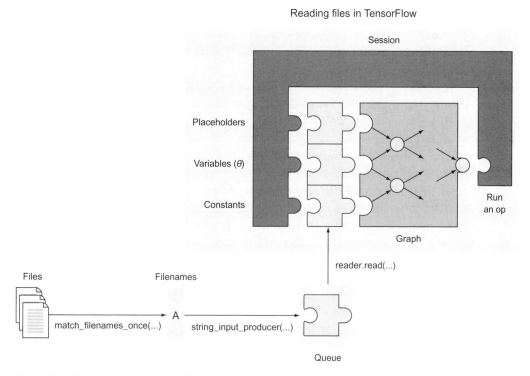

Figure 7.1 **You can use a queue in TensorFlow to read files. The queue is built into the TensorFlow framework, and you can use the `reader.read(…)` function to access (and dequeue) it.**

Listing 7.1 shows an implementation of reading files from disk in TensorFlow.

Listing 7.1 **Traversing a directory for data**

```
import tensorflow as tf

filenames = tf.train.match_filenames_once('./audio_dataset/*.wav')
count_num_files = tf.size(filenames)
filename_queue = tf.train.string_input_producer(filenames)
reader = tf.WholeFileReader()
filename, file_contents = reader.read(filename_queue)

with tf.Session() as sess:
    sess.run(tf.local_variables_initializer())
    num_files = sess.run(count_num_files)
```

Stores filenames that match a pattern

Runs the reader to extract file data

Natively reads a file in TensorFlow

Sets up a pipeline for retrieving filenames randomly

Counts the number of files

```
coord = tf.train.Coordinator()                              Initializes threads for
threads = tf.train.start_queue_runners(coord=coord)         the filename queue

for i in range(num_files):                         Loops through the
    audio_file = sess.run(filename)                data one by one
    print(audio_file)
```

7.2   *Extracting features from audio*

Machine-learning algorithms typically are designed to use feature vectors as input, but sound files use a different format. You need a way to extract features from sound files to create feature vectors.

It helps to understand how these files are represented. If you've ever seen a vinyl record, you've probably noticed the representation of audio as grooves indented in the disk. Our ears interpret audio from a series of vibrations through air. By recording the vibration properties, an algorithm can store sound in a data format.

The real world is continuous, but computers store data in discrete values. The sound is digitalized into a discrete representation through an analog-to-digital converter (ADC). You can think about sound as being fluctuation of a wave over time, but that data is too noisy and difficult to comprehend.

An equivalent way to represent a wave is to examine its frequencies at each time interval. This perspective is called the *frequency domain*. It's easy to convert between time domains and frequency domains by using a mathematical operation called a *discrete Fourier transform* (commonly implemented with an algorithm known as the *fast Fourier transform*, which you'll use to extract a feature vector from a sound).

A handy Python library can help you view audio in this frequency domain. Download it from http://mng.bz/X0J6, extract it, and then run the following command to set it up:

```
$ python setup.py install
```

> ### Python 2 required
>
> The BregmanToolkit is officially supported in Python 2. If you're using Jupyter Notebooks, you can access both versions of Python by following the directions outlined in the official Jupyter docs (http://mng.bz/ebvw).
>
> In particular, you can include Python 2 with the following commands:
>
> ```
> $ python2 -m pip install ipykernel
> $ python2 -m -ipykernel install --user
> ```

A sound may produce 12 kinds of pitches. In music terminology, the 12 pitches are C, C#, D, D#, E, F, F#, G, G#, A, A#, and B. Listing 7.2 shows how to retrieve the contribution of each pitch in a 0.1-second interval, resulting in a matrix with 12 rows. The number of columns grows as the length of the audio file increases. Specifically, there will be $10 \times t$ columns for a *t*-second audio. This matrix is also called a *chromagram* of the audio.

Listing 7.2 Representing audio in Python

Passes in the filename

```
from bregman.suite import *

def get_chromagram(audio_file):
    F = Chromagram(audio_file, nfft=16384, wfft=8192, nhop=2205)
    return F.X
```

Uses these parameters to describe 12 pitches every 0.1 second

Represents the values of a 12-dimensional vector 10 times per second

The chromagram output is a matrix, shown in figure 7.2. A sound clip can be read as a chromagram, and a chromagram is a recipe for generating a sound clip. Now you have a way to convert between audio and matrices. And as you've learned, most machine-learning algorithms accept feature vectors as a valid form of data. That said, the first machine-learning algorithm you'll look at is k-means clustering.

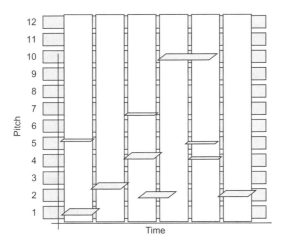

Figure 7.2 The chromagram matrix, where the x-axis represents time and the y-axis represents pitch class. The green parallelograms indicate the presence of that pitch at that time.

To run machine-learning algorithms on your chromagram, first you need to decide how you're going to represent a feature vector. One idea is to simplify the audio by looking only at the most significant pitch class per time interval, as shown in figure 7.3.

Then you count the number of times each pitch shows up in the audio file. Figure 7.4 shows this data as a histogram, forming a 12-dimensional vector. If you normalize the vector so that all the counts add up to 1, you can easily compare audio of different lengths. Note this approach is similar to the Bag of Words approach you used in chapter 6 to generate a histogram of word counts from text of arbitrary lengths.

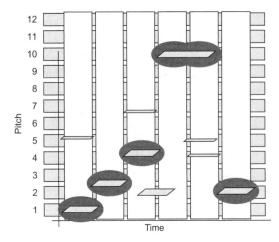

Figure 7.3   The most influential pitch at every time interval is highlighted. You can think of it as being the loudest pitch at each time interval.

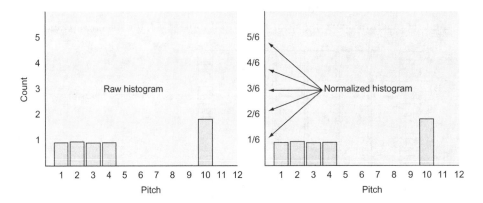

Figure 7.4   You count the frequency of loudest pitches heard at each interval to generate this histogram, which acts as your feature vector.

Exercise 7.2

What are some other ways to represent an audio clip as a feature vector?

Answer

You can visualize the audio clip as an image (such as a spectrogram), and use image-analysis techniques to extract image features.

Take a look at listing 7.3 to generate the histogram from figure 7.4, which is your feature vector.

Listing 7.3   Obtaining a dataset for k-means

```
import tensorflow as tf
import numpy as np
from bregman.suite import *


filenames = tf.train.match_filenames_once('./audio_dataset/*.wav')
count_num_files = tf.size(filenames)
filename_queue = tf.train.string_input_producer(filenames)
reader = tf.WholeFileReader()
filename, file_contents = reader.read(filename_queue)

chroma = tf.placeholder(tf.float32)
max_freqs = tf.argmax(chroma, 0)

def get_next_chromagram(sess):
    audio_file = sess.run(filename)
    F = Chromagram(audio_file, nfft=16384, wfft=8192, nhop=2205)
    return F.X

def extract_feature_vector(sess, chroma_data):
    num_features, num_samples = np.shape(chroma_data)
    freq_vals = sess.run(max_freqs, feed_dict={chroma: chroma_data})
    hist, bins = np.histogram(freq_vals, bins=range(num_features + 1))
    return hist.astype(float) / num_samples

def get_dataset(sess):
    num_files = sess.run(count_num_files)
    coord = tf.train.Coordinator()
    threads = tf.train.start_queue_runners(coord=coord)
    xs = []
    for _ in range(num_files):
        chroma_data = get_next_chromagram(sess)
        x = [extract_feature_vector(sess, chroma_data)]
        x = np.matrix(x)
        if len(xs) == 0:
            xs = x
        else:
            xs = np.vstack((xs, x))
    return xs
```

Creates an op to identify the pitch with the biggest contribution

Converts a chromagram into a feature vector

Constructs a matrix where each row is a data item

NOTE   All code listings are available from this book's website at http://mng.bz/yrEq and on GitHub at http://mng.bz/MoJn.

In keeping with what I've shown you in other chapters, after preparing your dataset, convince yourself that something is relatable among the chromagrams that listing 7.1 helps you read from disk and from which listing 7.3 generates a dataset. The dataset consists of five sounds corresponding to two different coughing sounds and three different screaming sounds. You can use your friendly neighborhood Matplotlib library to visualize the data and examine the *learnability* (unique proprieties of the underlying data) in listing 7.4. If you can spot something that relates among the sound files, there is a great chance that the machine-learning algorithm can as well.

You will create a set of labels P1–P12 for each of the 12 pitches in listing 7.4. Then, because you converted the data into a set of five matrices of size 1 × 12 in listing 7.3, you will flatten those matrices into 12 data points to visualize for each of the five chromagrams. The result of listing 7.4 is shown in figure 7.5.

Listing 7.4   Exploring your sound file chromagrams

```
labels=[]
for i in np.arange(12):                           Generate labels for each of
    labels.append("P"+str(i+1))                   the 12 pitch frequencies.

fig, ax = plt.subplots()
ind = np.arange(len(labels))
width = 0.15                                       Pick a different color for
colors = ['r', 'g', 'y', 'b', 'black']            each of the five sounds.
plots = []
                                                  Flatten the 1 × 12 matrices into
for i in range(X.shape[0]):                       12 points, one for each pitch.
    Xs = np.asarray(X[i]).reshape(-1)
    p = ax.bar(ind + i*width, Xs, width, color=colors[i])
    plots.append(p[0])

xticks = ind + width / (X.shape[0])
print(xticks)
ax.legend(tuple(plots), ('Cough1', 'Cough2', 'Scream1', 'Scream2', 'Scream3'))
ax.yaxis.set_units(inch)
ax.autoscale_view()                               Create a legend for the five sounds:
ax.set_xticks(xticks)                             two coughs, and three screams.
ax.set_xticklabels(labels)

ax.set_ylabel('Normalized freq coumt')
ax.set_xlabel('Pitch')
ax.set_title('Normalized frequency counts for Various Sounds')
plt.show()
```

Convince yourself that there are pitch similarities among the sounds by visually exploring figure 7.5. It's pretty clear that the vertical bars for the cough sounds have some correlation to pitches P1 and P5, and that scream sounds strongly relate on the vertical bars for pitches P5, P6, and P7. Other, less-obvious similarities are the relationship in P5 and P6 of coughs and screams. You'll see that it's sometimes easier to see the correlations if you visualize one sound at a time, such as in figure 7.6, but this example is a good start. There's definitely something to learn here, so let's see what the computer can tell us about how to cluster these files.

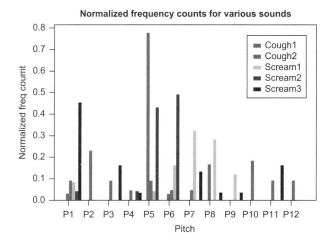

Figure 7.5 Exploring the five sounds—two coughs and three screams—and their relationship at the 12 pitches. If your eyes can spot a pattern, there's a great chance that the computer can too.

7.3 *Using k-means clustering*

The *k-means algorithm* is one of the oldest, yet most robust ways to cluster data. The *k* in *k-means* is a variable representing a natural number, so you can imagine 3-means clustering, 4-means clustering, or any other value for *k*. Thus, the first step in k-means clustering is choosing a value for *k*. To be concrete, let's pick $k = 3$. With that in mind, the goal of 3-means clustering is to divide the dataset into three categories (also called *clusters*).

Choosing the number of clusters

Choosing the right number of clusters often depends on the task. Suppose that you're planning an event for hundreds of people, both young and old. If you have the budget for only two entertainment options, you can use k-means clustering with $k = 2$ to separate the guests into two age groups. At other times, determining the value of *k* isn't as obvious. Automatically figuring out the value of *k* is a bit more complicated, so we won't touch on that much in this section. In simplified terms, a straightforward way of determining the best value of *k* is to iterate over a range of k-means simulations and apply a cost function to determine which value of *k* caused the best differentiation between clusters at the lowest value of *k*.

The k-means algorithm treats data points as points in space. If your dataset is a collection of guests at an event, you can represent each guest by their age. Thus, your dataset is a collection of feature vectors. In this case, each feature vector is 1D because you're considering only the age of the person.

For clustering music by the audio data, the data points are feature vectors from the audio files. If two points are close together, their audio features are similar. You want to discover which audio files belong in the same "neighborhood," because those clusters probably will be a good way to organize your music files.

The midpoint of all the points in a cluster is called its *centroid*. Depending on the audio features you choose to extract, a centroid could capture concepts such as loud sound, high-pitched sound, or saxophone-like sound. It's important to note that the k-means algorithm assigns nondescript labels, such as cluster 1, cluster 2, and cluster 3. Figure 7.6 shows examples of the sound data.

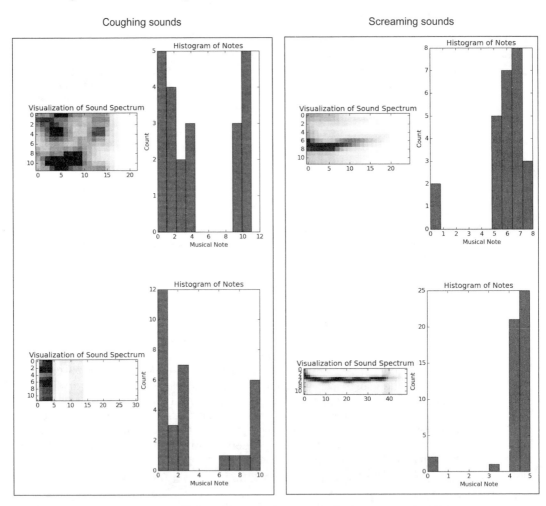

Figure 7.6   Four examples of audio files. The two on the right appear to have similar histograms, and the two on the left also have similar histograms. Your clustering algorithms will be able to group these sounds.

The k-means algorithm assigns a feature vector to one of the clusters by choosing the cluster whose centroid is closest to it. The k-means algorithm starts by guessing the cluster location and iteratively improves its guess over time. The algorithm either converges when it no longer improves the guesses or stops after a maximum number of attempts.

The heart of the algorithm consists of two tasks:

- *Assignment*—Assign each data item (feature vector) to a category of the closest centroid.
- *Recentering*—Calculate the midpoints of the newly updated clusters.

These two steps repeat to provide increasingly better clustering results, and the algorithm stops when it has repeated a desired number of times or when the assignments no longer change. Figure 7.7 illustrates the algorithm.

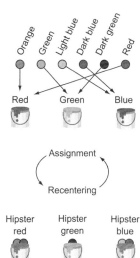

Figure 7.7 One iteration of the k-means algorithm. Suppose that you're clustering colors into three buckets (an informal way to say category). You can start with a guess of red, green, and blue to begin the assignment step. Then you update the bucket colors by averaging the colors that belong to each bucket. Repeat until the buckets no longer substantially change color, arriving at the color representing the centroid of each cluster.

Listing 7.5 shows how to implement the k-means algorithm by using the dataset generated in listing 7.3. For simplicity, choose $k = 2$, so you can easily verify that your algorithm partitions the audio files into two dissimilar categories. You'll use the first k vectors as initial guesses for centroids.

Listing 7.5 Implementing k-means

Decides the number of clusters

Declares the maximum number of iterations to run k-means

Chooses the initial guesses of cluster centroids

Assigns each data item to its nearest cluster

```
k = 2
max_iterations = 100

def initial_cluster_centroids(X, k):
    return X[0:k, :]

def assign_cluster(X, centroids):
    expanded_vectors = tf.expand_dims(X, 0)
    expanded_centroids = tf.expand_dims(centroids, 1)
    distances = tf.reduce_sum(tf.square(tf.subtract(expanded_vectors,
     expanded_centroids)), 2)
    mins = tf.argmin(distances, 0)
    return mins
```

```
def recompute_centroids(X, Y):
    sums = tf.unsorted_segment_sum(X, Y, k)
    counts = tf.unsorted_segment_sum(tf.ones_like(X), Y, k)
    return sums / counts

with tf.Session() as sess:
    sess.run(tf.global_variables_initializer())
    X = get_dataset(sess)
    centroids = initial_cluster_centroids(X, k)
    i, converged = 0, False
    while not converged and i < max_iterations:
        i += 1
        Y = assign_cluster(X, centroids)
        centroids = sess.run(recompute_centroids(X, Y))
    print(centroids)
```

Updates the cluster centroids to their midpoint

Iterates to find the best cluster locations

That's it! If you know the number of clusters and the feature vector representation, you can use listing 7.5 to cluster anything. In section 7.4, you'll apply clustering to audio snippets within an audio file.

7.4   *Segmenting audio*

In section 7.3, you clustered various audio files to group them automatically. This section is about using clustering algorithms within one audio file. Whereas the former process is called *clustering*, the latter process is referred to as *segmentation*. *Segmentation* is another word for *clustering*, but we often say *segment* instead of *cluster* when dividing a single image or audio file into separate components. Segmentation is similar to the way dividing a sentence into words is different from dividing a word into letters. Though segmentation and clustering share the general idea of breaking bigger pieces into smaller components, words are different from letters.

Suppose that you have a long audio file, maybe of a podcast or talk show. Imagine writing a machine-learning algorithm to identify which of two people is speaking in an audio interview. The goal of segmenting an audio file is to associate which parts of the audio clip belong to the same category. In this case, you'd have a category for each person, and the utterances made by each person should converge to their appropriate categories, as shown in figure 7.8.

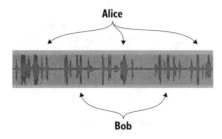

Figure 7.8   Audio segmentation is the process of labeling segments automatically.

Open a new source file, and follow along with listing 7.6, which will get you started by organizing the audio data for segmentation. The code splits an audio file into multiple segments of size `segment_size`. A long audio file would contain hundreds, if not thousands, of segments.

Listing 7.6 Organizing data for segmentation

Decides the number of clusters

```
import tensorflow as tf
import numpy as np
from bregman.suite import *

k = 2
segment_size = 50
max_iterations = 100

chroma = tf.placeholder(tf.float32)
max_freqs = tf.argmax(chroma, 0)

def get_chromagram(audio_file):
    F = Chromagram(audio_file, nfft=16384, wfft=8192, nhop=2205)
    return F.X

def get_dataset(sess, audio_file):
    chroma_data = get_chromagram(audio_file)
    print('chroma_data', np.shape(chroma_data))
    chroma_length = np.shape(chroma_data)[1]
    xs = []
    for i in range(chroma_length / segment_size):
        chroma_segment = chroma_data[:, i*segment_size:(i+1)*segment_size]
        x = extract_feature_vector(sess, chroma_segment)
        if len(xs) == 0:
            xs = x
        else:
            xs = np.vstack((xs, x))
    return xs
```

The smaller the segment size, the better the results (but slower performance).

Decides when to stop the iterations

Obtains a dataset by extracting segments of the audio as separate data items

Now run k-means clustering on this dataset to identify when segments are similar. The intention is that k-means will categorize similar-sounding segments with the same label. If two people have significantly different-sounding voices, their sound snippets will belong to different labels. Listing 7.7 illustrates how to apply segmentation to an audio clip.

Listing 7.7 Segmenting an audio clip

```
with tf.Session() as sess:
    X = get_dataset(sess, 'TalkingMachinesPodcast.wav')
    print(np.shape(X))
    centroids = initial_cluster_centroids(X, k)
    i, converged = 0, False
    while not converged and i < max_iterations:
```

Runs the k-means algorithm

```
        i += 1
        Y = assign_cluster(X, centroids)
        centroids = sess.run(recompute_centroids(X, Y))
        if i % 50 == 0:
            print('iteration', i)
    segments = sess.run(Y)                        ⟵───┐ Prints the labels for
    for i in range(len(segments)):                      each time interval
        seconds = (i * segment_size) / float(10)
        min, sec = divmod(seconds, 60)
        time_str = '{}m {}s'.format(min, sec)
        print(time_str, segments[i])
```

The output of running listing 7.7 is a list of timestamps and cluster IDs that correspond to who is talking during the podcast:

```
('0.0m 0.0s', 0)
('0.0m 2.5s', 1)
('0.0m 5.0s', 0)
('0.0m 7.5s', 1)
('0.0m 10.0s', 1)
('0.0m 12.5s', 1)
('0.0m 15.0s', 1)
('0.0m 17.5s', 0)
('0.0m 20.0s', 1)
('0.0m 22.5s', 1)
('0.0m 25.0s', 0)
('0.0m 27.5s', 0)
```

Exercise 7.3
How can you detect whether the clustering algorithm has converged (so that you can stop the algorithm early)?

Answer
One way is to monitor how the cluster centroids change and declare convergence when no more updates are necessary (such as when the difference in the size of the error isn't changing significantly between iterations). To do so, you'd need to calculate the size of the error and decide what constitutes *significantly*.

7.5   *Clustering with a self-organizing map*

A *self-organizing map* (SOM) is a model for representing data into a lower-dimensional space. In doing so, a SOM automatically shifts similar data items closer together. Suppose you're ordering pizza for a large group of people. You don't want to order the same type of pizza for every single person, because one might happen to prefer fancy pineapple with mushrooms and peppers for their toppings, and you may prefer anchovies with arugula and onions.

Each person's preference of toppings can be represented as a 3D vector. A SOM lets you embed these 3D vectors in two dimensions (as long as you define a distance metric between pizzas). Then a visualization of the 2D plot reveals good candidates for the number of clusters.

Although it may take longer to converge than the k-means algorithm, the SOM approach has no assumptions about the number of clusters. In the real world, it's hard to select a value for the number of clusters. Consider a gathering of people in which the clusters change over time, as shown in figure 7.9.

Figure 7.9 In the real world, we see groups of people in clusters all the time. Applying k-means requires knowing the number of clusters ahead of time. A more flexible tool is a SOM, which has no preconceptions about the number of clusters.

The SOM merely reinterprets the data as a structure conducive to clustering. The algorithm works as follows:

1 Design a grid of nodes. Each node holds a weight vector of the same dimension as a data item. The weights of each node are initialized to random numbers, typically from a standard normal distribution.
2 Show data items to the network one by one. For each data item, the network identifies the node whose weight vector most closely matches it. This node is called the *best matching unit* (BMU).

After the network identifies the BMU, all neighbors of the BMU are updated so their weight vectors move closer to the BMU's value. The closer nodes are affected more strongly than nodes farther away. Moreover, the number of neighbors around a BMU shrinks over time at a rate determined usually by trial and error. Figure 7.10 illustrates the algorithm.

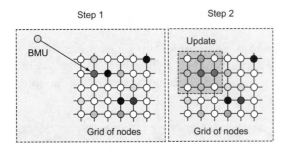

Figure 7.10 One iteration of the SOM algorithm. The first step is identifying the BMU, and the second is updating the neighboring nodes. You keep iterating these two steps with training data until certain convergence criteria are reached.

Listing 7.8 shows how to start implementing a SOM in TensorFlow. Follow along by opening a new source file.

Listing 7.8 Setting up the SOM algorithm

```
import tensorflow as tf
import numpy as np

class SOM:
    def __init__(self, width, height, dim):
        self.num_iters = 100
        self.width = width
        self.height = height
        self.dim = dim
        self.node_locs = self.get_locs()

        nodes = tf.Variable(tf.random_normal([width*height, dim]))
        self.nodes = nodes

        x = tf.placeholder(tf.float32, [dim])
        iter = tf.placeholder(tf.float32)

        self.x = x
        self.iter = iter

        bmu_loc = self.get_bmu_loc(x)

        self.propagate_nodes = self.get_propagation(bmu_loc, x, iter)
```

Each node is a vector of dimension dim. For a 2D grid, there are width × height nodes; get_locs is defined in listing 7.11.

These two ops are inputs at each iteration.

You'll need to access them from another method.

Finds the node that most closely matches the input (in listing 7.10)

Updates the values of the neighbors (in listing 7.9)

In listing 7.9, you define how to update neighboring weights, given the current time interval and BMU location. As time goes by, the BMU's neighboring weights are less influenced to change. That way, the weights gradually settle over time.

Listing 7.9 Defining how to update the values of neighbors

```
    def get_propagation(self, bmu_loc, x, iter):
        num_nodes = self.width * self.height
        rate = 1.0 - tf.div(iter, self.num_iters)
```

The rate decreases as iter increases. This value influences the alpha and sigma parameters.

```
                 alpha = rate * 0.5
                 sigma = rate * tf.to_float(tf.maximum(self.width, self.height)) / 2.
                 expanded_bmu_loc = tf.expand_dims(tf.to_float(bmu_loc), 0)   ◁────────┐
                 sqr_dists_from_bmu = tf.reduce_sum(
                   tf.square(tf.subtract(expanded_bmu_loc, self.node_locs)), 1)
                 neigh_factor =
                   tf.exp(-tf.div(sqr_dists_from_bmu, 2 * tf.square(sigma)))
                 rate = tf.multiply(alpha, neigh_factor)
                 rate_factor =
                   tf.stack([[tf.tile(tf.slice(rate, [i], [1]),
                             [self.dim]) for i in range(num_nodes)]])
                 nodes_diff = tf.multiply(
                   rate_factor,
                   tf.subtract(tf.stack([x for i in range(num_nodes)]), self.nodes))
                 update_nodes = tf.add(self.nodes, nodes_diff)   ◁───┐
                 return tf.assign(self.nodes, update_nodes)
```

Ensures that nodes closer to the BMU change more dramatically

Expands bmu_loc so you can efficiently compare it pairwise with each element of node_locs

Defines the updates

Returns an op to perform the updates

Listing 7.10 shows how to find the BMU location, given an input data item. It searches the grid of nodes to find the one with the closest match. This step is similar to the assignment step in k-means clustering, in which each node in the grid is a potential cluster centroid.

Listing 7.10   Getting the node location of the closest match

```
def get_bmu_loc(self, x):
    expanded_x = tf.expand_dims(x, 0)
    sqr_diff = tf.square(tf.subtract(expanded_x, self.nodes))
    dists = tf.reduce_sum(sqr_diff, 1)
    bmu_idx = tf.argmin(dists, 0)
    bmu_loc = tf.stack([tf.mod(bmu_idx, self.width), tf.div(bmu_idx,
    å self.width)])
    return bmu_loc
```

In listing 7.11, you create a helper method to generate a list of (x, y) locations on all the nodes in the grid.

Listing 7.11   Generating a matrix of points

```
def get_locs(self):
    locs = [[x, y]
            for y in range(self.height)
            for x in range(self.width)]
    return tf.to_float(locs)
```

Finally, let's define a method called `train` to run the algorithm, as shown in listing 7.12. First, you must set up the session and run the `global_variables_initializer` op. Next, you loop `num_iters` a certain number of times to update weights using the input data one by one. When the loop ends, you record the final node weights and their locations.

Listing 7.12   Running the SOM algorithm

```
def train(self, data):
    with tf.Session() as sess:
        sess.run(tf.global_variables_initializer())
        for i in range(self.num_iters):
            for data_x in data:
                sess.run(self.propagate_nodes, feed_dict={self.x: data_x,
                å self.iter: i})
        centroid_grid = [[] for i in range(self.width)]
        self.nodes_val = list(sess.run(self.nodes))
        self.locs_val = list(sess.run(self.node_locs))
        for i, l in enumerate(self.locs_val):
            centroid_grid[int(l[0])].append(self.nodes_val[i])
        self.centroid_grid = centroid_grid
```

That's it! Now let's see the algorithm in action. Test the implementation by showing the SOM some input. In listing 7.13, the input is a list of 3D feature vectors. By training the SOM, you'll discover clusters within the data. You'll use a 4 × 4 grid, but it's best to try various values to cross-validate the best grid size. Figure 7.11 shows the output of the code.

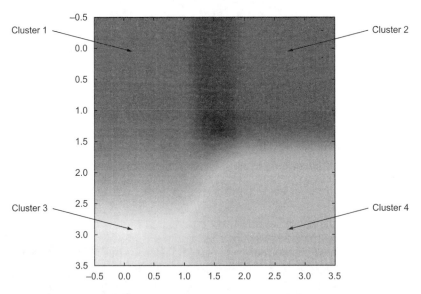

Figure 7.11   The SOM places all 3D data points in a 2D grid. From it, you can pick the cluster centroids (automatically or manually) and achieve clustering in an intuitive lower-dimensional space.

Listing 7.13   Testing the implementation and visualizing the results

```
from matplotlib import pyplot as plt
import numpy as np
from som import SOM
```

```
colors = np.array(
    [[0., 0., 1.],
     [0., 0., 0.95],
     [0., 0.05, 1.],
     [0., 1., 0.],
     [0., 0.95, 0.],
     [0., 1, 0.05],
     [1., 0., 0.],
     [1., 0.05, 0.],
     [1., 0., 0.05],
     [1., 1., 0.]])
som = SOM(4, 4, 3)    ◁────────   The grid size is 4 × 4, and
som.train(colors)                 the input dimension is 3.

plt.imshow(som.centroid_grid)
plt.show()
```

The SOM embeds higher-dimensional data in 2D to make clustering easy. This process acts as a handy preprocessing step. You can indicate the cluster centroids manually by observing the SOM's output, but it's also possible to find good centroid candidates automatically by observing the gradient of the weights. If you're adventurous, I suggest reading the famous paper "Clustering of the Self-Organizing Map" by Juha Vesanto and Esa Alhoniemi, at http://mng.bz/XzyS.

7.6   *Applying clustering*

You've already seen two practical applications of clustering: organizing music and segmenting an audio clip to label similar sounds. Clustering is especially helpful when the training dataset doesn't contain corresponding labels. As you know, such a situation characterizes unsupervised learning. Sometimes, data is too inconvenient to annotate.

Suppose that you want to understand sensor data from the accelerometer of a phone or smartwatch. At each time step, the accelerometer provides a 3D vector, but you have no idea whether the human is walking, standing, sitting, dancing, jogging, or so on. You can obtain such a dataset at http://mng.bz/rTMe.

To cluster the time-series data, you'll need to summarize the list of accelerometer vectors into a concise feature vector. One way is to generate a histogram of differences between consecutive magnitudes of the acceleration. The derivative of acceleration is called *jerk*, and you can apply the same operation to obtain a histogram outlining differences in jerk magnitudes.

This process of generating a histogram out of data is exactly like the preprocessing steps on audio data explained in this chapter. After you've transformed the histograms into feature vectors, you can use the code listings in this chapter (such as k-means in TensorFlow).

NOTE   Whereas previous chapters discussed supervised learning, this chapter focuses on unsupervised learning. In chapter 9, you'll see a machine-learning algorithm that is neither of the two. This algorithm is a modeling framework that doesn't get much attention from programmers but is the essential tool of statisticians for unveiling hidden factors in data.

Summary

- Clustering is an unsupervised machine-learning algorithm for discovering structure in data.
- One of the easiest algorithms to implement and understand is k-means clustering, which also performs well in terms of speed and accuracy.
- If the number of clusters isn't specified, you can use the SOM algorithm to view the data in a simplified perspective.

Inferring user activity from Android accelerometer data

This chapter covers

- Visualizing positional data from your phone in three dimensions along with time
- Performing exploratory data analysis and identifying patterns in Android phone users
- Automatically grouping Android phone users by their positional data using clustering
- Visualizing K-means clustering

Nowadays, we are pretty much inseparable from a small, thin, usually black device that connects us to one another and to the world: our mobile phones. These devices are computing marvels, miniaturized chips with powerful microprocessors that are much more powerful than desktop computers from a decade ago. Add to that capacious connections to Wi-Fi networks that allow broad connectivity to the

163

world and Bluetooth, which allows narrow and close-by secure connection to edge devices. Soon, Wi-Fi 5G and Bluetooth 6 will increase these connections to geographically disparate networks, to terabytes of data and to millions of interconnected devices making up the Internet of Things.

Also attached to those powerful phones are a variety of sensors, including cameras, temperature sensors, light-sensitive screens, and something perhaps little known to you before this chapter: accelerometers. An *accelerometer* detects and monitors vibration in rolling machines and can be used to obtain positional data in 3D space over time, which is 4D data. All cell phones are equipped with these sensors, which provide positional data in the following form:

(X, Y, Z, t)

As you walk, talk, climb stairs, and drive in your car, accelerometers collect and record this data in the cell phone's memory, usually a solid-state device with hundreds of gigabytes (GB) of information, soon be terabytes (TB). That data—your position in space-time as you perform various activities, such as walking, talking, and climbing—is recorded and can be used to infer those activities based on your position in space and time in an unsupervised fashion. You can conceptualize the positional data captured by the cell phone as shown in figure 8.1. A person moves in positive or negative X, Z on a plane, and the vertical position is captured by the Y-axis.

As I discussed in chapter 7, machine learning need not require labels to make predictions. You can do a lot by applying unsupervised methods such as k-means clustering and self-organizing map (SOM) to data points that naturally fit together. Like the Blu-ray discs that are lying all over your house after your kids threw them everywhere

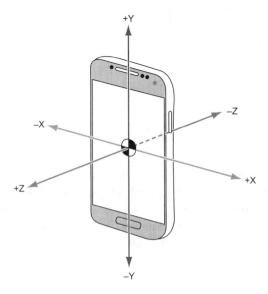

Figure 8.1   How (X, Y, Z) positional data captured by your cell phone looks in the real world. A person walks positively or negatively on the x- or z-axis in space over time, and when the person jumps or bends down, movement occurs on the y-axis.

(wait—that doesn't happen to you?), requiring organization and careful placement back in your media cabinet, there is a natural order in which you cluster things for organizational purposes. For those Blu-ray discs, the order might be by genre or actor.

But how can you classify or organize your positional data on your phone? That data is likely to have a natural organization; convince yourself of that. While you were running, jumping, or driving, all your positional data likely fit some trend or pattern. Perhaps the difference from point t_i to point t_{i+1} involves a sharp change in velocity or acceleration. Velocity and acceleration are the first and second derivative of position (X, Y, Z) in figure 8.1 with respect to time (t). Many researchers have discovered that jerk—the third derivative of position with respect to time—represents the rate of change of the force acting on a body. This jerk turns out to be the appropriate trending and change in motion when you shift activities, as captured by your positional data. The magnitude differences in jerk provide nice bins for clustering your time-based positional data in an unsupervised fashion; these clusters represent your motion activities, such as running, climbing, and walking.

In this chapter, you build on the k-means and SOM techniques you've already learned and apply then to real positional data. This data comes from the University of California at Irvine (UCI) and its Machine Learning Repository, which is a smorgasbord of open datasets to which you can apply machine-learning techniques to generate useful insights. The User Activity from Walking dataset is precisely the type of data to which you could apply TensorFlow and unsupervised clustering techniques. Let's get started!

8.1 *The User Activity from Walking dataset*

The User Activity from Walking dataset contains 22 participants and their associated Android-based positional data. The data was donated in March 2014 and has been accessed more than 69,000 times. The dataset was formed when the accelerometer in an Android phone positioned in the chest pocket of a participant collected (X, Y, Z, t) positional and time data. The participants walked in the wild and performed various activities along a predefined path. The data can be used for unsupervised inference of activity type. This dataset is a frequently used benchmark in the machine-learning domain because it provides challenges for identifying and authenticating people by using motion patterns.

You can download the dataset from http://mng.bz/aw5B. The dataset unzips into a set of files in a folder structure that looks like the following:

```
1.csv    10.csv   11.csv   12.csv   13.csv   14.csv   15.csv   16.csv   17.csv
         18.csv   19.csv   2.csv    20.csv   21.csv   22.csv   3.csv    4.csv
         5.csv    6.csv    7.csv    8.csv    9.csv    README
```

Each CSV file corresponds to one of the 22 participants, and the contents of the CSV files look like positional data of the form (t, X, Y, Z) shown in figure 8.2.

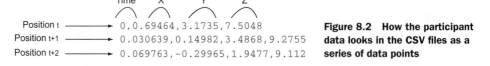

Figure 8.2   **How the participant data looks in the CSV files as a series of data points**

The first step to perform on this CSV data is to convert it to something that TensorFlow can use for machine learning: a NumPy dataset. To do that, you can use TensorFlow's `FileReader` API. You used this API in chapter 7 to extract feature vectors from the audio-file chromagrams and combine them to a NumPy dataset for clustering.

In this chapter, instead of creating feature vectors by turning sound into numbers with a fast Fourier transform, you convert the numbers you already have—positions in (X, Y, Z) space—to jerk magnitudes. You can use Pandas and its nifty dataframe API to read the participant CSV files into a big table structure in memory; then you can get NumPy arrays out of that structure. Using NumPy arrays as I've shown you in earlier chapters makes dealing with TensorFlow and machine learning much easier, because you can combine the 22 participants and their positional data into a TensorFlow-compatible NumPy matrix. The workflow can be generalized to the following form (figure 8.3):

1 Use TensorFlow's `FileReader` API to obtain the file contents and associated file names.

2 Extract a feature vector per file as a NumPy array, using a methodology such as a chromagram fast Fourier transformation or jerk magnitudes on positional data by calculating its *N*th-order derivatives.

3 Stack NumPy arrays vertically as a NumPy matrix, creating an N × M array where *N* is the number of samples and *M* is the number of features.

4 Perform clustering on the N × M NumPy matrix by using k-means, SOM, or some other technique.

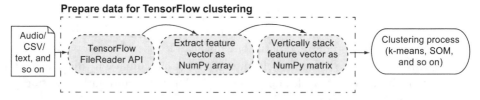

Figure 8.3   **The general methodology of preparing data for TensorFlow clustering, depicted left to right as input to the clustering process**

Listing 8.1 performs the first step in this workflow, traversing the CSV files by using TensorFlow and creating a pairwise set of the filename and its contents.

Listing 8.1   Obtaining the positional contents and filenames of the 22 participant CSVs

```
import tensorflow as tf
filenames = tf.train.match_filenames_once('./User Identification From Walking
➥ Activity/*.csv')
```
Creates a list of the participant CSV filenames

```
count_num_files = tf.size(filenames)
filename_queue = tf.train.string_input_producer(filenames)
reader = tf.WholeFileReader()
filename, file_contents = reader.read(filename_queue)
```

Counts the number of CSV filenames

Creates filename/content pairs for all participants

Reads the file contents by using the TensorFlow WholeFileReader API

To start clustering your positional data for the participants, you need a TensorFlow dataset to work with. Let's create one using the `FileReader` API from TensorFlow.

8.1.1 Creating the dataset

Keeping with what I showed you in chapter 7, you can structure your code by creating a `get_dataset` function, which relies on a `get_feature_vector` function (step 2 in the workflow shown in figure 8.3) to convert your raw CSV positional data to a feature vector for clustering. The implementation of this function calculates jerk and uses it as the feature vector; jerk is the third derivative of position with respect to time. When you've calculated jerk for all the participant data, you need to stack those feature vectors vertically into a big matrix that can be clustered (step 3 in the workflow in figure 8.3), which is the point of the `get_dataset` function.

Before you get started extracting your feature vector and computing jerk, a good machine-learning practice in general is to do some exploratory data analysis and see what type of information you are dealing with by inspecting it visually. To get some sample positional data that you can look at, you should try to sketch out the `get_dataset` function first. The CSV files, as you saw in figure 8.2, come with four columns (Time, XPos, YPos, and ZPos), so you can have Pandas name the columns in its dataframe accordingly. Don't worry that you haven't written your `extract_feature_vector` function yet. Check out the code in listing 8.2 to begin.

Listing 8.2 Converting the filename and contents to a NumPy matrix dataset

```
def get_dataset(sess):
    sess.run(tf.local_variables_initializer())
    num_files = sess.run(count_num_files)

    coord = tf.train.Coordinator()
    threads = tf.train.start_queue_runners(coord=coord)
    accel_files = []
    xs = []
    for i in range(num_files):
        accel_file = sess.run(filename)
        accel_file_frame = pd.read_csv(accel_file, header=None, sep=',',
                names = ["Time", "XPos", "YPos", "ZPos"])
        accel_files.append(accel_file_frame)
        print(accel_file)
        x = [extract_feature_vector(sess, accel_file_frame.values)]
        x = np.matrix(x)

        if len(xs) == 0:
```

Creates a TensorFlow session and counts the number of files needed to iterate through them

Reads the file contents into a Pandas dataframe with named columns and collects them in a list

Gets the filename by using TensorFlow

Extracts the feature vector

```
        xs = x
    else:
        xs = np.vstack((xs, x))        ◁——⌐ Stacks the vectors vertically
    return xs                               in a NumPy matrix
```

Before getting too deep into computing the feature vector, you can inspect the data from the Pandas dataframes you created in the `accel_files` variable. The X values from the positional data from the first two participants, for example, can be easily plotted with Matplotlib like so:

```
accel_files[0]["XPos"].plot.line()
accel_files[1]["XPos"].plot.line()
```

The results in figure 8.4, even only along the X dimension, show overlapping patterns, at least through the first 5,000 or so time steps along the x-axis. There is something for a machine-learning algorithm to learn.

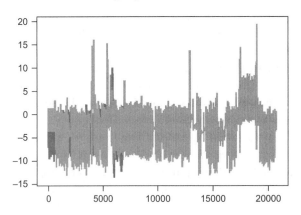

Figure 8.4   X positional data for the first two participants, using Pandas and Matplotlib. Overlap of points occurs abundantly in the initial 5,000 or so time steps (x-axis).

If you can spot a pattern, the machine-learning algorithm should be able to spot a similar pattern on all the dimensions. The algorithm should be able to identify that participants 1 and 2 have a similar X position for the first 5,000 time steps, for example. You can exploit this information by using TensorFlow and easily expand it to deal with all three positional dimensions, as I'll show you in the next section.

8.1.2   Computing jerk and extracting the feature vector

Let's start by computing jerk magnitudes on all your data. You can use the NumPy `np.diff` function, which computes `out = a[n+1] - a[n]` for all n in your data, leaving you an array of size n-1. If you had `foo = [1., 2., 3., 4., 5.]` and performed `np.diff(foo)`, the result would be `[1., 1., 1., 1.]`. Computing `np.diff` once gives you the first derivative of your input positional data (velocity); computing it a second time gives you the second derivative (acceleration), and so on. Because jerk is the third derivative of position with respect to time, you need to call `np.diff` three times, passing as input the result of each preceding call to the subsequent one. Because np.diff works with multidimensional input, it computes the difference for each dimension *M* in your *N* × *M* input matrix, and your input has three dimensions for *M*, a position consisting of samples of X, Y, and Z.

The next important step in exploring your CSV data is understanding the number of samples per participant, which corresponds to the *N* parameter in your *N* × 3 participant matrix. You can figure out the number of samples for each participant's data by taking the results of listing 8.1 (a pairwise set of 22 participant filenames and their contents) and then plotting a quick histogram of the number of points collected per participant, as shown in listing 8.3. The result, depicted in figure 8.5, shows a non-uniform distribution of positional data taken for the 22 participants, which means that your *N* is not equal for all participants and their input, at least to start. Don't fret; I'll show you how to normalize the samples.

Listing 8.3   Deciphering positional points per participant

Imports Matplotlib

```
import matplotlib.pyplot as plt
num_pts = [len(a_f) for a_f in accel_files]      ◁─┐ Counts number of points
plt.hist(num_pts)      ◁───┐                          per file in accel_files
                           │
                  Plots a histogram of uniform width of
                  number of points per participant file
```

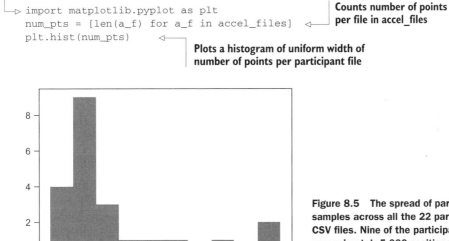

Figure 8.5   The spread of participant samples across all the 22 participant CSV files. Nine of the participants have approximately 5,000 positional samples, 1 has approximately 17,000 another 20,000, and so on.

This result is a problem, as it was in chapter 7, because the goal of clustering is to have one 1 × *M* feature vector represent each participant you want to cluster. One observation you can make is that across all the time steps in the positional data, there is a maximum or dominant jerk magnitude in each of the X, Y, Z positional dimensions. Going back to the definition of jerk—rate of change of the force acting on a body—selecting the maximum or dominant value for jerk in each of the three positional dimensions gives you the highest force in each of the three axes and the most responsible for influencing the switching motions from one activity to another. Selecting the max jerk magnitude per dimension per sample allows you to reduce your matrix to a size *N* × 1 matrix, giving you a single 1D set of points per participant.

To convert this matrix back to a 3D 1 × 3 matrix, you can perform a histogram count with three bins on the *N* sample max jerk magnitudes and then normalize by dividing by the number of samples *N* to produce your feature vector as a 1 × 3 matrix for each participant. Doing so results in an effective motion signature per participant for clustering representations of the positional data independent of the number of samples per participant. The code that performs this conversion is your `get_feature_vector` function. Listing 8.4 has the gory details.

Listing 8.4   Selecting and computing max jerk magnitudes per dimension

**Initializes the jerk matrix and TensorFlow operator
for computing max jerk for each dimension**

```
jerk = tf.placeholder(tf.float32)
max_jerk = tf.reduce_max(jerk, keepdims=True, axis=1)

def extract_feature_vector(sess, x):          ◁—— We don't need the time variable,
    x_s = x[:, 1:]                                   so consider only (X, Y, Z) of (t, X,
                                                     Y, Z) by chopping off t.

    v_X = np.diff(x_s, axis=0)          Computes velocity (v_X),
    a_X = np.diff(v_X, axis=0)          acceleration (a_X), and jerk (j_X)
    j_X = np.diff(a_X, axis=0)

    X = j_X                                  Number of samples is 1;
    mJerk = sess.run(max_jerk, feed_dict = {jerk: X})    number of features is 3.
    num_samples, num_features = np.shape(X)      ◁
    hist, bins = np.histogram(mJerk, bins=range(num_features + 1))
    return hist.astype(float) / num_samples      ◁
```

Computes max jerk by running TensorFlow (points to `mJerk = sess.run(...)` line)

Returns max jerk magnitude normalized by number of samples (total points)

You can convince yourself that in performing this data manipulation, there is still something to learn from plotting the resultant normalized jerk magnitudes with Matplotlib and inspecting them per participant sample for each of the 22 participants. Listing 8.5 sets up the plot to perform this exploratory data analysis. The first steps are creating a subplot for each participant and their 3D X, Y, Z normalized jerk magnitudes, using a different random color for each of the three bars per participant. As you can tell from figure 8.6, there is a definite pattern. The bars are closely aligned in certain dimensions for some participants, which means that the participants either changed motions to perform the same activity or shifted away from a particular activity that they were both performing. In other words, there are trends that you can spot, and so can a machine-learning algorithm for clustering. Now you are ready to cluster similar participants.

Listing 8.5   Visualizing the normalized jerk magnitudes

```
labels=['X', 'Y', 'Z']          ◁—— The three dimensions of
fig, ax = plt.subplots()                position in X, Y, and Z
ind = np.arange(len(labels))
```

```
width = 0.015
plots = []
colors = [np.random.rand(3,1).flatten() for i in range(num_samples)]

for i in range(num_samples):
    Xs = np.asarray(X[i]).reshape(-1)
    p = ax.bar(ind + i*width, Xs, width, color=colors[i])
    plots.append(p[0])

xticks = ind + width / (num_samples)
print(xticks)
ax.legend(tuple(plots), tuple(['P'+str(i+1) for i in range(num_samples)]),
    ncol=4)
ax.yaxis.set_units(inch)
ax.autoscale_view()
ax.set_xticks(xticks)
ax.set_xticklabels(labels)

ax.set_ylabel('Normalized jerk count')
ax.set_xlabel('Position (X, Y, Z)')
ax.set_title('Normalized jerk magnitude counts for Various Participants')
plt.show()
```

Adds a subplot of each 3-bar for all 22 participants

Picks a random color for each of the 3 bars for the 22 participants

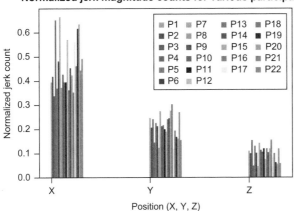

Figure 8.6 The normalized jerk magnitudes for all 22 participants in X, Y, Z dimensional space. As you can see, there is a definite pattern: participants' motions changed depending on their activity in X, Y, and Z.

8.2 *Clustering similar participants based on jerk magnitudes*

As you learned in chapter 7, k-means clustering is an unsupervised clustering approach with a single hyperparameter, K, that you can use to set the number of desired clusters. Normally, you could pick different values of K to see what happens and how closely the resulting clusters fit the data you provided. Because we normalized the maximum jerk magnitudes across thousands of data points in time for each participant, we are getting a sort of summary of the positional changes (jerk) over that time.

An easy value to pick for K to start with is 2, to see whether a natural dividing line exists between participants. Perhaps some participants had wild positional changes; they ran fast and then stopped, or went from doing nothing to jumping high in the air. These sudden changes in motion over time should yield high jerk magnitudes, compared with those of other participants who changed their motion gradually, slowing down before coming to a stop, for example, or walking or lightly jogging the entire time.

To that end, picking K = 2 implies there may be two natural bins of motion over time for our participants. Let's try it with TensorFlow. In chapter 7, I showed you how to use TensorFlow to implement a K-means algorithm and run it on your input NumPy matrix of feature vectors. You can carry forward the same code and apply it to the dataset resulting from calling the `get_dataset` function from listing 8.2.

Listing 8.6 adds functions defined in chapter 7 to implement k-means, runs the functions on your input participant data, and clusters the input data. To refresh your memory, first define the following:

- Hyperparameters, `k`, and `max_iterations`
- Number of clusters
- Maximum times you will update the centroids and assign points to new clusters based on their distances from the centroids

The `initial_cluster_centroids` function takes the first K points in the dataset as the initial cluster guesses, which could be random. Then the `assign_cluster` function uses TensorFlow's `expand_dims` function to create an additional dimension for computing the difference between points in the X dataset and the initially guessed centroids. Points farther from the centroids are likely not in the same cluster as those with similar distances.

Creating another dimension allows you to partition those distances into K clusters initially selected in the `expanded_centroids` variable, which stores the summed, squared distances between X points and the cluster centroids through each iteration of the algorithm.

Then TensorFlow's `argmin` function is applied to identify which dimension (0 to K) is the minimum distance and use that as a mask to identify a particular data point and its group. The data point and group masks are summed and divided by data-point count to achieve new centroids, which are an average distance from all the points in that group. The TensorFlow `unsorted_segment_sum` applies the centroid group mask to the specific points in that cluster. Then TensorFlow's `ones_like` creates a mask of count elements in each data point cluster and divides the summed distances of each data point from the centroid by the counts to get the new centroids.

Listing 8.6   Running k-means on the jerk magnitudes of all participants

Defines hyperparameters
```
k = 2
max_iterations = 100                                    Initially takes the first
                                                        K elements from X to
def initial_cluster_centroids(X, k):       ◁━━━━        be each centroid
```

```
                return X[0:k, :]

        def assign_cluster(X, centroids):
            expanded_vectors = tf.expand_dims(X, 0)
            expanded_centroids = tf.expand_dims(centroids, 1)
            distances = tf.reduce_sum(tf.square(tf.subtract(expanded_vectors,
            ⇒ expanded_centroids)), 2)
            mins = tf.argmin(distances, 0)
            return mins

        def recompute_centroids(X, Y):
            sums = tf.unsorted_segment_sum(X, Y, k)
            counts = tf.unsorted_segment_sum(tf.ones_like(X), Y, k)
            return sums / counts

        groups = None
        with tf.Session() as sess:
            X = get_dataset(sess)
            centroids = initial_cluster_centroids(X, k)
            i, converged = 0, False
            while not converged and i < max_iterations:
                i += 1
                Y = assign_cluster(X, centroids)
                centroids = sess.run(recompute_centroids(X, Y))
            print(centroids)
            groups = Y.eval()
            print(groups)
```

Creates an expanded dimension to handle computing the distances of each point from the centroid

Computes distances

Creates the group mask by selecting the min distance from each centroid

Creates an expanded dimension to split the distances into K groups from each centroid

Divides the summed distances by the number of data points and recomputes new centroids

Initializes TensorFlow

Sums the min distances for each data point by using the mask

Gets the initial dataset of participant normalized jerk magnitudes 22 × 3

Keeps clustering for 100 iterations and computing new center points

Prints the centroids and groups

After running k-means and the code in listing 8.6, you obtain the two centroid points and cluster masks: 0 indicates the first group; otherwise, the label is 1. You can also visualize the participants and the two clusters by using some simple Matplotlib scatter-point functionality. You can use your groups mask to index into the X dataset points by using 0s and 1s, and you can plot the centroid points as Xs, indicating the center of each group. Listing 8.7 has the code, and figure 8.7 plots the results. Though you can't be sure of the label for each cluster, it's clear that the participants' motion clearly fits the two different categories because there is a nice separation of participant data in each group.

```
[[0.40521887 0.23630463 0.11820933]
 [0.59834667 0.14981037 0.05972407]]
[0 0 0 1 0 0 1 0 0 0 0 1 0 0 0 0 1 0 1 1 0 1]
```

Listing 8.7   Visualizing the two participant motion clusters

Indexes the X data, using your groups mask

Plots the X center points, using the centroid points

```
plt.scatter([X[:, 0]], [X[:, 1]], c=groups, s=50, alpha=0.5)
plt.plot([centroids[:, 0]], [centroids[:, 1]], 'kx', markersize=15)
plt.show()
```

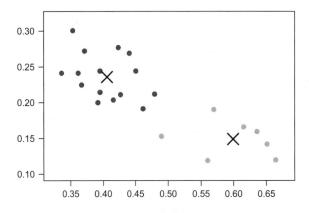

Figure 8.7   Two participant clusters of motion. Although you do not know the precise label for each cluster, you can see a clear delineation of the participants with similar motion over time.

You've used unsupervised clustering and the jerk magnitudes indicating participant motion to bin that motion into two categories. You aren't sure which category involves short, sudden motions and which is gradual motions, but you can leave that determination for a future classification activity.

Next, instead of looking across all the participant motion, I show you how to use k-means to partition a single participant's motion into motion categories. Onward!

8.3   *Different classes of user activity for a single participant*

I showed you in chapter 7 how to take a single sound file and perform segmentation on it, separating the speakers in that sound file at specific time periods and classifying them in different groups. You can do something similar with your positional-point data per participant by using TensorFlow and k-means clustering.

UCI's machine-learning repository, where the User Activity from Walking dataset that you are using in this chapter comes from, points to a source paper titled "Personalization and User Verification in Wearable Systems Using Biometric Walking Patterns." This paper states that the participants in the study performed five classes of activity: climbing, standing, walking, talking, and working. (You can obtain the source paper at http://mng.bz/ggQE.)

Logically, it makes sense that you could group segments of N samples of participant positional data for a single participant and then attempt to automatically partition and cluster the points—which represent accelerometer readings at a particular time—into the different motions that occurred during activities performed in the wild. You can take a single CSV file from the dataset and segment it positionally by using the hyperparameter `segment_size`. When the file is segmented, you can reuse your `extract_feature_vector` method from listing 8.4 to compute jerk magnitudes and their histograms for each segment of size 50 positional points to achieve representational position jerk magnitudes to cluster along the 5 possible classes of activities. Listing 8.8 creates a modified version of `get_dataset` using `segment_size` and thus is named `get_dataset_segemented`.

Listing 8.8 Segmenting a single participant CSV

```
segment_size = 50                    ◁——— Defines hyperparameters
def get_accel_data(accel_file):
    accel_file_frame = pd.read_csv(accel_file, header=None, sep=',',
                  names = ["Time", "XPos", "YPos", "ZPos"])
    return accel_file_frame.values

def get_dataset_segmented(sess, accel_file):
    accel_data = get_accel_data(accel_file)      ◁——— Gets the CSV positional data
    print('accel_data', np.shape(accel_data))
    accel_length = np.shape(accel_data)[0]    ◁——— Number of samples
    print('accel_length', accel_length)
    xs = []

    for i in range(accel_length / segment_size):
        accel_segment = accel_data[i*segment_size:(i+1)*segment_size, :] ◁——┐
        x = extract_feature_vector(sess, accel_segment)
        x = np.matrix(x)   ◁——┐
                               │ Stacks jerk magnitudes
        if len(xs) == 0:       │ into an N × 3 matrix
            xs = x             │ where N is num
        else:                  │ samples/segment size
            xs = np.vstack((xs, x))
    return accel_data, xs
```

Stacks jerk magnitudes into an N × 3 matrix where N is num samples/segment size

For each set of segment_size, slice off that number of points and extract jerk magnitudes.

After preparing your segmented dataset, you are ready to run TensorFlow again, this time with an $N \times 3$ matrix, where N is the number of samples / segment_size. When you run k-means with k = 5 this time, you are asking TensorFlow to cluster your representations of 50 positional points in time according to the different motions a participant could possibly be performing: climbing, standing, walking, talking, or working. The code looks similar to listing 8.6 but is modified slightly in listing 8.9.

Listing 8.9 Clustering a single participant file across different activity groups

```
k = 5                                ◁——┐
with tf.Session() as sess:              │ Climbing Stairs, Standing, Walking,
    tf.global_variables_initializer()   │ Talking, Working from the paper
    accel_data, X1 = get_dataset_segmented(sess, "./User Identification From
    ⮡ Walking Activity/11.csv")      ◁——┐
                                         │ You need only
    centroids = initial_cluster_centroids(X1, k)  │ one participant.
    i, converged = 0, False
    while not converged and i < max_iterations:
        i += 1
        Y1 = assign_cluster(X1, centroids)
        centroids = sess.run(recompute_centroids(X1, Y1))
        if i % 50 == 0:
            print('iteration', i)
    segments = sess.run(Y1)
    print('Num segments ', str(len(segments)))  ◁——┐ Prints the number of
    for i in range(len(segments)):                   │ segment—in this case, 112
```

```
seconds = (i * segment_size) / float(10)
seconds = accel_data[(i * segment_size)][0]
min, sec = divmod(seconds, 60)
time_str = '{}m {}s'.format(min, sec)
print(time_str, segments[i])
```

⟵ **Loops through the segments and prints the activity label, 0–4**

You'll want to visualize the result of running listing 8.9. Lo and behold, those 112 segments appear to have an interesting distribution of positional 50 time-step segments. The X group in the bottom left seems to have only a few segments by it. The three groups in the middle representing various activities seem to be the most dense, and the bottom far-right group has slightly more positional segments than the one at bottom left. You can see the result by running the code to generate figure 8.8:

```
plt.scatter([X1[:, 0]], [X1[:, 1]], c=segments, s=50, alpha=0.5)
plt.plot([centroids[:, 0]], [centroids[:, 1]], 'kx', markersize=15)
plt.show()
```

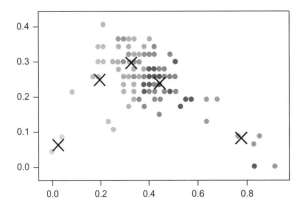

Figure 8.8   Different activities for a single participant based on the provided positional data

The challenge, of course, is knowing exactly what group label each X corresponds to, but that activity is best saved for when you can examine the properties of each motion group and perhaps try to characterize them against ground truth. Perhaps the jerk magnitudes closest to the bottom-left group correspond to gradual acceleration and are likely the walking activity. Only through separate analysis can you figure out which categories each label (0–4) corresponds to—walking, jumping, running, and so on—but it's pretty darned cool that machine learning and TensorFlow were able to partition the positional data into those groups automatically, without any ground truth!

Summary

- From your cell phone's positional data, a machine-learning algorithm using unsupervised machine learning and k-means clustering can infer what type of activity you were performing.
- TensorFlow can easily compute k-means, and you can apply your code from chapter 7 to it after transforming the data.

- Fingerprinting positional data is similar to fingerprinting text.
- Preparing and cleaning the data are key steps in machine learning.
- Using k-means clustering and segmenting an existing participant's data makes it easy to spot activity patterns, which is somewhat more difficult in a bigger group.

Hidden Markov models

If a rocket blows up, someone's probably going to get fired, so rocket scientists and engineers must be able to make confident decisions about all components and configurations. They do so by physical simulations and mathematical deduction from first principles. You, too, have solved science problems with pure logical thinking. Consider Boyle's law: pressure and volume of a gas are inversely related under a fixed temperature. You can make insightful inferences from these simple laws about the world that have been discovered. Recently, machine learning has started to play the role of an important sidekick to deductive reasoning.

Rocket science and *machine learning* aren't phrases that usually appear together except unless you literally walk a week in my shoes. (Check out my author bio!) But nowadays, modeling real-world sensor readings by using intelligent data-driven algorithms is more approachable in the aerospace industry. Also, the use of machine-learning techniques is flourishing in the health care and automotive industries. But why?

This influx can be partly attributed to better understanding of *interpretable* models, which are machine-learning models in which the learned parameters have clear interpretations. If a rocket blows up, for example, an interpretable model might help trace the root cause.

Exercise 9.1

What makes a model interpretable may be slightly subjective. What are your criteria for an interpretable model?

Answers

We like to refer to mathematical proofs as the de facto explanation technique. If one were to convince another of the truth of a mathematical theorem, a proof that irrefutably traces the steps of reasoning is sufficient.

This chapter is about exposing the hidden explanations behind observations. Consider a puppet master pulling strings to make a puppet appear to be alive. Analyzing only the motions of the puppet might lead to overly complicated conclusions about how it's possible for an inanimate object to move. After you notice the attached strings, you'll realize that a puppet master is the best explanation for the lifelike motions.

On that note, this chapter introduces *hidden Markov models* (HMMs), which reveal intuitive properties about the problem under study. The HMM is the "puppet master," which explains the observations. You model observations by using Markov chains, which are described in section 9.2.

Before reading in detail about Markov chains and HMMs, consider alternative models. In section 9.1, you'll see models that may not be interpretable.

9.1 *Example of a not-so-interpretable model*

One classic example of a black-box machine-learning algorithm that's difficult to interpret is image classification. In an image-classification task, the goal is to assign a label to each input image. More simply, image classification is often posed as a multiple-choice question: which one of the listed categories best describes the image? Machine-learning practitioners have made tremendous advancements in solving this problem, to the point where today's best image classifiers match human-level performance on certain datasets.

In chapter 14, you'll learn how to solve the problem of classifying images by using convolutional neural networks (CNNs), a class of machine-learning models that end up learning a lot of parameters. But those parameters are the problem with CNNs: what do each of the thousands, if not millions, of parameters mean? It's difficult to ask an image classifier why it made the decision that it did. All we have available are the learned parameters, which may not easily explain the reasoning behind the classification.

Machine learning sometimes gets the reputation of being a black-box tool that solves a specific problem without revealing how it arrives at its conclusion. The purpose of this chapter is to unveil an area of machine learning with an interpretable model. Specifically, you'll learn about the HMM and use TensorFlow to implement it.

9.2 *Markov model*

Andrey Markov was a Russian mathematician who studied the ways that systems change over time in the presence of randomness. Imagine gas particles bouncing around in the air. Tracking the position of each particle with Newtonian physics can get way too complicated, so introducing randomness helps simplify the physical model a little.

Markov realized that what helps simplify a random system even further is considering only a limited area around the gas particle to model it. Maybe a gas particle in Europe has barely any effect on a particle in the United States. So why not ignore it? **The mathematics is simplified when you look only at a nearby neighborhood instead of the entire system**. This notion is referred to as the *Markov property*.

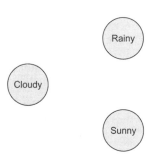

Consider modeling the weather. Meteorologists evaluate various conditions with thermometers, barometers, and anemometers to help predict the weather. They draw on brilliant insight and years of experience to do their job.

Let's use the Markov property to get started with a simple model. First, you identify the possible situations, or *states*, that you care to study. Figure 9.1 shows three weather states as nodes in a graph: Cloudy, Rainy, and Sunny.

Figure 9.1   Weather conditions (states) represented as nodes in a graph

Now that you have the states, you want to define how one state transforms into another. Modeling weather as a deterministic system is difficult. The conclusion that if it's sunny today, it'll certainly be sunny tomorrow isn't obvious. Instead, you can introduce randomness and say that if it's sunny today, there's a 90% chance that it'll be sunny tomorrow and a 10% chance that it'll be cloudy. The Markov property comes into play when you use only today's weather condition to predict tomorrow's (instead of using history).

Exercise 9.2

A robot that decides which action to perform based on only its current state is said to follow the Markov property. What are the advantages and disadvantages of such a decision-making process?

Answers

The Markov property is computationally easy to work with, but Markov models aren't able to generalize to situations that require accumulating a history of knowledge. Examples are models in which a trend over time is important or knowledge of more than one past state gives a better idea of what to expect next.

Figure 9.2 demonstrates the transitions as directed edges drawn between nodes, with the arrow pointing toward the next future state. Each edge has a weight representing the probability (such as a 30% chance that if today is rainy, tomorrow will be cloudy). The lack of an edge between two nodes is an elegant way of showing that the probability of that transformation is near zero. The transition probabilities can be learned from historical data, but for now, let's assume that they're given to us.

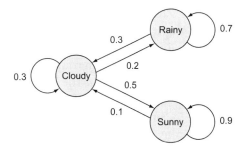

Figure 9.2 Transition probabilities between weather conditions are represented as directed edges.

If you have three states, you can represent the transitions as a 3×3 matrix. Each element of the matrix (at row i and column j) corresponds to the probability associated with the edge from node i to node j. In general, if you have N states, the *transition matrix* will be $N \times N$ in size; see figure 9.4 for an example.

We call this system a *Markov model*. Over time, a state changes using the transition probabilities defined in figure 9.2. In our example, Sunny has a 90% chance of Sunny again tomorrow, so we show an edge of probability 0.9, looping back to itself. There's a 10% chance of a sunny day being followed by a cloudy day, shown in the diagram as the edge 0.1, pointing from Sunny to Cloudy.

Figure 9.3 is another way to visualize how the states change, given the transition probabilities. This depiction is often called a *trellis diagram*, which turns out to be an essential tool, as you'll see later when we implement the TensorFlow algorithms.

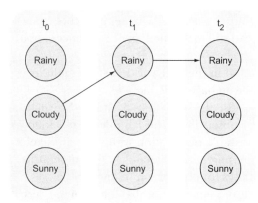

Figure 9.3 A trellis representation of the Markov system changing states over time

You've seen how TensorFlow code builds a graph to represent computation. It may be tempting to treat each node in a Markov model as a node in TensorFlow. But even though figures 9.2 and 9.3 nicely illustrate state transitions, figure 9.4 shows a more efficient way to implement them in code.

Remember that nodes in a TensorFlow graph are tensors, so you can represent a transition matrix (let's call it T) as a node in TensorFlow. Then you can apply mathematical operations on the TensorFlow node to achieve interesting results.

Suppose that you prefer sunny days over rainy ones, so you have a score associated with each day. You represent your scores for each state in a 3×1 matrix called s. Then multiplying the two matrices in TensorFlow with `tf.matmul(T*s)` gives the expected preference of transitioning from each state.

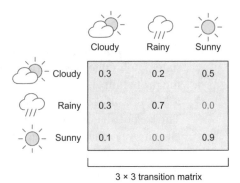

Figure 9.4   A transition matrix conveys the probabilities of a state from the left (rows) transitioning to a state at the top (columns).

Representing a scenario in a Markov model allows you to simplify greatly how you view the world. But frequently, it's difficult to measure the state of the world directly. Often, you have to use evidence from multiple observations to figure out the hidden meaning. That problem is what section 9.3 aims to solve.

9.3   Hidden Markov model

The Markov model defined in section 9.2 is convenient when all the states are observable, but that's not always the case. Consider having access to only the temperature readings of a town. Temperature isn't weather, but it's related. How, then, can you infer the weather from this indirect set of measurements?

Rainy weather most likely causes a lower temperature reading, whereas a sunny day most likely causes a higher temperature reading. With temperature knowledge and transition probabilities alone, you can still make intelligent inferences about the most likely weather.

Problems like this one are common in the real world. A state might leave traces of hints behind, and those hints are all you have available.

Models like these are HMMs because the true states of the world (such as whether it's raining or sunny) aren't directly observable. These hidden states follow a Markov model, and each state emits a measurable observation with a certain likelihood. The hidden state of Sunny, for example, might usually emit high temperature readings, but occasionally also emits low readings for one reason or another.

In an HMM, you have to define the emission probability, which is usually represented as a matrix called the *emission matrix*. The number of rows in the matrix is the number of states (Sunny, Cloudy, Rainy), and the number of columns is the number of observation types (Hot, Mild, Cold). Each element of the matrix is the probability associated with the emission.

The canonical way to visualize an HMM is to append observations to the trellis, as shown in figure 9.5.

Hidden states

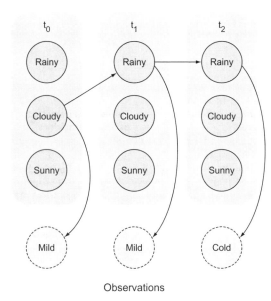

Observations

Figure 9.5   An HMM trellis showing how weather conditions might produce temperature readings

So that's *almost* it. The HMM is a description of transition probabilities, emission probabilities, and one more thing: initial probabilities. The *initial probability* is the probability that each state will happen without the model's previous knowledge. If you're modeling the weather in Los Angeles, perhaps the initial probability of Sunny would be much greater. Or let's say you're modeling the weather in Seattle; you know that you can set the initial probability of Rainy to something higher.

An HMM lets you understand a sequence of observations. In this weather-modeling scenario, you may ask about the probability of observing a certain sequence of temperature readings. I'll answer this question with the forward algorithm.

9.4   *Forward algorithm*

The *forward algorithm* computes the probability of an observation. Many permutations may cause a particular observation, so enumerating all possibilities the naïve way will take an exponentially long time to compute.

Instead, you can solve the problem by using *dynamic programming*, a strategy of breaking a complex problem into simple little ones and using a lookup table to cache the results. In your code, you'll save the lookup table as a NumPy array and feed it to a TensorFlow op to keep updating it.

As shown in listing 9.1, create an HMM class to capture the HMM parameters, which include the initial probability vector, transition probability matrix, and emission probability matrix.

Listing 9.1   Defining the HMM class

```
import numpy as np          Imports the
import tensorflow as tf     required libraries


class HMM(object):
    def __init__(self, initial_prob, trans_prob, obs_prob):
        self.N = np.size(initial_prob)
        self.initial_prob = initial_prob       Stores the parameters
        self.trans_prob = trans_prob           as method variables
        self.emission = tf.constant(obs_prob)

        assert self.initial_prob.shape == (self.N, 1)      Double-checks that
        assert self.trans_prob.shape == (self.N, self.N)   the shapes of all the
        assert obs_prob.shape[0] == self.N                 matrices make sense

        self.obs_idx = tf.placeholder(tf.int32)      Defines the placeholders used
        self.fwd = tf.placeholder(tf.float64)        for the forward algorithm
```

Next, you'll define a quick helper function to access a row from the emission matrix. The code in listing 9.2 is a helper function that obtains data efficiently from an arbitrary matrix. The `slice` function extracts a fraction of the original tensor. This function requires as input the relevant tensor, the starting location specified by a tensor, and the size of the slice specified by a tensor.

Listing 9.2   Creating a helper function to access an observation's emission probability

```
def get_emission(self, obs_idx):        Where to slice the        Performs
    slice_location = [0, obs_idx]       emission matrix           the slicing
    num_rows = tf.shape(self.emission)[0]                         operation
    slice_shape = [num_rows, 1]         The shape of the slice
    return tf.slice(self.emission, slice_location, slice_shape)
```

You need to define two TensorFlow ops. The first one, in listing 9.3, will be run only once to initialize the forward algorithm's cache.

Listing 9.3   Initializing the cache

```
def forward_init_op(self):
    obs_prob = self.get_emission(self.obs_idx)
    fwd = tf.multiply(self.initial_prob, obs_prob)
    return fwd
```

The next op updates the cache at each observation, as shown in listing 9.4. Running this code is often called *executing a forward step*. Although it looks as though this `forward_op` function takes no input, it depends on placeholder variables that need to be fed to the session. Specifically, `self.fwd` and `self.obs_idx` are the inputs to this function.

Listing 9.4 Updating the cache

```
def forward_op(self):
    transitions = tf.matmul(self.fwd,
 tf.transpose(self.get_emission(self.obs_idx)))
        weighted_transitions = transitions * self.trans_prob
        fwd = tf.reduce_sum(weighted_transitions, 0)
        return tf.reshape(fwd, tf.shape(self.fwd))
```

Outside the HMM class, let's define a function to run the forward algorithm, as shown in listing 9.5. The forward algorithm runs the forward step for each observation. In the end, it outputs a probability of observations.

Listing 9.5 Defining the forward algorithm, given an HMM

```
def forward_algorithm(sess, hmm, observations):
    fwd = sess.run(hmm.forward_init_op(), feed_dict={hmm.obs_idx:
 ➥ observations[0]})
    for t in range(1, len(observations)):
        fwd = sess.run(hmm.forward_op(), feed_dict={hmm.obs_idx:
 ➥ observations[t], hmm.fwd: fwd})
    prob = sess.run(tf.reduce_sum(fwd))
    return prob
```

In the main function, let's set up the HMM class by feeding it the initial probability vector, transition probability matrix, and emission probability matrix. For consistency, the example in listing 9.6 is lifted directly from the Wikipedia article on HMMs at http://mng.bz/8ztL, as shown in figure 9.6.

```
states = ('Rainy', 'Sunny')

observations = ('walk', 'shop', 'clean')

start_probability = {'Rainy': 0.6, 'Sunny': 0.4}

transition_probability = {
    'Rainy'  : {'Rainy': 0.7, 'Sunny': 0.3},
    'Sunny'  : {'Rainy': 0.4, 'Sunny': 0.6},
}

emission_probability = {
    'Rainy'  : {'walk': 0.1, 'shop': 0.4, 'clean': 0.5},
    'Sunny'  : {'walk': 0.6, 'shop': 0.3, 'clean': 0.1},
}
```

Figure 9.6 Screenshot of HMM example scenario

In general, the three concepts are defined as follows:

- *Initial probability vector*—Starting probability of the states
- *Transition probability matrix*—Probabilities associated with landing on the next states, given the current state
- *Emission probability matrix*—Likelihood of an observed state implying the state you're interested in has occurred

Given these matrices, you'll call the forward algorithm that you've defined (listing 9.6).

Listing 9.6   Defining the `HMM` and calling the forward algorithm

```
if __name__ == '__main__':
    initial_prob = np.array([[0.6],
                             [0.4]])

    trans_prob = np.array([[0.7, 0.3],
                           [0.4, 0.6]])

    obs_prob = np.array([[0.1, 0.4, 0.5],
                         [0.6, 0.3, 0.1]])

    hmm = HMM(initial_prob=initial_prob, trans_prob=trans_prob,
➥ obs_prob=obs_prob)

    observations = [0, 1, 1, 2, 1]
    with tf.Session() as sess:
        prob = forward_algorithm(sess, hmm, observations)
        print('Probability of observing {} is {}'.format(observations, prob))
```

When you run listing 9.6, the algorithm outputs the following:

```
Probability of observing [0, 1, 1, 2, 1] is 0.0045403
```

9.5   *Viterbi decoding*

The *Viterbi decoding algorithm* finds the most likely sequence of hidden states, given a sequence of observations. It requires a caching scheme similar to the forward algorithm. You'll name the cache `viterbi`. In the HMM constructor, append the line shown in listing 9.7.

Listing 9.7   Adding the Viterbi cache as a member variable

```
def __init__(self, initial_prob, trans_prob, obs_prob):
    ...
    ...
    ...
    self.viterbi = tf.placeholder(tf.float64)
```

In listing 9.8, you'll define a TensorFlow op to update the `viterbi` cache. This op will be a method in the HMM class.

Listing 9.8   Defining an op to update the forward cache

```
def decode_op(self):
        transitions = tf.matmul(self.viterbi,
      tf.transpose(self.get_emission(self.obs_idx)))
        weighted_transitions = transitions * self.trans_prob
        viterbi = tf.reduce_max(weighted_transitions, 0)
        return tf.reshape(viterbi, tf.shape(self.viterbi))
```

You'll also need an op to update the back pointers (listing 9.9).

Listing 9.9 Defining an op to update the back pointers

```
def backpt_op(self):
    back_transitions = tf.matmul(self.viterbi, np.ones((1, self.N)))
    weighted_back_transitions = back_transitions * self.trans_prob
    return tf.argmax(weighted_back_transitions, 0)
```

Finally, in listing 9.10, define the Viterbi decoding function outside the HMM.

Listing 9.10 Defining the Viterbi decoding algorithm

```
def viterbi_decode(sess, hmm, observations):
    viterbi = sess.run(hmm.forward_init_op(), feed_dict={hmm.obs:
     observations[0]})
    backpts = np.ones((hmm.N, len(observations)), 'int32') * -1
    for t in range(1, len(observations)):
        viterbi, backpt = sess.run([hmm.decode_op(), hmm.backpt_op()],
                            feed_dict={hmm.obs: observations[t],
                                       hmm.viterbi: viterbi})
        backpts[:, t] = backpt
    tokens = [viterbi[:, -1].argmax()]
    for i in range(len(observations) - 1, 0, -1):
        tokens.append(backpts[tokens[-1], i])
    return tokens[::-1]
```

You can run the code in listing 9.11 in the main function to evaluate the Viterbi decoding of an observation.

Listing 9.11 Running the Viterbi decode

```
seq = viterbi_decode(sess, hmm, observations)
print('Most likely hidden states are {}'.format(seq))
```

9.6 Uses of HMMs

Now that you've implemented the forward algorithm and Viterbi algorithm, let's take a look at interesting uses for your newfound power.

9.6.1 Modeling a video

Imagine being able to recognize a person based solely (no pun intended) on how they walk. Identifying people based on their gait is a pretty cool idea, but first, you need a model to recognize the gait. Consider an HMM in which the sequence of hidden states for a gait are (1) rest position, (2) right foot forward, (3) rest position, (4) left foot forward, and (5) rest position. The observed states are silhouettes of a person walking/jogging/running taken from a video clip. (A dataset of such examples is available at http://mng.bz/Tqfx.)

9.6.2 *Modeling DNA*

DNA is a sequence of nucleotides, and we're gradually learning more about its structure. One clever way to understand a long DNA string is to model the regions, if you know some probability about the order in which they appear. As a cloudy day is common after a rainy day, maybe a certain region on the DNA sequence (*start codon*) is more common before another region (*stop codon*).

9.6.3 *Modeling an image*

In handwriting recognition, we aim to retrieve the plaintext from an image of handwritten words. One approach is to resolve characters one at a time and then concatenate the results. You can use the insight that characters are written in sequences—words—to build an HMM. Knowing the previous character probably could help you rule out possibilities of the next character. The hidden states are the plaintext, and the observations are cropped images containing individual characters.

9.7 *Application of HMMs*

HMMs work best when you have an idea about what the hidden states are and how they change over time. Luckily, in the field of natural language processing, tagging a sentence's parts of speech can be solved with HMMs:

- A sequence of words in a sentence corresponds to the observations of the HMM. The sentence "Open the pod bay doors, HAL," for example, has six observed words.

- The hidden states are the parts of speech: verb, noun, adjective, and so on. The observed word *open* in the preceding example should correspond to the hidden state *verb*.

- The transition probabilities can be designed by the programmer or obtained through data. These probabilities represent the rules of the parts of speech. The probability that two verbs will occur one after another should be low, for example. By setting up a transition probability, you avoid having the algorithm brute-forcing all possibilities.

- The emitting probabilities of each word can be obtained from data. A traditional part-of-speech tagging dataset is called Moby; you can find it at www.gutenberg.org/ebooks/3203.

NOTE You now have what it takes to design your own experiments with HMMs. These models are powerful tools, and I urge you to try them on your own data. Predefine some transitions and emissions, and see whether you can recover hidden states. I hope that this chapter can get you started.

Summary

- A complicated, entangled system can be simplified with a Markov model.
- HMMs are particularly useful in real-world applications because most observations are measurements of hidden states.
- The forward and Viterbi algorithms are among the most common algorithms used on HMMs.

Part-of-speech tagging and word-sense disambiguation

This chapter covers

- Disambiguating language by predicting nouns, verbs, and adjectives from past data
- Making decisions and explaining them using hidden Markov models (HMMs)
- Using TensorFlow to model explainable problems and collect evidence
- Computing HMM initial, transition, and emission probabilities from existing data
- Creating a part-of-speech (PoS) tagger from your own data and larger corpora

You use language every day to communicate with others, and if you are like me, sometimes you scratch your head, especially if you are using the English language. English is known to have a ton of *exceptions* that make it difficult to teach non-native speakers, along with your little ones who are growing up trying to learn it themselves.

Context matters. Conversationally, you can use tools such as hand motions, facial expressions, and long pauses to convey additional context or meaning, but when you are reading language as written text, much of that context is missing, and there is a lot of ambiguity. *Parts of speech* (PoS) can help fill that missing context to disambiguate words and make sense of them in text. PoS tells you whether the word is being used is an action word (verb), whether it refers to an object (noun), whether it describes a noun (adjective), and so on.

Consider the two sentences in figure 10.1. In the first sentence—"I am hoping to engineer a future Mars rover vehicle!"—someone says they want to help engineer (build) the next Mars rover. The person who said it in real life was most definitely not interested in anything other than Mars and planetary science. The second sentence— "I love being an engineer and working at NASA JPL on Earth Science!"—uttered by a different person, is about enjoying working at the Jet Propulsion Laboratory, part of the National Aeronautics and Space Administration (NASA), where I work. The second sentence was said by someone who enjoys being an engineer at NASA working on earth-science projects.

I am hoping to engineer a future Mars rover vehicle!

I love being an engineer and working at NASA JPL on earth science!

Figure 10.1 Two sentences that require disambiguation

Here's the rub: both sentences use the word *engineer* in different ways. The first sentence uses *engineer* as a verb—an action—and the second sentence uses *engineer* as a noun to refer to his role. Verbs and nouns are different PoS in the English language, and deciding between a noun or a verb is not unique to English; PoS exist in many languages and delineate meaning among the words and characters in the text. But as you can see, the problem is that words and their (sense of) meaning—*word sense*, for short—frequently require disambiguation to provide the contextual cues you normally understood through spoken conversation or visual cues. Remember that when you are reading text, you don't have the benefit of hearing the inflection of someone's voice. You don't see visual cues to decide whether the person is saying that they want to build something that goes to Mars (using hand motions like hammering) or whether they're saying that enjoy working on earth-science projects (using hand motions to refer to the world around them).

The good news is that language scholars have long studied PoS across the humanities, mainly by reading literature and producing helpful guidance and rules that convey the particular PoS class a word can take on. Over the years, these scholars have examined many texts and recorded what they saw. One example of these efforts is Project Gutenberg (http://mng.bz/5pBB), which contains more than 200,000 words and dozens of PoS classes that those words could take on across a variety of written texts in the English language. You can think of the Gutenberg corpora as being a table of 200,000 English words; each word is a row and serves as the primary key, and the column values are the different PoS classes the word could take on (such as adjective or noun).

Try applying Gutenberg to the engineer sentences in figure 10.1, and the ambiguity will pop out at you. I've annotated the sentences with the PoS tag from Gutenberg for illustration (omitting the earth-science part from the first sentence for brevity):

```
I<Noun/> love<Adverb/> being<Verb/> an engineer<Noun/><Verb/>
and<Conjunction/> working at<Preposition/> NASA<Noun/> JPL<Noun/>.
I<Noun/> am<Adverb/> hoping<Verb/> to engineer<Noun/><Verb/> a future
Mars<Noun/> rover<Noun/> vehicle<Noun/>.
```

As you can clearly see, Gutenberg has told us that *engineer* can be either a noun or a verb. How can you look at the text and figure out automatically, using the surrounding context or by reading lots of similar text, what PoS class a particular word is with confidence, rather than guessing?

Machine learning and probabilistic models such as hidden Markov models (HMMs), which you learned about in chapter 9, can help you fill in some of that context by modeling the process of PoS tagging as an HMM problem. As an extremely early sketch, the *initial probabilities* are the probabilities that a particular PoS class will occur based on studying a set of input sentences. The *transition probabilities* are the probabilities of seeing a particular PoS class occur after another or set of classes in a particular order. Finally, the *emission or observable properties* are the probabilities of an ambiguous class like `Noun/Verb` being a noun or `Noun/Verb` being a verb, based on all other sentences your program has seen.

The great news is that all your code from chapter 9 is reusable here. The grand effort you spend in this chapter will prepare the data for machine learning, compute the model, and set up TensorFlow to do its thing! Let's get started. Before we jump into PoS tagging, though, I'll quickly review what the HMM is doing, using the Rainy or Sunny example from chapter 9. Follow me!

10.1 Review of HMM example: Rainy or Sunny

The Rainy/Sunny example from chapter 9 uses HMMs to model the hidden states of the weather if you could only ever observe indirect activities such as walking, shopping, or cleaning. To model the code as an HMM, you need the initial probabilities of the weather's being rainy or sunny—a 2×1 matrix. You need the transition probabilities of the weather's being rainy and then it being sunny (and vice versa)—a 2×2 matrix. And

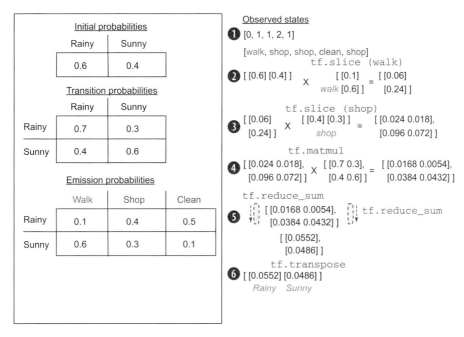

Figure 10.2 The left side is the HMM construction of the Rainy/Sunny example. The right side demonstrates how TensorFlow and our HMM class take in a set of observed states and accumulate the probabilities of those observed states occurring.

you need the probabilities of seeing the indirect actions, or emission probabilities, of walking, shopping, or cleaning for each of the hidden states Rainy and Sunny—a 3×2 matrix. The left side of figure 10.2 shows the construction of this problem.

Also in chapter 9, I showed you how to create an HMM class in Python and Tensor-Flow to represent the initialization of the initial, transition, and emission probabilities and then run the forward model to compute the overall probability of a sequence of events occurring (such as walk, shop, shop, clean) and then the next event as shop. This computation is shown on the right side of figure 10.2. TensorFlow operations shine in the development of the HMM class, in particular TensorFlow's lazy evaluation and graph construction process. Here's how:

- The HMM class acts as a proxy for constructing a graph of `tf.slice` operations that pull out specific emission probabilities based on the observation provided and `tf.matmul` operations that accumulate the forward model probabilities (steps 1–2, 2–3, and 3–4 from figure 10.2).
- The algorithm begins with initial probabilities and multiplies them by the emission probabilities based on the first observation index for the walk event on the right side of figure 10.2 (step 2).
- Next, the algorithm accumulates the forward model probabilities and prepares to iterate through the remaining observations (steps 4–6 in figure 10.2).

For each observation, the HMM class runs the forward model to execute the following steps repeatedly:

1. Use `tf.slice` to slice out the particular emission probability set for Rainy or Sunny based on the observation index and multiple those probabilities by the forward model (steps 1–3 in figure 10.2).

2. Accumulate (through matrix multiplication or `tf.matmul`) the forward model probabilities for each hidden state, based on multiplying the forward model by the transition probabilities (step 4 in figure 10.2).

3. Use `tf.reduce_sum` to accumulate for each choice, Rainy and Sunny, the agglomerative probability of being in those states based on the observations and `tf.transpose` to return the Rainy/Sunny matrix to the original forward model structure (steps 5–6 in figure 10.2).

Listing 10.1 creates the HMM class and then runs the forward model. This listing maps to the visual steps 1–6 (figure 10.2), and you can see the first iteration unfolding for rainy and sunny weather as a series of transformations on the right side of figure 10.2.

Listing 10.1 The HMM class and forward model

```
class HMM(object):
    def __init__(self, initial_prob, trans_prob, obs_prob):
        self.N = np.size(initial_prob)
        self.initial_prob = initial_prob
        self.trans_prob = trans_prob
        self.emission = tf.constant(obs_prob)
        assert self.initial_prob.shape == (self.N, 1)
        assert self.trans_prob.shape == (self.N, self.N)
        assert obs_prob.shape[0] == self.N
        self.obs_idx = tf.placeholder(tf.int32)
        self.fwd = tf.placeholder(tf.float64)

    def get_emission(self, obs_idx):
        slice_location = [0, obs_idx]
        num_rows = tf.shape(self.emission)[0]
        slice_shape = [num_rows, 1]
        return tf.slice(self.emission, slice_location, slice_shape)

    def forward_init_op(self):
        obs_prob = self.get_emission(self.obs_idx)
        fwd = tf.multiply(self.initial_prob, obs_prob)
        return fwd

    def forward_op(self):
        transitions = tf.matmul(self.fwd,
        tf.transpose(self.get_emission(self.obs_idx)))
        weighted_transitions = transitions * self.trans_prob
        fwd = tf.reduce_sum(weighted_transitions, 0)
        return tf.reshape(fwd, tf.shape(self.fwd))

def forward_algorithm(sess, hmm, observations):
```

Initializes the model with initial probabilities, emission probabilities, and transition probabilities

Uses tf.slice to extract the emission probabilities corresponding to the observation index

Runs the first forward operation on the first observation and accumulates forward model

Accumulates through multiplication the emission probabilities and transition probabilities for an observation

Runs the forward model on observation 2 and beyond, accumulating probabilities

```
fwd = sess.run(hmm.forward_init_op(),
 feed_dict={hmm.obs_idx:observations[0]})
for t in range(1, len(observations)):
    fwd = sess.run(hmm.forward_op(),
 feed_dict={hmm.obs_idx:observations[t], hmm.fwd: fwd})
prob = sess.run(tf.reduce_sum(fwd))
return prob
```

To use the forward model, you create the initial probabilities, transition probabilities, and emission probabilities and then feed them to the HMM class, as shown in listing 10.2. The output of the program is the accumulated probability of seeing those specific indirect observations (or emissions) in that particular order.

Listing 10.2   Running the HMM class with the Rainy/Sunny example

```
initial_prob = np.array([[0.6],[0.4]])    ⬅        Creates the initial NumPy arrays
trans_prob = np.array([[0.7, 0.3],                 representing initial, transition,
                       [0.4, 0.6]])                and emission probabilities
obs_prob = np.array([[0.1, 0.4, 0.5],
                     [0.6, 0.3, 0.1]])
hmm = HMM(initial_prob=initial_prob, trans_prob=trans_prob,
➡   obs_prob=obs_prob)
observations = [0, 1, 1, 2, 1]    ⬅        Walk, shop, shop, clean, and shop observations
with tf.Session() as sess:
    prob = forward_algorithm(sess, hmm, observations)
    print('Probability of observing {} is {}'.format(observations, prob))
```

Runs the forward model and prints the accumulated
probability of those events occurring

Recall from chapter 9 that the Viterbi algorithm is a simple specialization of the HMM model and class that keeps track of the transitions between states through back pointers and accumulates the probable transition between states, given a set of observations. Instead of providing the cumulative probability of a set of states occurring, the Viterbi algorithm provides the most probable hidden state for each indirect observed emission state. In other words, it provides the most probable state (Rainy or Sunny) for each indirect observation of walk, shop, shop, clean, and shop. You will make direct use the Viterbi algorithm later in the chapter because you will want to predict the PoS for a given ambiguity class. Specifically, you will want to know whether the PoS is a noun or a verb, if given an ambiguity class Noun/Verb.

Now that our HMM review is done, it's time to put together our initial ambiguous PoS tagger.

10.2   PoS tagging

PoS tagging can be generalized to the problem of taking input sentences and then trying to disambiguate the ambiguous parts of speech. The Moby project is one of the largest free phonetic databases and is mirrored as part of Project Gutenberg. The Moby effort contains the file mobypos.txt, which is a database of words in English and the PoSes they can take. The file (available at http://mng.bz/6Ado) needs to be parsed because it's a set of lines in which each line begins with the word that the database knows about and is followed by a set of tags (such as \A\N) that correspond to parts of speech—in this case adjective (\A) and noun (\N). The mapping of PoS tags to mobypos.txt annotations is shown in listing 10.3, and you will reuse this mapping in the remainder of the chapter. Words appear in mobypos.txt in the following form:

```
word\PoSTag1\PoSTag2
```

A concrete example follows:

```
abdominous\A
```

According to mobypos.txt, the English word *abdominous* has a single PoS use as an adjective.

Listing 10.3 PoS tag mapping for mobypos.txt

```
pos_tags = {                              ◁──── The PoS tags defined in Project
    "N" : "Noun",                               Gutenberg as part of mobypos.txt
    "p" : "Plural",
    "h" : "Noun Phrase",
    "V" : "Verb (usu participle)",
    "t" : "Verb (transitive)",
    "i" : "Verb (intransitive)",
    "A" : "Adjective",
    "v" : "Adverb",
    "C" : "Conjunction",
    "P" : "Preposition",
    "!" : "Interjection",
    "r" : "Pronoun",
    "D" : "Definite Article",
    "I" : "Indefinite Article",      ◁── The PoS
    "o" : "Nominative"                    tag keys

    }                           The PoS tag values
pos_headers = pos_tags.keys()            Add end-of-sentence tag
pt_vals = [*pos_tags.values()]   ◁───    because you will use it later for
pt_vals += ["sent"]    ◁──               computing initial probabilities.
```

You can find the full documentation on Project Gutenberg's PoS database below the heading Database Legend at http://mng.bz/oROd.

To get started disambiguating word sense with uing TensorFlow and HMMs, you are going to need some words. Luckily for you, I've got a set of thriving youngsters and a wife who are replete with sayings and phrases that beg for disambiguation. While compiling this book, I listened to some of the things they said and jotted down a few for your perusal. I hope that those of you who have preteen children should get a kick out of these:

- "There is tissue in the bathroom!"
- "What do you want it for?"
- "I really enjoy playing Fortnite, it's an amazing game!"
- "The tissue is coming out mommy, what should I use it for?"
- "We are really interested in the Keto diet, do you know the best way to start it?"

Now I'll show you how to start using Project Gutenberg and mobypos.txt to label the PoS. The first step is creating a function to parse the full mobypos.txt file and load it into a Python variable. Because parsing the file amounts to reading line by line, building a table of words and their PoS classes, the simple function in listing 10.4 does the trick. The function returns pos_words, which is the database of English words and their PoS classes along with pos_tag_counts—a summary of PoS tags and their overall occurrences.

Listing 10.4   Parsing the mobypos.txt file into a PoS database

```
import tqdm

def parse_pos_file(pos_file):
    with open(pos_file, 'r') as pf:
        ftext = pf.readlines()          ▷ Reads mobypos.txt line by line
        for line in tqdm(ftext):        ◁── Uses TQDM to print progress while parsing each line
            l_split = line.split('\\')  ◁── Splits the line by the word and its remaining classes after the '\' symbol
            word = l_split[0]
            classes=[]
            u_classes = l_split[1].strip()
            for i in range(0, len(u_classes)):
                if not u_classes[i] in pos_tags:   ◁── Occasionally, there are PoS classes that you will want to ignore or are unknown, so skip them.
                    print("Unknown pos tag: "+u_classes[i]+" from line "+line)
                    continue
                classes.append(u_classes[i])
        pos_words[word] = classes       ▷ Joins the English word to its set of PoS classes
        for c in classes:
            if c in pos_tag_counts:
                cnt = pos_tag_counts[c]      ⎫
                cnt = cnt + 1                ⎬ Accumulates totals of PoS tags in the corpora
            else:                            ⎪
                cnt = 1                      ⎪
            pos_tag_counts[c] = cnt          ⎭
```

When you execute the parse_pos_file function and obtain pos_words and pos_tag_counts, you can analyze the distribution of PoS tags across the project Gutenberg corpora to see whether anything jumps out at you. In particular, you see a few frequently occurring PoS tags and many that do not occur frequently and likely will not appear when you're tagging sentence text. The simple Matplotlib listing in listing 10.5 reveals the PoS tag distribution (figure 10.3).

Listing 10.5   Distribution of PoS tags across Project Gutenberg

```
pos_lists = sorted(pos_tag_counts.items())     ◁——— Sorted by key, returns a list
plists = []
for i in range(0, len(pos_lists)):
    t = pos_lists[i]                                     Creates a list of
    plists.append((pos_tags[t[0]], t[1]))    ◁——┘       tuples of (tag, count)

x, y = zip(*plists)          ◁——┐
plt.xticks(rotation=90)          │  Unpacks a list of
plt.xlabel("PoS Tag")            │  pairs into two tuples
plt.ylabel("Count")
plt.title("Distribution of PoS tags in Gutenberg corpus")
plt.bar(x, y)
plt.show()          ◁——— Visualizes the plot
```

NOTE   Adjective, noun, noun phrase, verb (usu.—short for *usually*—participle), plural, verb (transitive) and adverb are the most frequently occurring PoS tags in the corpora.

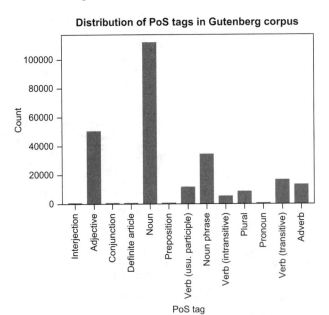

Figure 10.3   The distribution of PoS tags in the Project Gutenberg corpus

You may also wonder what percentage of English words have multiple PoS classes assigned to them, so that you can get a feel in general for what requires disambiguation, at least according to Project Gutenberg. Listing 10.6 provides an answer that may surprise you: about 6.5%.

Listing 10.6　Computing the percentage of English words with multiple PoS classes

```
                                      Divides words with more
Counts the number of words that       than one PoS class by the
have more than one PoS class          total number of words
pc_mc = 0                                                    Prints the resulting
for w in pos_words:                                                    percentage
    if len(pos_words[w]) > 1:
        pc_mc = pc_mc +1
pct = (pc_mc * 1.) / (len(pos_words.keys()) * 1.)
print("Percentage of words assigned to multiple classes: {:.0%}".format(pct))
```

It's important to note that of those 6.5% of words with multiple PoS classes assigned to them, many classes include the most frequently occurring words in the language. Overall, word-sense disambiguation is needed. You'll see soon how much it's needed. Before we get to that topic, though, I want you to see the big picture.

10.2.1　The big picture: Training and predicting PoS with HMMs

It's worth taking a step back to consider what the HMM and TensorFlow are providing to the PoS tagger. As I mentioned earlier, PoS tagging can be generalized to the problem of trying to disambiguate ambiguous parts of speech when the PoS tagger can't figure out whether a word should have a noun, verb, or other PoS tag.

Similar to the other machine-learning processes that you have encountered in this book, the process of creating an HMM to predict the unambiguous PoS tag involves a set of training steps. In those steps, you need to create a TensorFlow-based HMM model; in turn, you need a way of learning the initial probabilities, transition probabilities, and emission probabilities. You provide the HMM some text as input (such as a set of sentences). The first part of training involves running a PoS tagger that will tag the words in those sentences in an ambiguous way, as I showed you with Project Gutenberg earlier. After running the PoS tagger and obtaining annotated ambiguous text, you can ask for human feedback to disambiguate the output of the tagger. Doing so yields a training set of three parallel corpora of data that you can use to construct your HMM model:

- Input text such as sentences
- Annotated sentences with ambiguous PoS tags
- Annotated sentences with disambiguated PoS tags based on human feedback

Given those corpora, the HMM model probabilities can be computed as follows:

1 Construct a bigram matrix of transition counts.
2 Calculate the transition probabilities for each tag.
3 Compute the emission probabilities.

You construct a bigram matrix of transition counts per PoS tags or a matrix counting how many times the pairwise sets of PoS tags follow one another, and vice versa. The rows of the matrix are the list of PoS tags, and the columns are the list of PoS tags—hence the term *bigram* (a pair of consecutive units, words, or phrases). The table may look something like figure 10.4.

Matrix of transition counts							
	Second tag						
First tag	**verb**	**noun**	**det**	**prn**	**pr**	**adj**	**sent**
verb	0	1	1	0	2	1	0
noun	1	0	0	0	1	1	3
det	0	4	0	0	0	0	0
prn	0	0	0	0	0	0	0
pr	0	1	2	0	0	0	0
adj	0	0	0	0	0	0	2
sent	3	0	1	0	0	0	0

Figure 10.4   An example bigram matrix of transition counts for PoS

Then you take the counts of one PoS tag occurring after another and sum them. The transition probabilities are the cell values divided by the sum of the values in that particular row. Then, for the initial probabilities, you take the computed transition probabilities in the row corresponding to the end-of-sentence tag (sent) in figure 10.4. That row of probabilities is the perfect set of initial probabilities because the probability of a PoS tag occurring in that row is the probability of it occurring at the beginning of a sentence or after the end-of-sentence tag, such as the final row highlighted in figure 10.5.

Finally, you compute the emission probabilities by computing the ratio of ambiguous PoS tags and their count of occurrences in the ambiguous corpus to the user-provided tags in the disambiguated corpus. If, in the user-provided disambiguated corpus, a word

Matrix of transition probabilities (A)							
	Second tag (γ_j)						
First tag (γ_i)	**verb**	**noun**	**det**	**prn**	**pr**	**adj**	**sent**
verb	0	0.2	0.2	0	0.4	0.2	0
noun	0.16	0	0	0	0.16	0.16	0.5
det	0	1	0	0	0	0	0
prn	0	0	0	0	0	0	0
pr	0	0.3	0.6	0	0	0	0
adj	0	0	0	0	0	0	1
sent[3]	0.75	0	0.25	0	0	0	0

Figure 10.5   The initial probabilities are those computed transition probabilities for PoS tags in the end-of-sentence/beginning-of-sentence tag (sent).

should be tagged as a verb seven times, and the PoS ambiguous corpus tagged it as Noun/Verb three times, `Adjective` two times, and `Noun` two times, the emission probability of `Noun/Verb` if the hidden state is truly `Noun` is 3 divided by 7 or 43%, and so on.

Given this construction, you can build your initial, transition, and emission matrices and then run your HMM, using the TensorFlow code in listing 10.1 and the Viterbi algorithm, which can tell you the actual hidden states given observed states. In this case, the hidden states are the true PoS tags, and the observed tags are the ambiguity-class PoS tags. Figure 10.6 summarizes this discussion and pinpoints how TensorFlow and HMMs can help you disambiguate text.

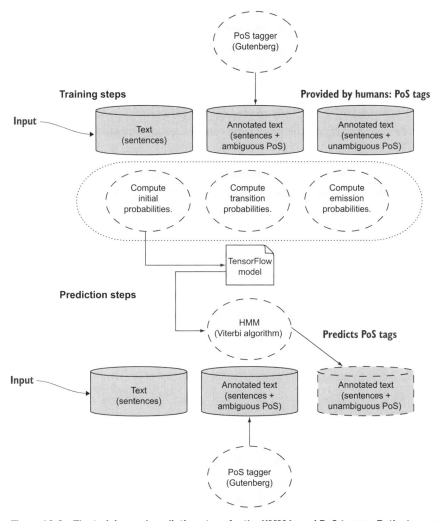

Figure 10.6   The training and prediction steps for the HMM-based PoS tagger. Both steps require input text (sentences), and the PoS tagger annotates them ambiguously. In the training portion, humans provide unambiguous PoS for the input sentences to train the HMM on. In the prediction stage, the HMM predicts the unambiguous PoS. The input text, annotated text with ambiguous PoS, and annotated text with disambiguated PoS form the three corpora needed to build an HMM.

Now that I've gone over the machine-learning problem setup, you can get your coding fingers ready to write the function to perform initial PoS tagging and generate the ambiguous corpora.

10.2.2 Generating the ambiguity PoS tagged dataset

In the field of natural language processing, the process of taking in text and then analyzing it for its PoS is called *morphological analysis.* If you consider the sentences that my children said earlier and then perform morphological analysis on them, you'll have the first two of three corpora needed to start PoS tagging. Remember that the output of the morphological analysis is the ambiguous PoS text.

To perform the analysis, you can use the Python Natural Language ToolKit (NLTK) library, which provides handy text analysis code for reuse. The `word_tokenize` function breaks a sentence into individual words. Then you can check each word against the `pos_words` dictionary you computed in listing 10.4. For each ambiguity, you get a word with multiple PoS tags, so you'll need to collect and output them as part of the input word. In listing 10.7, you'll create an `analyse` function that performs the morphological analysis step and returns the ambiguously tagged sentences.

Listing 10.7   Performing morphological analysis on input sentences

```
import nltk
from nltk.tokenize import word_tokenize        ◁——┐   Imports NLTK and tokenizes
                                                    │   the input sentence
def analyse(txt):                                   │
    words = word_tokenize(txt)        ◁────────────┘
    words_and_tags = []
    for i in range(0, len(words)):
        w = words[i]
        w_and_tag = w
        if w in pos_words:
            for c in pos_words[w]:
                w_and_tag = w_and_tag + "<" + pos_tags[c] + "/>"
        elif w in end_of_sent_punc:
            w_and_tag = w_and_tag + "<sent/>"        ◁──┐  If the word is the end-of-sentence
        words_and_tags.append(w_and_tag)                │  tag, add that special PoS.
    return " ".join(words_and_tags)        ◁──┐  Returns the analyzed words and
                                               │  their PoSes joined by whitespace
```

Iterates through each word points to `for i in range(0, len(words)):`

Creates a combined string of the word and its PoS tag points to `w_and_tag = w`

If the word is known to the PoS tags from Project Gutenberg, check its possible PoS.

Running the code in listing 10.7 produces a list of Python strings. You can run `analyse` on each of those strings to generate the first two parts of the parallel corpora. For the third part of the corpora, you need an expert to disambiguate the PoS tags for you and tell you the right answer. For a handful of sentences, it's almost trivial to identify whether the person was referring to the word as a noun or verb, or other PoS class. Because I collected the data for you, I also provided the disambiguated PoS tags that you can teach TensorFlow (in the `tagged_sample_sentences` list). Later, you will see that having more knowledge and tagged data helps, but for now, you'll be fine. Lo and behold, listing 10.8 combines the three parallel corpora and prepares them for you. Following the construction of the three corpora, you can use the Python Pandas library to create a dataframe, which in turn you will use to extract a NumPy array of probabilities. Then, after the probabilities are extracted, the code in listing 10.9 will help subset out the initial, transition, and emission probabilities for each corpus and store the results in a dataframe.

Listing 10.8   Creating the parallel corpora of sentences, analyzed and tagged

```
sample_sentences = [
    "There is tissue in the bathroom!",
    "What do you want it for?",
    "I really enjoy playing Fortnite, it's an amazing game!",
    "The tissue is coming out mommy, what should I use it for?",
    "We are really interested in the Keto diet, do you know the best way to
    start it?"
]

sample_sentences_a = [analyse(s) for s in sample_sentences]
tagged_sample_sentences = [
    "There is<Verb (usu participle)/> tissue<Noun/> in<Preposition/>
    the<Definite Article/> bathroom<Noun/> !<sent/>",
    "What do<Verb (transitive)/> you<Pronoun/> want<Verb (transitive)/>
    it<Noun/> for<Preposition/> ?<sent/>",
    "I<Pronoun/> really<Adverb/> enjoy<Verb (transitive)/> playing Fortnite ,
    it<Pronoun/> 's an<Definite Article/> amazing<Adjective/> game<Noun/>
    !<sent/>",
    "The tissue<Noun/> is<Verb (usu participle)/> coming<Adjective/>
    out<Adverb/> mommy<Noun/> , what<Definite Article/> should<Verb (usu
    participle)/> I<Pronoun/> use<Verb (usu participle)/> it<Pronoun/>
    for<Preposition/> ?<sent/>",
    "We are<Verb (usu participle)/> really<Adverb/> interested<Adjective/>
    in<Preposition/> the<Definite Article/> Keto diet<Noun/> , do<Verb (usu
    participle)/> you<Pronoun/> know<Verb (usu participle)/> the<Definite
    Article/> best<Adjective/> way<Noun/> to<Preposition/> start<Verb (usu
    participle)/> it<Pronoun/> ?<sent/>"
]
```

The input sentences I collected → (points to `sample_sentences`)

Runs analyse on the sentences and stores the analyzed data in a list → (points to `sample_sentences_a`)

The disambiguated PoS tags I provided

Listing 10.9   Building a Pandas dataframe of the parallel corpora

```
import pandas as pd
def build_pos_df(untagged, analyzed, tagged):
    pos_df = pd.DataFrame(columns=['Untagged', 'Analyzed', 'Tagged'])
    for i in range(0, len(untagged)):
        pos_df = pos_df.append({"Untagged":untagged[i],
     "Analyzed":analyzed[i], "Tagged": tagged[i]}, ignore_index=True)

    return pos_df

pos_df = build_pos_df(sample_sentences, sample_sentences_a,
    tagged_sample_sentences)
```

Creates a function for building the dataframe → (points to `def build_pos_df`)

Iterates through each of the five sentences and adds each element from the three parallel corpora

Returns the dataframe

Using the Pandas dataframe construct allows you to call df.head and interactively inspect the sentences, their morphological analyzed tags, and human-provided tags in a Jupyter notebook to keep track of the data you are working with. You can easily slice out a column or row to work with; even better for your purposes, you can get a NumPy array back. You see an example of calling df.head in figure 10.7.

	Untagged	Analyzed	Tagged
0	There is tissue in the bathroom!	There is<Verb (usu participle)/> tissue<Noun/>...	There is<Verb (usu participle)/> tissue<Noun/>...
1	What do you want it for?	What do<Verb (usu participle)/><Verb (transiti...	What do<Verb (transitive)/> you<Pronoun/> want...
2	I really enjoy playing Fortnite, it's an amazi...	I<Pronoun/> really<Adverb/><Interjection/> enj...	I<Pronoun/> really<Adverb/> enjoy<Verb (transi...
3	The tissue is coming out mommy, what should I ...	The tissue<Noun/><Verb (transitive)/> is<Verb ...	The tissue<Noun/> is<Verb (usu participle)/> c...
4	We are really interested in the Keto diet, do ...	We are<Verb (usu participle)/><Noun/> really<A...	We are<Verb (usu participle)/> really<Adverb/>...

Figure 10.7 **Easily view your three parallel corpora with Pandas: the untagged original sentences, the (morphologically) analyzed ambiguous corpora, and the user-provided tagged corpora without ambiguity.**

Next, I'll show you how to process the dataframe and create the initial probabilities, transition probabilities, and emission probabilities. Then you will apply the HMM class to predict the disambiguated PoS classes.

10.3 *Algorithms for building the HMM for PoS disambiguation*

Computing the emission, transition, and initial probability matrices proves to be a fairly straightforward activity, given your Pandas dataframe. You can slice out a column (such as Analyzed in figure 10.7) corresponding to the morphologically analyzed sentences and then extract all the tags from them. As it turns out, taking the analyzed and tagged sentences and extracting out the PoS tags is a needed utility function. The function compute_tags in listing 10.10 enumerates all the sentences in one of your dataframe's analyzed or tagged columns and extracts the PoS tags positionally.

Listing 10.10 **Extracting tags from a sentence dataframe**

```
def compute_tags(df_col):
    all_tags = []                          ◁─── Initializes the list of tags to
                                                return—a list of tags in the order
    for row in df_col:                          in which they were encountered
        tags = []
        tag = None
        tag_list = None
                                                     Catches the end-of-tag value and decides
        for i in range(0, len(row)):                 whether there is another tag or whether
            if row[i] == "<":                                              to add this tag
                tag = ""
            elif i+1 < len(row) and row[i] == "/" and row[i+1] == ">":  ◁─
                if i+2 < len(row) and row[i+2] == "<":
                    if tag_list == None:                      If there are two
                        tag_list = []                         <Noun><Verb> tags
                                                              (ambiguous), add both tags.
                    tag_list.append(tag)
```

Enumerates the sentences in the dataframe and for each sentence, enumerates its characters

```
                          tag = None
Catches the        ┌──▷ else:
end-of-tag value and   │     if tag_list != None and len(tag_list) > 0:
decides whether there  │         tag_list.append(tag)
is another tag or      │         tags.append(tag_list)
whether to add this tag│         tag_list = None
                       │         tag = None
                             else:
                                 tags.append(tag)
                                 tag = None


             else:
                 if tag != None:          │ Collects the
                     tag = tag + row[i]   │ tag value
         all_tags.append(tags)
         tags = None
         tag = None
         tag_list = None


     return all_tags
                                           │ Extracts the analyzed tags
                                           │ (a_all_tags), and human-tagged tags
 a_all_tags = compute_tags(pos_df['Analyzed']) │ (t_all_tags) for all parallel sentences
 t_all_tags = compute_tags(pos_df['Tagged'])
```

Armed with `compute_tags` and the extracted analyzed tags (`a_all_tags`) and extracted human-tagged tags (`t_all_tags`), you are ready to begin computing the transition probability matrix. You will use `t_all_tags` to build a matrix of bigram PoS sentence occurrence counts, as shown in figure 10.4. Pandas can help you construct such an occurrence matrix. You already have a set of the valid PoS tags from Project Gutenberg (listing 10.3): the `pt_vals` variable. If you were to print the values from that variable, you'd see something like this:

```
print([*pt_vals])
['Noun',
 'Plural',
 'Noun Phrase',
 'Verb (usu participle)',
 'Verb (transitive)',
 'Verb (intransitive)',
 'Adjective',
 'Adverb',
 'Conjunction',
 'Preposition',
 'Interjection',
 'Pronoun',
 'Definite Article',
 'Indefinite Article',
 'Nominative',
 'sent']
```

Your matrix of PoS tag occurrence counts is a bigram matrix in which the columns are a tag. The column `FirstPOS`, followed by PoS tags from `pt_vals`, makes up the columns, and the rows are the same values as shown in figure 10.4. If you make the dataframe indexed by the value of FirstPoS, you can easily use the PoS tag as a key for slicing the dataframe, such as dividing a column by its summed values. Listing 10.11 builds the uninitialized (all cells' value 0) transition probability matrix.

Listing 10.11   Computing the transition probability matrix

```
def build_trans(pt_vals):
    trans_df = pd.DataFrame(columns=["FirstPoS"] + pt_vals)
    trans_df.set_index('FirstPoS')
    for i in range(0, len(pt_vals)):
        pt_data = {}
        pt_data["FirstPoS"] = pt_vals[i]
        for j in range(0, len(pt_vals)):
            pt = pt_vals[j]
            pt_data[pt] = 0
        trans_df = trans_df.append(pt_data, ignore_index=True)
    return trans_df
```

Constructs the dataframe with column FirstPoS representing the first PoS tag of the two

Creates the dataframe index on PoS tag

Returns the transition probability matrix dataframe

Initializes the count to zero

When you have the uninitialized dataframe, you need to count the occurrence of PoS tags in your tagged sentence corpora. Luckily for you, this data was captured in t_all_tags, which you computed in listing 10.10. A simple algorithm can capture the counts of the PoS tags for the transition count matrix from the tagged corpus. You need to iterate for all sentences the captured PoS tags, capture the tags that are co-occurring, and then sum their occurrences. The two special cases are the beginning of the sentences after the first sentence (preceded by as end-of-sentence tag) and the final sentence (which ends with a sent PoS tag). Because the dataframe is a pass by reference, you can update its count values (the cnt variable at the specified array [row_idx, col_idx]) to fill the cell counts. The function compute_trans_matrix in listing 10.12 does the heavy lifting for you.

Listing 10.12   Counting the occurrence of PoS tags in the tagged corpus

Iterates each sentence in the PoS tagged corpus dataframe

```
def compute_trans_matrix(t_df, tags):
    for j in range(0, len(pos_df['Tagged'])):
        s = pos_df['Tagged'][j]
        tt_idx = []
        for i in range(0, len(tags[j])):
            tt_idx.append(tags[j][i])
            if j > 0 and i == 0:
                row_idx = "sent"
                col_idx = tags[j][i]
                cnt = t_df.loc[t_df.FirstPoS==row_idx, col_idx]
                cnt = cnt + 1
                t_df.loc[t_df.FirstPoS==row_idx, col_idx] = cnt
```

Initializes the row, column index (tt_idx) to a blank list. The column index will have only two PoS tags.

Iterates the tags for this sentence from the tagged corpus

For any sentence after the first and the first tag, the first element is always the end-of-sentence tag from the preceding sentence.

Adds the first element of the row, column index as the current PoS tag for the sentence

Increments count at row index and column index

```
         ┌─▷ if len(tt_idx) == 2:
         │        row_idx = tt_idx[0]
         │        col_idx = tt_idx[1]
         │        cnt = t_df.loc[t_df.FirstPoS==row_idx, col_idx]
         └─▷     cnt = cnt + 1
                 t_df.loc[t_df.FirstPoS==row_idx, col_idx] = cnt
                 tt_idx.clear()
            elif len(tt_idx) == 1 and tags[j][i] == "sent":    ◁────────────┐
                 row_idx = tags[j][i-1]
                 col_idx = tags[j][i]
                 cnt = t_df.loc[t_df.FirstPoS==row_idx, col_idx]
                 cnt = cnt + 1
                 t_df.loc[t_df.FirstPoS==row_idx, col_idx] = cnt
                 tt_idx.clear()
```

If we have two elements for row, column index, we are ready to increment the count there.

If we've reached the end-of-sentence PoS tag for the column, we grab the preceding tag for our row index and increment the count.

When you have the counts of the co-occurring PoS tags in the matrix, you need to do a little bit of postprocessing to turn them into probabilities. You sum the counts for each row in the PoS bigram count matrix and then divide each cell count in that row by the sum. This process computes the transition probabilities and the initial probabilities. Because quite a few steps are involved, I captured the key parts in figure 10.8, which is a handy reference for looking at listing 10.13.

Listing 10.13 Postprocessing the transition probability matrix

Computes the initial zero count transition probability matrix

Drops the FirstPoS column as it is not needed (corresponds to figure 10.8 step 3)

Adds the sum column—figure 10.8 step 2—and sums counts horizontally for each row

```
compute_trans_matrix(trans_df, t_all_tags)
    just_trans_df = trans_df.drop(columns='FirstPoS')    ◁
    just_trans_df['sum'] = just_trans_df.sum(axis=1)    ◁
    just_trans_df.loc[just_trans_df['sum']==0., 'sum'] = .001
    trans_prob_df = just_trans_df.loc[:,"Noun":"sent"].div(just_trans_df['sum'],
    ⟱  axis=0)    ◁
```

Avoid divide by zero if there are zero counts and divide by a really small number instead.

Create a new dataframe without the sum column and perform the division in place for each cell for all valid PoS tags between Noun and sent by the values in the sum column.

Phew! That was a lot of work. Now you will work on the emission probabilities. Aside from a couple of more algorithms, the process is fairly straightforward, and it's the last thing that you need to do before running the HMM.

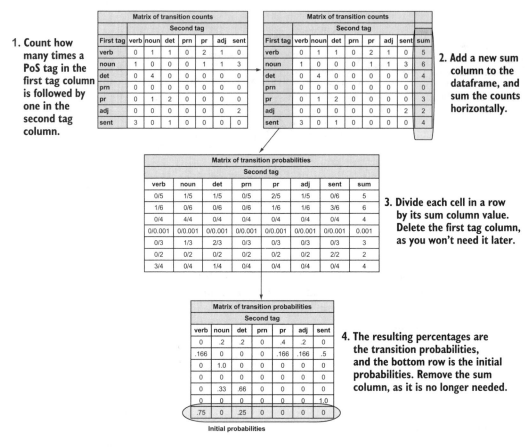

Figure 10.8   The operational steps 1–4 to compute on your Pandas dataframe and turn transition counts into transition probabilities and initial probabilities

10.3.1   *Generating the emission probabilities*

You can generate the emission probabilities by creating a bigram matrix of emission probabilities from construction, similar to the one you created in section 10.3. The major difference is that instead of listing only the valid PoS tags for each row, you also list the *ambiguity* classes—classes such as Noun/Verb, Noun/Adjective/Verb, and Verb/Adverb. See, the whole point of the HMM is to deal with ambiguity. You can't observe the hidden state of Noun or Verb directly, so instead you observe the ambiguous class with some emission probability, which you can learn from construction. The matrix of emission probability counts is constructed as follows:

The rows are the ambiguity classes followed by the valid PoS tags from the tagged corpus. These rows are the emission variables that you observe instead of the hidden states. The columns are the valid PoS tags from the tagged corpus, corresponding to what the hidden unambiguous PoS class would be if you could observe it directly.

The cell values for first and second tag are the number of times that an ambiguity class was seen (for the first tag) in the morphological analyzed sentence corpus divided by the total number of times the actual PoS tag appeared in the tagged corpus.

So if `Noun/Verb` appeared four times in the morphologically analyzed corpus and was definitively tagged as `Verb` in the tagged corpus, you take the total number of times `Verb` appeared in the tagged corpus, such as six, and you get 4/6, or .66. Of the six times that a PoS tag was a `Verb` in the tagged corpus, four times the PoS tagger ambiguously thought that the word was a `Noun/Verb` during morphological analysis.

The remainder of the ambiguity classes can be computed the same way. You'll whip up a `build_emission` function in listing 10.14 to create the initial emission matrix with placeholders of 0; then, as before, you'll create a function to process the analyzed and tagged corpora and fill in the emission probabilities.

Listing 10.14 Constructing the initial emission count matrix

Adds the First part of speech (PoS) index for the data frame and the columnar values corresponding to the tagged corpus valid PoS

```
def build_emission(pt_vals, a_all_tags):
    emission_df = pd.DataFrame(columns=["FirstPoS"] + pt_vals)
    emission_df.set_index('FirstPoS')

    amb_classes = {}
    for r in a_all_tags:
        for t in r:
            if type(t) == list:
                am_class = str(t)
                if not am_class in amb_classes:
                    amb_classes[am_class] = "yes"

    amb_classes_k = sorted(amb_classes.keys())

    for ambck in amb_classes_k:
        em_data = {}
        em_data["FirstPoS"] = ambck
        for j in range(0, len(pt_vals)):
            em = pt_vals[j]
            em_data[em] = 0
        emission_df = emission_df.append(em_data, ignore_index=True)

    for i in range(0, len(pt_vals)):
        em_data = {}
        em_data["FirstPoS"] = pt_vals[i]
        for j in range(0, len(pt_vals)):
            em = pt_vals[j]
            em_data[em] = 0
        emission_df = emission_df.append(em_data, ignore_index=True)

    return (emission_df, amb_classes_k)
```

After extracting all tags, collect them as keys in a dictionary.

Sorts the collected ambiguity classes, which are the keys in the dictionary amb_classes

Adds the ambiguity classes as the rows in the emission probability matrix

Adds the remaining PoS classes as rows, though you will flag a 1 because you need only the ambiguity classes

Given the output of `build_emission`, which is the `emission_df` or emission dataframe, along with the identified ambiguity classes, you can perform the simple algorithm discussed earlier to fill the emission probability matrix that you see in listing 10.15 as a start. To recap, you will compute the times that a tag in the tagged corpus—such as `Verb`—had ambiguity in the morphological analyzed corpora and identified the PoS tag as `Noun/Verb` because the model was unsure. The ratio of the amount of times that happens, given all the occurrences of `Verb` in the tagged corpus, is the emission probability to see the ambiguity class `Noun/Verb`. Listing 10.15 creates the initial counts in the matrix of PoS ambiguity classes.

Listing 10.15   Constructing the emission count matrix

```
def compute_emission(e_df, t_tags, a_tags):
    for j in range(0, len(t_tags)):
        for i in range(0, len(t_tags[j])):
            a_tag = a_tags[j][i]        ◄─── The analyzed
            t_tag = t_tags[j][i]             ambiguous PoS tag

            if type(a_tag) == list:    The ambiguity classes will be of type list because
                a_tag_str = str(a_tag)   there will be multiple possible tags for them.
                row_idx = a_tag_str      Convert to a string, and use it to index the
                col_idx = t_tag             row_idx/col_idx to update its count.
                cnt = e_df.loc[e_df.FirstPoS==row_idx, col_idx]
                cnt = cnt + 1
                e_df.loc[e_df.FirstPoS==row_idx, col_idx] = cnt
            else:
                if a_tag != t_tag:
                    continue       ◄─── Should never happen; tags don't
                else:                   agree from analyzed and tagged
                    row_idx = a_tag       corpora.
                    col_idx = t_tag
                    cnt = e_df.loc[e_df.FirstPoS==row_idx, col_idx]
                    if (cnt < 1).bool():
                        cnt = cnt + 1
                        e_df.loc[e_df.FirstPoS==row_idx, col_idx] = cnt
                    else:
                        continue
```

The human-tagged corpora PoS tag (annotation pointing to `t_tag = t_tags[j][i]`)

Update the count of ambiguous PoS class to 1 only one time; otherwise, skip updating it. (annotation pointing to `continue`)

To convert the emission count matrix to the emission probability matrix, you again do some minimal postprocessing. Because you need to figure out the total count of tags in the tagged corpora, it makes sense to write a helper function to compute it and save the result as a dictionary of `tag name:count`. The `count_tagged` function in listing 10.16 performs this task. The function is generic and can count from either the tagged corpora or the analyzed corpora (which will be useful later).

Listing 10.16   Computing the count of tags in the tagged corpora

```
def count_tagged(tags):
    tag_counts = {}
    cnt = 0
```

```
                    for i in range(0, len(tags)):
                        row = tags[i]
                        for t in row:
                            if type(t) == list:
                                for tt in t:
                                    if tt in tag_counts:
                                        cnt = tag_counts[tt]
                                        cnt = cnt + 1
                                        tag_counts[tt] = cnt
                                    else:
                                        tag_counts[tt] = 1
                            else:
                                if t in tag_counts:
                                    cnt = tag_counts[t]
                                    cnt = cnt + 1
                                    tag_counts[t] = cnt
                                else:
                                    tag_counts[t] = 1
                    return tag_counts
```

Gets all the tags for a sentence → `row = tags[i]`

Iterates the tags, if a list; then it's an ambiguity class and captures its subtag counts

Otherwise, sums the counts → `else:`

After one other bit of postprocessing, you can finish computing the emission probabilities in the dataframe. This processing (listing 10.17) performs the divide step in each cell with the computed tag counts.

Listing 10.17   Dividing each emission ambiguity class count by the tagged corpora tag count

```
def emission_div_by_tag_counts(emission_df, amb_classes_k, tag_counts):
    for pt in pt_vals:
        for ambck in amb_classes_k:
            row_idx = str(ambck)
            col_idx = pt

            if pt in tag_counts:
                tcnt = tag_counts[pt]
                if tcnt > 0:
                    emission_df.loc[emission_df.FirstPoS==row_idx, col_idx] =
                    ➥ emission_df.loc[emission_df.FirstPoS==row_idx,
                    ➥ col_idx] / tcnt
```

Collects the row index (the ambiguity class) and the column index (the PoS tag)

Grabs the count of the particular PoS tag

Divides the count of the ambiguity class by the PoS-tagged corpora tag count

Now you are ready to compute the emission probabilities dataframe fully. The process is fairly trivial at this point; you chain your processing steps, as shown in listing 10.18. Build the initial zero'ed emission dataframe with PoS tags from the tagged corpus as columns and ambiguity classes as rows from the analyzed corpus. Then you count the occurrence of ambiguity classes compared with the tagged corpora analog, and compute the ratio of those counts to the total number of times the unambiguous PoS class appeared in the tagged corpora. The code is shown in listing 10.18.

Listing 10.18   Computing the emission probability dataframe

Builds the zero'ed-out
emission count dataframe

Computes
the counts
of ambiguity
classes

```
(emission_df, amb_classes_k) = build_emission(pt_vals, a_all_tags)
compute_emission(emission_df, t_all_tags, a_all_tags)
tag_counts = count_tagged(t_all_tags)
emission_div_by_tag_counts(emission_df, amb_classes_k, tag_counts)
just_emission_df = emission_df.drop(columns='FirstPoS')
```

Computes the total counts of
PoS tags in the tagged corpora

Drops the FirstPoS
index column

Divides the ambiguity
class counts by
unambiguous PoS class
total count and removes
the sum column

Now that you have all three probabilities computed, you can finally run the HMM! I'll show you how in section 10.4.

10.4   *Running the HMM and evaluating its output*

You've written all the necessary code (which turned out to be quite a bit) to prepare your three parallel corpora and to use those corpora as training input for your HMM in TensorFlow. It's time to see the fruits of your labor. Recall that you have two Pandas dataframes at this point: just_trans_df, and just_emission_df. The row in just_trans_df corresponding to the sentence (sent) tag is the initial probabilities, as already mentioned, so you have all three pieces of data for your HMM model.

But as you remember, you need NumPy arrays for TensorFlow to work its magic. The good news is that these arrays are crazy simple to get out of Pandas dataframes with the handy helper function .values, which returns a NumPy array of values for the matrix inside. Coupled with the .astype('float64') function, you have an easy way to grab all three of the NumPy arrays you need. The code in listing 10.19 handles this task for you. The only tricky part is transposing the values from the emission probabilities to ensure that it is indexed by PoS tag and not ambiguity class. (In short, you flip the rows and columns.)

Listing 10.19   Getting the NumPy arrays for your HMM

Gets the sent row values and
returns a NumPy array (16, 1)

Gets the transition
probabilities as a
(16, 16) NumPy
array

```
initial_prob = trans_prob_df.loc[15].values.astype('float64')
initial_prob = initial_prob.reshape((len(initial_prob), 1))
trans_prob = trans_prob_df.values.astype('float64')
obs_prob = just_emission_df.T.values.astype('float64')
```

Gets the emission probabilities by transposing the (36, 16) array of
PoS ambiguity classes into a (16, 36) array indexed by PoS class

The code in listing 10.19 gives you three NumPy arrays of size (16, 1), (16, 16), and (16, 36) for initial probabilities, transition probabilities, and emission probabilities, respectively. With these arrays, you can use your TensorFlow HMM class and run the Viterbi algorithm to reveal the hidden states, which are the actual PoS tags, given the ambiguities.

One helper function you need to write is a simple way to convent a sentence to its PoS ambiguity class observations. You can use the original emission dataframe you made to look up the index of a particular observed PoS tag/ambiguity class from the morphologically analyzed corpus and then collect those indexes in a list. You also need the reverse function that converts predicted indices to their corresponding PoS tag. Listing 10.20 handles these tasks for you.

Listing 10.20 Converting a sentence to its PoS ambiguity class observations

```
def sent_to_obs(emission_df, pos_df, a_all_tags, sent_num):
    obs = []
    sent = pos_df['Untagged'][sent_num]        Gets the sentence and its
    tags = a_all_tags[sent_num]                PoS tags/ambiguity classes
    for t in tags:
        idx = str(t)
        obs.append(int(emission_df.loc[emission_df.FirstPoS==idx].index[0]))
    return obs                                                   Gets the index of
                                                                 observation from the
def seq_to_pos(seq):     ◁──┐ Takes a predicted set of PoS       emission dataframe
    tags = []                 indices and returns the PoS
    for s in seq:             tag name
        tags.append(pt_vals[s])  Computes the PoS tag names
                                 and returns them as a list for
    return tags                  all predicted observations
```

Now you can get your HMM and run it on a random sentence from the initial five that I curated for you. I picked sentence index 3, shown in its ambiguous analyzed form first and in its tagged disambiguated form second:

```
The tissue<Noun/><Verb (transitive)/> is<Verb (usu participle)/>
coming<Adjective/><Noun/>
out<Adverb/><Preposition/><Interjection/><Noun/><Verb (transitive)/><Verb
(intransitive)/> mommy<Noun/> , what<Definite
Article/><Adverb/><Pronoun/><Interjection/> should<Verb (usu participle)/>
I<Pronoun/> use<Verb (usu participle)/><Verb (transitive)/><Noun/>
it<Pronoun/><Noun/> for<Preposition/><Conjunction/> ?<sent/>
The tissue<Noun/> is<Verb (usu participle)/> coming<Adjective/> out<Adverb/>
mommy<Noun/> , what<Definite Article/> should<Verb (usu participle)/>
I<Pronoun/> use<Verb (usu participle)/> it<Pronoun/> for<Preposition/>
?<sent/>
```

Without further ado, you can run your TensorFlow HMM class. Give it a try in listing 10.21.

Listing 10.21   Running the HMM on your parallel corpora

The index of the third sentence in the morphologically analyzed parallel corpora

Converts the sentence's PoS ambiguity classes to observation indices from the emission matrix, or [9, 23, 1, 3, 20, 4, 23, 31, 18, 14, 13, 35]

```
sent_index = 3
observations = sent_to_obs(emission_df, pos_df, a_all_tags, sent_index)

hmm = HMM(initial_prob=initial_prob, trans_prob=trans_prob, obs_prob=obs_prob)
with tf.Session() as sess:
    seq = viterbi_decode(sess, hmm, observations)
    print('Most likely hidden states are {}'.format(seq))
    print(seq_to_pos(seq))
```

Runs the Viterbi algorithm and predicts the most likely hidden states

Converts the predicted internal state indices to PoS tags

Initializes the TensorFlow HMM model with the computed initial, emission, and transition probabilities

When you run listing 10.21, you get some interesting results:

```
Most likely hidden states are [0, 3, 0, 0, 0, 0, 0, 0, 0, 0, 0, 0]
['Noun', 'Verb (usu participle)', 'Noun', 'Noun', 'Noun', 'Noun', 'Noun',
'Noun', 'Noun', 'Noun', 'Noun', 'Noun']
```

If you compare the predicted output, you see that the first two tags were predicted correctly, but after that, every other hidden state was predicted to be Noun, which is clearly wrong. Why did the code make those incorrect predictions? The answer boils down to lack of data and the algorithm's ability to make confident predictions. It's the age-old machine-learning issue: without enough data, the model isn't finely tuned. The model can make predictions but has not seen enough examples to delineate the necessary PoS tag classes properly. How can you address this problem?

One way would be to jot down a whole bunch more sentences and then go through each sentence with a PoS tagger like Gutenberg. Afterward, I could disambiguate the ambiguity classes myself.

Incentivizing data collection

The process of incentivizing collection of annotations has taken off in the past decade. Predicted by Tim Berners-Lee in his famous 2001 *Scientific American* article on the semantic web (https://www.scientificamerican.com/article/the-semantic-web), organizations have been trying to crowdsource valuable annotations from users forever. Berners-Lee thought that the benefit of having an intelligent agent handle your calendar, much as Siri does today, would be enough to get regular web users to write well-curated XML annotations for web pages, an expectation that failed miserably. Later, social media companies persuaded users to provide annotations for web content by giving them a cool service to keep in touch with their relatives, family members, and social connections. They overperformed and collected an amazing social corpus by providing the right incentive. In this case, as much as I love you guys, I didn't have the time to collect more than a handful of PoS annotations. Luckily for you, many other people have already done that. Read on to find out how to use their work.

This solution is possible, especially given the current times, when the little ones are around the house a great deal more often. But why invest human labor when there are plenty of other sources of tagged corpora? One such source is the Brown Corpus that's part of the PNLTK.

10.5 Getting more training data from the Brown Corpus

The Brown Corpus is the first million-word electronic corpus of English words collected from more than 500 sources of information, such as news and editorials, created in 1961 at Brown University. The corpus is organized by genre, annotated with PoS tags and other structures. You can read more about the corpus at https://www.nltk.org/book/ch02.html.

The Brown Corpus has various text articles, organized by genre or chapter, that contain annotated sentences. You can pull out 100 sentences and their corresponding PoS tags from chapter 7 of the corpus, for example (listing 10.22). One caveat is that not all corpora are tagged with the same PoS tag set. Instead of using the Project Gutenberg set of PoS tags—the 16 that you have seen thus far in this chapter—the Brown Corpus is tagged with the Universal tag set, a set of 14 PoS tags defined by Slav Petrov, Dipanjan Das, and Ryan McDonald in a 2011 paper (https://arxiv.org/abs/1104.2086). You see an example of the Universal tag set output classes, which instead of short codes and descriptions such as `"A"` : `"Adjective"`, as you see in Project Gutenberg, you get `"ADJ"` : `"Adjective"`. I've done the heavy lifting for you, though, mapping a subset of the overlap between the tag sets and recorded it in listing 10.23. In the future, you can decide to map more of the overlap, but the listing gives you an idea of the process.

> **Listing 10.22 Exploring PoS tags from 100 sentences in the Brown Corpus**

Imports the Brown Corpus and its PoS tags in the Universal tag set

```
import nltk
nltk.download('brown')
nltk.download('universal_tagset')
from nltk.corpus import brown

print(brown.tagged_sents('ch07', tagset='universal'))
print(len(brown.tagged_sents('ch07', tagset='universal')))
```

Prints the PoS tagged sentences from chapter 7 in the Brown Corpus to discern the format

Prints the number of sentences from chapter 7 (122)

The output from listing 10.22 is worth a look to get a feel for how the Brown Corpus is recorded, because you are going to process it and prepare it in a dataframe as you did for my small set of example sentences. The output is a set of lists; each list contains a tuple corresponding to the word and its associated PoS tag from the Universal tag set. Because these assignments are unambiguous, you can treat them as your user-provided tagged corpora from the set of three parallel corpora that you need to train the disambiguated PoS tagger. The mapping of the Universal tag set to the Gutenberg tags is provided in listing 10.23.

```
[[('Special', 'ADJ'), ('districts', 'NOUN'), ('in', 'ADP'), ('Rhode',
    'NOUN'), ('island', 'NOUN'), ('.', '.')], [('It', 'PRON'), ('is',
    'VERB'), ('not', 'ADV'), ('within', 'ADP'), ('the', 'DET'), ('scope',
    'NOUN'), ('of', 'ADP'), ('this', 'DET'), ('report', 'NOUN'), ('to',
    'PRT'), ('elaborate', 'VERB'), ('in', 'ADP'), ('any', 'DET'), ('great',
    'ADJ'), ('detail', 'NOUN'), ('upon', 'ADP'), ('special', 'ADJ'),
    ('districts', 'NOUN'), ('in', 'ADP'), ('Rhode', 'NOUN'), ('Island',
    'NOUN'), ('.', '.')], ...]
```

Listing 10.23 Mapping of Universal tag set to Project Gutenberg tag set

```
univ_tagset = {                          ◁——  The set of tag identifiers and
    "ADJ"     : "Adjective",                   full names for PoS tags from
    "ADP"     : "Adposition",                  the Universal tag set
    "ADV"     : "Adverb",
    "CONJ"    : "Conjunction",
    "DET"     : "Determiner",
    "NOUN"    : "Noun",
    "NUM"     : "Numeral",
    "PRT"     : "Particle",
    "PRON"    : "Pronoun",
    "VERB"    : "Verb",
    "."       : "Punctuation marks",
    "X"       : "Other"
}

univ_gutenberg_map = {   ◁——  The mapping of overlapping tags from Project
    "ADJ"   : "A",             Gutenberg to consider in the Universal tag set
    "ADV"   : "v",             keyed by the Universal tag set identifier
    "CONJ"  : "C",
    "NOUN"  : "N",
    "PRON"  : "r",
    "VERB"  : "V",
    "."     : "sent"                            Creates a reverse index by Project
}                                               Gutenberg short PoS tag identifier

univ_gutenberg_map_r = {v: k for k, v in univ_gutenberg_map.items()}   ◁——┘
```

With the mapping of overlap between the Project Gutenberg and Universal tag sets, you have the tagged corpus. But you need a way to remove the tags and get back to the original sentences so you can run them through Project Gutenberg and get the ambiguous sentences for use in training your parallel corpora. NLTK provides a handy untag function that takes care of this task. Run untag on a tagged sentence; it returns the original sentence (without the tuples). So you have the original sentences and the annotated tagged corpora, but you need to make a simple update to your morphological analyzer to handle the mapping between Project Gutenberg and the Universal tag sets.

The handy analyse function that you wrote in listing 10.7 needs some updating in a few areas:

- white_list *variable*—The ability to take in the Gutenberg to universal tag-set mapping and use it to map from the Gutenberg PoS ambiguous tagger so that your pos_words mapping represents to the corresponding universal tag set.
- tagged_sent *variable*—The tagged sentences with existing PoS tags from the NLTK annotations, used to ensure that you consider only the universal tag-set ground-truth tags for which there are corresponding Gutenberg tags.
- map_tags *variable*—Some valid universal tag-set PoS tags don't have a Gutenberg corollary, so I took the liberty of mapping them for you. DET (for *determinant*), for example, doesn't have a great mapping in Gutenberg, so I mapped it to CONJ (for *conjunction*) for you. This example could use improving, but for illustrative purposes, it works fine.

Listing 10.24 has the updated analyse function that will handle and create all three parallel corpora from the Brown Corpus.

Listing 10.24 Updating the analyse function to learn the three parallel corpora from Brown

```
def analyse(txt, white_list=None, tagged_sent=None):
    map_tags = {                              ◁──── Remaps some tags from the Universal
        "ADP" : "ADJ",                              tag set to Project Gutenberg tags that
        "DET" : "CONJ",                             aren't equivalent
        "NUM" : "NOUN",
        "PRT" : "CONJ"
    }
    words = word_tokenize(txt)◁──┐  Tokenizes the sentence
    words_and_tags = []          │  into words by using NLTK
    wl_keys = None
    if white_list != None:       ◁────┐  Whitelist is the allowable set of tags that Project
        wl_keys = white_list.keys()    │  Gutenberg and Universal tag set both recognize.
        white_list_r = {v: k for k, v in white_list.items()}
        wlr_keys = white_list_r.keys()   ◁──┐
                                            │  Creates a reverse index of
                                            │  the whitelist by identifier
    for i in range(0, len(words)):
        w = words[i]
        w_and_tag = w
        if w in pos_words:
            for c in pos_words[w]:
                if wl_keys != None:
                    if c not in wl_keys:   │ The PoS tag isn't in the
                        continue           │ whitelist, so skip it.
                    else:
                        if tagged_sent != None:
                            if tagged_sent[i][1] in white_list_r:  ◁──┐
                                ttag = white_list_r[tagged_sent[i][1]]
                                if ttag != "sent":
                                    if ttag in pos_words[w]:
                                        w_and_tag += "<"+pos_tags[ttag]+"/>"
                                    else:
                                        w_and_tag += "<"+pos_tags[c]+"/>"
                        else:
                            if tagged_sent[i][0] == ".":
```

Tagged_sent is the set of actual tags from a truth set for this sentence.

The PoS tag isn't in the whitelist, so skip it.

If the tag is in the whitelist, consider it.

The tagged corpus tag disagrees with label set, so pick the PoS tag for its corresponding identifier in Project Gutenberg.

```
                                        w_and_tag += "<"+ttag+"/>"
                              break
  Tagged annotation ┌──▷ else:
  doesn't correspond │         mt = map_tags[tagged_sent[i][1]]
     to Gutenberg.   │         ttag = white_list_r[mt]
                     │         if ttag in pos_words[w]:
                                   w_and_tag += "<"+pos_tags[ttag]+"/>"
                              else:
                         w_and_tag += "<"+pos_tags[c]+"/>"
                         break

            else:
                w_and_tag = w_and_tag + "<" + pos_tags[c] + "/>"
         else:
             w_and_tag = w_and_tag + "<" + pos_tags[c] + "/>"

     elif w in end_of_sent_punc:
         w_and_tag = w_and_tag + "<sent/>"

     words_and_tags.append(w_and_tag)
  return " ".join(words_and_tags)
```

Now you can create the three parallel corpora. I grabbed the first 100 of 132 sentences from the Brown Corpus to perform the training. This process can be computationally intensive because these sentences are 20 times the data you were using before, and there are many more tags to use to update your HMM model. In practice, this approach would scale even better if you fed it *all* of the Brown Corpus from various chapters, but this way, you'll get a real-world example and won't have to wait hours for it to run. Listing 10.25 sets up the parallel corpora and creates the new PoS dataframe for training.

Listing 10.25   Preparing the Brown Corpus for training

```
brown_train = brown.tagged_sents('ch07', tagset='universal')[0:100] first
➥ 100 sentences
brown_train_u = [" ".join(untag(brown_train[i])) for i in range(0,
➥ len(brown_train))]
brown_train_a = [analyse(" ".join(untag(brown_train[i])),
➥ white_list=univ_gutenberg_map_r) for i in range(0, len(brown_train))]
brown_train_t = [analyse(" ".join(untag(brown_train[i])),
➥ white_list=univ_gutenberg_map_r, tagged_sent=brown_train[i]) for i in
➥ range(0, len(brown_train))]

new_pos_df = build_pos_df(brown_train_u, brown_train_a, brown_train_t)
all_n_a_tags = compute_tags(new_pos_df['Analyzed'])
all_n_t_tags = compute_tags(new_pos_df['Tagged'])
```

To remind you of where you are in the process of making better PoS disambiguation predictions, it's worthwhile to recap. You saw that my limited sentences didn't have enough PoS tags and tagged corpora to learn from. By using NLTK and datasets like the Brown Corpus, which has thousands of tagged sentences and corpora, you embarked down a path of learning the parallel corpora from 100 Brown sentences.

You couldn't use the sentences directly; the `analyse` function required updating to take into account the fact that Brown and other corpora use a different PoS tag set from the Project Gutenberg corpus tag set. I showed you how to create a mapping to take that fact into account and to make sure that the Gutenberg PoS tagger morphologically analyzed only the sentence and output tags that were present in the Brown tags. In listing 10.25, you used this information to get back to your PoS dataframe of three parallel corpora and to extract the analyzed and tagged corpora PoS tags. You've completed steps 1 and 2 of figure 10.9.

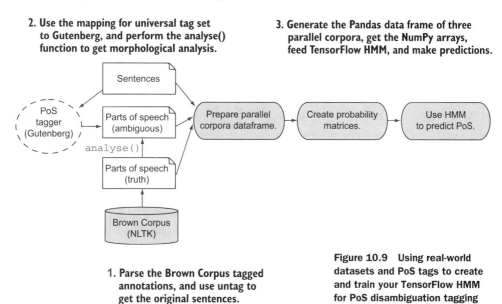

2. Use the mapping for universal tag set to Gutenberg, and perform the analyse() function to get morphological analysis.

3. Generate the Pandas data frame of three parallel corpora, get the NumPy arrays, feed TensorFlow HMM, and make predictions.

1. Parse the Brown Corpus tagged annotations, and use untag to get the original sentences.

Figure 10.9   Using real-world datasets and PoS tags to create and train your TensorFlow HMM for PoS disambiguation tagging

To get to step 3 in figure 10.9, you need to run the algorithms on the Pandas dataframe representing the three parallel corpora and generate the transition, initial, and emission matrices. You did this on the small five-sentence dataset, so you can use those existing functions and run them again on the dataframe to get ready for the HMM (listing 10.26).

Listing 10.26   Generating the transition and emission count matrices

```
n_trans_df = build_trans(pt_vals)                        ◁──── Builds the transition matrix
compute_trans_matrix(n_trans_df, all_n_t_tags)
n_just_trans_df = n_trans_df.drop(columns='FirstPoS')
n_just_trans_df['sum'] = n_just_trans_df.sum(axis=1)              Avoids dividing
n_just_trans_df.loc[n_just_trans_df['sum']==0., 'sum'] = .001 ◁── by zero
n_trans_prob_df =
    n_just_trans_df.loc[:,"Noun":"sent"].div(n_just_trans_df['sum'], axis=0)
```

```
(n_emission_df, n_amb_classes_k) = build_emission(pt_vals, all_n_a_tags)
compute_emission(n_emission_df, all_n_t_tags, all_n_a_tags)
n_tag_counts = count_tagged(all_n_t_tags)
emission_div_by_tag_counts(n_emission_df, n_amb_classes_k, n_tag_counts)
n_just_emission_df = n_emission_df.drop(columns='FirstPoS')
```

Builds the emission matrix

With the transition and emission matrices built, you extract the NumPy arrays and load the HMM model. Again, you grab the location of the last PoS tag. Because there are 16 columns and the dataframe is indexed by 0, it is index 15 for the initial probabilities row. Then extract the values of the transition and emission probabilities from their respective dataframes (listing 10.27).

Listing 10.27 Generating the NumPy arrays

Extracts the initial probabilities from the sent PoS row in the transition probabilities of shape (16, 1)

Extracts the transition probabilities of shape (16, 16).

```
n_initial_prob = n_trans_prob_df.loc[15].values.astype('float64')
n_initial_prob = n_initial_prob.reshape((len(n_initial_prob), 1))
n_trans_prob = n_trans_prob_df.values.astype('float64')
n_obs_prob = n_just_emission_df.T.values.astype('float64')
```

Extracts the emission probabilities of shape (16, 50).

Next, in listing 10.28, I picked a sentence randomly again. I picked the sentence at index 3 for illustration but could have picked any from the Brown Corpus. The sentence is shown in its original form, ambiguous analyzed form, and tagged form for your perusal:

```
There are forty-seven special district governments in Rhode Island (excluding
two regional school districts, four housing authorities, and the Kent County
Water Authority).

There are<Verb (usu participle)/><Noun/> forty-seven<Noun/><Adjective/>
special<Adjective/><Noun/> district<Noun/> governments
in<Adverb/><Adjective/><Noun/> Rhode<Noun/> Island<Noun/> ( excluding
two<Noun/> regional<Adjective/> school<Noun/> districts , four<Noun/>
housing<Noun/> authorities , and<Conjunction/><Noun/> the<Adverb/>
Kent<Noun/> County Water Authority ) .<sent/>

There are<Verb (usu participle)/> forty-seven<Noun/> special<Adjective/>
district<Noun/> governments in<Adjective/> Rhode<Noun/> Island<Noun/>
( excluding two<Noun/> regional<Adjective/> school<Noun/> districts ,
four<Noun/> housing<Noun/> authorities , and<Conjunction/> the<Adverb/>
Kent<Noun/> County Water Authority ) .
```

The code in listing 10.28 runs the sentence through the TensorFlow HMM PoS disambiguation step. It should look familiar because it is basically the same as listing 10.21.

Listing 10.28　Picking a sentence and running the HMM

Selects the sentence
at index 3

Converts the ambiguous PoS tags to evidence
observations from their indices [33, 23, 7, 34,
11, 34, 34, 34, 40, 34, 34, 34, 21, 41, 34, 49]

```
sent_index =
observations = sent_to_obs(n_emission_df, new_pos_df, all_n_a_tags,
    sent_index)

hmm = HMM(initial_prob=n_initial_prob, trans_prob=n_trans_prob,
    obs_prob=n_obs_prob)
with tf.Session() as sess:
    seq = viterbi_decode(sess, hmm, observations)
    print('Most likely hidden states are {}'.format(seq))
    print(seq_to_pos(seq))
```

Creates the HMM with the learned initial, transition,
and emission probabilities from the Brown Corpus

Outputs the predicted
hidden states

Runs TensorFlow and makes predictions
to disambiguate the PoS tags

Running the HMM this time generates a few valid predictions of elements besides Nouns, in particular two more PoS predictions:

```
Most likely hidden states are [3, 0, 6, 0, 6, 0, 0, 0, 6, 0, 0, 0, 0, 0, 0, 0]
['Verb (usu participle)', 'Noun', 'Adjective', 'Noun', 'Adjective', 'Noun',
'Noun', 'Noun', 'Adjective', 'Noun', 'Noun', 'Noun', 'Noun', 'Noun', 'Noun',
'Noun']
```

The challenge with HMMs is the same as that in any machine-learning model: the more examples you show, the better the representational variables represent even unforeseen cases. Because Nouns tend to surround many of the other PoS tags in sentence structure, they will be the most selected or highly probable guess. That said, our HMM from the Brown Corpus *seems* to perform better than our five-sentence example, which represented a handful of PoS tags and their co-occurrences. There were 50 PoS tags and ambiguity classes this time compared with 36 in the first example, so you can deduce that you've seen more ambiguity examples and trained your TensorFlow model to recognize them.

You can do better in terms of showing that your model improved with more data, however. Let's measure it!

10.6　*Defining error bars and metrics for PoS tagging*

A simple way to compute how well your PoS tagger is doing is to define a couple of simple metrics. The first metric is the per-line or per-sentence error rate, which boils down to how many tags your PoS tagger predicted correctly. This metric is measured as

$$\frac{min(|TL_p \cap TL_t|, |TL_t|)}{TL_t}$$

where TL_p is the predicted PoS tags for the sentence or line L and TL_t is the actual tagged PoS tags for the sentence or line L. The equation takes the number of tags predicted correctly out of the total possible tags. Then it divides by the total amount of valid tags to predict. This type of equation is commonly known as a *containment equation* because the numerator represents how much the prediction captured what was *contained* in the denominator out of the valid tags to predict. The per-sentence error rate is useful for measuring the accuracy of your algorithm, and you can add a hyperparameter that is the acceptable threshold per sentence that you will allow. After experimenting with the Brown Corpus, I've determined that a threshold value of .4, or 40%, is an acceptable rate for each sentence. The algorithm considers a sentence to be correct if it correctly predicted at least 60% of the PoS tags.

Another metric you can use to evaluate your PoS tagger captures all diffs for all sentences and then computes the total number of diffs compared with the total number of PoS tags to predict for all sentences. This technique can provide an overall accuracy assessment for your algorithm. Running listing 10.29 tells you that your HMM predicted 73 of the total 100 sentences correctly (73%) with a 40% threshold error rate, and that overall, your algorithm incorrectly identified only 254 of a possible 1,219 PoS tags it could predict, yielding overall accuracy of 79%. Not bad! You were right: your model performed better.

Try running TensorFlow and your HMM again, this time capturing these metrics as shown in listing 10.29.

Listing 10.29   Capturing and printing per-sentence error rate, diffs, and overall accuracy

Reinitializes TensorFlow

Records the per-line/per-sentence error rate results for each line

Defines the metrics you want to capture

Runs TensorFlow and the HMM for 100 sentences in the Brown Corpus

Computes per-line error rate and adds it to line_diffs

Defines the per-line error_rate threshold

Saves the number of PoS tags possible

Saves the number of PoS tag diffs

Counts how many sentences were predicted correctly based on the error_rate threshold

Prints the number of total diffs, total possible PoS tags, and overall accuracy

```
with tf.Session() as sess:
    num_diffs_t = 0
    num_tags_t = 0
    line_diffs = []
    for i in tqdm(range(0, len(brown_train))):
        observations = sent_to_obs(n_emission_df, new_pos_df, all_n_a_tags, i)
        seq = viterbi_decode(sess, hmm, observations)
        sq_pos = seq_to_pos(seq)
        diff_list = intersection(sq_pos, all_n_t_tags[i])
        line_diffs.append((min(len(diff_list),len(all_n_t_tags[i])) * 1.) /
            (len(all_n_t_tags[i]) * 1.))
        num_diffs_t += min(len(diff_list), len(all_n_t_tags[i]))
        num_tags_t += len(all_n_t_tags[i])
    p_l_error_rate = 0.4
    num_right = len([df for df in line_diffs if df < p_l_error_rate])
    print("Num Lines Correct(threshold=%f) %d" % (p_l_error_rate, num_right))
    print("Accuracy {0:.0%}".format(num_right*1. / 100.))

    print("Total diffs", num_diffs_t)
    print("Num Tags Total", num_tags_t)
    print("Overall Accuracy {0:.0%}".format(1 - (num_diffs_t*1. /
        num_tags_t*1.)))
```

One last thing you can do is visualize the fruits of your labor, taking a look at the per-line error rate graphically with Matplotlib. After you develop a good PoS tagger, it's worth looking for any particular trends on certain sentences. Listing 10.30 and figure 10.10 show the Matplotlib Python code and the output of the visualized error rate.

Evaluating the graph about every 20 sentences or so, the PoS tagger performs horribly. But overall, the performance is strong. This situation could warrant further evaluation. You could shuffle your sentences in the Brown Corpus, for example, or inspect the underperforming sentences to determine whether they are representative of PoS tags that you haven't learned well. But I will leave that analysis for a later date. You've done a great job sticking with me in this chapter and learning a real-world application of HMMs. Onward!

Listing 10.30 Using Matplotlib to visualize the per-line error rate

```
l_d_lists = sorted([(i, line_diffs[i]) for i in range(0, len(line_diffs))])    ⟵  Sorted by key, returns a
d_lists = []                                                                          list of tuples of the form
for i in range(0, len(l_d_lists)):                                                     (line num, error rate)
    t = l_d_lists[i]
    d_lists.append((t[0], t[1]))

x, y = zip(*d_lists)    ⟵  Unpacks a list of pairs
plt.xlabel("Line Number")      into two tuples
plt.ylabel("Error rate")
plt.title("Distribution of per sentence error rate")
plt.bar(x, y)
plt.show()    ⟵  Shows the plot
```

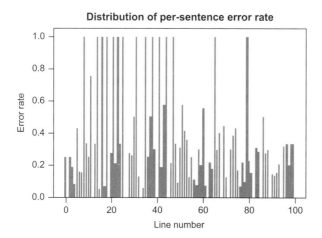

Figure 10.10 The per-line error rate for your PoS disambiguation tagger

Summary

- Word-sense disambiguation occurs in everyday life, and you can use machine learning and TensorFlow to perform it.
- Labeled data is available; you need methods of setting it up for a machine-learning problem by using HMMs.
- HMMs are explainable models that accumulate probabilistic evidence and guide decisions based on possible states that the evidence represents.

Part 3

The neural network paradigm

The past 10 years in machine-learning research have been deeply influenced by smart people turning their attention to the brain and the way it works. With capacious terrestrial computing and graphical processing units (GPUs) that optimize machine-learning code speed and deployment by orders of magnitude, both older models and newer approaches that are computationally difficult to empirically test are widely available, democratized by the cloud, not hidden and usable only by big web companies.

As it turns out, modeling how to think, hear, see, and speak based on the brain, and taking those models and easily deploying them, sharing them, retraining and adapting them, and using them have yielded many advances, such as the intelligent digital assistant in your smartphone or a home assistant device that can order food or turn the channel to your favorite program based on your talking to it and its talking to you.

These machine-learning models are called *neural networks*. Neural networks are modeled based on your brain, which contains networks of connected neurons. The recent release of models like GPT-3 that automatically generate believable news articles, plays, tweets, and you name it feels like the beginning of the (r)evolution.

TensorFlow is optimized for creating neural networks and getting them deployed and evaluated. This part of the book shows you how to create, train, and evaluate some of the neural networks most commonly used today to touch, see, speak, and hear.

11
A peek into autoencoders

This chapter covers
- Getting to know neural networks
- Designing autoencoders
- Representing images by using an autoencoder

Have you ever heard a person humming a melody and identified the song? That might be easy for you, but I'm comically tone-deaf when it comes to music. Humming is an approximation of a song. An even better approximation could be singing. Include some instrumentals, and sometimes, a cover of a song sounds indistinguishable from the original.

Instead of songs, in this chapter you'll approximate functions. *Functions* are a general notion of relations between inputs and outputs. In machine learning, you typically want to find the function that relates inputs to outputs. Finding the best possible function fit is difficult, but approximating the function is much easier.

Conveniently, artificial neural networks (ANNs) are a model in machine learning that can approximate any function. As you've learned, your model is a function that gives the output you're looking for, given the inputs you have. In machine-learning terms, given training data, you want to build a neural network model that best approximates the implicit function that might have generated the data—one that might not give you the exact answer but that's good enough to be useful.

So far, you've generated models by explicitly designing a function, whether it be linear; polynomial; or something more complicated, like softmax regression or hidden Markov models (HMMs). Neural networks enable a little bit of leeway when it comes to picking out the right function and, consequently, the right model. In theory, a neural network can model general-purpose types of transformation, in which you don't need to know much at all about the function being modeled.

After section 11.1 introduces neural networks, you'll learn how to use autoencoders, which encode data into smaller, faster representations (section 11.2).

11.1 Neural networks

If you've heard about neural networks, you've probably seen diagrams of nodes and edges connected in a complicated mesh. That visualization is inspired mostly by biology—specifically, neurons in the brain. It's also a convenient way to visualize functions, such as $f(x) = w \times x + b$, as shown in figure 11.1.

As a reminder, a *linear model* is set of linear functions, such as $f(x) = w \times x + b$, where (w, b) is the vector of parameters. The learning algorithm drifts around the values of w and b until it finds a combination that best matches the data. After the algorithm successfully converges, it'll find the best possible linear function to describe the data.

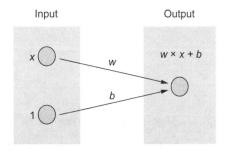

Figure 11.1   A graphical representation of the linear equation $f(x) = w \times x + b$. The nodes are represented as circles, and edges are represented as arrows. The values on the edges are often called *weights*, and they act as a multiplication on the input. When two arrows lead to the same node, they act as a summation of the inputs.

Linear is a good place to start, but the real world isn't always that pretty. Thus, we dive into the type of machine learning responsible for TensorFlow's inception. This chapter is your introduction to a type of model called an *ANN*, which can approximate arbitrary functions (not only linear ones).

Exercise 11.1
Is $f(x) = |x|$ a linear function?

Answer
No. It's two linear functions stitched together at zero, not a single straight line.

To incorporate the concept of nonlinearity, it's effective to apply a nonlinear function, called the *activation function*, to each neuron's output. Three of the most commonly used activation functions are *sigmoid* (sig), *hyperbolic tangent* (tan), and a type of *ramp* function called a *Rectifying Linear Unit* (ReLU), all plotted in figure 11.2.

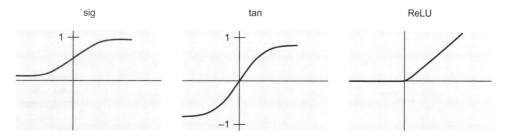

Figure 11.2   Use nonlinear functions such as sig, tan, and ReLU to introduce nonlinearity to your models.

You don't have to worry too much about which activation function is better under what circumstances. The answer is still an active research topic. Feel free to experiment with the three functions shown in figure 11.2. Usually, the best one is chosen by using cross-validation to determine which one gives the best model, given the dataset you're working with. Remember your confusion matrix in chapter 5? You test which model gives the fewest false positives or false negatives, or whatever other criterion best suits your needs.

The sigmoid function isn't new to you. As you may recall, the logistic regression classifier in chapters 5 and 6 applied this sigmoid function to the linear function $w \times x + b$. The neural network model in figure 11.3 represents the function $f(x) = \text{sig}(w \times x + b)$. The function is a one-input, one-output network, where w and b are the parameters of this model.

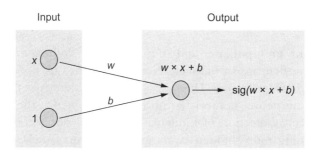

Figure 11.3   A nonlinear function, such as sigmoid, is applied to the output of a node.

If you have two inputs ($x1$ and $x2$), you can modify your neural network to look like the one in figure 11.4. Given training data and a cost function, the parameters to be learned are $w1$, $w2$, and b. When you're trying to model data, having multiple inputs to a function is common. Image classification takes the entire image (pixel by pixel) as the input, for example.

Naturally, you can generalize to an arbitrary number of inputs ($x1$, $x2$, ..., xn). The corresponding neural network represents the function $f(x1, ..., xn) = \text{sig}(wn \times xn + ... + w1 \times x1 + b)$, as shown in figure 11.5.

Input   Output

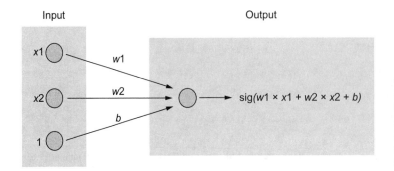

Figure 11.4   A two-input network will have three parameters (*w*1, *w*2, and *b*). Multiple lines leading to the same node indicate summation.

Input   Output

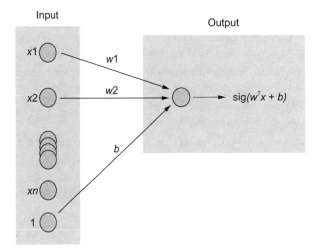

Figure 11.5   The input dimension can be arbitrarily long. Each pixel in a grayscale image can have a corresponding input *x1*, for example. This neural network uses all inputs to generate a single output number, which you might use for regression or classification. The notation *w*^{T} means that you're transposing *w*, which is an *n* × 1 vector, into a 1 × *n* vector. That way, you can properly multiply it with *x* (which has the dimensions *n* × 1). Such a matrix multiplication is also called a *dot product*, and it yields a scalar (1D) value.

So far, you've dealt with only an input layer and an output layer. Nothing's stopping you from arbitrarily adding neurons in between. Neurons that are used as neither input nor output are called *hidden neurons*. These neurons are hidden from the input and output interfaces of the neural network, so no one can influence their values directly. A *hidden layer* is any collection of hidden neurons that don't connect, as shown in figure 11.6. Adding more hidden layers greatly improves the expressive power of the network.

As long as the activation function is something nonlinear, a neural network with at least one hidden layer can approximate arbitrary functions. In linear models, no matter what parameters are learned, the function remains linear. The nonlinear neural network model with a hidden layer, on the other hand, is flexible enough to approximately represent any function. What a time to be alive!

TensorFlow comes with many helper functions that help you obtain the parameters of a neural network in an efficient way. You'll see how to invoke those tools in this chapter when you start using your first neural network architecture: an autoencoder.

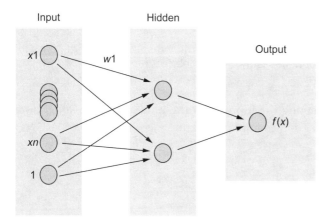

Figure 11.6 Nodes that don't interface to both the input and the output are called *hidden neurons*. A *hidden layer* is a collection of hidden units that aren't connected.

11.2 *Autoencoders*

An *autoencoder* is a type of neural network that tries to learn parameters that make the output as close to the input as possible. An obvious way to do so is to return the input directly, as shown in figure 11.7.

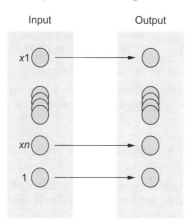

Figure 11.7 If you want to create a network in which the input equals the output, you can connect the corresponding nodes and set each parameter's weight to 1.

But an autoencoder is more interesting than that. It contains a small hidden layer! If that hidden layer has a smaller dimension than the input, the hidden layer is a compression of your data, called *encoding*.

Encoding data in the real world

A couple of audio formats are out there, but the most popular may be MP3 because of its relatively small file size. You may have already guessed that such efficient storage comes with a trade-off. The algorithm to generate an MP3 file takes original uncompressed audio and shrinks it to a much smaller file that sounds approximately the same to your ears. But it's *lossy*, meaning that you won't be able to completely recover the original uncompressed audio from the encoded version.

(continued)
Similarly, in this chapter, we want to reduce the dimensionality of the data to make it more workable but not necessarily create a perfect reproduction.

The process of reconstructing the input from the hidden layer is called *decoding*. Figure 11.8 shows an exaggerated example of an autoencoder.

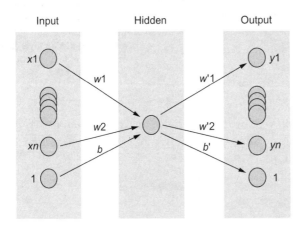

Figure 11.8   Here, you introduce a restriction to a network that tries to reconstruct its input. Data will pass through a narrow channel, as illustrated by the hidden layer. In this example, there's only one node in the hidden layer. This network is trying to encode (and decode) an *n*-dimensional input signal into one dimension, which will likely be difficult in practice.

Encoding is a great way to reduce the dimensions of the input. If you can represent a 256×256 image in 100 hidden nodes, for example, you've reduced each data item by a factor of thousands.

Exercise 11.2
Let *x* denote the input vector (x1, x2, ..., xn), and let *y* denote the output vector (y1, y2, ..., yn). Last, let *w* and *w'* denote the encoder and decoder weights, respectively. What's a possible cost function to train this neural network?

Answer
See the loss function in listing 11.3.

It makes sense to use an object-oriented programming style to implement an autoencoder. That way, you can reuse the class in other applications without worrying about tightly coupled code. Creating your code as outlined in listing 11.1 helps you build deeper architectures, such as a *stacked autoencoder*, which has been known to perform better empirically.

   TIP   Generally, with neural networks, adding more hidden layers seems to improve performance if you have enough data to not overfit the model.

Listing 11.1 Python class schema

```
class Autoencoder:
    def __init__(self, input_dim, hidden_dim):  ⟵—— Initializes variables

    def train(self, data):  ⟵—— Trains on a dataset

    def test(self, data):  ⟵—— Tests on some new data
```

Open a new Python source file, and call it autoencoder.py. This file will define the autoencoder class that you'll use from a separate piece of code.

The constructor will set up all the TensorFlow variables, placeholders, optimizers, and operators. Anything that doesn't immediately need a session can go in the constructor. Because you're dealing with two sets of weights and biases (one for the encoding step and the other for the decoding step), you can use TensorFlow's tf.name scopes to disambiguate a variable's name.

Listing 11.2 shows an example of defining a variable within a named scope. Now you can seamlessly save and restore this variable without worrying about name collisions.

Listing 11.2 Using name scopes

```
with tf.name_scope('encode'):
    weights = tf.Variable(tf.random_normal([input_dim, hidden_dim],
    ➡ dtype=tf.float32), name='weights')
    biases = tf.Variable(tf.zeros([hidden_dim]), name='biases')
```

Moving on, implement the constructor, as shown in listing 11.3.

Listing 11.3 The autoencoder class

```
import tensorflow as tf
import numpy as np
                                                     Hyperparameter
                                                     of the optimizer      Defines the weights
class Autoencoder:                                                         and biases under a
    def __init__(self, input_dim, hidden_dim, epoch=250,                   name scope so you
        learning_rate=0.001):                                             can tell them apart
Number of     self.epoch = epoch                                          from the decoder's
learning      self.learning_rate = learning_rate  ⟵——                     weights and biases
cycles

Defines the
input layer  x = tf.placeholder(dtype=tf.float32, shape=[None, input_dim])
dataset
             with tf.name_scope('encode'):                        ⟵——
                 weights = tf.Variable(tf.random_normal([input_dim, hidden_dim],
                 ➡ dtype=tf.float32), name='weights')
The              biases = tf.Variable(tf.zeros([hidden_dim]), name='biases')
decoder's        encoded = tf.nn.tanh(tf.matmul(x, weights) + biases)
weights and  with tf.name_scope('decode'):
biases are       weights = tf.Variable(tf.random_normal([hidden_dim, input_dim],
defined          ➡ dtype=tf.float32), name='weights')
under this       biases = tf.Variable(tf.zeros([input_dim]), name='biases')
name scope.
```

```
        decoded = tf.matmul(encoded, weights) + biases

        self.x = x
        self.encoded = encoded          These will be
        self.decoded = decoded          method variables.         Defines the
                                                                  reconstruction cost
        self.loss = tf.sqrt(tf.reduce_mean(tf.square(tf.subtract(self.x,
     ➡    self.decoded))))                                    ←
        self.train_op =
     tf.train.RMSPropOptimizer(self.learning_rate).minimize(self.loss)  ←
        self.saver = tf.train.Saver()
                                                            Chooses the optimizer
```

Sets up a saver to save model parameters as they're being learned

Defines the reconstruction cost

Chooses the optimizer

Now, in listing 11.4, you'll define a class method called `train` that will receive a dataset and learn parameters to minimize its loss.

Listing 11.4 Training the autoencoder

```
    def train(self, data):                          Starts a TensorFlow
        num_samples = len(data)                     session and initializes
        with tf.Session() as sess:                  all variables
            sess.run(tf.global_variables_initializer())
            for i in range(self.epoch):
                for j in range(num_samples):
                    l, _ = sess.run([self.loss, self.train_op],
                ➡        feed_dict={self.x: [data[j]]})       Prints the
                if i % 10 == 0:                               reconstruction
                    print('epoch {0}: loss = {1}'.format(i, l))   error once
                    self.saver.save(sess, './model.ckpt')    every 10 cycles
            self.saver.save(sess, './model.ckpt')
                                                      Saves the learned
                                                      parameters to file
```

Iterates through the number of cycles defined in the constructor

One sample at a time, trains the neural network on a data item

Now you have enough code to design an algorithm that learns an autoencoder from arbitrary data. Before you start using this class, create one more method. As shown in listing 11.5, the `test` method lets you evaluate the autoencoder on new data.

Listing 11.5 Testing the model on data

```
    def test(self, data):                        Loads the learned
        with tf.Session() as sess:               parameters
            self.saver.restore(sess, './model.ckpt')   ←
            hidden, reconstructed = sess.run([self.encoded, self.decoded],
        feed_dict={self.x: data})        ←
            print('input', data)                Reconstructs the input
            print('compressed', hidden)
            print('reconstructed', reconstructed)
            return reconstructed
```

Finally, create a new Python source file called main.py, and use your `autoencoder` class, as shown in listing 11.6.

Listing 11.6 Using your autoencoder class

```
from autoencoder import Autoencoder
from sklearn import datasets

hidden_dim = 1
data = datasets.load_iris().data
input_dim = len(data[0])
ae = Autoencoder(input_dim, hidden_dim)
ae.train(data)
ae.test([[8, 4, 6, 2]])
```

Running the train function will output debug info about how the loss decreases over the epochs. The test function shows info about the encoding and decoding process:

```
('input', [[8, 4, 6, 2]])
('compressed', array([[ 0.78238308]], dtype=float32))
('reconstructed', array([[ 6.87756062,   2.79838109,   6.25144577,
➡ 2.23120356]], dtype=float32))
```

Notice that you're able to compress a 4D vector into 1D and then decode it back into a 4D vector with some loss in data.

11.3 Batch training

Training a network one sample at a time is the safest bet if you're not pressed for time. But if your network training is taking longer than desired, one solution is to train it with multiple data inputs at a time, called *batch training*.

Typically, as the batch size increases, the algorithm speeds up but has a lower likelihood of converging successfully. The comparison between batch size and successful convergence is a double-edged sword. Go wield it in listing 11.7. You'll use that helper function later.

Listing 11.7 Batch helper function

```
def get_batch(X, size):
    a = np.random.choice(len(X), size, replace=False)
    return X[a]
```

To use batch learning, you'll need to modify the train method from listing 11.4. The batch version, shown in listing 11.8, inserts an additional inner loop for each batch of data. Typically, the number of batch iterations should be enough so that all data is covered in the same epoch.

Listing 11.8 Batch learning

```
def train(self, data, batch_size=10):
    with tf.Session() as sess:
        sess.run(tf.global_variables_initializer())
```

```
                    for i in range(self.epoch):
Loops through  ┌─▷      for j in range(500):
various batch   │           batch_data = get_batch(data, self.batch_size)       ◁──────
selections      │           l, _ = sess.run([self.loss, self.train_op],
                │        ➠  feed_dict={self.x: batch_data})              Runs the
                        if i % 10 == 0:                                  optimizer on
                            print('epoch {0}: loss = {1}'.format(i, l))  a randomly
                            self.saver.save(sess, './model.ckpt')        selected
                    self.saver.save(sess, './model.ckpt')                batch
```

11.4   *Working with images*

Most neural networks, like your autoencoder, accept only 1D input. Pixels of an image, on the other hand, are indexed by both rows and columns. Moreover, if a pixel is in color, it has a value for its red, green, and blue concentrations, as shown in figure 11.9.

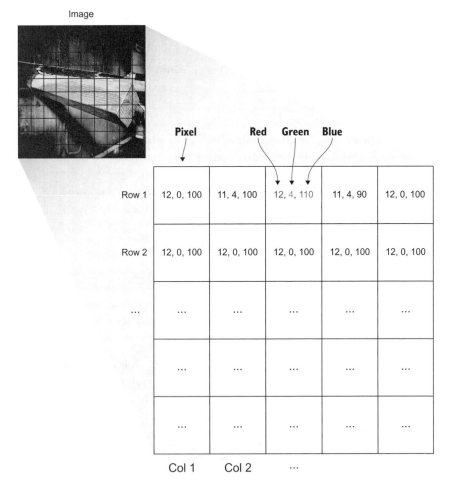

Figure 11.9   **A colored image is composed of pixels, and each pixel contains values for red, green, and blue.**

A convenient way to manage the higher dimensions of an image involves two steps:

1 Convert the image to grayscale. Merge the values of red, green, and blue into the *pixel intensity*, which is a weighted average of the color values.
2 Rearrange the image into row-major order. *Row-major order* stores an array as a longer, single-dimension set; you put all the dimensions of an array on the end of the first dimension, which allows you to index the image by one number instead of two. If an image is 3 × 3 pixels, you rearrange it into the structure shown in figure 11.10.

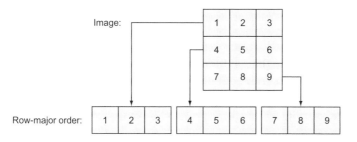

Figure 11.10   An image can be represented in row-major order. That way, you can represent a 2D structure as a 1D structure.

You can use images in TensorFlow in many ways. If you have pictures lying around on your hard drive, you can load them by using SciPy, which comes with TensorFlow. Listing 11.9 shows you how to load an image in grayscale, resize it, and represent it in row-major order.

Listing 11.9   Loading images

```
from scipy.misc import imread, imresize

gray_image = imread(filepath, True)            ◁—— Loads an image as grayscale
small_gray_image = imresize(gray_image, 1. / 8.)   ◁—— Resizes it to something smaller
x = small_gray_image.flatten()                 ◁—— Converts it to a 1D structure
```

Image processing is a lively field of research, so datasets are readily available for you to use, instead of using your own limited images. A dataset called CIFAR-10, for example, contains 60,000 labeled images, each 32 × 32.

Exercise 11.3
Can you name other online image datasets? Search online for more.
Answer
Perhaps the most-used dataset in the deep-learning community is ImageNet (www .image-net.org). You can also find a great list at http://deeplearning.net/datasets.

Download the Python dataset from www.cs.toronto.edu/~kriz/cifar.html. Place the extracted cifar-10-batches-py folder in your working directory. Listing 11.10 is from the CIFAR-10 web page; add the code to a new file called main_ imgs.py.

Listing 11.10 Reading from the extracted CIFAR-10 dataset

```
import pickle

def unpickle(file):          ←──┐ Reads the CIFAR-10 file,
    fo = open(file, 'rb')          returning the loaded dictionary
    dict = pickle.load(fo, encoding='latin1')
    fo.close()
    return dict
```

You can read each of the dataset files by using the unpickle function created in listing 11.10. The CIFAR-10 dataset contains six files, each prefixed with data_batch_ and followed by a number. Each file contains information about the image data and corresponding label. Listing 11.11 shows how to loop through all the files and append the datasets to memory.

Listing 11.11 Reading all CIFAR-10 files to memory

```
import numpy as np

names = unpickle('./cifar-10-batches-py/batches.meta')['label_names']
data, labels = [], []
for i in range(1, 6):                          ←── Loops through the six files
    filename = './cifar-10-batches-py/data_batch_' + str(i)
    batch_data = unpickle(filename)
    if len(data) > 0:
        data = np.vstack((data, batch_data['data']))
        labels = np.hstack((labels, batch_data['labels']))
    else:
        data = batch_data['data']
        labels = batch_data['labels']
```

Loads the file to obtain a Python dictionary

The rows of a data sample represent each sample, so you stack it vertically.

Labels are 1D, so you stack them horizontally.

Each image is represented as a series of red pixels, followed by green pixels and then blue pixels. Listing 11.12 creates a helper function to convert the image to grayscale by averaging the red, green, and blue values.

NOTE You can achieve more-realistic grayscale in other ways, but this approach of averaging the three values gets the job done. Human perception is more sensitive to green light, so in some other versions of grayscaling, green values might have a higher weight in the averaging.

Listing 11.12 Converting CIFAR-10 image to grayscale

```
def grayscale(a):
    return a.reshape(a.shape[0], 3, 32, 32).mean(1).reshape(a.shape[0], -1)

data = grayscale(data)
```

Finally, collect all images of a certain class, such as horse. You'll run your autoencoder on all pictures of horses, as shown in listing 11.13.

Listing 11.13 Setting up the autoencoder

```
from autoencoder import Autoencoder

x = np.matrix(data)
y = np.array(labels)

horse_indices = np.where(y == 7)[0]          ◁——  Selects horse (label 7) from
                                                   the set of indices to use to
                                                   index into the data array x
horse_x = x[horse_indices]

print(np.shape(horse_x))          ◁——  A matrix of size (5000, 3072), 5,000
                                        images and 32 × 32*3 channels
input_dim = np.shape(horse_x)[1]        (R,G,B), or 3,072 values
hidden_dim = 100
ae = Autoencoder(input_dim, hidden_dim)
ae.train(horse_x)
```

Now you can encode images similar to your training dataset into 100 numbers. This autoencoder model is one of the simplest, so clearly, the encoding will be lossy. Beware: running this code may take up to 10 minutes. The output will trace loss values of every 10 epochs:

```
epoch 0: loss = 99.8635025024
epoch 10: loss = 35.3869667053
epoch 20: loss = 15.9411172867
epoch 30: loss = 7.66391372681
epoch 40: loss = 1.39575612545
epoch 50: loss = 0.00389165547676
epoch 60: loss = 0.00203850422986
epoch 70: loss = 0.00186171964742
epoch 80: loss = 0.00231492402963
epoch 90: loss = 0.00166488380637
epoch 100: loss = 0.00172081717756
epoch 110: loss = 0.0018497039564
epoch 120: loss = 0.00220602494664
epoch 130: loss = 0.00179589167237
epoch 140: loss = 0.00122790911701
epoch 150: loss = 0.0027100709267
epoch 160: loss = 0.00213225837797
epoch 170: loss = 0.00215123943053
epoch 180: loss = 0.00148373935372
epoch 190: loss = 0.00171591725666
```

See the book's website (http://mng.bz/nzpa) or GitHub repo (http://mng.bz/v9m7) for a full example of the output.

11.5 *Application of autoencoders*

This chapter introduced the most straightforward type of autoencoder, but other variants have been studied, each with their benefits and applications. Let's take a look at a few:

- A *stacked autoencoder* starts the same way that a normal autoencoder does. It learns the encoding for an input into a smaller hidden layer by minimizing the reconstruction error. Then the hidden layer is treated as the input to a new autoencoder that tries to encode the first layer of hidden neurons to an even smaller layer (the second layer of hidden neurons). This process continues as desired. Often, the learned encoding weights are used as initial values for solving regression or classification problems in a deep neural network architecture.

- A *denoising autoencoder* receives a noised-up input instead of the original input and tries to "denoise" it. The cost function is no longer used to minimize the reconstruction error. Now you're trying to minimize the error between the denoised image and the original image. The intuition is that our human minds can still comprehend a photograph even with scratches or markings on it. If a machine can also see through the noised input to recover the original data, maybe it has a better understanding of the data. Denoising models have been shown to better capture salient features of an image.

- A *variational autoencoder* can generate new natural images, given the hidden variables directly. Let's say you encode a picture of a man as a 100D vector and then a picture of a woman as another 100D vector. You can take the average of the two vectors, run it through the decoder, and produce a reasonable image that represents a person who's between a man and a woman. This generative power of the variational autoencoder is derived from a type of probabilistic model called a *Bayesian network*. It's also some of the technology used in modern deep fakes and generative adversarial networks.

Summary

- A neural network is useful when a linear model is ineffective for describing the dataset.
- Autoencoders are unsupervised learning algorithms that try to reproduce their inputs and in doing so reveal interesting structure about the data.
- Images can easily be fed as input to a neural network by flattening and grayscaling.

Applying autoencoders: The CIFAR-10 image dataset

This chapter covers

- Navigating and understanding the structure of the CIFAR-10 image dataset
- Building an autoencoder model to represent different CIFAR-10 image classes
- Applying the CIFAR-10 autoencoder as an image classifier
- Implementing a stacked and denoising autoencoder on CIFAR-10 images

Autoencoders are powerful tools for learning arbitrary functions that transform input into output without having the full set of rules to do so. Autoencoders get their names from their function: learning a representation of the input much smaller than its size, which means *encoding* input data using less knowledge and then *decoding* that internal representation to get approximately back to its original input.

When the input is an image, autoencoders have many useful applications. Compression is one, such as using 100 neurons in a hidden layer and formatting your 2D image input in row-order format (chapter 11). With averaging for the red, green, and blue channels, the autoencoder learns a representation of the image and is able to encode a $32 \times 32 \times 3$ height × width × channel image, or 3,072 pixel intensities into 100 numbers, which is a reduction of 30x in data. How's that for compression? Though you trained a network to demonstrate this use case in chapter 11, you did not explore the resulting learned representation of the images, but you will in this chapter.

Classification is also possible by using the autoencoder's representation. You could train the autoencoder on a set of horse images from a labeled training dataset like the Canadian Institute for Advanced Research (CIFAR)-10 data and then compare the autoencoder's representation of a horse—those 100 numbers, trained and weighted on many samples—with that the autoencoder's learned representation for another image class, such as `frog`. The representation will be different, and you can use it as a compact way to classify (and cluster) the image types. Also, if you can classify samples with a strong representation, you can detect anomalous samples and thus detect automatically when some set of data in the series is different or perform anomaly detection. You explore these uses of autoencoders in this chapter, which focuses on the CIFAR-10 dataset.

As I hinted at the end of chapter 11, there are different types of autoencoders, including a stacked autoencoder, which uses more than one hidden layer and supports a deep architecture for classification. Also, denoising autoencoders try to noise up the input, such as an image, and see whether the network can still learn a more robust representation that's resilient to image imperfections. You'll play with both of those concepts in this chapter.

12.1 What is CIFAR-10?

CIFAR-10 gets its name from its 10 image classes, including `automobile`, `plane`, and `frog`. CIFAR-10 is a powerful tool of labeled images selected from the 80 million Tiny Images dataset of size 32×32 and in three-channel RGB format. Each image represents 3,072 pixels in full color and 1,024 pixels in grayscale. You can read more about Tiny Images at https://people.csail.mit.edu/torralba/publications/80millionImages.pdf.

Before you get too deep into autoencoder representations, it's worthwhile to explore the CIFAR-10 dataset in detail.

CIFAR-10 is divided into a training and a test dataset, which is a good practice, as I have been preaching to you. Following in the vein of reserving approximately 80% of the data for training and 20% of the data for testing, the dataset consists of 60,000 images divided into 50,000 training and 10,000 test images. Each image class—airplane, automobile, bird, cat, deer, dog, frog, horse, ship, and truck—has 6,000 representative samples in the dataset. The training set includes 5,000 random samples of each class, and the test set includes 1,000 random samples of the data for each of the 10 classes. The data is formatted on disk in binary file format for Python, Matlab,

To grayscale or not to grayscale

You may be wondering why you used grayscale for images in chapters 10 and 11 instead of the full RGB values. Maybe the color property is something you want your neural network to learn, so why remove R(ed), G(reen) and B(lue), and replace them with grayscale? The answer lies in dimensionality reduction. Reducing to grayscale reduces the number of required learned parameters by a factor of 3, which helps in training and learning without sacrificing much. That's not to say that you'll never want to train a neural network on color as a feature. When you try to find a yellow cup in a picture that also has blue and red cups, you have to use color. But for your work in this chapter, the autoencoder will be happy enough with a third less data, and so will your computer's CPU fan.

and C programming users. The 50,000-image training dataset is broken into five batches, each with 10,000 images, and the training file batch is a single file of 10,000 images in random order. Figure 12.1 shows a visual representation of CIFAR-10 and and its 10 classes, with randomly selected images.

In chapter 11, you built an `autoencoder` class that took in a CIFAR-10 batch of images of the `horse` class; then it learned a representation of the images so that it

Figure 12.1   Ten randomly picked samples for each of CIFAR-10's image classes.

could reduce each 1,024-pixel (32 × 32 in grayscale) image to 100 numbers. How well did the encoding perform? You explore that topic in section 12.1.1 as you refresh your memory of the autoencoder class.

12.1.1 Evaluating your CIFAR-10 autoencoder

The CIFAR-10 autoencoder class that you built in chapter 11 had a single hidden layer of size 100 neurons, took as input a 5000 × 1024 vector of training images, encoded the input using tf.matmul and a hidden layer of size 1024 × 100, and decoded the hidden layer using an output layer of 100 × 1024. The autoencoder class trained using 1,000 epochs and a user-specified batch size, and also provided methods to test the process by printing the values of the hidden neurons or the encoding and then the decoded representation of the original input values. Listing 12.1 shows the class and its utility methods.

Listing 12.1   The autoencoder class

Gets a randomly selected batch of size from X using indices, selecting only unique samples because replace=False

```
def get_batch(X, size):
    a = np.random.choice(len(X), size, replace=False)
    return X[a]

class Autoencoder:
    def __init__(self, input_dim, hidden_dim, epoch=1000, batch_size=50,
        learning_rate=0.001):
        self.epoch = epoch
        self.batch_size = batch_size
        self.learning_rate = learning_rate

        x = tf.placeholder(dtype=tf.float32, shape=[None, input_dim])
        with tf.name_scope('encode'):
            weights = tf.Variable(tf.random_normal([input_dim, hidden_dim],
                dtype=tf.float32), name='weights')
            biases = tf.Variable(tf.zeros([hidden_dim]), name='biases')
            encoded = tf.nn.sigmoid(tf.matmul(x, weights) + biases)
        with tf.name_scope('decode'):
            weights = tf.Variable(tf.random_normal([hidden_dim, input_dim],
                dtype=tf.float32), name='weights')
            biases = tf.Variable(tf.zeros([input_dim]), name='biases')
            decoded = tf.matmul(encoded, weights) + biases

        self.x = x
        self.encoded = encoded
        self.decoded = decoded

        self.loss = tf.sqrt(tf.reduce_mean(tf.square(tf.subtract(self.x,
            self.decoded))))
        self.train_op =
            tf.train.RMSPropOptimizer(self.learning_rate).minimize(self.loss)
        self.saver = tf.train.Saver()
```

Reuses weights and biases using tf.scope construct for the encoding step

Creates encoding of size input_dim, hidden_dim

Decodes encoding from hidden_dim back to input_dim using learned weights

Uses root mean-squared error (RMSE) as the loss function and optimizer

Reuses a saver to save and restore the model

```
    def train(self, data):
        with tf.Session() as sess:
            sess.run(tf.global_variables_initializer())
            for i in range(self.epoch):
                for j in range(np.shape(data)[0] // self.batch_size):
                    batch_data = get_batch(data, self.batch_size)
                    l, _ = sess.run([self.loss, self.train_op],
                        feed_dict={self.x: batch_data})
                if i % 10 == 0:
                    print('epoch {0}: loss = {1}'.format(i, l))
                    self.saver.save(sess, './model.ckpt')
            self.saver.save(sess, './model.ckpt')

    def test(self, data):
        with tf.Session() as sess:
            self.saver.restore(sess, './model.ckpt')
            hidden, reconstructed = sess.run([self.encoded, self.decoded],
                feed_dict={self.x: data})
        print('input', data)
        print('compressed', hidden)
        print('reconstructed', reconstructed)
        return reconstructed
```

Iterates by num batches or floor(dataset size/batch_size) for each epoch and train

Computes the encoding and decoding layers and output, and prints their values

Though you ran this class in chapter 11, you didn't look at the input to it or the output from the decoding step to check out how well it learned a representation of the input. To do so, you can use the code from chapter 11, which is recommended on the CIFAR-10 website as an easy way to read the Python-formatted data stored in the Pickle format. Pickle is a Python library for compact binary representation that serializes a Python object into a byte stream and then provides methods to deserialize the object back into an active Python dynamic object from that byte stream. You can use the unpickle function and associated dataset loading code, such as the greyscale function, which converts the 50,000 training three-channel RGB images into one-channel grayscale images by taking the mean of the RGB values for each image. The rest of the CIFAR-10 loading code iterates through the downloaded five 10,000-image training files. The files are in the Python pickle format; the data is stored in a Python dictionary with key data and the key labels with valid values (0–9) for the 10 image classes. The 10 image-class names are populated into the names variable read from the Python pickle batches.meta file and include the values automobile, bird, and so on. Each of the five sets of 10,000 images and labels is vertically and horizontally stacked on two NumPy arrays—data of size (50000,1024) and labels (5000,), respectively—and made available for training. Listing 12.2 gets the CIFAR-10 data ready for the Autoencoder.

Listing 12.2   Getting the CIFAR-10 data ready for the Autoencoder

```
def unpickle(file):
    fo = open(file, 'rb')
    dict = pickle.load(fo, encoding='latin1')
    fo.close()
```

Loads a CIFAR-10 batch Pickle file. There are five files for training and one for test, of size 10,000 images and labels each.

```
                return dict  ◁──┤ The return from loading by        Converts 3-channel RGB image
                                 │ Pickle is a Python dictionary,    input into 1-channel grayscale
            def grayscale(a):    │ with keys data and labels.       by averaging the RGB values
                return a.reshape(a.shape[0], 3, 32, 32).mean(1).reshape(a.shape[0], -1)  ◁──┘
```

```
         ▷  names = unpickle('./cifar-10-batches-py/batches.meta')['label_names']
            data, labels = [], []
            for i in range(1, 6):                               Iterates through the five
                filename = './cifar-10-batches-py/data_batch_' + str(i)   batches for training and
                batch_data = unpickle(filename)                 unpickles the data
The named    if len(data) > 0:
image classes    data = np.vstack((data, batch_data['data']))
indexed by       labels = np.hstack((labels, batch_data['labels']))   Data is vertically stacked
each label   else:                                              into (50000,1024), and
index from       data = batch_data['data']                      labels are horizontally
labels           labels = batch_data['labels']   Applies the    stacked into (50000, )
            data = grayscale(data)          ◁──  grayscale function   after the first iteration.
                                                 on the (50000,1024)
                                                 array of image data
```

With the image data from CIFAR-10 loaded into the `data` array, the `labels` in the associated named array and the `names` array giving you the image classes associated with the label values, you can look at a particular class of images, such as `horse`, as you did in chapter 11. After selecting the indices of the image data that have the `horse` class by first selecting the indices of all the horse labels from the labels array, you can use those indices to index into the data array for label `ID=7` (horse). Then you can display a few horse images from the set of 50,000—5,000 for each class in training—and also another 10,000 for testing (1,000 for each class), using Matplotlib (listing 12.3).

Listing 12.3 Selecting the set of 5,000 horse images and displaying them

```
Converts the data to a NumPy        Converts the labels to a      Uses np.where to
matrix for the Autoencoder later    NumPy array through           select the indices
                                    an explicit cast so you       of the horse labels
 ▷ x = np.matrix(data)              can use np.where              (class ID=7)
   y = np.array(labels)        ◁──
   horse_indices = np.where(y == 7)[0]   ◁──
   horse_x = x[horse_indices]                              ◁──
   print('Some examples of horse images we will feed to the autoencoder for
   ➥ training')                                            Uses the horse indices to
   plt.rcParams['figure.figsize'] = (10, 10)               index into the image data
   num_examples = 5                                        of size (5000,1024)
   for i in range(num_examples):
       horse_img = np.reshape(horse_x[i, :], (32, 32))
       plt.subplot(1, num_examples, i+1)                  Displays the
       plt.imshow(horse_img, cmap='Greys_r')              horse image
   plt.show()
Sets up Matplot lib to print five
images of horses of size 10,10
```

The resulting output is shown in figure 12.2. Now you can see the CIFAR-10 images you used your autoencoder to learn a representation of.

Some examples of horse images we will feed to the autoencoder for training

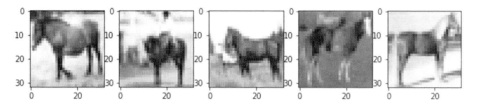

Figure 12.2   The first five horse images returned from the set of 5,000 samples in CIFAR-10 training data

Now review listing 12.4, which has the small snippet of code required to train your 100-neuron autoencoder to learn the representation of those horse images. You'll need to run your TensorFlow-trained autoencoder.

Listing 12.4   Training your `Autoencoder`

Input dimensions are sized 1024 (32 × 32) grayscale CIFAR-10 image.

```
input_dim = np.shape(horse_x)[1]
hidden_dim = 100
ae = Autoencoder(input_dim, hidden_dim)
ae.train(horse_x)
```

Use hidden neurons as the encoding size to train up the Autoencoder on the horse images.

Next, I'll show you how to use your learned representation to evaluate how well your encoding process did and how well it captures the `horse` image class.

12.2   *Autoencoders as classifiers*

It's probably worth reviewing the steps that you completed to build your autoencoder and get the CIFAR-10 data ready for loading. I'll summarize them for you:

1   Load the 50,000 training images for CIFAR-10. There are 5,000 sample images for each of the 10 classes of images. The images and their associated labels are read from Python's Pickle binary representation.

2   Each CIFAR-10 image is of 32 × 32, with three channels, or one value for red, green, and blue pixels. You converted the three channels to one-channel grayscale by averaging their three values.

3   You created an `autoencoder` class with a single hidden layer with 100 neurons, which took as input the set of 5,000 images with 1,024 pixels of grayscale intensity and reduced the size in a hidden layer to 100 values during the encoding step. The encoding step uses TensorFlow, learns via training, and uses root mean-squared error (RMSE) as the loss function and associated optimizer to learn the encoding weights (W_e) and biases (B_e) for your hidden layer encoding.

4   The decoding portion of your autoencoder also learns associated weights (W_d) and biases (B_d) and is codified in the `test` function, which you'll use in this section. You'll also create a `classify` function that will show off the learned representation of horse images that your network managed.

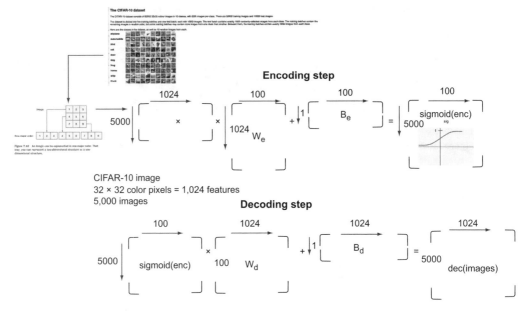

Figure 12.3   The overall CIFAR-10 autoencoding process. Images of size 32 × 32 with three channels are reshaped to 1,024 grayscale pixels.

The learned representation of your image data is the encoding hidden layer and its associated learned weights in your autoencoder. The overall process flow is shown in figure 12.3.

Now let's see some information about the learned encoding of images. You can use the `Autoencoder.test` function to print the values of the hidden layer and its values for reconstructing the inputs. You can try it on the 1000 test CIFAR-10 horse images, but first, you'll have to load the images (listing 12.5). CIFAR-10's test data comes in Python Pickle format. Loading it and converting it to grayscale should be familiar, as should selecting the `horse` class indices (class `ID=7`) and selecting the horse images from the 1,000-image test set. Then you will run `Autoencoder.test` to get an idea of how well the autoencoder performed. As you may remember from listing 12.1, the `test` function loads the hidden encoded layer, runs the decoder step, and shows the original input values.

Listing 12.5   Loading test CIFAR-10 images and evaluating the `Autoencoder`

Loads the pickled 10,000 test images for CIFAR-10 by reading the 'data' and 'labels' keys from the resulting deserialized dictionary

Selects the indices of the horse class ID=7 and indexes into the image data array for the 1,000 horse images

```
test_data = unpickle('./cifar-10-batches-py/test_batch')
test_x = grayscale(test_data['data'])
test_labels = np.array(test_data['labels'])
test_horse_indices = np.where(test_labels==7)[0]
test_horse = test_x[test_horse_indices]
ae.test(test_horse)
```

Runs the Autoencoder test method to evaluate the Autoencoder

The output from running listing 12.5 follows:

```
input [[ 34.          60.66666667  36.33333333 ...    5.            3.66666667
     5.        ]
 [111.66666667 120.         116.          ... 205.66666667 204.33333333
  206.        ]
 [ 48.33333333  66.66666667  86.66666667 ... 135.33333333 133.66666667
  140.        ]
 ...
 [ 29.          43.33333333  58.66666667 ... 151.         151.33333333
  147.33333333]
 [100.66666667 108.66666667 109.66666667 ... 143.33333333 128.66666667
   85.33333333]
 [ 75.33333333 104.66666667 106.33333333 ... 108.33333333  63.66666667
   26.33333333]]
compressed [[0. 1. 1. ... 1. 1. 1.]
 [0. 1. 1. ... 1. 1. 1.]
 [1. 1. 1. ... 1. 1. 1.]
 ...
 [0. 1. 1. ... 1. 1. 1.]
 [0. 1. 1. ... 1. 1. 1.]
 [1. 1. 1. ... 1. 1. 1.]]
reconstructed [[ 88.69392   93.134995  93.69954  ...  49.1538    53.48016
   57.427284]
 [104.61283  101.96864  102.228165 ... 159.11684  158.36711  159.06337 ]
 [205.88844  204.99907  205.80833  ... 106.32716  107.85627  110.11922 ]
 ...
 [ 77.93032   76.28443   76.910736 ... 139.74327  139.15686  138.78288 ]
 [171.00897  170.47668  172.95482  ... 149.24767  148.32034  151.43066 ]
 [185.52625  183.34001  182.78853  ... 125.33179  127.04839  129.3505  ]]
```

Python and NumPy does the lovely summarization:

- Each test horse image of the 1,000 includes 1,024 image pixels, so each row in the `input` is 1,024 numbers.
- The `compressed` layer is 100 neurons, turned on (`1.`) or off (`0.`).
- The `reconstructed` values are the values restored after the decode step of the autoencoder.

A quick scan of the reconstruction for image values shows quite a variance. The first three numbers in the original input image—34, 60.66666667, and 36.33333333—are reconstructed as 88.69392, 93.134995, 93.69954 by the autoencoder. Similar differences exist in other images and in other pixels, but don't get too worked up about them. The autoencoder was trained by default for only 100 epochs, with a learning rate of 0.001. As I explained in earlier chapters, hyperparameter tuning is an active area of research. You can tweak these hyperparameters and obtain better values. You could even do other optimizations and tricks that I will teach you when convolutional neural networks (CNNs) and data augmentation come into the picture, but for now, using the `test` method is a quick-and-dirty way to evaluate the autoencoder. A better way may be to visualize the learned representation of the images compared with their originals and visually compare how well they match. I'll show you how, but first, I'll demonstrate another computational method to evaluate the autoencoder.

12.2.1 *Using the autoencoder as a classifier via loss*

Comparing the values from the reconstructed images with the original input shows a variance between the reconstructed pixel values and the original pixel values. This variance is easily measured with the loss function set up to guide the autoencoder during training. You used RMSE. RMSE is the difference between the model-generated data and the input, squared, reduced to a scalar via the mean average and then the square root of that. RMSE is a nice distance measure for evaluating loss for training. Even better, it's a good classification indication, because as it turns out, images that belong to a particular image class have a similar loss from the model value when compared with the original value.

Horse images have a particular loss, airplane images have a different loss, and so on. You can test this intuition by adding a simple method to the `autoencoder` class: `classify`. This method's job will be to compute the loss function for the `horse` class and then compare the loss generated for those images with that of the loss for the other image classes and see whether there is a difference. Listing 12.6 adds the `classify` method to the `autoencoder` class and returns the hidden and reconstructed layers for later use.

Listing 12.6   `Autoencoder.classify` comparing loss across classes

```
def classify(self, data, labels):                         Initializes the
    with tf.Session() as sess:                            TensorFlow trained
        sess.run(tf.global_variables_initializer())      model and loads it
        self.saver.restore(sess, './model.ckpt')
        hidden, reconstructed = sess.run([self.encoded, self.decoded],
        ➥ feed_dict={self.x: data})                        Uses NumPy to compute the
        reconstructed = reconstructed[0]                         loss RMSE for all images
        loss = np.sqrt(np.mean(np.square(data - reconstructed), axis=1))
        horse_indices = np.where(labels == 7)[0]
        not_horse_indices = np.where(labels != 7)[0]
        horse_loss = np.mean(loss[horse_indices])
        not_horse_loss = np.mean(loss[not_horse_indices])
        print('horse', horse_loss)
        print('not horse', not_horse_loss)
        return hidden
```

Obtains the hidden (encoded) layer and its reconstruction for use in computing loss

Prints the horse loss and the not horse loss from the classifier

Computes the indices of the horse images and the indices of all other classes, and computes the mean loss value across all images (horse or not horse)

Following is the output from listing 12.6:

```
horse 63.19770728235271
not horse 61.771580430829474
```

And though not staggering, the loss value from image to reconstruction for `horse` is clearly different and statistically significant compared with that of the other image classes. So although the autoencoder may not have enough experience to reconstruct the image with little loss, it learned enough of a representation of horse images to be able to distinguish their structure from that of the other nine image classes in CIFAR-10. Cool!

Now you can look at the difference in the reconstruction of some of the images. A little Matplotlib goes a long way. You can take the hidden layer returned from the `classify` function and a small `decode` method to your autoencoder, which will generate the reconstruction for a particular encoded image and reconvert it from 1,024 pixels to a 32 × 32 grayscale image. The code is in listing 12.7.

Listing 12.7 The decode method to convert an encoded image back to CIFAR-10

```
def decode(self, encoding):
    with tf.Session() as sess:
        sess.run(tf.global_variables_initializer())
        self.saver.restore(sess, './model.ckpt')
        reconstructed = sess.run(self.decoded, feed_dict={self.encoded:
        ➥ encoding})
    img = np.reshape(reconstructed, (32, 32))
    return img
```

Loads TensorFlow and the stored Autoencoder model to generate the image reconstruction

Reshapes the reconstructed 1,024-pixel array into a 32 × 32 grayscale image and returns it

---

After you run that code, you can use Matplotlib (listing 12.8) to generate a set of reconstructions of the first 20 horse images from the CIFAR-10 test dataset, with the original images on the left and what the autoencoder "sees" on the right.

Listing 12.8 Evaluating and visualizing CIFAR-10 reconstructed horse images

Iterates through the first 20 test horse images from CIFAR-10

```
plt.rcParams['figure.figsize'] = (100, 100)
plt.figure()
for i in range(20):
    plt.subplot(20, 2, i*2 + 1)
    original_img = np.reshape(test_horse[i, :], (32, 32))
    plt.imshow(original_img, cmap='Greys_r')

    plt.subplot(20, 2, i*2 + 2)
    reconstructed_img = ae.decode([encodings_horse[i]])
    plt.imshow(reconstructed_img, cmap='Greys_r')

plt.show()
```

Sets up the Matplotlib plot to be a set of 100 × 100 figure areas (rows)

For each CIFAR-10 test horse image, shows it on the left side of the column

Shows the plot

For each CIFAR-10 test horse image, shows the autoencoder reconstruction on the right side of the column

---

Figure 12.4 shows the results.

Figure 12.4   A subset of the output from listing 12.8 showing 3 of the first 20 CIFAR-10 test horse images: the original CIFAR-10 test horse image on the left and what the autoencoder "sees" on the right

Now that you have both numerical and visual ways of evaluating your autoencoder, I'll show you another type of autoencoder: the denoising autoencoder.

The results of examining the autoencoder representation on the right side of figure 12.4 are fascinating if you think about them. Based on a few of the representations on the right, the autoencoder clearly has some basic understanding of the horse features versus the background and the general shape of the object. I typically think of an autoencoder representation as being what you would think about when you close your eyes and try to reimagine something you saw in the distant past. Sometimes, imagination allows you to remember the recent future fairly well, but many of your representations of the distant past look like the autoencoder-generated images on the right side of figure 12.4—basic features, shapes, and differentiation with background, but not perfect reconstructions by any means. If an autoencoder can learn to take imperfection into account when remembering the images, it can build a more resilient model. That's where the denoising autoencoder comes in to play.

12.3   *Denoising autoencoders*

In real life, we humans use our minds to think about something for a while and improve the way that we remember it. Suppose that you are trying to remember playing fetch with your family dog, and you struggle to remember what he looked like or the black patch of fur under his rosy nose. Seeing more dogs with black patches in a similar area or with slightly different patches, perhaps of different colors, might trigger a better reconstruction in your memory.

Part of the reason is that our minds build visual models that get better by seeing more examples. I'll discuss this topic more in chapter 14, which covers CNNs, which are a learning approach and network architecture focused on delineating lower- and higher-level image features. Additional images that are extremely similar to the one you are trying to recall—such as an old pet, perhaps—help you focus on the important features of that image. More examples of dissimilar images help too. Images with noise in them—such as variations in light, hue, contrast, or other repeatable differences— build a more resilient model and memory of the original image.

Drawing from this inspiration, denoising autoencoders introduce some noise by passing pixel values through a Gaussian function or randomly masking some pixels by turning them off (or on) from the original image to build a more resilient, robust representation of the image your network is trying to learn. You need to modify the autoencoder original class only slightly to create a denoising autoencoder and try it on your CIFAR-10 data. Listing 12.9 sets up the `Denoiser` class with a slight modification to the function to obtain batch data. Your `Denoiser` will maintain a parallel noised version of the input and as such will need to account for it in batch functions and throughout the remainder of the class. Most of the other methods you will recall from the `autoencoder` class—`train`, `test`, `classify`, and `decode`—work the same way as in the other listings in this chapter except for `train`, highlighted in listing 12.11.

Listing 12.9 The denoiser autoencoder

```
def get_batch_n(X, Xn, size):
    a = np.random.choice(len(X), size, replace=False)
    return X[a], Xn[a]
```
Gets a batch of training data input, along with its noised version

```
class Denoiser:

    def __init__(self, input_dim, hidden_dim, epoch=10000, batch_size=50,
        learning_rate=0.001):
        self.epoch = epoch
        self.batch_size = batch_size
        self.learning_rate = learning_rate

        self.x = tf.placeholder(dtype=tf.float32, shape=[None, input_dim],
            name='x')
        self.x_noised = tf.placeholder(dtype=tf.float32, shape=[None,
            input_dim], name='x_noised')
        with tf.name_scope('encode'):
            self.weights1 = tf.Variable(tf.random_normal([input_dim,
                hidden_dim], dtype=tf.float32), name='weights')
            self.biases1 = tf.Variable(tf.zeros([hidden_dim]), name='biases')
            self.encoded = tf.nn.sigmoid(tf.matmul(self.x_noised,
                self.weights1) + self.biases1, name='encoded')
        with tf.name_scope('decode'):
            weights = tf.Variable(tf.random_normal([hidden_dim, input_dim],
                dtype=tf.float32), name='weights')
            biases = tf.Variable(tf.zeros([input_dim]), name='biases')
            self.decoded = tf.matmul(self.encoded, weights) + biases
        self.loss = tf.sqrt(tf.reduce_mean(tf.square(tf.subtract(self.x,
            self.decoded))))
        self.train_op =
            tf.train.AdamOptimizer(self.learning_rate).minimize(self.loss)
        self.saver = tf.train.Saver()
```

Creates the weights and biases and encoded data layer, using the sigmoid function

Sets up the placeholder for the noised version of the input data

Creates the weights and biases and decoded data layer for emitting the learned representation

Sets up the loss and training operation using the AdamOptimizer

---

The biggest difference in the setup for the denoiser is the storage of a parallel Tensor-Flow placeholder for the noised-up version of the input data that the encoding step uses instead of the original input. You could take a few approaches. You could use a

Gaussian function and sample random pixels and mask out the input pixels according to some frequency, for example. These random pixels are—you guessed it—another hyperparameter in the machine learning modeling process. There isn't a best approach, so experiment with methods and pick the best one for your use case. Your `Denoiser` will implement two noise approaches—Gaussian and random mask—in listing 12.10.

Listing 12.10 The `add_noise` method for your `Denoiser`

```
def add_noise(self, data, noise_type='mask-0.2'):
    if noise_type == 'gaussian':
        n = np.random.normal(0, 0.1, np.shape(data))      Adds a value between 0 and
        return data + n                                    0.1 along a Gaussian random
    if 'mask' in noise_type:                               function to each pixel
        frac = float(noise_type.split('-')[1])
        temp = np.copy(data)
        for i in temp:
            n = np.random.choice(len(i), round(frac * len(i)), replace=False)
            i[n] = 0
        return temp        ◁——— Returns the noised data
```

Picks some percentage provided by frac of the overall input pixels to set to value 0 randomly

With noised data, the `train` method uses the `get_batch_n` method, which returns noised and regular batch input data for training. Additionally, the remaining methods for `test`, `classify`, and `decode` are unchanged other than to provide the noised data so that the appropriate tensors can be returned. Listing 12.11 completes the `Denoiser` class with the exception of the `decode` function, which is the same as that of listing 12.7.

Listing 12.11 The rest of the `Denoiser` class

```
def train(self, data):                            Creates a noised version of the
    data_noised = self.add_noise(data)   ◁——┘     data with the add_noise function
        with tf.Session() as sess:
            sess.run(tf.global_variables_initializer())
            for i in range(self.epoch):
                for j in range(50):
                    batch_data, batch_data_noised = get_batch_n(data,
                        data_noised, self.batch_size)
                    l, _ = sess.run([self.loss, self.train_op],
                        feed_dict={self.x: batch_data, self.x_noised:
                        batch_data_noised})
                if i % 10 == 0:
                    print('epoch {0}: loss = {1}'.format(i, l))
                    self.saver.save(sess, './model.ckpt')
                    epoch_time = int(time.time())
            self.saver.save(sess, './model.ckpt')

def test(self, data):
    with tf.Session() as sess:
        self.saver.restore(sess, './model.ckpt')
```

Creates a new TensorFlow session for training

Uses the noised data

```
            data_noised = self.add_noise(data)
            hidden, reconstructed = sess.run([self.encoded, self.decoded],
                feed_dict={self.x: data, self.x_noised:data_noised})
        print('input', data)
        print('compressed', hidden)
        print('reconstructed', reconstructed)
        return reconstructed

    def classify(self, data, labels):
        with tf.Session() as sess:
            sess.run(tf.global_variables_initializer())
            self.saver.restore(sess, './model.ckpt')
            data_noised = self.add_noise(data)
            hidden, reconstructed = sess.run([self.encoded, self.decoded],
                feed_dict={self.x: data, self.x_noised:data_noised})
            reconstructed = reconstructed[0]
            print('reconstructed', np.shape(reconstructed))
            loss = np.sqrt(np.mean(np.square(data - reconstructed), axis=1))
            print('loss', np.shape(loss))
            horse_indices = np.where(labels == 7)[0]
            not_horse_indices = np.where(labels != 7)[0]
            horse_loss = np.mean(loss[horse_indices])
            not_horse_loss = np.mean(loss[not_horse_indices])
            print('horse', horse_loss)
            print('not horse', not_horse_loss)
            return hidden
```

> **Gets a noised version of the data for testing and classification**

One thing that you will notice when looking at the output of the test function is that with only 1,000 test samples and noise, the `Denoiser` has lost some of its early gains in classification power and ability to distinguish among image classes because there is little difference in mean loss between the `horse` and `not horse` classes:

```
data (10000, 1024)
reconstructed (1024,)
loss (10000,)
horse 61.12571251705483
not horse 61.106683374373304
```

But not to worry, because over time, the `Denoiser` autoencoder will learn a more robust model of the image features, resilient to fluctuations and imperfections in training data, to develop a more solid model. You need more data than CIFAR-10 has for you for the `horse` class at the moment. Figure 12.5 shows the image representation of what the `Denoiser` learns for three of the first 20 horse images from the CIFAR-10 test set (on the left). There's one more autoencoder to learn about: the stacked or deep autoencoder. Onward to the finish line!

Figure 12.5   The noised version of the autoencoder and its representations (right) of the original CIFAR-10 test horse images (left)

12.4   *Stacked deep autoencoders*

Another class of autoencoders is referred to as *stacked* or *deep autoencoders*. Instead of having a single hidden layer that handles the encoding step on the input end and ends the decoding with a single layer of hidden neurons on the output end, stacked autoencoders have several layers of hidden neurons, using the previous layer to parameterize and tune the learned representation of the future layers. Future layers in these autoencoders have fewer neurons. The goal is to create and learn the optimal settings for an even more compressed interpretation of your input data.

In practice, each hidden layer in the stacked autoencoder learns a parameterization of a set of optimal features to achieve optimal compressed representation in the adjacent layers. You could think of each layer as representing a set of higher-order features, and because you don't know precisely what they are yet, this concept is a useful way to simplify the complexity of the problem. In chapter 14, you'll explore some ways to visualize these representations, but for now, the lesson from chapter 11 holds: as you add more hidden neurons that are not linear, your autoencoder can learn and represent any function. Now you can take input and make it even smaller!

Your `StackedAutoencoder` class is a fairly straightforward adaption of the previous autoencoders, as you see in listing 12.12. You will create hidden layers with neurons amounting to half of the provided input. The first hidden layer is `input_dim /2`, the second is `input_dim /4`, and so on. With three hidden layers by default, your autoencoder learns an encoding that is a fourth the size of the original input, so for CIFAR-10, it learns a representation of the input with 256 numbers. The last hidden layer is sized `input_dim /2`, and the final output layer is size `input_dim`. The class methods are similar to previous autoencoders except that they operate on the N-1 encoding layer of the architecture.

Listing 12.12   The `StackedAutoencoder` class

Creates a StackedAutoencoder with 3 hidden layers, batch size of 250, and learning rate 0.01, and trains for 100 epochs

```
class StackedAutoencoder:
    def __init__(self, input_dim, num_hidden_layers=3, epoch=100,
    ⮕ batch_size=250, learning_rate=0.01):
        self.epoch = epoch
        self.batch_size = batch_size
        self.learning_rate = learning_rate
        self.idim = [None]*num_hidden_layers
        self.hdim = [None]*num_hidden_layers
        self.hidden = [None]*num_hidden_layers
        self.weights = [None]*num_hidden_layers
        self.biases = [None]*num_hidden_layers
```

Number of hidden neurons for each hidden layer

The weights for each hidden layer

Input dimensions for each hidden layer

The tensors representing each hidden layer activated by the act function (tf.nn.relu)

The biases for each hidden layer

```
x = tf.placeholder(dtype=tf.float32, shape=[None, input_dim])
initializer=tf.variance_scaling_initializer()
output_dim = input_dim
act=tf.nn.relu
```

Uses the tf.nn.relu (rectifying linear unit) activation function

Inputs dimensions, initially the size of the input and then the output from the previous hidden layer

Performs the network construction input to hidden layers

```
for i in range(0, num_hidden_layers):
    self.idim[i] = int(input_dim / (2*i)) if i else input_dim
    self.hdim[i] = int(input_dim / (2*(i+1))) if i <
        num_hidden_layers-1 else int(input_dim/2)
    print('%s, weights [%d, %d] biases %d' % ("hidden layer "
        +str(i+1) if i else "input to hidden layer 1", self.idim[i],
        self.hdim[i], self.hdim[i]))
    self.weights[i] = tf.Variable(initializer([self.idim[i],
        self.hdim[i]]), dtype=tf.float32, name='weights'+str(i))
    self.biases[i] = tf.Variable(tf.zeros([self.hdim[i]]),
        name='biases'+str(i))
```

Number of hidden neurons (input_dim /2) for each hidden layer

```
    if i == 0:
        self.hidden[i] = act(tf.matmul(x, self.weights[i]) +
            self.biases[i])
    else:
        self.hidden[i] = act(tf.matmul(self.hidden[i-1],
            self.weights[i]) + self.biases[i])
```

The hidden layer is the matrix multiplication of the input × weights plus the biases, or the previous layer encoding × weights plus the biases.

```
#output layer
print('output layer, weights [%d, %d] biases %d' %
    (self.hdim[num_hidden_layers-1], output_dim, output_dim))
self.output_weight =
    tf.Variable(initializer([self.hdim[num_hidden_layers-1],
    output_dim]), dtype=tf.float32, name='output_weight')
self.output_bias = tf.Variable(tf.zeros([output_dim]),
    name='output_bias')
self.output_layer = act(tf.matmul(self.hidden[num_hidden_layers-1],
    self.output_weight)+self.output_bias)
```

Creates the output layer, which is of dimension layer N-1 × output size, or original input size.

```
self.x = x
self.loss = tf.reduce_mean(tf.square(self.output_layer-self.x))
self.train_op =
    tf.train.AdamOptimizer(self.learning_rate).minimize(self.loss)
self.saver = tf.train.Saver()
```

The `train` method is fairly straightforward, though I introduce you briefly to the TensorFlow `Dataset` API, a powerful system for easily manipulating and preparing data for training. Instead of rewriting the same batch method over and over, you can use `tf.Dataset` and its methods to batch and shuffle the data (in a randomized fashion) to prepare it for training. You'll see other useful methods in chapter 14. The key takeaways for `tf.Dataset` are the ability to automatically set `shuffle` and `batch` parameters ahead of time and then to use an iterator to get batches of size `batch_size` that are automatically shuffled in random order so that your network doesn't memorize the order of the input data. When the iterator is exhausted, you are done with the epoch, and you can catch a `tf.errors.OutOfRangeException` to account for this case.

Listing 12.13 The `train` method for `StackedAutoencoder` and `tf.Dataset`

```
def train(self, data):                                    Creates a new tf.Dataset from tensor slices in this
    features = data                                        case, the input data a NumPy array
    features_placeholder = tf.placeholder(features.dtype, features.shape)
    dataset =
    ➥ tf.data.Dataset.from_tensor_slices((features_placeholder))
    dataset = dataset.shuffle(buffer_size=100)    ◄
    dataset = dataset.batch(self.batch_size)              Sets the shuffle size for
                                                           randomized sample
    with tf.Session() as sess:                             selection from the input
        sess.run(tf.global_variables_initializer())
        for i in range(self.epoch):
            batch_num=0
            iter = dataset.make_initializable_iterator()
            sess.run(iter.initializer, feed_dict={features_placeholder:
            ➥ features})
            iter_op = iter.get_next()    ◄
                                                 Gets the next batch of size
                                                 randomly shuffled from the
            while True:                          original input set
                try:
                    batch_data = sess.run(iter_op)
                    l, _ = sess.run([self.loss, self.train_op],
                    ➥ feed_dict={self.x: batch_data})
                    batch_num += 1
                except tf.errors.OutOfRangeError:
                    break

            print('epoch {0}: loss = {1}'.format(i, l))
            self.saver.save(sess, './model.ckpt')
```

Sets the size of the batch in each batch training step

Uses an iterator that can be initialized with the input data in each batch

Catches the exception, indicating that the dataset has been exhausted in this epoch, and then moves to the save epoch after saving the mode

TensorFlow's Dataset API is elegant and simplifies common batch-training techniques, as you saw with the `train` method in listing 12.13. The rest of the `StackedAutoencoder` is more or less the same as the other autoencoders, except that you use the N-1 layer encodings for classification and for the decoding step. Listing 12.14 defines the rest of the class.

Listing 12.14 The rest of the `StackedAutoencoder` method

```
def test(self, data):                                     Computes the last layer before output,
    with tf.Session() as sess:                             based on the input, and then decodes
        self.saver.restore(sess, './model.ckpt')                          that layer
        hidden, reconstructed = sess.run([self.hidden[num_hidden_layers-1],
        ➥ self.output_layer], feed_dict={self.x: data})
        print('input', data)
        print('compressed', hidden)
        print('reconstructed', reconstructed)    ◄        Prints the activated N-1
        return reconstructed                               layer neuron values
```

Prints the input data

Prints the reconstructed data

```
def classify(self, data, labels):
    with tf.Session() as sess:
        sess.run(tf.global_variables_initializer())
        self.saver.restore(sess, './model.ckpt')
        hidden, reconstructed = sess.run([self.hidden[num_hidden_layers-1],
            self.output_layer], feed_dict={self.x: data})
        reconstructed = reconstructed[0]
        print('reconstructed', np.shape(reconstructed))
        loss = np.sqrt(np.mean(np.square(data - reconstructed), axis=1))
        print('loss', np.shape(loss))
        horse_indices = np.where(labels == 7)[0]
        not_horse_indices = np.where(labels != 7)[0]
        horse_loss = np.mean(loss[horse_indices])
        not_horse_loss = np.mean(loss[not_horse_indices])
        print('horse', horse_loss)
        print('not horse', not_horse_loss)
        return hidden

def decode(self, encoding):
    with tf.Session() as sess:
        sess.run(tf.global_variables_initializer())
        self.saver.restore(sess, './model.ckpt')
        reconstructed = sess.run(self.output_layer,
    feed_dict={self.hidden[num_hidden_layers-1]: encoding})
        img = np.reshape(reconstructed, (32, 32))
        return img
```

Uses the last N-1 layer for classification → [points to `hidden, reconstructed = sess.run(...)` line]

Prints the loss from the horse test class → [points to `print('horse', horse_loss)` line]

Prints the loss from all other image classes ← [points to `print('not horse', not_horse_loss)` line]

Uses the N-1 layer to obtain the output layer and returns the reconstructed 32 × 32 image ← [points to `feed_dict={self.hidden[num_hidden_layers-1]: encoding})` line]

The output of the test method shows that the `StackedEncoder` N-1 layer encodings are enough to delineate between the horse class and other image classes, though the encodings show less variation than the original autoencoder. Interestingly enough, though, the reconstructed images show a more compact overall representation of features, and some grainy higher-order features are present in the masked-out artifacts on the right side of the representations of the original CIFAR-test horse images in figure 12.6.

```
reconstructed (1024,)
loss (10000,)
horse 65.17236194056699
not horse 64.06345316293603
```

Now that you have explored different autoencoders and their benefits and trade-offs for classification and detection related to images, you're all set to apply them to other real datasets!

Figure 12.6   Stacked autoencoder representations (right) of the three CIFAR-10 test images (left). Higher order features are visible in masked-out grainy areas.

Summary

- Autoencoders can be used to classify, sort, and cluster images by learning a representation of them with neural network hidden layers.
- CIFAR-10 is a widely used image dataset with 10 classes of images (including `horse`, `bird`, and `automobile`). CIFAR-10 includes 5,000 images per class for training (50,000 total) and 10,000 total images for testing (1,000 per class).
- Specializations of autoencoders can be used to learn more robust representations of input such as images by handling noise in data features or by using denser architectures with more layers. These autoencoders are called denoising and stacked autoencoders.
- You can evaluate autoencoders on image data by comparing the learned representation values with their original results by hand or by using Matplotlib and other helper libraries.

Reinforcement learning

13

Humans learn from experiences (or at least *should*). You didn't get so charming by accident. Years of positive compliments as well as negative criticism have all helped shape who you are today. This chapter is about designing a machine-learning system driven by criticisms and rewards.

You learn what makes people happy, for example, by interacting with friends, family members, or even strangers, and you figure out how to ride a bike by trying out various muscle movements until riding clicks. When you perform actions, you're sometimes rewarded immediately. Finding a good restaurant nearby might yield instant gratification, for example. At other times, the reward doesn't appear right away; you might have to travel a long distance to find an exceptional place to eat. *Reinforcement learning* is about choosing the right actions, given any state—such as in figure 13.1, which shows a person making decisions to arrive at their destination.

Moreover, suppose that on your drive from home to work, you always choose the same route. But one day, your curiosity takes over, and you decide to try a different path in the hope of shortening your commute. This dilemma—trying new routes or sticking to the best-known route—is an example of *exploration versus exploitation*.

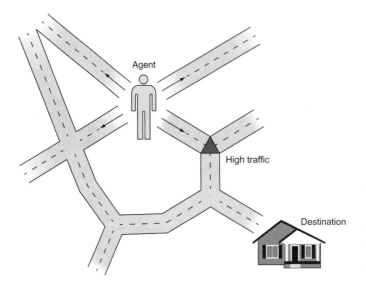

Figure 13.1 A person navigating to reach a destination in the midst of traffic and unexpected situations is a problem setup for reinforcement learning.

NOTE Why is the trade-off between trying new things and sticking with old ones called *exploration versus exploitation*? Exploration makes sense, but you can think of exploitation as exploiting your knowledge of the status quo by sticking with what you know.

All these examples can be unified under a general formulation: performing an action in a scenario can yield a reward. A more technical term for scenario is *state*. And we call the collection of all possible states a *state space*. Performing an action causes the state to change. This shouldn't be too unfamiliar to you if you remember chapters 9 and 10, which deal with hidden Markov models (HMMs). You transitioned from state to state in those chapters based on observations. But what series of actions yields the highest expected rewards?

13.1 *Formal notions*

Whereas supervised and unsupervised learning appear at opposite ends of the spectrum, reinforcement learning (RL) exists somewhere in the middle. It's not supervised learning, because the training data comes from the algorithm deciding between exploration and exploitation. And it's not unsupervised, because the algorithm receives feedback from the environment. As long as you're in a situation in which performing an action in a state produces a reward, you can use reinforcement learning to discover a good sequence of actions to take to maximize expected rewards.

You may notice that reinforcement-learning lingo involves anthropomorphizing the algorithm into taking *actions* in *situations* to *receive rewards*. The algorithm is often referred to as an *agent* that acts with the environment. It shouldn't be a surprise that much of reinforcement-learning theory is applied in robotics. Figure 13.2 demonstrates the interplay among states, actions, and rewards.

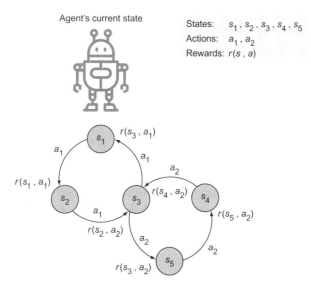

Agent's current state

States: s_1, s_2, s_3, s_4, s_5
Actions: a_1, a_2
Rewards: $r(s, a)$

Figure 13.2 Actions are represented by arrows, and states are represented by circles. Performing an action on a state produces a reward. If you start at state s_1, you can perform action a_1 to obtain a reward $r(s_1, a_1)$.

Do humans use reinforcement learning?

Reinforcement learning seems to be the best way to explain how to perform the next action based on the current situation. Perhaps humans behave the same way biologically. But let's not get ahead of ourselves; consider the following example.

Sometimes, humans act without thinking. If I'm thirsty, I might instinctively grab a cup of water to quench my thirst. I don't iterate through all possible joint motions in my head and choose the optimal one after thorough calculations.

Most important, the actions we make aren't characterized solely by our observations at each moment. Otherwise, we're no smarter than bacteria, which act deterministically given their environment. There seems to be a lot more going on, and a simple RL model might not explain human behavior fully.

A robot performs actions to change states. But how does it decide which action to take? Section 13.1.1 introduces a new concept to answer this question.

13.1.1 Policy

Everyone cleans their room differently. Some people start by making their bed. I prefer cleaning my room clockwise so I don't miss a corner. Have you ever seen a robotic vacuum cleaner, such as a Roomba? Someone programmed a strategy the robot can follow to clean any room. In reinforcement-learning lingo, the way that an agent decides which action to take is a *policy*: the set of actions that determines the next state (figure 13.3).

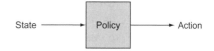

Figure 13.3 A policy suggests which action to take, given a state.

The goal of reinforcement learning is to discover a good policy. A common way to create that policy is to observe the long-term consequences of actions at each state. The *reward* is the measure of the outcome of taking an action. The best possible policy is called the *optimal policy*, which is the Holy Grail of reinforcement learning. The optimal policy tells you the optimal action, given any state—but as in real life, it may not provide the highest reward at the moment.

If you measure the reward by looking at the immediate consequence—the state of things after taking the action—it's easy to calculate. This strategy is called the *greedy strategy*. But it's not always a good idea to "greedily" choose the action that provides the best immediate reward. When you're cleaning your room, for example, you might make your bed first, because the room looks neater with the bed made. But if another goal is to wash your sheets, making the bed first may not be the best overall strategy. You need to look at the results of the next few actions and the eventual end state to come up with the optimal approach. Similarly, in chess, grabbing your opponent's queen may maximize the points for the pieces on the board—but if it puts you in checkmate five moves later, it isn't the best possible move.

Limitations of (Markovian) reinforcement learning

Most RL formulations assume that you can figure out the best action to take from knowing the current state, instead of considering the longer-term history of states and actions that got you there. This approach to making decisions is called *Markovian*, and the general framework is often referred to as the *Markov decision process* (MDP). I hinted at this earlier.

Situations in which the state sufficiently captures what to do next can be modeled with the RL algorithms discussed in this chapter. But most real-world situations aren't Markovian and therefore need a more realistic approach, such as a hierarchical representation of states and actions. In a grossly oversimplified sense, hierarchical models are like context-free grammars, whereas MDPs are like finite-state machines. The expressive leap of modeling a problem as an MDP to something more hierarchical can dramatically improve the effectiveness of the planning algorithm.

You can also choose an action arbitrarily, which is a *random policy*. If you come up with a policy to solve a reinforcement-learning problem, it's often a good idea to double-check that your learned policy performs better than both the random and greedy policies, which are often called a *baseline*.

13.1.2 *Utility*

The long-term reward is called a *utility*. If you know the utility of performing an action at a state, learning the policy is easy with reinforcement learning. To decide which action to take, you select the action that produces the highest utility. The hard part, as you might have guessed, is uncovering these utility values.

The utility of performing an action (a) at a state (s) is written as a function $Q(s, a)$, called the *utility function*, shown in figure 13.4.

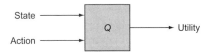

Figure 13.4   **Given a state and the action taken, applying a utility function Q predicts the expected and the total rewards: the immediate reward (next state) plus rewards gained later by following an optimal policy.**

> **Exercise 13.1**
>
> If you were given the utility function Q(s, a), how could you use it to derive a policy function?
>
> **Answer**
>
> Policy(s) = argmax_a Q(s, a)

An elegant way to calculate the utility of a particular state-action pair (s, a) is to recursively consider the utilities of future actions. The utility of your current action is influenced not only by the immediate reward, but also by the next best action, as shown in the following formula. In the formula, s' is the next state, and a' denotes the next action. The reward of taking action a in state s is denoted by $r(s, a)$:

$$Q(s, a) = r(s, a) + \gamma\max Q(s', a')$$

Here, γ is a hyperparameter that you get to choose, called the *discount factor*. If γ is 0, the agent chooses the action that maximizes the immediate reward. Higher values of γ will make the agent put more importance on considering long-term consequences. You can read the formula as "the value of this action is the immediate reward provided by taking this action, added to the discount factor times the best thing that can happen after that."

Looking to future rewards is one type of hyperparameter you can play with, but there's another. In some applications of reinforcement learning, newly available information might be more important than historical records, or vice versa. If a robot is expected to learn to solve tasks quickly but not necessarily optimally, you might want to set a faster learning rate. Or if a robot is allowed more time to explore and exploit, you might tune down the learning rate. Let's call the learning rate α, and change the utility function as follows (noting that when $\alpha = 1$, the equations are identical):

$$Q(s, a) \leftarrow Q(s, a) + \alpha\ (r(s, a) + \gamma\max Q(s', a') - Q(s, a))$$

Reinforcement learning can be solved if you know the Q-function: $Q(s, a)$. Conveniently for us, *neural networks* (chapters 11 and 12) approximate functions, given enough training data. TensorFlow is the perfect tool to deal with neural networks because it comes with many essential algorithms that simplify neural-network implementation.

13.2 *Applying reinforcement learning*

Application of reinforcement learning requires defining a way to retrieve rewards after an action is taken from a state. A stock-market trader fits these requirements easily, because buying and selling a stock changes the state of the trader (cash on hand), and each action generates a reward (or loss).

Exercise 13.2

What are some possible disadvantages of using reinforcement learning for buying and selling stocks?

Answer

By performing actions in the market, such as buying or selling shares, you could end up influencing the market, causing it to change dramatically from your training data.

The states in this situation are a vector containing information about the current budget, the current number of stocks, and a recent history of stock prices (the last 200 stock prices). Each state is a 202-dimensional vector.

For simplicity, the only three actions are buy, sell, and hold:

- Buying a stock at the current stock price decreases the budget while incrementing the current stock count.
- Selling a stock trades it in for money at the current share price.
- Holding does neither thing. This action waits a single time period and yields no reward.

Figure 13.5 demonstrates one possible policy, given stock market data.

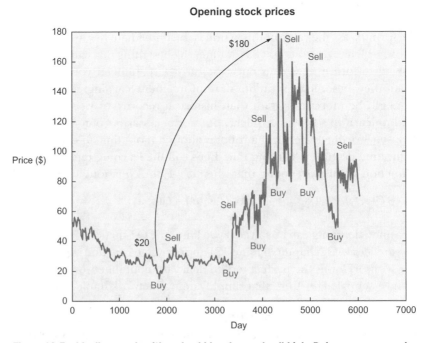

Opening stock prices

Figure 13.5 Ideally, our algorithm should buy low and sell high. Doing so once, as shown here, might yield a reward of around $160. But the real profit rolls in when you buy and sell more frequently. Have you ever heard the term *high-frequency trading*? This type of trading involves buying low and selling high as frequently as possible to maximize profits within a given period.

The goal is to learn a policy that gains the maximum net worth from trading in a stock market. Wouldn't that be cool? Let's do it!

13.3 *Implementing reinforcement learning*

To gather stock prices, you'll use the `ystockquote` library in Python. You can install it by using `pip` or follow the official guide (https://github.com/cgoldberg/ystockquote). The command to install it with `pip` is as follows:

```
$ pip install ystockquote
```

With that library installed, let's import all the relevant libraries (listing 13.1).

Listing 13.1 Importing relevant libraries

For obtaining stock-price raw data

```
import ystockquote
from matplotlib import pyplot as plt
import numpy as np
import tensorflow as tf
import random
```

For plotting stock prices

For numeric manipulation and machine learning

Create a helper function to get stock prices by using the `ystockquote` library. The library requires three pieces of information: share symbol, start date, and end date. When you pick each of the three values, you'll get a list of numbers representing the share prices in that period by day.

If you choose start and end dates that are too far apart, fetching that data will take some time. It might be a good idea to save (cache) the data to disk so that you can load it locally next time. Listing 13.2 shows to use the library and cache the data.

Listing 13.2 Helper function to get prices

```
def get_prices(share_symbol, start_date, end_date,
               cache_filename='stock_prices.npy', force=False):
    try:
        if force:
            raise IOError
        else:
            stock_prices = np.load(cache_filename)
    except IOError:
        stock_hist = ystockquote.get_historical_prices(share_symbol,
            start_date, end_date)
        stock_prices = []
        for day in sorted(stock_hist.keys()):
            stock_val = stock_hist[day]['Open']
            stock_prices.append(stock_val)
        stock_prices = np.asarray(stock_prices)
        np.save(cache_filename, stock_prices)

    return stock_prices.astype(float)
```

Tries to load the data from file if it has already been computed

Retrieves stock prices from the library

Extracts only relevant info from the raw data

Caches the result

As a sanity check, it's a good idea to visualize the stock-price data. Create a plot, and save it to disk (listing 13.3).

Listing 13.3   Helper function to plot the stock prices

```
def plot_prices(prices):
    plt.title('Opening stock prices')
    plt.xlabel('day')
    plt.ylabel('price ($)')
    plt.plot(prices)
    plt.savefig('prices.png')
    plt.show()
```

You can grab some data and visualize it by using listing 13.4.

Listing 13.4   Getting data and visualizing it

```
if __name__ == '__main__':
    prices = get_prices('MSFT', '1992-07-22', '2016-07-22', force=True)
    plot_prices(prices)
```

Figure 13.6 shows the chart produced by running listing 13.4.

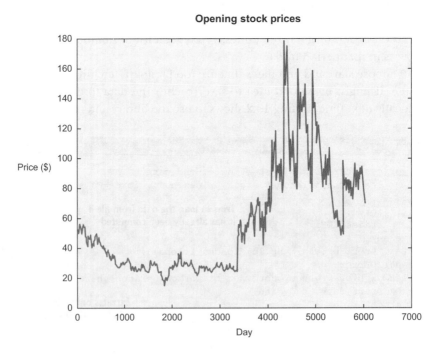

Figure 13.6   This chart summarizes the opening stock prices of Microsoft (MSFT) from July 22, 1992, to July 22, 2016. Wouldn't it have been nice to buy around day 3,000 and sell around day 5,000? Let's see whether our code can learn to buy, sell, and hold to make optimal gain.

Most reinforcement-learning algorithms follow similar implementation patterns. As a result, it's a good idea to create a class with the relevant methods to reference later, such as an abstract class or interface. See listing 13.5 for an example and figure 13.7 for an illustration. Reinforcement learning needs two well-defined operations: how to select an action and how to improve the utility Q-function.

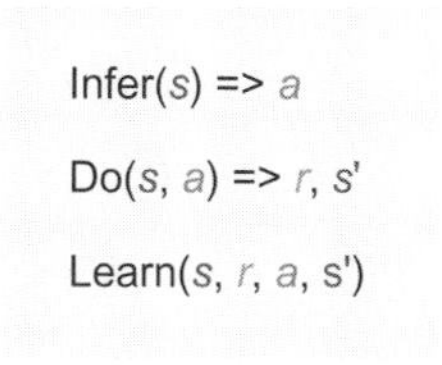

Infer(s) => a

Do(s, a) => r, s'

Learn(s, r, a, s')

Figure 13.7 Most reinforcement-learning algorithms boil down to three main steps: infer, do, and learn. During the first step, the algorithm selects the best action (a), given a state (s), using the knowledge it has so far. Next, it does the action to find out the reward (r) as well as the next state (s'). Then it improves its understanding of the world by using the newly acquired knowledge (s, r, a, s').

Listing 13.5 Defining a superclass for all decision policies

```
class DecisionPolicy:
    def select_action(self, current_state):      Given a state, the decision policy will
        pass                                      calculate the next action to take.

    def update_q(self, state, action, reward, next_state):   Improves the
        pass                                                  Q-function from a
                                                              new experience of
                                                              taking an action
```

Next, let's inherit from this superclass to implement a policy in which decisions are made at random, otherwise known as a *random decision policy*. You need to define only the select_action method, which randomly picks an action without even looking at the state. Listing 13.6 shows how to implement it.

Listing 13.6 Implementing a random decision policy

```
class RandomDecisionPolicy(DecisionPolicy):      Inherits from DecisionPolicy
    def __init__(self, actions):                 to implement its functions
        self.actions = actions

    def select_action(self, current_state):      Randomly chooses
        action = random.choice(self.actions)     the next action
        return action
```

In listing 13.7, you assume that a policy is given to you (such as the one from listing 13.6) and run it on the real-world stock-price data. This function takes care of exploration and exploitation at each interval of time. Figure 13.8 illustrates the algorithm from listing 13.7.

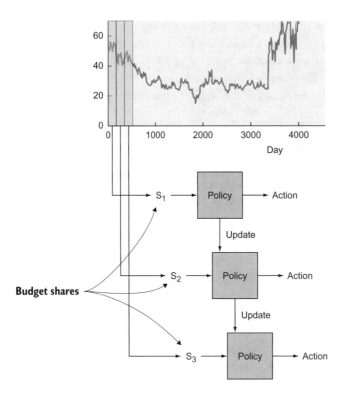

Figure 13.8 A rolling window of a certain size iterates through the stock prices, as shown by the chart segmented into states S_1, S_2, and S_3. The policy suggests an action to take: you may choose to exploit it or randomly explore another action. As you get rewards for performing an action, you can update the policy function over time.

Listing 13.7 Using a given policy to make decisions and returning the performance

```
def run_simulation(policy, initial_budget, initial_num_stocks, prices, hist):
    budget = initial_budget
    num_stocks = initial_num_stocks
    share_value = 0
    transitions = list()
    for i in range(len(prices) - hist - 1):
        if i % 1000 == 0:
            print('progress {:.2f}%'.format(float(100*i) /
            ➥ (len(prices) - hist - 1)))
        current_state = np.asmatrix(np.hstack((prices[i:i+hist], budget,
        ➥ num_stocks)))
        current_portfolio = budget + num_stocks * share_value
        action = policy.select_action(current_state, i)
        share_value = float(prices[i + hist])
        if action == 'Buy' and budget >= share_value:
            budget -= share_value
            num_stocks += 1
        elif action == 'Sell' and num_stocks > 0:
            budget += share_value
            num_stocks -= 1
        else:
            action = 'Hold'
        new_portfolio = budget + num_stocks * share_value
```

Initializes values that depend on computing the net worth of a portfolio

The state is a hist + 2D vector. You'll force it to be a NumPy matrix.

Calculates the portfolio value

Selects an action from the current policy

Updates portfolio values based on action

Computes a new portfolio value after taking action

Computes the reward from taking an action at a state

```
reward = new_portfolio - current_portfolio
next_state = np.asmatrix(np.hstack(((prices[i+1:i+hist+1], budget,
    num_stocks)))
transitions.append((current_state, action, reward, next_state))
policy.update_q(current_state, action, reward, next_state)
```

Updates the policy after experiencing a new action

```
    portfolio = budget + num_stocks * share_value
    return portfolio
```

Computes the final portfolio worth

To obtain a more robust measurement of success, run the simulation a couple of times and average the results (listing 13.8). Doing so may take a while (perhaps 5 minutes), but your results will be more reliable.

Listing 13.8 Running multiple simulations to calculate average performance

```
def run_simulations(policy, budget, num_stocks, prices, hist):
    num_tries = 10
    final_portfolios = list()
    for i in range(num_tries):
        final_portfolio = run_simulation(policy, budget, num_stocks, prices,
            hist)
        final_portfolios.append(final_portfolio)
        print('Final portfolio: ${}'.format(final_portfolio))
    plt.title('Final Portfolio Value')
    plt.xlabel('Simulation #')
    plt.ylabel('Net worth')
    plt.plot(final_portfolios)
    plt.show()
```

Decides the number of times to rerun the simulations

Stores the portfolio worth of each run in this array

Runs this simulation

In the `main` function, append the lines in listing 13.9 to define the decision policy, then run simulations to see how the policy performs.

Listing 13.9 Defining the decision policy

Defines the list of actions the agent can take

```
if __name__ == '__main__':
    prices = get_prices('MSFT', '1992-07-22', '2016-07-22')
    plot_prices(prices)
    actions = ['Buy', 'Sell', 'Hold']
    hist = 3
    policy = RandomDecisionPolicy(actions)
    budget = 100000.0
    num_stocks = 0
    run_simulations(policy, budget, num_stocks, prices, hist)
```

Initializes a random decision policy

Sets the initial amount of money available to use

Sets the number of stocks already owned

Runs simulations multiple times to compute the expected value of your final net worth

Now that you have a baseline to compare your results, let's implement a neural network approach to learn the Q-function. The decision policy is often called the *Q-learning decision policy.* Listing 13.10 introduces a new hyperparameter, `epsilon`, to keep the solution from getting "stuck" when applying the same action over and over. The lower the value of `epsilon`, the more often it will randomly explore new actions. The Q-function is defined by the function depicted in figure 13.9.

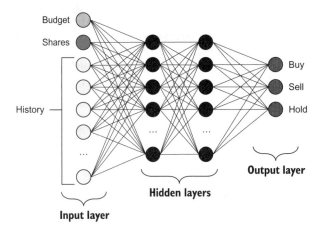

Figure 13.9   input is the state space vector, with three outputs: one for each output's Q-value.

Exercise 13.3

What other possible factors that your state-space representation ignores can affect the stock prices? How could you factor them into the simulation?

Answer

Stock prices depend on a variety of factors, including general market trends, breaking news, and specific industry trends. Each of these factors, once quantified, could be applied to the model as an additional dimension.

Listing 13.10   Implementing a more intelligent decision policy

```
class QLearningDecisionPolicy(DecisionPolicy):
    def __init__(self, actions, input_dim):
        self.epsilon = 0.95                              Sets the hyperparameters
        self.gamma = 0.3                                 from the Q-function
        self.actions = actions
        output_dim = len(actions)          Sets the number of hidden
        h1_dim = 20                        nodes in the neural networks

        self.x = tf.placeholder(tf.float32, [None, input_dim])
        self.y = tf.placeholder(tf.float32, [output_dim])
        W1 = tf.Variable(tf.random_normal([input_dim, h1_dim]))
        b1 = tf.Variable(tf.constant(0.1, shape=[h1_dim]))          Designs the
        h1 = tf.nn.relu(tf.matmul(self.x, W1) + b1)                 neural network
        W2 = tf.Variable(tf.random_normal([h1_dim, output_dim]))    architecture
        b2 = tf.Variable(tf.constant(0.1, shape=[output_dim]))
```

Defines the input and output tensors

Defines the op to compute the utility

Sets up the session and initializes variables

Exploits the best option with probability epsilon

Sets the loss as the square error

Uses an optimizer to update model parameters to minimize the loss

Explores a random option with probability 1 – epsilon

Updates the Q-function by updating its model parameters

```
        self.q = tf.nn.relu(tf.matmul(h1, W2) + b2)

        loss = tf.square(self.y - self.q)
        self.train_op = tf.train.AdagradOptimizer(0.01).minimize(loss)
        self.sess = tf.Session()
        self.sess.run(tf.global_variables_initializer())

    def select_action(self, current_state, step):
        threshold = min(self.epsilon, step / 1000.)
        if random.random() < threshold:
            # Exploit best option with probability epsilon
            action_q_vals = self.sess.run(self.q, feed_dict={self.x:
                current_state})
            action_idx = np.argmax(action_q_vals)
            action = self.actions[action_idx]
        else:
            # Explore random option with probability 1 - epsilon
            action = self.actions[random.randint(0, len(self.actions) - 1)]
        return action

    def update_q(self, state, action, reward, next_state):
        action_q_vals = self.sess.run(self.q, feed_dict={self.x: state})
        next_action_q_vals = self.sess.run(self.q, feed_dict={self.x:
            next_state})
        next_action_idx = np.argmax(next_action_q_vals)
        current_action_idx = self.actions.index(action)
        action_q_vals[0, current_action_idx] = reward + self.gamma *
            next_action_q_vals[0, next_action_idx]
        action_q_vals = np.squeeze(np.asarray(action_q_vals))
        self.sess.run(self.train_op, feed_dict={self.x: state, self.y:
            action_q_vals})
```

The output from the entire script is shown in figure 13.10. Two key functions are part of the QLearningDecisionPolicy: update_q and select_action, which implement the learned value of actions over time. Five percent of the time, the functions yield a random action. In select_action, every 1,000 or so prices, the function forces a random action and exploration as defined by self.epsilon. In update_q, the agent takes the current state and next desired action as defined by the argmax of q policy value for those states. Because the algorithm is initialized with a Q-function and weights with tf.random_normal, it will take some actions over time for the agent to start to realize the true longer-term reward, but then again, that realization is the point. The agent starts with a random understanding, takes actions, and learns the optimal policy over the simulation.

You can imagine the neural network for the Q-policy function learning to resemble the flow shown in figure 13.11. X is your input, representing the history of three stock prices along with the current balance and number of stocks. The first hidden layer (20, 1) learns a history over time of the reward for particular actions, and the second hidden layer (3, 1) maps those actions to the probability of Buy, Sell, Hold at any time.

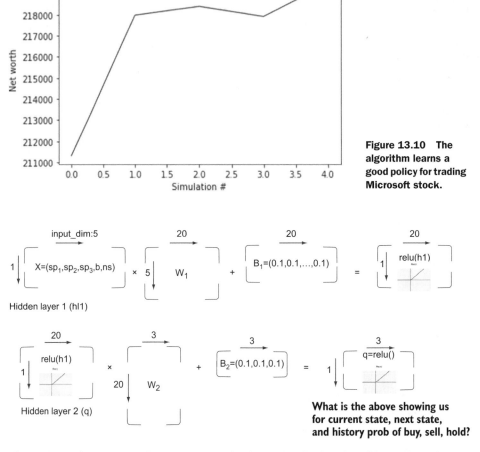

Figure 13.10 The algorithm learns a good policy for trading Microsoft stock.

Figure 13.11   The neural architecture construction for the Q-policy function with two hidden layers

13.4   *Exploring other applications of reinforcement learning*

Reinforcement learning is more common than you might expect. It's too easy to forget that it exists when you've learned supervised- and unsupervised-learning methods. But the following examples will open your eyes to successful uses of RL by Google:

- *Game playing*—In February 2015, Google developed a reinforcement-learning system called Deep RL to learn how to play arcade video games from the Atari 2600 console. Unlike most RL solutions, this algorithm had a high-dimensional input; it perceived the raw frame-by-frame images of the video game. That way, the same algorithm could work with any video game without much reprogramming or reconfiguring.

- *More game playing*—In January 2016, Google released a paper about an AI agent that was capable of winning the board game Go. The game is known to be unpredictable because of the enormous number of possible configurations (even more than in chess!), but this algorithm, using RL, could beat top human Go players. The latest version, AlphaGo Zero, was released in late 2017 and was able to beat the earlier version consistently—100 games to 0—in only 40 days of training. AlphaGo Zero will be considerably better than its 2017 performance by the time you read this book.

- *Robotics and control*—In March 2016, Google demonstrated a way for a robot to learn how to grab an object via many examples. Google collected more than 800,000 grasp attempts by using multiple robots and developed a model to grasp arbitrary objects. Impressively, the robots were capable of grasping an object with the help of camera input alone. Learning the simple concept of grasping an object required aggregating the knowledge of many robots, spending many days in brute-force attempts until enough patterns were detected. Clearly, robots have a long way to go to be able to generalize, but this project is an interesting start nonetheless.

NOTE Now that you've applied reinforcement learning to the stock market, it's time for you to drop out of school or quit your job and start gaming the system—your payoff, dear reader, for making it this far into the book! I'm kidding. The actual stock market is a much more complicated beast, but the techniques in this chapter generalize to many situations.

Summary

- Reinforcement learning is a natural tool for problems that can be framed by states that change due to actions taken by an agent to discover rewards.

- Implementing the reinforcement-learning algorithm requires three primary steps: infer the best action from the current state, perform the action, and learn from the results.

- Q-learning is an approach to solving reinforcement learning whereby you develop an algorithm to approximate the utility function (Q-function). After a good enough approximation is found, you can start inferring the best actions to take from each state.

Convolutional neural networks

This chapter covers

- Examining the components of a convolutional neural network
- Classifying natural images using deep learning
- Improving neural network performance—tips and tricks

Grocery shopping after an exhausting day is a taxing experience. My eyes get bombarded with too much information. Sales, coupons, colors, toddlers, flashing lights, and crowded aisles are a few examples of all the signals forwarded to my visual cortex, whether or not I try to pay attention. The visual system absorbs an abundance of information.

Ever heard the phrase "A picture is worth a thousand words"? That might be true for you or me, but can a machine find meaning within images as well? The photoreceptor cells in our retinas pick up wavelengths of light, but that information doesn't seem to propagate up to our consciousness. After all, I can't put into words exactly what wavelengths of lights I'm picking up. Similarly, a camera picks up pixels, yet we want to squeeze out some form of higher-level knowledge instead, such as names or locations of objects. How do we get from pixels to human-level perception?

To achieve intelligent meaning from raw sensory input with machine learning, you'll design a neural network model. In previous chapters, you've seen a few types of neural network models, such as fully connected ones (chapter 13) and autoencoders (chapters 11 and 12). In this chapter, you'll meet another type of model: a *convolutional neural network* (CNN), which performs exceptionally well on images and other sensory data such as audio. A CNN model can reliably classify what object is being displayed in an image, for example.

The CNN model that you'll implement in this chapter will learn how to classify images to one of ten candidate categories from the CIFAR-10 dataset (chapters 11 and 12). In effect, "A picture is worth only *one* word" out of only 10 possibilities. It's a tiny step toward human-level perception, but you have to start somewhere, right?

14.1 *Drawback of neural networks*

Machine learning constitutes an eternal struggle: designing a model that's expressive enough to represent the data, yet not so flexible that it overfits and memorizes the patterns. Neural networks are proposed as a way to improve that expressive power, yet as you may guess, they often suffer from the pitfalls of overfitting.

> **NOTE** Overfitting occurs when your learned model performs exceptionally well on the training dataset, yet tends to perform poorly on the test dataset. The model is likely too flexible for what little data is available, and it ends up more or less memorizing the training data.

A quick-and-dirty heuristic you can use to compare the flexibility of two machine-learning models is to count the number of parameters to be learned. As shown in figure 14.1, a fully connected neural network that takes in a 256×256 image and maps it to a layer of 10 neurons will have $256 \times 256 \times 10 = 655{,}360$ parameters! Compare that with a model with perhaps only five parameters. It's likely that the fully connected neural network can represent more complex data than the model with five parameters.

Section 14.2 introduces CNNs, which are a clever way to reduce the number of parameters. Instead of dealing with a fully connected network that would have to learn many more parameters individually, you can take the CNN approach, reusing the same parameter multiple times to reduce the number of learned weights.

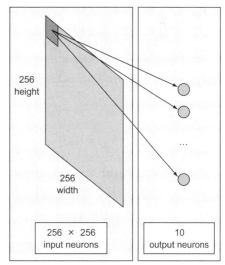

Figure 14.1   In a fully connected network, each pixel of an image is treated as an input. For a grayscale image of size 256 × 256, that's 256 × 256 neurons. Connecting each neuron to 10 outputs yields 256 × 256 × 10 = 655,360 weights.

14.2 Convolutional neural networks

The big idea behind CNNs is that a local understanding of an image is good enough. The practical benefit is that having fewer parameters greatly improves the time it takes to learn, as well as reduces the amount of data required to train the model. The time improvement sometimes comes at the cost of accuracy, however.

Instead of a fully connected network of weights from each pixel, a CNN has enough weights to look at a small patch of the image. Imagine that you're reading a book by using a magnifying glass; eventually, you read the whole page, but you look at only a small patch of the page at any given time.

Consider a 256 × 256 image. Instead of processing the whole image at the same time, your Tensor-Flow code can efficiently scan it chunk by chunk—say, a 5 × 5 window that slides along the image (usually left to right and top to bottom), as shown in figure 14.2. How "quickly" it slides is called its *stride length*. A stride length of 2, for example, means that the 5 × 5 sliding window moves 2 pixels at a time until it spans the entire image. In TensorFlow, you can easily adjust the stride length and window size by using the built-in library functions, as you'll soon see.

This 5 × 5 window has an associated 5 × 5 matrix of weights.

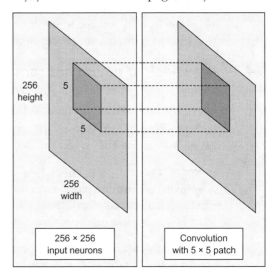

Figure 14.2   Convolving a 5 × 5 patch over an image (left) produces another image (right). In this case, the produced image is the same size as the original. Converting an original image to a convolved image requires only 5 × 5 = 25 parameters.

> **NOTE**   A *convolution* is a weighted sum of the pixel values of the image, as the window slides across the whole image. This convolution process throughout an image with a weight matrix produces another image of the same size, depending on the convention. *Convolving* is the process of applying a convolution.

The sliding-window shenanigans happen on the *convolution layer* of the neural network. A typical CNN has multiple convolution layers. Each convolutional layer typically generates many alternate convolutions, so the weight matrix is a tensor of 5 × 5 × *n*, where *n* is the number of convolutions.

Suppose that an image goes through a convolution layer on a weight matrix of 5 × 5 × 64. This layer generates 64 convolutions by sliding a 5 × 5 window. Therefore, this model has 5 × 5 × 64 (= 1,600) parameters, which is remarkably fewer parameters than a fully connected network, which has 256 × 256 (= 65,536).

The beauty of the CNN is that the number of parameters is independent of the size of the original image. You can run the same CNN on a 300 × 300 image, and the number of parameters won't change on the convolution layer!

14.3 Preparing the image

To start implementing CNNs in TensorFlow, you need to obtain some images to work with. The code listings in this section help you set up a training dataset for the remainder of the chapter.

First, download the CIFAR-10 dataset from www.cs.toronto.edu/~kriz/cifar-10-python.tar.gz; if you need to, review chapters 11 and 12 for more information on it. This dataset contains 60,000 images, split into 10 categories, which makes it a great resource for classification tasks, as I showed you in those chapters. Extract that file to your working directory. Figure 14.3 shows examples of images from the dataset.

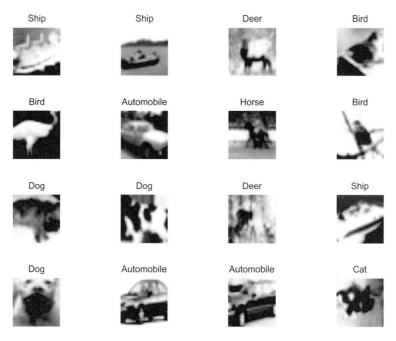

Figure 14.3 Images from the CIFAR-10 dataset. Because they're only 32 × 32, they're a bit difficult to see, but you can recognize some of the objects.

You used the CIFAR-10 dataset in chapter 12, so pull up that code again. Listing 14.1 comes straight from the CIFAR-10 documentation at www.cs.toronto.edu/~kriz/cifar.html. Place the code in a file called cifar_tools.py.

Listing 14.1   Loading images from a CIFAR-10 file in Python

```python
import pickle

def unpickle(file):
    fo = open(file, 'rb')
    dict = pickle.load(fo, encoding='latin1')
    fo.close()
    return dict
```

Neural networks are already prone to overfitting, so it's essential that you do as much as you can to minimize that error. For that reason, always remember to clean the data before processing it. You've seen by now that data cleaning and pipelines are sometimes the majority of the work.

Cleaning data is a core process in the machine-learning pipeline. Listing 14.2 implements the following three steps for cleaning a dataset of images:

1   If you have an image in color, try converting it to grayscale to lower the dimensionality of the input data and consequently lower the number of parameters.

2   Consider center-cropping the image, because the edges of an image might provide no useful information.

3   Normalize your input by subtracting the mean and dividing by the standard deviation of each data sample so that the gradients during backpropagation don't change too dramatically.

Listing 14.2 shows how to clean a dataset of images by using these techniques.

Listing 14.2   Cleaning data

Reorganizes the data so it's a 32 × 32 matrix with three channels

```python
import numpy as np

def clean(data):
    imgs = data.reshape(data.shape[0], 3, 32, 32)
    grayscale_imgs = imgs.mean(1)
    cropped_imgs = grayscale_imgs[:, 4:28, 4:28]
    img_data = cropped_imgs.reshape(data.shape[0], -1)
    img_size = np.shape(img_data)[1]
    means = np.mean(img_data, axis=1)
    meansT = means.reshape(len(means), 1)
    stds = np.std(img_data, axis=1)
    stdsT = stds.reshape(len(stds), 1)
    adj_stds = np.maximum(stdsT, 1.0 / np.sqrt(img_size))
    normalized = (img_data - meansT) / adj_stds
    return normalized
```

Grayscales the image by averaging the color intensities

Crops the 32 × 32 image to a 24 × 24 image to reduce parameters

Normalizes the pixels' values by subtracting the mean and dividing by standard deviation

Collect all the images from CIFAR-10 into memory, and run your cleaning function on them. Listing 14.3 sets up a convenient method to read, clean, and structure your data for use in TensorFlow. Include this code in cifar_tools.py as well.

Listing 14.3 Preprocessing all CIFAR-10 files

```
def read_data(directory):
    names = unpickle('{}/batches.meta'.format(directory))['label_names']
    print('names', names)

    data, labels = [], []
    for i in range(1, 6):
        filename = '{}/data_batch_{}'.format(directory, i)
        batch_data = unpickle(filename)
        if len(data) > 0:
            data = np.vstack((data, batch_data['data']))
            labels = np.hstack((labels, batch_data['labels']))
        else:
            data = batch_data['data']
            labels = batch_data['labels']

    print(np.shape(data), np.shape(labels))

    data = clean(data)
    data = data.astype(np.float32)
    return names, data, labels
```

In another file called using_cifar.py, you can use the method by importing cifar_tools. Listings 14.4 and 14.5 show how to sample a few images from the dataset and visualize them.

Listing 14.4 Using the `cifar_tools` helper function

```
import cifar_tools

names, data, labels = \
    cifar_tools.read_data('your/location/to/cifar-10-batches-py')
```

You can randomly select a few images and draw them along their corresponding label. Listing 14.5 does exactly that, giving you a better understanding of the type of data you'll be dealing with.

Listing 14.5 Visualizing images from the dataset

```
import numpy as np
import matplotlib.pyplot as plt
import random

def show_some_examples(names, data, labels):
    plt.figure()
    rows, cols = 4, 4                                          ◁─── Change to as many
    random_idxs = random.sample(range(len(data)), rows * cols) ◁───┐ rows and columns
    for i in range(rows * cols):                                   │ as you desire.
        plt.subplot(rows, cols, i + 1)                             │ Randomly pick
        j = random_idxs[i]                                         │ images from
        plt.title(names[labels[j]])                               │ the dataset
                                                                   │ to show
```

```
        img = np.reshape(data[j, :], (24, 24))
        plt.imshow(img, cmap='Greys_r')
        plt.axis('off')
    plt.tight_layout()
    plt.savefig('cifar_examples.png')

show_some_examples(names, data, labels)
```

By running this code, you'll generate a file called cifar_examples.png that will look similar to figure 14.3 earlier in this section.

14.3.1 Generating filters

In this section, you'll convolve an image with a couple of random 5 × 5 patches, also called *filters*. This step is an important one in a CNN, so you'll carefully examine how the data transforms. To understand a CNN model for image processing, it's wise to observe the way that an image filter transforms an image. Filters extract useful image features such as edges and shapes. You can train a machine-learning model on these features.

Remember that a feature vector indicates how you represent a data point. When you apply a filter to an image, the corresponding point in the transformed image is a feature—a feature that says, "When you apply this filter to this point, it has this new value." The more filters you use on an image, the greater the dimensionality of the feature vector. The overall goal is to balance the number of filters that reduce the dimensionality while still capturing the important features in the original image.

Open a new file called conv_visuals.py. Let's randomly initialize 32 filters. You'll do so by defining a variable called W of size 5 × 5 × 1 × 32. The first two dimensions correspond to the filter size; the last dimension corresponds to the 32 convolutions. The 1 in the variable's size corresponds to the input dimension, because the conv2d function is capable of convolving images of multiple channels. (In this example, you care about only grayscale images, so the number of input channels is 1.) Listing 14.6 provides the code to generate filters, which are shown in figure 14.4.

Listing 14.6 Generating and visualizing random filters

```
W = tf.Variable(tf.random_normal([5, 5, 1, 32]))    ◁─── Defines the tensor representing
                                                          the random filters

def show_weights(W, filename=None):
    plt.figure()
    rows, cols = 4, 8                    ◁─────  Defines enough rows and columns
    for i in range(np.shape(W)[3]):             to show the 32 figures in figure 14.4
        img = W[:, :, 0, i]
        plt.subplot(rows, cols, i + 1)
        plt.imshow(img, cmap='Greys_r', interpolation='none')
        plt.axis('off')
    if filename:
        plt.savefig(filename)
    else:
        plt.show()
```

Visualizes each filter matrix

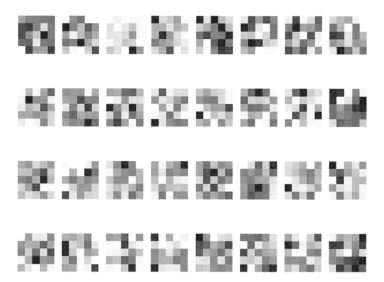

Figure 14.4 Each of these 32 randomly initialized matrices is size 5 × 5. The matrices represent the filters you'll use to convolve an input image.

Exercise 14.1

What would you change in listing 14.6 to generate 64 filters of size 3 × 3?

Answer

```
W = tf.Variable(tf.random_normal([3, 3, 1, 64]))
```

Use a session, as shown in listing 14.7, and initialize some weights by using the `global_variables_initializer` op. Call the `show_weights` function to visualize random filters, as shown in figure 14.4.

Listing 14.7 Using a session to initialize weights

```
with tf.Session() as sess:
    sess.run(tf.global_variables_initializer())

    W_val = sess.run(W)
    show_weights(W_val, 'step0_weights.png')
```

14.3.2 Convolving using filters

Section 14.3.1 showed you how to prepare filters to use. In this section, you'll use Tensor-Flow's convolve function on your randomly generated filters. Listing 14.8 sets up code to visualize the convolution outputs. You'll use it later, as you used `show_weights`.

Listing 14.8   Showing convolution results

```
def show_conv_results(data, filename=None):
    plt.figure()
    rows, cols = 4, 8
    for i in range(np.shape(data)[3]):
        img = data[0, :, :, i]
        plt.subplot(rows, cols, i + 1)
        plt.imshow(img, cmap='Greys_r', interpolation='none')
        plt.axis('off')
    if filename:
        plt.savefig(filename)
    else:
        plt.show()
```

Unlike in listing 14.6, the tensor shape is different; it's not the weights, but the resulting image.

Suppose that you have an example input image, such as the one shown in figure 14.5. You can convolve the 24 × 24 image by using 5 × 5 filters to produce many convolved images. All these convolutions are unique perspectives on the same image. These perspectives work together to comprehend the object that exists in the image. Listing 14.9 shows how to perform this task step by step.

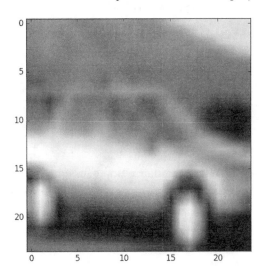

Figure 14.5   An example 24 × 24 image from the CIFAR-10 dataset

Listing 14.9   Visualizing convolutions

```
raw_data = data[4, :]
raw_img = np.reshape(raw_data, (24, 24))
plt.figure()
plt.imshow(raw_img, cmap='Greys_r')
plt.savefig('input_image.png')

x = tf.reshape(raw_data, shape=[-1, 24, 24, 1])
```

Gets an image from the CIFAR dataset and visualizes it

Defines the input tensor for the 24 × 24 image

```
b = tf.Variable(tf.random_normal([32]))
conv = tf.nn.conv2d(x, W, strides=[1, 1, 1, 1], padding='SAME')
conv_with_b = tf.nn.bias_add(conv, b)
conv_out = tf.nn.relu(conv_with_b)

with tf.Session() as sess:
    sess.run(tf.global_variables_initializer())

    conv_val = sess.run(conv)
    show_conv_results(conv_val, 'step1_convs.png')
    print(np.shape(conv_val))

conv_out_val = sess.run(conv_out)
    show_conv_results(conv_out_val, 'step2_conv_outs.png')
    print(np.shape(conv_out_val))
```

Defines the filters and corresponding parameters

Runs the convolution on the selected image

Finally, by running the `conv2d` function in TensorFlow, you get the 32 images in figure 14.6. The idea of convolving images is that each of the 32 convolutions captures different features of the image.

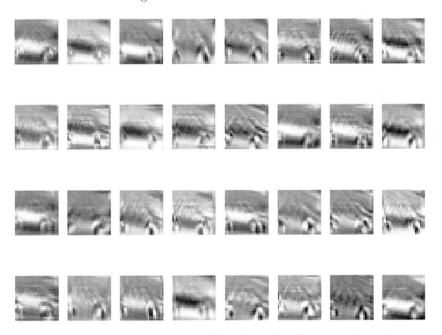

Figure 14.6   **Resulting images from convolving the random filters on an image of a car**

With the addition of a bias term and an activation function such as `relu` (see listing 14.12 for an example), the convolution layer of the network behaves nonlinearly, which improves its expressiveness. Figure 14.7 shows what each of the 32 convolution outputs becomes.

Figure 14.7   After you add a bias term and an activation function, the resulting convolutions can capture more-powerful patterns within images.

14.3.3 *Max pooling*

After a convolution layer extracts useful features, it's usually a good idea to reduce the size of the convolved outputs. Rescaling or subsampling a convolved output helps reduce the number of parameters, which in turn can help prevent overfitting the data.

This concept is the main idea behind *max pooling*, which sweeps a window across an image and picks the pixel with the maximum value. Depending on the stride length, the resulting image is a fraction of the size of the original. This technique is useful because it lessens the dimensionality of the data, reducing the number of parameters in future steps.

Exercise 14.2

Let's say you want to max pool over a 32 × 32 image. If the window size is 2 × 2 and the stride length is 2, how big will the resulting max-pooled image be?

Answer

The 2 × 2 window would need to move 16 times in each direction to span the 32 × 32 image, so the image would shrink by half: 16 × 16. Because it shrank by half in both dimensions, the image is one-fourth the size of the original image (½ × ½).

Place listing 14.10 within the `Session` context.

```
k = 2
maxpool = tf.nn.max_pool(conv_out,
                         ksize=[1, k, k, 1],
                         strides=[1, k, k, 1],
                         padding='SAME')

with tf.Session() as sess:
    maxpool_val = sess.run(maxpool)
    show_conv_results(maxpool_val, 'step3_maxpool.png')
    print(np.shape(maxpool_val))
```

As a result of running this code, the max-pooling function halves the image size and produces lower-resolution convolved outputs, as shown in figure 14.8.

Figure 14.8 After `maxpool` runs, the convolved outputs are halved in size, making the algorithm computationally faster without losing too much information.

You have the tools necessary to implement the full CNN. In section 14.4, you'll finally train the classifier.

14.4   *Implementing a CNN in TensorFlow*

A CNN has multiple layers of convolutions and max pooling. The convolution layer offers different perspectives on the image, and the max-pooling layer simplifies the computations by reducing the dimensionality without losing too much information.

Consider a full-size 256×256 image convolved by a 5×5 filter into 64 convolutions. As shown in figure 14.9, each convolution is subsampled by using max pooling to produce 64 smaller convolved images of size 128×128.

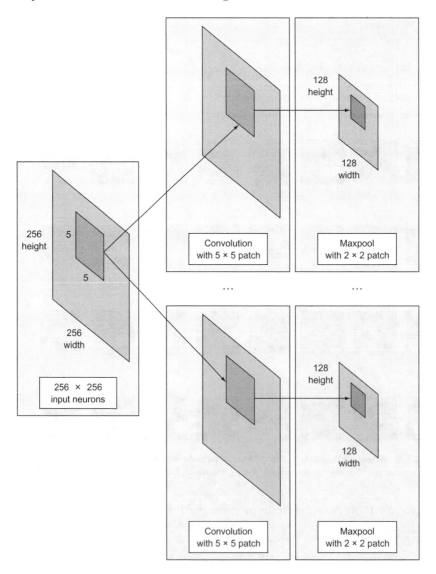

Figure 14.9   An input image is convolved by multiple 5 × 5 filters. The convolution layer includes an added bias term with an activation function, resulting in 5 × 5 + 5 = 30 parameters. Next, a max-pooling layer reduces the dimensionality of the data (which requires no extra parameters).

Now that you know how to make filters and use the convolution op, let's create a new source file. You'll start by defining all your variables. In listing 14.11, import all libraries, load the dataset, and define all variables.

Listing 14.11 Setting up CNN weights

```
import numpy as np
import matplotlib.pyplot as plt
import cifar_tools
import tensorflow as tf
names, data, labels = \
    cifar_tools.read_data('/home/binroot/res/cifar-10-batches-py')
```
�
Loads the dataset

```
x = tf.placeholder(tf.float32, [None, 24 * 24])
y = tf.placeholder(tf.float32, [None, len(names)])
```
| **Defines the input and output placeholders**

```
W1 = tf.Variable(tf.random_normal([5, 5, 1, 64]))
b1 = tf.Variable(tf.random_normal([64]))
```
| **Applies 64 convolutions of window size 5 × 5**

```
W2 = tf.Variable(tf.random_normal([5, 5, 64, 64]))
b2 = tf.Variable(tf.random_normal([64]))
```
| **Applies 64 more convolutions of window size 5 × 5**

```
W3 = tf.Variable(tf.random_normal([6*6*64, 1024]))
b3 = tf.Variable(tf.random_normal([1024]))
```
| **Introduces a fully connected layer**

```
W_out = tf.Variable(tf.random_normal([1024, len(names)]))
b_out = tf.Variable(tf.random_normal([len(names)]))
```
| **Defines the variables for a fully connected linear layer**

In listing 14.12, you define a helper function to perform a convolution, add a bias term, and then add an activation function. Together, these three steps form a convolution layer of the network.

Listing 14.12 Creating a convolution layer

```
def conv_layer(x, W, b):
    conv = tf.nn.conv2d(x, W, strides=[1, 1, 1, 1], padding='SAME')
    conv_with_b = tf.nn.bias_add(conv, b)
    conv_out = tf.nn.relu(conv_with_b)
    return conv_out
```

Listing 14.13 shows how to define the max-pool layer by specifying the kernel and stride size.

Listing 14.13 Creating a max-pool layer

```
def maxpool_layer(conv, k=2):
    return tf.nn.max_pool(conv, ksize=[1, k, k, 1], strides=[1, k, k, 1],
    ⮡ padding='SAME')
```

You can stack together the convolution and max-pool layers to define the CNN architecture. Listing 14.14 defines a possible CNN model. The last layer typically is a fully connected network connected to each of the 10 output neurons.

Listing 14.14   The full CNN model

```
def model():                                            Constructs the first
    x_reshaped = tf.reshape(x, shape=[-1, 24, 24, 1])   layer of convolution
                                                        and max pooling
    conv_out1 = conv_layer(x_reshaped, W1, b1)
    maxpool_out1 = maxpool_layer(conv_out1)
    norm1 = tf.nn.lrn(maxpool_out1, 4, bias=1.0, alpha=0.001 / 9.0,
    ➥ beta=0.75)

    conv_out2 = conv_layer(norm1, W2, b2)
    norm2 = tf.nn.lrn(conv_out2, 4, bias=1.0, alpha=0.001 / 9.0, beta=0.75)
    maxpool_out2 = maxpool_layer(norm2)
                                                        Constructs the
                                                        second layer
    maxpool_reshaped = tf.reshape(maxpool_out2, [-1,
    ➥ W3.get_shape().as_list()[0]])                    Constructs the concluding
    local = tf.add(tf.matmul(maxpool_reshaped, W3), b3)  fully connected layers
    local_out = tf.nn.relu(local)

    out = tf.add(tf.matmul(local_out, W_out), b_out)
    return out
```

14.4.1 *Measuring performance*

With a neural network architecture designed, the next step is defining a cost function that you want to minimize. You'll use TensorFlow's `softmax_cross_entropy_with_logits` function, which is best described by the official documentation at http://mng.bz/4Blw:

> *[The function* `softmax_cross_entropy_with_logits`*] measures the probability error in discrete classification tasks in which the classes are mutually exclusive (each entry is in exactly one class). For example, each CIFAR-10 image is labeled with one and only one label: an image can be a dog or a truck, but not both.*

Because an image can belong to one of ten possible labels, you'll represent that choice as a 10D vector. All elements of this vector have a value of 0 except the element that corresponds to the label, which will have a value of 1. This representation, as you've seen in earlier chapters, is called *one-hot encoding*.

As shown in listing 14.15, you'll calculate the cost via the cross-entropy loss function I mentioned in chapter 6. This code returns the probability error for your classification. Note that the code works only for simple classifications—those in which your classes are mutually exclusive. (A truck can't also be a dog, for example.) You can employ many types of optimizers, but in this example, you stick with the AdamOptimizer, which is a fast, simple optimizer described in detail at http://mng.bz/QxJG.

It may be worth playing around with the arguments in real-world applications, but the AdamOptimizer works well off-the-shelf.

Listing 14.15   Defining ops to measure cost and accuracy

```
model_op = model()                    Defines the                  Defines the training
                                      classification               op to minimize the
cost = tf.reduce_mean(      ◄─        loss function                loss function
    tf.nn.softmax_cross_entropy_with_logits(logits=model_op, labels=y)
)

train_op = tf.train.AdamOptimizer(learning_rate=0.001).minimize(cost)   ◄───

correct_pred = tf.equal(tf.argmax(model_op, 1), tf.argmax(y, 1))
accuracy = tf.reduce_mean(tf.cast(correct_pred, tf.float32))
```

Finally, in section 14.4.2, you'll run the training op to minimize the cost of the neural network. Doing so multiple times throughout the dataset will teach the optimal weights (or parameters).

14.4.2 *Training the classifier*

In listing 14.16, you'll loop through the dataset of images in small batches to train the neural network. Over time, the weights will slowly converge to a local optimum to predict the training images accurately.

Listing 14.16   Training the neural network by using the CIFAR-10 dataset

```
with tf.Session() as sess:
    sess.run(tf.global_variables_initializer())
    onehot_labels = tf.one_hot(labels, len(names), on_value=1., off_value=0.,
    ➡ axis=-1)
    onehot_vals = sess.run(onehot_labels)
    batch_size = len(data) // 200
    print('batch size', batch_size)           Loops through 1,000 epochs
    for j in range(0, 1000):         ◄───
        print('EPOCH', j)
        for i in range(0, len(data), batch_size):  ◄──── Trains the network in batches
            batch_data = data[i:i+batch_size, :]
            batch_onehot_vals = onehot_vals[i:i+batch_size, :]
            _, accuracy_val = sess.run([train_op, accuracy], feed_dict={x:
            ➡ batch_data, y: batch_onehot_vals})
            if i % 1000 == 0:
                print(i, accuracy_val)
        print('DONE WITH EPOCH')
```

That's it! You've successfully designed a CNN to classify images. Beware: training the CNN might take a lot more than 10 minutes. If you're running this code on CPU, it might even take hours! Can you imagine discovering a bug in your code after a day of waiting? That's why deep-learning researchers use powerful computers and GPUs to speed computations.

14.5 *Tips and tricks to improve performance*

The CNN you developed in this chapter is a simple approach to solving the problem of image classification, but many techniques can improve performance after you finish your first working prototype:

- *Augmenting data*—From a single image, you can easily generate new training images. As a start, flip an image horizontally or vertically, and you can quadruple your dataset size. You can also adjust the brightness of the image or the hue to ensure that the neural network generalizes to other fluctuations. You may even want to add random noise to the image to make the classifier robust to small occlusions. Scaling the image up or down can also be helpful; having exactly the same-sized items in your training images will almost guarantee overfitting.

- *Early stopping*—Keep track of the training and testing errors while you train the neural network. At first, both types of errors should dwindle slowly, because the network is learning. But sometimes, test errors go back up, which signals that the neural network has started overfitting on the training data and is unable to generalize to previously unseen input. You should stop the training the moment you witness this phenomenon.

- *Regularizing weights*—Another way to combat overfitting is to add a regularization term to the cost function. You've seen regularization in previous chapters, and the same concepts apply here.

- *Dropout*—TensorFlow comes with a handy `tf.nn.dropout` function, which can be applied to any layer of the network to reduce overfitting. The function turns off a randomly selected number of neurons in that layer during training so that the network is redundant and robust to inferring output.

- *Deeper architecture*—A deeper architecture results from adding more hidden layers to the neural network. If you have enough training data, adding more hidden layers has been shown to improve performance. The network will take more time to train, however.

Exercise 14.3

After the first iteration of this CNN architecture, try applying a couple of tips and tricks mentioned in this chapter.

Answer

Fine-tuning is part of the process, unfortunately. You should begin by adjusting the hyperparameters and retraining the algorithm until you find the setting that works best.

14.6 *Application of CNNs*

CNNs blossom when the input contains sensor data from audio or images. Images in particular are of major interest in industry. When you sign up for a social network, for example, you usually upload a profile photo, not an audio recording of yourself saying "Hello." Humans seem to be naturally entertained by photos, so you can experiment to see how CNNs can be used to detect faces in images.

The overall CNN architecture can be as simple or as complicated as you desire. You should start simple and gradually tune your model until you're satisfied. There's no one correct path, because facial recognition isn't completely solved. Researchers are still publishing papers that one-up previous state-of-the-art solutions.

Your first step should be obtaining a dataset of images. One of the largest datasets of arbitrary images is ImageNet (http://image-net.org). Here, you can find negative examples for your binary classifier. To obtain positive examples of faces, you can find numerous datasets at the following sites that specialize in human faces:

- VGG-Face Dataset (http://www.robots.ox.ac.uk/~vgg/data/vgg_face)
- Face Detection Data Set and Benchmark (FDDB) (http://vis-www.cs.umass.edu/fddb)
- Databases for Face Detection and Pose Estimation (http://mng.bz/X0Jv)
- YouTube Faces Database (www.cs.tau.ac.il/~wolf/ytfaces)

Summary

- CNNs make assumptions that capturing the local patterns of a signal is sufficient to characterize that signal and thus reduce the number of parameters of a neural network.
- Cleaning data is vital to the performance of most machine-learning models. The hour you spend to write code that cleans data is nothing compared with the amount of time it can take for a neural network to learn that cleaning function by itself.

15

Building a real-world CNN: VGG-Face and VGG-Face Lite

This chapter covers

- Augmenting data for training a convolution neural network (CNN)
- Tuning a CNN by using dropout and batch normalization and evaluating performance
- Building an accurate CNN for object recognition with CIFAR-10 and facial identification

Convolutional neural network (CNN) architectures are useful tools for analyzing images and for differentiating their features. Lines or curves may indicate your favorite automobile, or the indicator might be a particular higher-level feature, such as the green coloring present in most frog pictures. More complex indicators might be a freckle near your left nostril or the curvature of your chin passed down through generations of your family.

Humans have become adept through the years at picking out these identifying features, and it's fine to wonder why. Humans have grown accustomed to looking at billions of example images shown to them since birth and then receiving feedback about what they are seeing in those images. Remember your mom repeating the word *ball* while showing you a ball? There's a good chance that you remember *some* time she said it. What about the time you saw another ball of a slightly different shape or color and said, "Ball"?

Perhaps the toddler version of yourself, upon being handed a new action figure of a caped superhero, asked whether that figure was Superman. It wasn't, but it was another hero that looked similar. Why did you think it was Superman? The cape, the dark hair, and a possible triangle near the chest with some sort of symbol in it were image features that looked familiar. Your biological neural network fired with the input image, retrieving the label that was reinforced over time when your parents provided it to you verbally. When you were handed a new toy, you spit out the label, and your parents corrected you. ("No, honey, it's Shazam. It looks like Superman, though; I can totally understand why you thought that!") Boom—a label was added based on the slightly different features, and you moved on to learning more.

This process is similar to the way you train CNNs, which allow a computer program to capture higher- and lower-order features automatically and use them to differentiate among images. As you learned in chapter 14, those features are represented by convolutional filters, which are the learned parameters of the network.

Training CNNs to learn those parameters is no easy task due to a variety of factors:

- *Accessibility of training data*—To be realistic and accurate, a CNN needs boatloads of training data with lots of feature variations so that the filters can capture them. Likewise, lots of filters are required to represent those features. As a human, you've probably seen billions of images in your lifetime, with lots of repetition of classes, colors, objects, and people. Your label assignments get better over time, and so does the CNN.

- *Deeper neural architectures and more feature delineation*—These architectures help CNNs differentiate among images that have great parity. If your CNN has learned what a human is versus a bird, how does it separate different *kinds* of humans, such as those with wavy or curly hair, or with fair or tan skin? Deeper architectures require your network to learn more parameters, but it has more *capacity* to represent the feature variations and, as such, will take *much* longer to train.

- *Preventing memorization and learning more resilient representations*—Training a robust CNN means preventing the network from memorizing features for objects or people from the training data. This process also ensures that your network is open to new interpretations of objects and people in those images that have slightly different representations of those features that it may see in the wild, breaking its simply trained understanding.

All these issues are required to make a CNN useful tools for solving problems in the real world, as you see in figure 15.1.

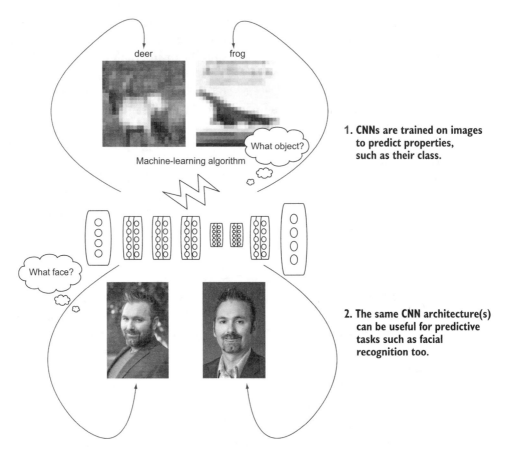

Figure 15.1   CNN architectures help a machine-learning algorithm label an image. Whether you are trying to label an object or someone's face, the same CNN architectures can perform the task.

In this chapter, I'll show you how to build resilient CNN architectures by using Tensor-Flow, beginning with something you're familiar with: the Canadian Institute for Advanced Research (CIFAR-10) dataset of automobiles, planes, ships, birds, and so on. This dataset is representative enough of the real world that to make them accurate, you need to make the optimizations in the basic CNN architectures that I showed you in chapter 14.

Additionally, you will build a facial-detection CNN system by using the Visual Geometry Group (VGG) Face model. That CNN, when given one of 2,622 possible celebrity faces, will identify with high accuracy which celebrity the face belongs to. The CNN can even handle different poses, lighting, makeup (or no makeup), glasses (or no glasses), hats (or no hats), and loads of other properties in the images. Let's get started building real-world CNNs!

15.1   *Making a real-world CNN architecture for CIFAR-10*

The CIFAR-10 dataset should be familiar because you used it in chapters 11 and 12. It contains 50,000 images for training, representing 5,000 images per each of 10 classes of object—airplane, automobile, bird, cat, deer, dog, frog, horse, ship, and truck—and 10,000 test images (1,000 per class). In chapter 14, I showed you how to construct a shallow network CNN with a few layers to classify CIFAR-10 images into one of the 10 classes.

The CIFAR-10 dataset was collected by Alex Krizhevsky, Vinod Nair, and Geoffrey Hinton. Krizhevsky is the author of a seminal paper on CNNs, "ImageNet Classification with Deep Convolutional Neural Networks" (http://www.cs.toronto.edu/~hinton/absps/imagenet.pdf). The paper, cited more than 40,000 times, proposes what became known as AlexNet, which is Krizhevsky's famous CNN architecture for image processing named after him. In addition to being used for CIFAR-10, AlexNet was used to win the ImageNet 2012 challenge. (ImageNet is a corpus of millions of images labeled with the WordNet taxonomy with 1,000 classes of objects; CIFAR-10 is the subset of that with 10 object classes.)

AlexNet employs several important optimizations beyond the CNNs you constructed in chapter 14. In particular, it proposes a deeper architecture with many more convolutional filters to capture higher- and lower-order features (figure 15.2). Those optimizations include the following:

- Deeper architectures and more convolutional layers with associated filters and capacity
- The use of data augmentation (rotating an image, flipping it left and right, or randomly cropping it)
- The application of a technique called *dropout*, which randomly turns off neurons in a particular layer so that the architecture learns a more resilient representation of the input

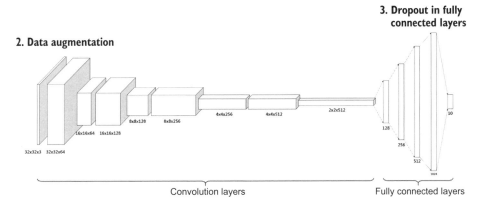

Figure 15.2   The famous AlexNet CNN architecture for object classification on the CIFAR data

You can implement these optimizations starting from the shallow CIFAR-10 CNN you created in chapter 14. To begin, review the read data functions that handle loading the CIFAR-10 50,000 training images; then convert them to grayscale to reduce the number of learned parameters. Don't worry; you'll deal with color images a bit later in the chapter when you build a facial recognition CNN.

15.1.1 Loading and preparing the CIFAR-10 image data

CIFAR-10 data is in Python Pickle format, so you'll need functions to read that pickle format back into Python dictionaries—one for the $32 \times 32 \times 50000$ image data and another for the 1×50000 labels. Additionally, you'll need to prepare and clean the data up a bit, a task that I want to emphasize strongly. You'll do the following things:

1 Create a function to clean the data and normalize the image variance by dividing by the mean image values.
2 Crop the images to the centers, and reduce background noise.
3 Convert the images to grayscale to reduce the dimensionality and increase learning efficiency in the network.

You'll copy those functions forward in listing 15.1 and get your images and labels ready for training. Note that these optimizations ease learning and training. You could omit doing some of them, but your training might take forever to converge or perhaps would never converge quickly to optimal learned parameters. You perform this cleaning to aid the learning process.

Listing 15.1 Loading and preparing CIFAR-10 training images and labels

```
def unpickle(file):
    fo = open(file, 'rb')
    dict = pickle.load(fo, encoding='latin1')   ◁──┐ Loads the pickled
    fo.close()                                      │ dictionary
    return dict                                  ◁──┘

def clean(data):
    imgs = data.reshape(data.shape[0], 3, 32, 32)   ┐ The grayscale image is the
    grayscale_imgs = imgs.mean(1)                ◁──┘ mean of the R,G,B axes.
    cropped_imgs = grayscale_imgs[:, 4:28, 4:28]   ◁── Crops the images
    img_data = cropped_imgs.reshape(imgs.shape[0], -1)
    img_size = np.shape(img_data)[1]
    means = np.mean(img_data, axis=1)
    meansT = means.reshape(len(means), 1)
    stds = np.std(img_data, axis=1)
    stdsT = stds.reshape(len(stds), 1)
    adj_stds = np.maximum(stdsT, 1.0 / np.sqrt(img_size))
    normalized = (img_data - meansT) / adj_stds
    return normalized
```

Crops the images (annotation for `cropped_imgs = grayscale_imgs[:, 4:28, 4:28]`)

Subtracts the image means and divides by the standard deviation so that the images are not too sensitive to high variation, and eases learning (annotation for the block from `means` through `normalized`)

The data-reading function saves the existing image data and labels if you've loaded them before by using NumPy's npy compact binary format to store NumPy arrays. This way, after you've processed, cleaned, and loaded the images and their labels, you don't have to bother waiting for those functions to complete again before training, because they can take quite a while to complete.

But I've got a GPU!

Graphical processing units (GPUs) have changed the game in terms of neural networks and training them for deep learning tasks such as prediction and classification. Optimized over the years for instructions related to graphical processing that were originally in video games, the operations that GPUs support—matrix multiplications—have found a friend in matrix-hungry machine-learning algorithms. GPUs do not really help you in traditional CPU-oriented operations, however, or in operations involving disk input and output (I/O) such as loading cached data from disk. The good news? Machine-learning frameworks including TensorFlow know which operations to optimize for the GPU and which ones are fine for the CPU, and they allocate those operations accordingly. Don't get too excited about your GPU for the data preparation part(s), though, because you are still I/O-bound.

Listing 15.2 loads the image data and labels for CIFAR-10. Note that it also includes the augment function, which I'll discuss in section 15.1.2.

Listing 15.2 Loading CIFAR-10 image data and labels

```
def read_data(directory):
    data_file = 'aug_data.npy'          Caches the NumPy arrays for image data and labels using
    labels_file = 'aug_labels.npy'      these filenames or loads them if the files do not exist

    names = unpickle('{}/batches.meta'.format(directory))['label_names']
    print('names', names)
    data, labels = [], []

    if os.path.exists(data_file) and os.path.isfile(data_file) and
      os.path.exists(labels_file) and os.path.isfile(labels_file):
        print('Loading data from cache files {} and {}'.format(data_file,
         labels_file))
            data = np.load(data_file)
            labels = np.load(labels_file)
    else:
        for i in range(1, 6):
            filename = '{}/data_batch_{}'.format(directory, i)
            batch_data = unpickle(filename)
            if len(data) > 0:
                data = np.vstack((data, batch_data['data']))
                labels = np.hstack((labels, batch_data['labels']))
            else:
                data = batch_data['data']
                labels = batch_data['labels']
        data, labels = augment(data, labels)       Performs data augmentation
        data = clean(data)                          as shown in section 15.2
```

Cleans the image data by normalizing the image variance and converting to grayscale

```
data = data.astype(np.float32)
np.save('aug_data.npy', data)
np.save('aug_labels.npy', labels)

print(np.shape(data), np.shape(labels))

return names, data, labels
```

Saves the resultant loaded data in NPY cache files so that you don't have to recompute them

With the functions built to get the data loading pipeline going, next I'll explain how to handle data augmentation for your CIFAR-10 CNN.

15.1.2 *Performing data augmentation*

CIFAR-10 is a static dataset. The dataset was collected with great effort and is used all over the world. No one is collecting and adding images to the dataset at the moment; instead, everyone uses it as-is. CIFAR-10 has 10 classes of objects, such as birds, and for those objects, it captures many of the variations you would expect in real life, such as a bird taking off in flight, a bird on the ground, or perhaps a bird pecking or making some traditional eating movement. The dataset doesn't include *all variations* of *all* birds and what they may be doing, however. Consider a bird taking flight and rising to the top-left portion of the image. An analogous image you could imagine would be of a bird making the same ascension movement to the top right of the image. Or the image could be flipped from left to right. You could imagine a bird in flight in the top portion of the image, but not the bottom, and flip the image from top to bottom or rotate it. Consider seeing a bird far away versus close-up, or when it's sunny or a bit darker before dusk. The possibilities are endless!

As you've learned so far, the CNN's job is to use filters to represent higher- and lower-order image features in the network. Those features are heavily influenced by foreground, background, object position, rotation, and so on. To account for the variational features in images that you'll find in real life, you use data augmentation. *Data augmentation* takes a static dataset and represents the variation in images by applying these transformations randomly to images in the dataset during training, augmenting your static data with new images. Given enough training epochs and based on batch size (a hyperparameter), you can use data augmentation to significantly increase the variation and learnability of your dataset. Take that bird image ascending left, and flip it to the right during some of the training epochs. Take the bird landing at dusk, and change the image contrast to make it brighter during other epochs. These changes allow the network to account for further variation in images in its learned parameters, making it more resilient to unseen images in real life that will have these variations—all without having to collect new images, which could be costly or perhaps impossible.

You'll implement a few of these augmentations in listings 15.3 and 15.4. In particular, you'll implement the image flip left/right; then you'll add some random noise to the image called *contrast*. *Contrast* is also referred to as *salt-and-pepper* or *black-and-white* randomly masked pixels, as shown in the sp_noise function in listing 15.3.

Listing 15.3 **Simple salt-and-pepper noise for the image**

Adds salt (0 value, or white) and pepper (255 value, or black) noise to image. prob is the probability of the noise.

```
def sp_noise(image,prob):
    output = np.zeros(image.shape,np.float32)
    thres = 1 - prob                          ◁─────  Decides the threshold
    for i in range(image.shape[0]):                   for setting the pixel to
        for j in range(image.shape[1]):               black (255) or white (0)
            rdn = random.random()
            if rdn < prob:
                output[i][j] = 0.
            elif rdn > thres:
                output[i][j] = 255.
            else:
                output[i][j] = image[i][j]
    return output
```

Returns the salted image

You can use NumPy's random function and then set hyperparameters for the probability of flipping the image and for salt and pepper, set to 5% for both parameters in listing 15.4. You can play around with these values (they are hyperparameters) because they control how much extra training data you will generate. More data is always better, but it can grow your dataset significantly.

Listing 15.4 **Achieving data augmentation for CIFAR-10 images**

5% chance of flipping the image each time

```
def augment(img_data, img_labels):
    imgs = img_data.reshape(img_data.shape[0], 3, 32, 32)
    flip_pct = 0.05
    salt_pct = 0.05          ◁─────  5% chance of applying the
    noise_pct = 0.15  ◁              salt/pepper to the image

    orig_size = len(imgs)           Amount of noise or salt/pepper
    for i in tqdm(range(0, orig_size)):   (15% in the image)
                                                                    Random flip UD
                                                                    (which will in effect
                                                                    do the left/right flip)
        if random.random() < flip_pct:    ◁──────────────────┘
            im_flip = np.expand_dims(np.flipud(imgs[i]), axis=0)
            imgs = np.vstack((imgs, im_flip))
            img_labels = np.hstack((img_labels, img_labels[i]))

        if random.random() < salt_pct:
            im_salt = np.expand_dims(sp_noise(imgs[i], noise_pct), axis=0)
            imgs = np.vstack((imgs, im_salt))
            img_labels = np.hstack((img_labels, img_labels[i]))    Returns the
                                                                    augmented
    return imgs.reshape(imgs.shape[0], -1), img_labels   ◁─────    image data
```

Adds the flipped image and label

Random salt and pepper for the image

You can double-check whether your image dataset is properly augmented by plotting a random image from training beyond image 50,000. I chose 52,002, but you can inspect others. The following code uses Matplotlib to print a 24 × 24 grayscale augmented image from CIFAR-10, as shown in figure 15.3. Note that the count of images begins at index 0; hence, the index for image 52,002 is 52,001.

```
plt.figure()
plt.title("Image of "+str(names[labels[y]]))
img = np.reshape(data[52001, :], (24,24))
plt.imshow(img, cmap='Greys_r')
plt.axis('off')
plt.tight_layout()
```

Figure 15.3   A flipped (to the right) image of an automobile, likely with salted contrast

Now, with your augmented dataset, you're ready to construct a deeper CIFAR-10 CNN model to capture those image features.

15.2   *Building a deeper CNN architecture for CIFAR-10*

The CNN architecture you constructed in chapter 14 was a shallow architecture with only two convolutional layers and one fully connected layer leading to the output layer for image class prediction. The CNN worked, but if you evaluated it against the CIFAR-10 test labels by generating a receiver operating characteristic (ROC) curve, as I've shown you in earlier chapters, it would not sufficiently differentiate among classes of CIFAR-10 test images and would do even worse evaluating unseen data randomly collected from the internet. How poorly the shallow architecture would perform, I'll leave as an exercise for you. Instead, in this section I'll focus on how you can build a better architecture and evaluate its performance.

One big reason for the poor performance has to do with what machine-learning theorists call *model capacity*. In shallow architectures, the network lacks the necessary capacity to capture variance between higher- and lower-order image features that properly distinguish among image classes. Without the necessary amount of weights for your machine-learning model to learn, the model can't separate the variance in the images; therefore, it can't properly discern large and small differences in input images of different classes.

Take the example of a frog versus an automobile. Frogs and cars have a similar feature: four shapes toward the bottom of the image (figure 15.4). Those shapes in frogs—feet—are flatter and, depending on sitting orientation, can be spaced in different ways. In a car with four tires, these shapes are circular and more stationary, and they can't reorient themselves as the frog's feet do. Without the capacity to learn these parameters, a CNN with shallow architecture can't tell the difference between these features, and the input image is close enough to a car that the output neurons may fire on the `automobile` class and not the `frog` class. With extra weights and neurons, the network may figure out that the top-left outward shape is more indicative

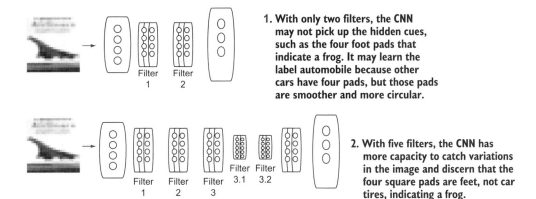

1. **With only two filters, the CNN may not pick up the hidden cues, such as the four foot pads that indicate a frog. It may learn the label automobile because other cars have four pads, but those pads are smoother and more circular.**

2. **With five filters, the CNN has more capacity to catch variations in the image and discern that the four square pads are feet, not car tires, indicating a frog.**

Figure 15.4 An input CIFAR-10 training image—a frog—run first through a shallow network and then through a dense network. The shallow network thinks that the image is a car; the dense network learns that the image is a frog.

of animals and frogs than it is of cars—a key feature that would update the network's understanding and cause it to flag the image as a frog instead of an automobile.

If your neural architecture lacks the capacity to learn these variations, in the form of weights to train and update based on training data and labels, your model won't be able to learn these simple differences. You can think of the model filters as being tunable parameters that distinguish between the big-deal and smaller-deal differences in the images.

Even humans may need some reinforcement

A simple experiment that I conducted while writing this book yielded some interesting results. I showed a picture of the frog in figure 15.4 to a few members of my family and asked them to identify the image in a context-free manner, without telling them the labels.

Was it a dinosaur? The Loch Ness Monster? A boomerang?

Providing a choice of two labels—automobile or frog—produced better results. The point is that even humans, with our dense neural architectures, may need label retraining or possibly more data augmentation.

The AlexNet model gives you a road map showing how many features are necessary to delineate all the features in the CIFAR-10 dataset and improve its accuracy significantly. In fact, AlexNet goes well beyond CIFAR-10; it contains enough capacity that if it's given enough input data and training, it performs well on the much larger ImageNet dataset, which has 1,000 classes of input images and millions of training samples. AlexNet's architecture will suffice as a model for a denser architecture with the capacity needed to improve the model accuracy for CIFAR-10.

Listing 15.5 isn't exactly AlexNet; I omitted a couple of filters that will reduce the amount of training time and memory needed for your computer without sacrificing noticeable accuracy. You'll make these types of choices while training machine-learning models. Some of these choices will vary based on your access to high-capacity or cloud computing, or whether you are working only on your laptop.

The function `model()` takes as input the CIFAR-10 image, a hyperparameter called `keep_prob`, and a function called `tf.nn.dropout` that I'll explain in section 15.2.1. The model construction uses TensorFlow's 2D convolutional filter function, which takes as input four convolutional filters, as follows:

```
conv1_filter = tf.Variable(tf.truncated_normal(shape=[3, 3, 1, 64], mean=0,
➥ stddev=0.08))
conv2_filter = tf.Variable(tf.truncated_normal(shape=[3, 3, 64, 128], mean=0,
➥ stddev=0.08))
conv3_filter = tf.Variable(tf.truncated_normal(shape=[5, 5, 128, 256],
➥ mean=0, stddev=0.08))
conv4_filter = tf.Variable(tf.truncated_normal(shape=[5, 5, 256, 512],
➥ mean=0, stddev=0.08))
```

Recall from chapter 14 that the filters are of the shape [x, y, c, n], where [x, y] is the window size for the convolutional patch, c is the number of image channels (1 for grayscale), and n is the number of filters. So your dense model uses four filters, with a 3×3 window patch size for the first two layers, 5×5 for the last two layers, 1 channel for grayscale input, 64 filters in the first convolutional layer, 128 filters in the second, 256 in the third, and 512 in the fourth layer.

> **NOTE** The choices of these architectural properties of the network are elaborated in the Krizhevsky paper. But I'll note that it's an active area of research and something that in itself is best left to the latest papers in machine learning for constructing neural architectures. In this chapter, we're going to follow the prescribed models.

The latter portion of the model construction uses some higher-level TensorFlow functions to create neural network layers. The function `tf.contrib.layers.fully_connected` creates fully connected layers to interpret the learned feature parameters and output the CIFAR-10 image labels.

To begin, reshape the input image from CIFAR's $32 \times 32 \times 1$ (1024 pixels) to [24 × 24 × 1] input, mainly to reduce the number of parameters and lessen the burden on your local computing resources. If you've got a machine more powerful than a laptop, you can experiment with this parameter, so feel free to tweak the size upward. To each convolutional filter, you'll apply a 1-pixel stride and the same padding, and convert the output to neurons via the rectifying linear unit (ReLU) activation function. Each layer includes max pooling to further reduce the learned parameter space through averaging, and you'll use batch normalization to make the statistics in each layer easier to learn. The convolutional layers are flattened into a 1D layer of parameters representing the fully connected layers; then they are mapped into the final 10-class softmax output predictions to round out the model.

Listing 15.5   A denser CNN architecture for CIFAR-10 modeled on AlexNet

Reshapes into [24 × 24 × 1] input

```
def model(x, keep_prob):
    x_reshaped = tf.reshape(x, shape=[-1, 24, 24, 1])

    conv1 = tf.nn.conv2d(x_reshaped, conv1_filter, strides=[1,1,1,1],
        padding='SAME')
    conv1 = tf.nn.relu(conv1)
    conv1_pool = tf.nn.max_pool(conv1, ksize=[1,2,2,1], strides=[1,2,2,1],
        padding='SAME')
    conv1_bn = tf.layers.batch_normalization(conv1_pool

    conv2 = tf.nn.conv2d(conv1_bn, conv2_filter, strides=[1,1,1,1],
        padding='SAME')
    conv2 = tf.nn.relu(conv2)
    conv2_pool = tf.nn.max_pool(conv2, ksize=[1,2,2,1], strides=[1,2,2,1],
        padding='SAME')
    conv2_bn = tf.layers.batch_normalization(conv2_pool)

    conv3 = tf.nn.conv2d(conv2_bn, conv3_filter, strides=[1,1,1,1],
        padding='SAME')
    conv3 = tf.nn.relu(conv3)
    conv3_pool = tf.nn.max_pool(conv3, ksize=[1,2,2,1], strides=[1,2,2,1],
        padding='SAME')
    conv3_bn = tf.layers.batch_normalization(conv3_pool)

    conv4 = tf.nn.conv2d(conv3_bn, conv4_filter, strides=[1,1,1,1],
        padding='SAME')
    conv4 = tf.nn.relu(conv4)
    conv4_pool = tf.nn.max_pool(conv4, ksize=[1,2,2,1], strides=[1,2,2,1],
        padding='SAME')
    conv4_bn = tf.layers.batch_normalization(conv4_pool)

    flat = tf.contrib.layers.flatten(conv4_bn)

    full1 = tf.contrib.layers.fully_connected(inputs=flat, num_outputs=128,
        activation_fn=tf.nn.relu)
    full1 = tf.nn.dropout(full1, keep_prob)
    full1 = tf.layers.batch_normalization(full1)

    full2 = tf.contrib.layers.fully_connected(inputs=full1, num_outputs=256,
        activation_fn=tf.nn.relu)
    full2 = tf.nn.dropout(full2, keep_prob)
    full2 = tf.layers.batch_normalization(full2)

    full3 = tf.contrib.layers.fully_connected(inputs=full2, num_outputs=512,
        activation_fn=tf.nn.relu)
    full3 = tf.nn.dropout(full3, keep_prob)
    full3 = tf.layers.batch_normalization(full3)
```

Applies the filters

Uses the ReLU activation function for the neurons

Applies max pooling

Uses batch normalization to make the statistics in each layer easier to learn

Flattens the neurons into a 1D layer

```
full4 = tf.contrib.layers.fully_connected(inputs=full3, num_outputs=1024,
➥ activation_fn=tf.nn.relu)
full4 = tf.nn.dropout(full4, keep_prob)
full4 = tf.layers.batch_normalization(full4)

out = tf.contrib.layers.fully_connected(inputs=full4, num_outputs=10,
➥ activation_fn=None)
return out
```

Maps the hidden-layer neurons to the final 10-class softmax output predictions

Now that you've got the model built, I'll show you how to make it more resilient to variations in input during training.

15.2.1 CNN optimizations for increasing learned parameter resilience

The model function also uses two other optimizations: *batch normalization* and *dropout*. There are plenty of more-detailed mathematical explanations for the utility and purpose of batch normalization, which I'll leave to you to research. The simple way to explain batch normalization is as a mathematical function that ensures learned parameters in each layer are easier to train and not overfit to the input images, which themselves are already normalized (converted to grayscale, divided by the image mean, and so on). In short, batch normalization eases training and accelerates model convergence to optimal parameters. The good news is that TensorFlow hides all the mathematical complexity and gives you an easy utility function to apply this technique.

> **TIP**   If you want to read more about batch normalization, consider this informative article: http://mng.bz/yrxB.

For dropout, the key intuition is similar to data augmentation in the sense that you want to make the CNN learned parameters more resilient (less sensitive) to imperfections in the input, as in real life. Even if you squint, distort the image you are seeing, you can still make out the objects in it, up to a point. This phenomenon means that you can distort an image and still reinforce the learned labels. Dropout goes a step further by forcing the network to randomly forget or mask the internal neurons for their learned values while reinforcing the output labels during training. Dropout randomly turns off neurons during training with probability (1-keep_prob), where keep_prob is the second parameter input to the model() function from listing 15.5.

Dropout causes the network to learn hardened weights and parameters that are resilient to imperfections or variations in the training process. So, similar to noising an image as you saw in chapter 12 and still learning more robust weights in spite of the distortion, dropout operates similarly and masks the *internal* world of the network. In other words, dropout randomly disables its own hidden neurons during training so that what it learns ends up being more resilient independent of the input. The technique has proved to be effective in the construction of neural networks because with enough epochs and training time, the network learns to deal with internal failure and still recall the correct labels and tuning parameters.

Ever forget something that you remembered later? Dropout helped!

This happens all the time, at least to me. I was trying to remember the label for an input image, *stroller*, the other day after discussing something that happened on my daily walk with my wife and kids. I kept referring to the stroller as the "pushing cart." Eventually I focused, and there it came: *stroller*. I had no reinforcement from my wife, who was internally laughing uncontrollably, I'm sure. Over the years, I'm sure that my internal network layers are set up with dropout to allow recollection, even if not immediately. Aren't biologically-inspired computer models grand?

Now it's time to train your optimized CNN and see whether you can do better than the initial shallow network you trained in chapter 14.

15.3 *Training and applying a better CIFAR-10 CNN*

With the well-curated CIFAR-10 input dataset, data augmentation, cleaning, and normalization complete, and given your resilient biologically inspired CNN model, you're ready for some training with TensorFlow. Consider the optimization steps for building a CNN, highlighted in figure 15.5. Thus far, I've covered the ways you can have optimal data for training and some steps for model representation to ensure capacity, memory, resilience, and convergence for training.

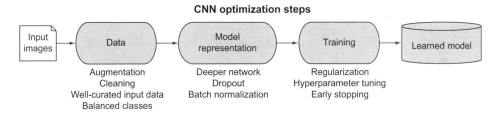

Figure 15.5   Optimization steps for building a CNN and what you can do in each stage from data to learned model

The training step also has optimizations that you can apply, as covered in previous chapters. You may recall that regularization is a technique in training that influences better learned parameters by penalizing exploration of nonoptimal parameter values during training. Regularization applies to input images as well as to numerical and text inputs. That's the beauty of machine learning and of TensorFlow: everything is an input tensor or matrix of numbers.

Listing 15.6 sets up the training process by rescaling the CIFAR 32×32 RGB images to 24×24 grayscale. Training is set up as follows:

- Using 1,000 epochs with a 0.001 learning rate
- Dropping out neurons with 30% probability, using L2 regularization
- Applying the AdamOptimizer technique

The rationales for selecting these tunable training parameters could be chapters in their own right and are covered in detail elsewhere. As I mention throughout the book, you should experiment by changing these values to see how they affect the overall experience during training:

- Length of training time
- Amount of GPU and memory used while processing
- Ability to converge to an optimal result

For now, these parameters will allow you to complete training, even on a laptop with a CPU and no GPU. I should warn you, though: training a network this dense can take a day or more.

Listing 15.6   Setting up the training process for your CIFAR-10 dense CNN

Removes previous weights, bias, and inputs

Input of size (50000,576), or 50,000 24 × 24 images

Input of size (50000,10), or 50,000 class labels for the 10 classes

```
tf.reset_default_graph()
names, data, labels = read_data('./cifar-10-batches-py')
x = tf.placeholder(tf.float32, [None, 24 * 24], name='input_x')
y = tf.placeholder(tf.float32, [None, len(names)], name='output_y')
keep_prob = tf.placeholder(tf.float32, name='keep_prob')
epochs = 1000
keep_probability = 0.7
learning_rate = 0.001
model_op = model(x, keep_probability)
model_ops = tf.identity(model_op, name='logits')
beta = 0.1
weights = [conv1_filter, conv2_filter, conv3_filter, conv4_filter]
regularizer = tf.nn.l2_loss(weights[0])
for w in range(1, len(weights)):
    regularizer = regularizer + tf.nn.l2_loss(weights[w])

cost = tf.reduce_mean(tf.nn.softmax_cross_entropy_with_logits(logits=model_op,
    labels=y))
cost = tf.reduce_mean(cost + beta * regularizer)
train_op = tf.train.AdamOptimizer(learning_rate=learning_rate).minimize(cost)
correct_pred = tf.equal(tf.argmax(model_op, 1), tf.argmax(y, 1))
accuracy = tf.reduce_mean(tf.cast(correct_pred, tf.float32),
    name='accuracy')
```

Defines the hyperparameter for dropout. Neurons in layers where this is applied will be set to 0 with probability 1-keep_prob.

Trains for 1,000 epochs with learning rate 0.001

Defines the model and enables you to look it up with the name 'logits' from disk after training

Uses the Adam-Optimizer

Measures accuracy and the number of correct predictions

Applies regularization by adding the weights together, applying a hyperparameter beta to them, and adding to the cost for L2 regularization

---

Now that the training process is defined, you can train your model (listing 15.7). I've included a few options that take advantage of a GPU if one is available in your system. Note if you have a GPU, the training can complete in a few hours rather than days. The listing code also saves your trained model so you can load it for predictions and generate the ROC curve for evaluation later.

Listing 15.7   Executing the deep CNN training for CIFAR-10

Allows for GPU to be used and for growth in GPU memory

Creates a saver for your TensorFlow model to store it to disk

```
config = tf.ConfigProto()
config.gpu_options.allow_growth = True
with tf.Session(config=config) as sess:
    sess.run(tf.global_variables_initializer())
    saver = tf.train.Saver()
    onehot_labels = tf.one_hot(labels, len(names), on_value=1., off_value=0.,
    axis=-1)
    onehot_vals = sess.run(onehot_labels)
    batch_size = len(data) // 200
    print('batch size', batch_size)
    for j in tqdm(range(0, epochs)):
        for i in range(0, len(data), batch_size):
            batch_data = data[i:i+batch_size, :]
            batch_onehot_vals = onehot_vals[i:i+batch_size, :]
            _, accuracy_val = sess.run([train_op, accuracy],
            feed_dict={x:batch_data, y: batch_onehot_vals})
        print(j, accuracy_val)

    saver.save(sess,
    './cifar10-cnn-tf1n-ia-dropout-reg-dense-'+str(epochs)+'epochs.ckpt')
```

Converts the 10 CIFAR-10 label names to one-hot labels

Divides your training into batches (may be greater than 200 due to data augmentation)

Trains and visually shows progress using the TQDM library

Saves the model

Go ahead and get a cup of coffee, as they say in the science community. This code is going to take a while to run as your network does the following:

- Generates automatic additional examples of the input data and images
- Learns a more resilient representation, both externally through augmentation and internally by randomly turning off neurons 30% of the time
- Captures more variations using its four convolutional filters, and distinguishes between the CIFAR-10 image classes
- Trains faster and with higher probability of finding optimal weights via regularization and batch normalization

15.4   Testing and evaluating your CNN for CIFAR-10

OK, it's hours or maybe days later, and you're back. I know, I know—why did I subject you to this torture? Yes, I'm sorry that running this code on your laptop crashed all your other programs. At least you've got your trained model now, and it's time to try it.

To do that, you'll need a prediction function. Using your learned model to make predictions involves some steps similar to training. First, you need to make sure that your input is a 24 × 24 single-channel grayscale image. If so, you can load your trained model from disk and obtain a few key pieces of information from running your input image through it:

- The output logits, which you'll run a `tf.nn.softmax` over to get predictions for all 10 image classes from CIFAR-10.

- The dimension with the highest softmax value is the output predicted class. You can get this dimension with an np.argmax call that returns the highest-value column index in a row. The associated confidence for this prediction is the output of its softmax value. The np.argmax call obtains and returns the selected highest confidence class (class_num), its name (bird, automobile, and so on), the confidence or softmax value, and the full set of confidences for all classes. Listing 15.8 creates the predict function to allow you to call the classifier.

Listing 15.8   Making predictions of CIFAR-10 classes from input images

```
def predict(img_data):
    class_num, class_name, confidence = None, None, 0.
    with tf.Session() as sess:
        loaded_graph = tf.Graph()          ◁── Gets a pointer to the
                                               default TensorFlow graph                    Loads model
                                                                                            into the graph
            with tf.Session(graph=loaded_graph) as sess:
                loader = tf.train.import_meta_graph('./cifar10-cnn-tf1n-ia-
                ➥ dropout-reg-dense-'+str(epochs)+'epochs.ckpt' + '.meta')
                loader.restore(sess, './cifar10-cnn-tf1n-ia-dropout-reg-dense-
                ➥ '+str(epochs)+'epochs.ckpt')

                loaded_logits = loaded_graph.get_tensor_by_name('logits:0')
                logits_out = sess.run(tf.nn.softmax(loaded_logits),
                ➥ feed_dict={'input_x:0': img_data.reshape((1, 24*24))})
                class_num = np.argmax(logits_out, axis=1)[0]
                class_name = names[class_num]
                confidence = logits_out[0,class_num]
                all_preds = logits_out
            return (class_num, class_name, confidence, all_preds)
```

Gets tensors from loaded model ──▷

Runs the model using its learned weights; gets the output logits and runs the softmax function over them

Returns highest confidence class number, name, and predictions

You can test your prediction function by applying it to the third training image from CIFAR-10: a deer (figure 15.6).

The following code loads the model and obtains the class number, its name, the confidence in the prediction, and the full set of predictions for this image:

```
class_num, class_name, confidence, all_preds =
➥ predict(data[3])
print('Class Num', class_num)
print('Class', class_name)
print('Confidence', confidence)
print('All Predictions', str(all_preds))
```

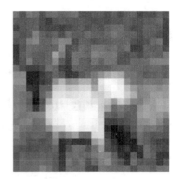

Figure 15.6   An image of a deer from CIFAR-10

Because it's a softmax, you get a confidence score in the model's prediction for all 10 CIFAR-10 classes. So your model is 93% confident (0.9301368 value) this image is a picture of a deer. The next-highest beliefs are class 6 (frog) with confidence ~3%— a virtual tie between classes 2 (bird) and 5 (dog) at ~1%, respectively. The drop-off in confidence between `deer` and the latter three classes is statistically significant (90%+ points):

```
INFO:tensorflow:Restoring parameters from ./cifar10-cnn-tf1n-ia-dropout-reg-
⇨ dense-1000epochs.ckpt
Class Num 4
Class deer
Confidence 0.9301368
All Predictions [[6.24996528e-06 5.14547166e-04 1.39211295e-02 6.32673642e-03
   9.30136800e-01 1.21700075e-02 3.20204385e-02 4.65520751e-03
   2.48217111e-05 2.24148083e-04]]
```

That result is a nice confidence-booster for a single image from the training data, but how well does your deep CNN with optimizations perform on the unseen test data from CIFAR-10? You can build a simple evaluation function that will run your new model across all the test data and output prediction accuracy. You can load the model the same way. This time, give the model the full set of 10,000 test images and 10,000 test labels (1,000 per class); count the number of times that the model predicted correctly; and store 1 for each correct entry and 0 otherwise. Overall accuracy, then, is the mean of that prediction array for all the images. Listing 15.9 has the full evaluation of the deep CNN on the CIFAR-10 test data.

Listing 15.9 Running your deep CNN across CIFAR-10's test data

```
def get_test_accuracy(test_data, test_names, test_labels):
    class_num, class_name, confidence = None, None, 0.
    with tf.Session() as sess:
        loaded_graph = tf.Graph()

        with tf.Session(graph=loaded_graph) as sess:
            loader = tf.train.import_meta_graph('./cifar10-cnn-tf1n-ia-
            ⇨ dropout-reg-dense-'+str(epochs)+'epochs.ckpt' + '.meta')
            loader.restore(sess, './cifar10-cnn-tf1n-ia-dropout-reg-dense-
            ⇨ '+str(epochs)+'epochs.ckpt')

            loaded_x = loaded_graph.get_tensor_by_name('input_x:0')
            loaded_y = loaded_graph.get_tensor_by_name('output_y:0')
            loaded_logits = loaded_graph.get_tensor_by_name('logits:0')
            loaded_acc = loaded_graph.get_tensor_by_name('accuracy:0')
            onehot_test_labels = tf.one_hot(test_labels, len(test_names),
            ⇨ on_value=1., off_value=0., axis=-1).eval()
            test_logits_out = sess.run(tf.nn.softmax(loaded_logits),
            ⇨ feed_dict={'input_x:0': test_data, "output_y:0"
            ⇨ :onehot_test_labels, "keep_prob:0": 1.0})
            test_correct_pred = tf.equal(tf.argmax(test_logits_out, 1),
            ⇨ tf.argmax(onehot_test_labels, 1))
            test_accuracy = tf.reduce_mean(tf.cast(test_correct_pred,
            ⇨ tf.float32))

            print('Test accuracy %f' % (test_accuracy.eval()))
```

Loads the model — `loader.restore(...)`

Gets tensors from loaded model

Applies the model given the input test images and test labels

Counts how many times the model agreed with the one-hot test labels, storing 1 for each correct prediction and 0 otherwise

Measures average accuracy by computing the mean

```
predictions = tf.argmax(test_logits_out, 1).eval()
return (predictions, tf.cast(test_correct_pred,
  ➥ tf.float32).eval(), onehot_test_labels)
```

**Returns the predictions, the correct prediction
counts, and the one-hot test labels**

Run listing 15.9 with the following simple invocation:

```
predict_vals, test_correct_preds, onehot_test_lbls =
  ➥ get_test_accuracy(test_data, test_names, test_labels)
```

The command produces the following output:

```
Test accuracy 0.647800
```

Next, I'll discuss how you can evaluate the accuracy of your CNN. A familiar technique
will re-appear: ROC curves.

15.4.1 *CIFAR-10 accuracy results and ROC curves*

Normally, producing a test accuracy overall of ~65% on 10,000 images wouldn't feel
great. Did you improve your model by training a deep CNN with optimizations? In fact,
you have to dig a little deeper to find out, because your model's accuracy is more than
right or wrong for a particular image class; each time, you are predicting across 10
classes, and because it's a softmax, getting a label wrong may not have been *that* wrong.

What if the label was bird, and your model predicted the highest confidence class
label as deer at 93%, but its next-highest confidence, 91%, was bird? Sure, you got the
test answer wrong, but you weren't far off. If your model uniformly was less confident
in all the remaining classes, you could say that it is performing well overall because
one of the top two predictions was correct. Scaling this result out, if it always happens,
you will have poor overall accuracy. But considering the top-k (k is a hyperparameter)
predictions, your model performs quite well and is sensitive to the right image class.
Perhaps the model is missing the capacity to distinguish between a deer and a bird, or
perhaps you do not have enough training examples or data augmentation for the
model to distinguish between them.

You apply a ROC curve to evaluate the true-positive rate against the false-positive
rate of your predictions and look at the micro-average across all the classes to evaluate.
The ROC curve shows you how well your model is performing based on distinguishing
between classes in the full CIFAR-10 test data, which is a more appropriate measure of
model performance on multiclass classification problems. You can use your friendly
neighborhood Matplotlib and SK-learn libraries, as I've shown you throughout
the book.

The SK-learn libraries provide functionality to compute the ROC curve based on
the false-positive rate (fpr) and true-positive rate (tpr), and to compute the area
under the curve (AUC). Then Matplotlib provides plotting and graphical functionality to display the results. Note the np.ravel() function in listing 15.10, which provides

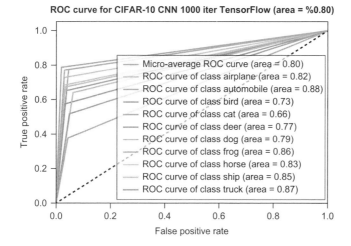

Figure 15.7 The ROC curve for your **CIFAR-10** deep CNN model. Overall, it performed quite well across all classes except `cat`, `bird`, and `deer`.

ROC curve generation; plotting code is used to return a continuous flattened NumPy array. The output of running the ROC curve-generation code in listing 15.10 is shown in figure 15.7.

The ROC curve shows that the model performed excellently for most classes and better than average for a few of them (`cat`, `bird`, and `deer`).

Listing 15.10 CIFAR-10 ROC curve

Uses SK-learn's label_binarize function to create
one-hot prediction values and test labels to compare

```
from sklearn.preprocessing import label_binarize
from sklearn.metrics import roc_curve, auc
outcome_test = label_binarize(test_labels, classes=[0, 1, 2, 3, 4, 5, 6, 7,
    8, 9])
predictions_test = label_binarize(predict_vals, classes=[0, 1, 2, 3, 4, 5, 6,
    7, 8, 9])

fpr = dict()          ◁──┐  Computes ROC curve and
tpr = dict()             │  ROC area for each class
roc_auc = dict()
for i in range(n_classes):
    fpr[i], tpr[i], _ = roc_curve(outcome_test[:, i], predictions_test[:, i])
    roc_auc[i] = auc(fpr[i], tpr[i])

fpr["micro"], tpr["micro"], _ = roc_curve(outcome_test.ravel(),
    predictions_test.ravel())
roc_auc["micro"] = auc(fpr["micro"], tpr["micro"])   ◁──┐  Computes micro-
                                                         average ROC curve
plt.figure()                          Plot of a ROC curve for a   and ROC area
    plt.plot(fpr["micro"], tpr["micro"],      specific class
            label='micro-average ROC curve (area = {0:0.2f})'
Plots ROC curve          ''.format(roc_auc["micro"]))
    for i in range(n_classes):
```

```
            plt.plot(fpr[i], tpr[i], label='ROC curve of class {0} (area = {1:0.2f})'
                                    ''.format(test_names[i], roc_auc[i]))
plt.plot([0, 1], [0, 1], 'k--')
plt.xlim([0.0, 1.0])
plt.ylim([0.0, 1.05])
plt.xlabel('False Positive Rate')
plt.ylabel('True Positive Rate')
roc_mean = np.mean(np.fromiter(roc_auc.values(), dtype=float))
plt.title('ROC curve for CIFAR-10 CNN '+str(epochs)+' iter Tensorflow (area =
➥ %{0:0.2f})'.format(roc_mean))
plt.legend(loc="lower right")         Displays the micro-average
plt.show()                            ROC curve across all classes
```

So although your model's test accuracy left you feeling a little bummed (~65%), the model is performing quite well, with an 80% overall micro-average ROC across all classes. Also, the model has exceptional performance on all classes except cat, bird, and deer. The model does a good job of distinguishing among different image classes and likely has some confident responses for the top two or three predictions, even if it didn't always get the top one right. I explore that topic more in section 15.4.2.

15.4.2 Evaluating the softmax predictions per class

You can go even further by looking at the softmax predictions per class to see your model trying to decide between classes. Instead of an ROC curve, imagine for each image prediction a horizontal bar chart, with a softmax bar value of 0 to 1 for each possible predicted class. The softmax-based bar chart is like watching your model try to figure out what class it believes is most correct. The softmax process also shows what classes the model was deciding among for the top spot prediction versus what classes it was throwing out or wasn't confident in.

With some effort, you can create a function that will show you this chart. You wouldn't want to run the function on tens of thousands of images, but you can test the model on a few images outside your train-and-test set. I curated a list of nine random image URLs across six of the CIFAR-10 classes for this purpose. These images are of a frog, three ships, two trucks, a cat, a horse, and a car. The simple URLs (listing 15.11) are followed by calls to the predict function to run your model on each image.

Listing 15.11   Unseen evaluation URLs from the internet for your CNN

```
predict_urls = [
    'http://www.torontozoo.com/adoptapond/guide_images/Green%20Frog.jpg',
    'https://cdn.cnn.com/cnnnext/dam/assets/160205192735-01-best-cruise-
    ➥ ships-disney-dream-super-169.jpg',
    'https://www.sailboston.com/wp-content/uploads/2016/11/amerigo-
    ➥ vespucci.jpg',
'https://upload.wikimedia.org/wikipedia/commons/d/d9/Motorboat_at_Kankaria_
➥ lake.JPG',
'https://media.wired.com/photos/5b9c3d5e7d9d332cf364ad66/master/pass/
➥ AV-Trucks-187479297.jpg',
    'https://images.schoolspecialty.com/images/1581176_ecommfullsize.jpg',
```

```
'https://img.purch.com/w/660/aHR0cDovL3d3dy5saXZlc2NpZW5jZS5jb20vaW1hZ2VzL2kv
➥ MDAwLzEwNC84MTkvb3JpZ2luYWwvY3V0ZS1raXR0ZW4uanBn',
    'https://thehorse.com/wp-content/uploads/2017/01/iStock-510488648.jpg',
'http://media.wired.com/photos/5d09594a62bcb0c9752779d9/master/w_2560%2Cc_lim
➥ it/Transpo_G70_TA-518126.jpg'
]
```

Note that the `predict` function has been altered slightly in listing 15.12 to prepare the online image for your network (converting it to 24 × 24 grayscale via the OpenCV library) and to read the image by using the SK-learn library and its `imread` function.

Listing 15.12 A `predict` function for images in the wild

```
from skimage.io import imread          Reads the image at
def predict_img_url(url):              the specified URL and
    image = color.rgb2gray(imread(url))  ◁── converts it to grayscale
    new_size = 24,24
    image = cv2.resize(image, new_size, interpolation=cv2.INTER_CUBIC)   ◁─
    images = np.expand_dims(image, axis=0)
    im_data = images.astype(np.float32)      Rescales the image to 24,24, using
    prediction = predict(im_data[0])  ◁─     intercubic interpolation and OpenCV
    return prediction
                          Runs the prepared image against your
                          network and returns the prediction
```

The following snippet runs the function against all the random images:

```
preds=[]
for url in predict_urls:
    pred = predict_img_url(url)
    preds.append(pred)
```

With the predictions made and softmax values returned, you can make an `evaluate_model` function that does the following:

- Grabs the image data from the internet and rescales to 24,24 grayscale to display each image
- Shows the output softmax predictions right next to the rescaled grayscale images to show you how much confidence the network had in each class

Listing 15.13 shows the `evaluate_model` function, and figure 15.8 shows a partial screenshot of the output for a few of the images. The model appears to be sensitive to whether it is classifying animals, objects, or vehicles, but on the third ship, it has some trouble deciding between the second and third guesses for each class. This test can be useful for evaluating the sensitivities of your model to specific image features. Evaluating your CNN model by using a per-class confidence figure like the one shown in figure 15.8 provides a guide for tuning the CNN by expanding capacity to capture missing features.

The test could also suggest that you need to change your data augmentation approach or to tweak the hyperparameters for dropout or regularization. Functions

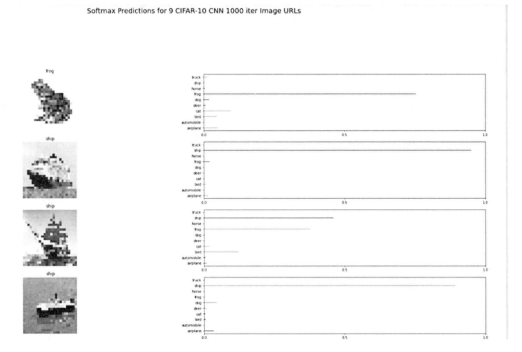

Figure 15.8   Output of the evaluate_model function, showing the model deciding among four of the image URLs and their associated class labels

such as evaluate_model are a necessity for improving your deep CNN and providing a road map to debugging and investigating it.

The code in listing 15.13 produces figure 15.8. First, it prepares the images, using the OpenCV and SK-learn libraries to convert them to grayscale; next, it resizes the images to 24 × 24. Then the evaluate_model function stacks the images vertically as a matrix. For each prediction, the function shows the image to be classified; to the right is a horizontal bar chart of the softmax predictions that the model derived for each class it knows about.

Listing 15.13   The evaluate_model function for CIFAR-10

```
def evaluate_model(urls, predicted):
    im_data = []
    for url in urls:
        image = color.rgb2gray(imread(url))
        new_size = 24,24
        image = cv2.resize(image, new_size, interpolation=cv2.INTER_CUBIC)
        images = np.expand_dims(image, axis=0)
        if len(im_data) > 0:
            im_data = np.vstack((im_data, images.astype(np.float32)))
        else:
            im_data = images.astype(np.float32)
```

Prepares
the images

```
n_predictions = len(predicted)
fig, axies = plt.subplots(nrows=n_predictions, ncols=2, figsize=(24, 24))
fig.tight_layout()
fig.suptitle('Softmax Predictions for '+str(len(predicted))+' CIFAR-10
  ➥ CNN '+str(epochs)+' iter Image URLs', fontsize=20, y=1.1)

n_predictions = 10
margin = 0.05
ind = np.arange(n_predictions)
width = (1. - 2. * margin) / n_predictions

for i in range(0, len(im_data)):
    pred_names = names
    pred_values = predicted[i][3][0]
    correct_name = predicted[i][1]

    axies[i][0].imshow(im_data[i], cmap='Greys_r')
    axies[i][0].set_title(correct_name)
    axies[i][0].set_axis_off()

    axies[i][1].barh(ind + margin, pred_values, width)
    axies[i][1].set_yticks(ind + margin)
    axies[i][1].set_yticklabels(pred_names)
    axies[i][1].set_xticks([0, 0.5, 1.0])
```

> Shows the image and its predicted class name

> Shows the bar chart next to the image

Now that you've created a model with 80% micro-average ROC accuracy on CIFAR-10, you've significantly improved on the shallow CNN you built in chapter 14. The good news? Those improvements can also translate to a similar problem: facial recognition, which is another image classification problem with a similar construction. Instead of providing images containing 10 classes of objects sized 32 × 32 as input, you will provide images sized 244 × 244, containing images of 2,622 celebrity faces as input, and try to classify the label as one of those 2,622 celebrities. Everything you've learned thus far in the chapter can help you create the VGG-Face model.

15.5 Building VGG-Face for facial recognition

The problem of facial recognition has been studied for decades and in recent years has become newsworthy for various reasons. In 2015, Oxford's Visual Geometry Group (VGG), fresh from creating deep CNN networks for use in the ImageNet challenge, attempted to reapply its CNN network, called VGG, to the problem of celebrity facial recognition. The members of the VGG group wrote a seminal paper called "Deep Face Recognition" and published the results of their work to identify celebrity faces through a deep CNN. The paper is available at http://mng.bz/MomW.

The authors—Omkar M. Parkhi, Andrea Vedaldi, and Andrew Zisserman—built a dataset of 2,622 celebrity faces (some of which are shown in figure 15.9) in various poses with varying backgrounds. The dataset after initial collection was further culled, using human curators to sort through and curate 1,000 URLs for each of the celebrities. In the end, the authors created a dataset of 2,622,000 images for use in a deep

CNN that detected celebrity faces. The network used 13 convolutional filters and comprised 37 layers, the last layer being a fully connected layer emitting a softmax probability value corresponding to which of the 2,622 celebrities the input image corresponds to.

Figure 15.9   A few of the faces and poses like those you would see in the VGG-Face dataset.

In my attempts to re-create this network for this book, I found several challenges that I will summarize for you:

- More than 50% of the data, largely from 2015, doesn't exist anymore. The VGG group published the URLs to the data it used, but the internet moved on, so the URLs pointed to images that no longer existed.
- Collecting the remaining data that existed—around 1,250,000 images—required a sophisticated crawling technique, URL validation, and the use of a supercomputer over a few weeks, employing both trial and error and manual curation.
- The resulting data had a mean image sample average of ~477 images per class—much less than the original 1,000 images per class that made data augmentation more necessary but also reduced its effectiveness.
- Even this updated VGG-Face Lite dataset that I collected was ~90 GB, which is huge, hard to run on a laptop, and doesn't fit into memory. Also, the size of the dataset severely limited the batch-size parameter because laptops, GPUs, and even supercomputers don't have infinite memory.
- Dealing with images of size 244 × 244 and full-color RGB channels requires the deep network and its 13 filters to capture the higher- and lower-order features needed to distinguish among so many output classes (2,622).

I could list many other issues in collecting an updated version of this dataset and in testing and building a deep CNN for it based on the VGG-Face paper, but I won't. Summarizing the data collection issues here wouldn't add much color other than the points I've already made about the importance of data cleaning, augmentation, and preparation to machine learning.

> **Why don't machine-learning researchers provide their data?**
>
> The short answer is that it's complicated. It would have been nice to download the original 2015 VGG-Face dataset of 2 million images and start training instead of having to re-collect only the remaining subset. But there are likely legal and other issues related to open data collection and how that data is used. A lot of image datasets provide only the image URLs, or if you do get the images, they're a small subset with a lot of legalese to read. This situation makes it difficult to reproduce machine-learning models and is a problem that plagues the community even today. The only solution is to prepare a well-curated dataset and to provide a recipe for re-collecting it.

The good news is that I've got a dataset that you can use to perform facial identification and to build your own version of VGG-Face, which I'll call VGG-Face Lite, a subset of four celebrities that will run on your computer and illustrate the architecture. Then I'll show you how to use the full model to make predictions with TensorFlow's Estimator API.

15.5.1 Picking a subset of VGG-Face for training VGG-Face Lite

I randomly selected a set of four celebrities from the updated VGG-Face dataset based on average number of samples, trying to find a representative subset of features, backgrounds, and learnability for the model. There are other sets of four that I could have picked, but for the purposes of getting the model trained, this one works fine. I used four random celebrities to train the model. You can grab a small subset of the VGG-Face dataset, containing 244 × 244 images, at http://mng.bz/awy7.

The subset has 1,903 total images arranged in directories that contain the celebrities' first and last names concatenated with the underscore character: `Firstname_Lastname`. Unzip the images into a top-level folder called vgg_face.

Earlier in the chapter, you developed functionality for image dataset augmentation on your own, using lower-level NumPy functions for introducing salt-and-pepper noise and for flipping images left and right. This time, I'll show you how to use TensorFlow's robust capabilities to do the same thing. I'll also introduce you to TensorFlow's powerful Dataset API, which provides native capabilities for batching, repeating data over epochs, and combining data and labels into a powerful construct for learning. Hand-in-hand with the Dataset API is TensorFlow's support for data augmentation through its graph structure, which I'll show you in section 15.5.2.

15.5.2 *TensorFlow's Dataset API and data augmentation*

Whether or not you use TensorFlow's native constructs to iterate over datasets or prepare them for machine learning, or whether you combine functionality from libraries such as SK-learn and NumPy, TensorFlow works well with the results for training and prediction tasks.

It's worthwhile to explore TensorFlow's capabilities in this area. TensorFlow provides a powerful Dataset API that uses its great properties for lazy evaluation and graph-based operations in dataset preparation and processing. These features come in handy for batching, data augmentation, epoch management, and other preparation and training tasks, which you can perform by making a few calls to the Dataset API.

To begin, you'll need a TensorFlow dataset. You'll start preparing this dataset by gathering the initial image paths for the 1,903 images and 4 celebrities (listing 15.14). The images are in the form index_244x244.png and stored in BGR (blue, green, red) format.

> **Listing 15.14 Gathering image paths for the VGG-Face Lite TensorFlow dataset**

```
data_root_orig = './vgg-face'
data_root = pathlib.Path(data_root_orig)                      The four celebrities
celebs_to_test = ['CelebA, 'CelebB', 'CelebC', 'CelebD']  ◁──┘ you will train on
all_image_paths = []
for c in celebs_to_test:                                      Selects all the
    all_image_paths += list(data_root.glob(c+'/*'))  ◁──┘ images in each

all_image_paths_c = []
for p in all_image_paths:
    path_str = os.path.basename(str(p))
    if path_str.startswith('._'):      ◁──┐
        print('Rejecting '+str(p))         Ignores hidden
    else:                                  files and appends
        all_image_paths_c.append(p)  ◁──┘  images
                                                         Shuffles image paths
                                                         so that the network
all_image_paths = all_image_paths_c                      doesn't remember
all_image_paths = [str(path) for path in all_image_paths] the actual order
random.shuffle(all_image_paths)                  ◁────────┘

image_count = len(all_image_paths)   ◁──── Counts the images (1,903)
```

With the set of image paths defined and associated labels for the four celebrities, you can begin to construct your TensorFlow dataset by using its Dataset API. In section 15.1, you wrote a lot of your own data augmentation by using lower-level NumPy constructs. This data augmentation code operated on image matrices. Now I'll show you how to create new code to perform the same functionality with TensorFlow's API.

TensorFlow provides elegant support for data augmentation. The functions are provided by the `tf.image` package. This package includes `tf.image.random_flip_left_right` to flip the images at random; `tf.image_random_brightness` and `tf.image.random_contrast` change background hues and perform augmentation similar to salt and pepper, which you implemented by hand earlier in the chapter. What's more, rather than directly altering the images and generating new training images that expand your dataset, data augmentation provided by TensorFlow's API is a lazy-evaluated graph construct that creates the augmented image only when it's invoked.

You can use TensorFlow's Dataset API, which includes full support for shuffling, batching, and repetition for epochs to arbitrarily provide data augmentation at random without creating physical new data to store in memory or on disk. Also, the augmentation happens only at run time during training and is deallocated when your Python code completes running.

To begin using the augmentation capabilities, write a preprocess_image function that takes in a VGG-Face Lite image sized 244 × 244 in BGR format and returns an image tensor to be modified only during execution. You can think of the tensor as being the same as the image, but it's much more powerful. The result is a tensor representing a graph of operations that will execute at runtime during training. You can also pipeline augmentation techniques together and have TensorFlow run them randomly as you iterate through batches and epochs during training.

One other thing that TensorFlow can do is image standardization or cleaning to divide by the mean value to ease training. TensorFlow's tf.image.per_image_ standardization function returns a tensor after invocation. Because tensor operations are graphs, you can combine these operations on the original input image. Your preprocess_image function pipelines the following operations, shown in listing 15.15:

- Convert the image to RGB format instead of BGR.
- Randomly flip the image from left to right.
- Randomly apply brightness to the image.
- Randomly create image contrast (similar to salt and pepper).
- Randomly rotate the image by 90 degrees.
- Apply fixed image standardization and divide by the mean variance of pixels.

Listing 15.15   Image dataset augmentation with TensorFlow

```
IMAGE_SIZE=244
def preprocess_image(image, distort=True):             Images are stored
    image = tf.image.decode_png(image, channels=3)     in files with BGR to
    image = image[..., ::-1]                            convert to RGB.
    image = tf.image.resize(image, [IMAGE_SIZE, IMAGE_SIZE])

    if distort:
        image = tf.image.random_flip_left_right(image)
        image = tf.image.random_brightness(image, max_delta=63)
        image = tf.image.random_contrast(image, lower=0.2, upper=1.8)

        rotate_pct = 0.5 # 50% of the time do a rotation between 0 to 90
            degrees
        if random.random() < rotate_pct:
```

Resizes the image to 244 × 244

Applies random flip (L-R), brightness, contrast, and rotation to the image, using tensor graph

```
        degrees = random.randint(0, 90)
        image = tf.contrib.image.rotate(image, degrees * math.pi / 180,
        ⮡ interpolation='BILINEAR')

    image = (tf.cast(image, tf.float32) - 127.5)/128.0    ◁─

    image = tf.image.per_image_standardization(image)

    return image
```

> **Fixed standardization for the image and subtract off the mean and divide by the variance of the pixels**

With your image data augmentation `function preprocess_image` returning a tensor graph of operations to apply during training, you're nearly ready to create your Tensor-Flow dataset. First, you need to split the input data into training and testing sets, using a 70/30 split:

```
def get_training_and_testing_sets(file_list):
    split = 0.7
    split_index = math.floor(len(file_list) * split)
    training = file_list[:split_index]
    testing = file_list[split_index:]
    return training, testing
```

You can use `get_training_and_testing_sets` to split your image path list into a 70/30 split, with 70% of the images to be used for training and the other 30% for testing. You'll also need to prepare your labels and the image paths to construct the overall dataset. One easy way to do that is to iterate the folders that correspond to the celebrity names and then assign each celebrity name an index from 0 to 4:

```
label_names = sorted(celebs_to_test)
label_to_index = dict((name, index) for index,name in enumerate(label_names))
all_image_labels = [label_to_index[pathlib.Path(path).parent.name]
                    for path in all_image_paths]
```

Finally, you can generate your image paths and your labels for training and testing by calling the `get_training_and_testing_sets` function to split them:

```
train_paths, test_paths = get_training_and_testing_sets(all_image_paths)
train_labels, test_labels = get_training_and_testing_sets(all_image_labels)
```

Now you are ready to create your TensorFlow dataset.

15.5.3 Creating a TensorFlow dataset

Datasets in TensorFlow are also lazily-executed graphs of operations that can be constructed in various ways. One easy way is to provide a set of existing data slices that can be operated over to yield a new dataset tensor. If you provide `train_paths` as input to TensorFlow's `tf.data.Dataset.from_tensor_slices` function, for example, the function will yield a TensorFlow `Dataset` object: a graph of operations that will execute at runtime and provide the wrapped paths to images. Then, if you pass that `Dataset` object to the `tf.data.Dataset.map` function, you can further construct your TensorFlow `Dataset` graph as follows.

The `tf.data.Dataset.map` function takes as input a function to run in parallel across each iterable item in the dataset, so you can use the `preprocess_image` function from listing 15.15. That function returns another `Dataset` object that corresponds to the image paths that have been run through the data augmentation operations.

Remember operations such as image flipping, random brightness, contrast, and random rotation? Giving `tf.data.Dataset.map` a copy of the `preprocess_image` function creates a graph of operations to be applied to each image path in the `Dataset`. Finally, the TensorFlow `Dataset` API provides a `zip` method that combines two datasets, with each entry being an enumeration of each item pair from the two datasets.

Again, all these operations are lazily executed, so you are building up a graph of operations to execute only when you iterate or perform some other operation on the dataset in a TensorFlow session. Figure 15.10 shows the resulting Dataset pipeline that combines data augmentation on the input images from the VGG-Face paths and their labels, which are the directory names that contain the images.

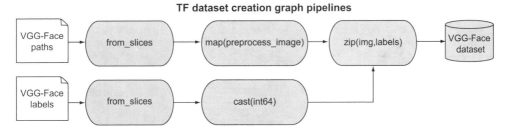

Figure 15.10 The TensorFlow `Dataset` API pipeline to combine the VGG-Face image paths with data augmentation and the image labels (the directories that contain each image from the path)

The code in listing 15.16 implements the process shown in figure 15.10, creating a train and test TensorFlow dataset for VGG-Face images and labels named `train_image_label_ds` and `val_image_label_ds`, respectively. You will use these datasets during the training process, which I'll explain in section 15.5.4. The Dataset API will come in handy for training too, because operations that you had to implement by hand before—such as batching, prefetching, and repetition during epochs—are provided natively by TensorFlow.

Listing 15.16 Creating the VGG-Face val and train datasets

Divides into 70/30 train/test split for
the input image paths and input labels

```
train_paths, test_paths = get_training_and_testing_sets(all_image_paths)
train_labels, test_labels = get_training_and_testing_sets(all_image_labels)
```

Creates initial Dataset from the mage paths for train and test

Executes the map function to create a new Dataset that applies the data augmentation steps to train and test images

```
train_path_ds = tf.data.Dataset.from_tensor_slices(train_paths)
val_path_ds = tf.data.Dataset.from_tensor_slices(test_paths)
train_image_ds = train_path_ds.map(load_and_preprocess_image,
⇒ num_parallel_calls=AUTOTUNE)
val_image_ds = val_path_ds.map(load_image, num_parallel_calls=AUTOTUNE)
val_label_ds = tf.data.Dataset.from_tensor_slices(tf.cast(test_labels,
⇒ tf.int64))
train_label_ds = tf.data.Dataset.from_tensor_slices(tf.cast(train_labels,
⇒ tf.int64))
train_image_label_ds = tf.data.Dataset.zip((train_image_ds, train_label_ds))
val_image_label_ds = tf.data.Dataset.zip((val_image_ds, val_label_ds))
```

Creates a dataset by casting the train and test labels to int64 values

Zips the augmented image data and the labels into datasets for train and val/test

If you were to inspect the results of applying the data augmentation, you might see a randomly flipped image of celebrity A, a high-contrast black-and-white photo of celebrity B, or perhaps a slightly rotated picture of celebrity C. Some of these augmentations are shown in figure 15.11.

Random rotate and L-R flip   Random contrast   Random flip L-R

Figure 15.11   Results of data augmentation with the TensorFlow Dataset API

Now that you have your TensorFlow `Dataset` graph prepared, it's time to configure your dataset with typical training hyperparameters, such as batch size and shufflings. The cool part about the `Dataset` API is that you do this all beforehand by setting properties on the `Dataset` object to execute during training.

15.5.4 *Training using TensorFlow datasets*

With the TensorFlow dataset graph you created for VGG-Face, you've got a combined lazily-executable graph representing your data augmentation operations that will execute only when you iterate and realize each entry in the dataset with a TensorFlow session. The power of the dataset API shows itself during the training and setup process.

Because you've got a dataset, you can perform explicit operations on it, such as defining ahead of time what batch size you want in each iteration when you perform training. You can also define ahead of time that you would like to shuffle the dataset so that you are guaranteed to get the dataset in a different order in each epoch. You do this so that the network doesn't memorize the order of the dataset, which can happen as it tries to optimize the weights. Seeing the same image in the same order may never allow the train operation to achieve a particular optimization step during backpropagation and the weight updates it needs to achieve an optimal result. So you can turn on shuffling in your dataset ahead of time (listing 15.17). You can also tell your dataset to repeat a certain number of times, obviating the need to use a loop for epochs. The power of the TensorFlow Dataset API is front and center in listing 15.17.

The listing also sets up the Dataset API to use a batch size of 128. The more images you have per batch, the more memory your CPU and GPU (if you have one) will use, so you'll have to play with this number. Additionally, the more images you have per batch, the less randomness and the fewer chances the training operation will have to update the weights for the learned parameters in each epoch. You'll shuffle the dataset by using a buffer size, which is the length of the input, ensuring that the whole dataset is shuffled only once in each epoch. Finally, you prefetch the data on your dataset, which allows it to gather data during the training operation when the graph is finally executing, optimizing, reducing I/O waiting, and taking advantage of TensorFlow's parallelism. All these features are possible because of the `Dataset` API.

With the datasets created for training and validation, it's time to build the model for VGG-Face Lite.

Listing 15.17 Preparing the VGG-Face TensorFlow dataset for training

Shuffles the entire dataset of training images and validation images for testing during each epoch

Uses the batch size of 128 images/labels during training, ensuring ~11 epochs because there are 1,903 images and 70% are used for training

```
BATCH_SIZE=128
train_ds= train_image_label_ds.shuffle(buffer_size=len(train_paths))
val_ds = val_image_label_ds.shuffle(buffer_size=len(test_paths))

train_ds = train_ds.batch(BATCH_SIZE)
val_ds = val_ds.batch(len(test_paths))

train_ds = train_ds.prefetch(buffer_size=AUTOTUNE)
val_ds = val_ds.prefetch(buffer_size=AUTOTUNE)
```

Uses the remaining 30% of images for validation and batches the whole set for validation

Prefetch lets the dataset fetch batches in the background while the model is training.

Now that you've parameterized your TensorFlow `Dataset` graph for training, you'll get to the actual running of the training process. Follow me to section 15.5.5!

15.5.5 VGG-Face Lite model and training

The full VGG-Face model includes 37 layers and is a deep network model taking gigabytes of memory to load the model graph after training for predictions. If I were sure that you had access to supercomputing and cloud resources, we'd reimplement the model. But I'm not sure, so instead, we'll chop off a few of the filters and layers for something that you'll be able to train in about a day on your laptop. Even without a GPU, the model will perform with exceptional accuracy for the four celebrity faces.

VGG-Face Lite uses five convolutional filters and is a 10-layer deep network that takes advantages of the some optimizations discussed in this chapter, such as batch normalization. One other thing you can do to speed training and learning is to rescale your image sizes to 64×64. This rescaling reduces the amount of learning that your model must do by decreasing the input pixels by a factor of ~4. You can bet that if the computer program can learn the differentiation in smaller-scale images, you can start to scale it up to larger ones. The output of the CNN model is which of the four celebrity-face classes the input image corresponds to.

The model architecture is shown in listing 15.18. The first portion defines the convolutional filters in full RGB three-channel space and then uses 64 convolutional filters, followed by 64, 128, 128, and 256 filters for learning. These filters correspond to the 4D parameter in convolution filters conv1_2 through conv3_1 in listing 15.18. The output fully connected layer is 128 neurons, which are mapped to the four output classes via a softmax in the final output. In the first input filter, the third parameter is the RGB 3 channel because you will use color images.

Listing 15.18   The VGG-Face Lite model

Defines convolutional filters (five of them)

```
conv1_1_filter = tf.Variable(tf.random_normal(shape=[3, 3, 3, 64], mean=0,
➥ stddev=10e-2))
conv1_2_filter = tf.Variable(tf.random_normal(shape=[3, 3, 64, 64], mean=0,
➥ stddev=10e-2))
conv2_1_filter = tf.Variable(tf.random_normal(shape=[3, 3, 64, 128], mean=0,
➥ stddev=10e-2))
conv2_2_filter = tf.Variable(tf.random_normal(shape=[3, 3, 128, 128], mean=0,
➥ stddev=10e-2))
conv3_1_filter = tf.Variable(tf.random_normal(shape=[3, 3, 128, 256], mean=0,
➥ stddev=10e-2))
                                                 Defines the model function for VGG-Face Lite
def model(x, keep_prob):          ◁────────
    conv1_1 = tf.nn.conv2d(x, conv1_1_filter, strides=[1,1,1,1],
    ➥ padding='SAME')
    conv1_1 = tf.nn.relu(conv1_1)
    conv1_2 = tf.nn.conv2d(conv1_1, conv1_2_filter, strides=[1,1,1,1],
    ➥ padding='SAME')
    conv1_2 = tf.nn.relu(conv1_2)
    conv1_pool = tf.nn.max_pool(conv1_2, ksize=[1,2,2,1], strides=[1,2,2,1],
    ➥ padding='SAME')
    conv1_bn = tf.layers.batch_normalization(conv1_pool)

    conv2_1 = tf.nn.conv2d(conv1_bn, conv2_1_filter, strides=[1,1,1,1],
    ➥ padding='SAME')
    conv2_1 = tf.nn.relu(conv2_1)
    conv2_2 = tf.nn.conv2d(conv2_1, conv2_2_filter, strides=[1,1,1,1],
    ➥ padding='SAME')
    conv2_2 = tf.nn.relu(conv2_2)
```

```
conv2_pool = tf.nn.max_pool(conv2_2, ksize=[1,2,2,1], strides=[1,2,2,1],
➥ padding='SAME')
conv2_bn = tf.layers.batch_normalization(conv2_pool)

conv3_1 = tf.nn.conv2d(conv2_pool, conv3_1_filter, strides=[1,1,1,1],
➥ padding='SAME')
conv3_1 = tf.nn.relu(conv3_1)
conv3_pool = tf.nn.max_pool(conv3_1, ksize=[1,2,2,1], strides=[1,2,2,1],
➥ padding='SAME')
conv3_bn = tf.layers.batch_normalization(conv3_pool)

flat = tf.contrib.layers.flatten(conv3_bn)
full1 = tf.contrib.layers.fully_connected(inputs=flat, num_outputs=128,
➥ activation_fn=tf.nn.relu)
full1 = tf.nn.dropout(full1, keep_prob)          ⟵┐ Uses dropout only in the last layer
full1 = tf.layers.batch_normalization(full1)

out = tf.contrib.layers.fully_connected(inputs=full1, num_outputs=4,
➥ activation_fn=None)
return out                  ⟵── Returns the logits of the model
```

With the model defined, you can move on to set up the hyperparameters for training. You can use hyperparameters similar to those in your CIFAR-10 object recognition model. In practice, you would experiment with these hyperparameters to obtain the optimal values. But for the purposes of this example, these parameters should allow you to complete training in about a day.

One new hyperparameter to try is exponential weight decay, which uses the overall global training epoch step as an influence factor in decreasing the learning weight. Over time, your network will make smaller learning steps and try to hone in on an optimal value. Combined with the ADAMOptimizer, weight decay has been shown to help CNNs converge on optimal learning parameters. TensorFlow provides easy-to-use optimizers that you can experiment with. Associated techniques such as weight decay are fairly simple to test with the framework, as shown in listing 15.19.

> **Listing 15.19 Setting up the hyperparameters for VGG-Face Lite model training**

N three-channel RGB images
of input N × 64 × 64 × 3

Output of length N
images N × 4 classes

```
IMAGE_SIZE=64
x = tf.placeholder(tf.float32, [None, IMAGE_SIZE, IMAGE_SIZE, 3],
➥ name='input_x')
y = tf.placeholder(tf.float32, [None, len(label_names)], name='output_y')   ⟵┐
keep_prob = tf.placeholder(tf.float32, name='keep_prob')
global_step = tf.Variable(0, name='global_step', trainable=False)

epochs = 1000                        Uses 0.5 dropout per the
keep_probability = 0.5      ⟵──┐    deep facial recognition paper
starter_learning_rate = 0.001
learning_rate =
➥ tf.compat.v1.train.exponential_decay(starter_learning_rate,global_step,
```

```
⇒ 100000, 0.96, staircase=True)
model_op = model(x, keep_probability)                           Names logits tensor so
model_ops = tf.identity(model_op, name='logits') ⇐──┐          that can be loaded from
beta = 0.01                                                     disk after training
weights = [conv1_1_filter, conv1_2_filter, conv2_1_filter, conv2_2_filter,
⇒ conv3_1_filter]
regularizer = tf.nn.l2_loss(weights[0])
for w in range(1, len(weights)):
    regularizer = regularizer + tf.nn.l2_loss(weights[w])                Implements L2
                                                                         regularization
cost =
⇒ tf.reduce_mean(tf.nn.softmax_cross_entropy_with_logits(logits=model_op,
⇒ labels=y))
cost = tf.reduce_mean(cost + beta * regularizer)                     ⇐────────
train_op = tf.train.AdamOptimizer(learning_rate=learning_rate, beta1=0.9,
⇒ beta2=0.999, epsilon=0.1).minimize(cost, global_step=global_step)
correct_pred = tf.equal(tf.argmax(model_op, 1), tf.argmax(y, 1))
accuracy = tf.reduce_mean(tf.cast(correct_pred, tf.float32), name='accuracy')
```

**Uses exponential weight
decay to set learning rate**

The model definition and hyperparameters for implementing facial recognition are similar to those used for CIFAR-10 object detection. Whether you are trying to build CNN architectures to learn facial features or object features, the same techniques apply. You create deeper networks by adding filters and layers, experimenting with rescaling and sizing the images. You can use dropout to enable more-resilient architectures and data augmentation to take static datasets and create new data. Augmentation is performed with TensorFlow's powerful `Dataset` API.

In section 15.5.6, you'll train the network and learn something new, watching the training for early stopping by performing validation accuracy checks on unseen data for training every few epochs. This technique will give you better understanding during network training and help you understand the influence of validation accuracy and loss.

15.5.6 *Training and evaluating VGG-Face Lite*

During training, one optimization you can do is using validation loss instead of training accuracy to measure how well your model is converging. The theory is simple. If you separate your train and validation data—perhaps using a 70/30 split, as you are for VGG-Face Lite—your validation loss should decrease while your train accuracy increases. Modeling train and validation loss are the common convex intersecting curves that you've probably seen when people try to explain deep learning. The top-right descending curve is the validation loss, and the bottom-left curve ascending in a polynomial or exponential path is the training accuracy.

You can measure your validation loss by testing it and printing it every so often during training epochs. The code in listing 15.20 prints the following:

- Validation loss and accuracy every five epochs
- Training accuracy every epoch (to give you a feel for how your model is performing)

Note that training the model will likely take up to 36 hours on a CPU laptop and a few hours on a machine with a GPU.

Another important point in the listing is the use of the TensorFlow `Dataset` API. You create an iterator with the `make_one_shot_iterator()` function, which uses the preset parameters for batch size and a prefetch buffer to consume a batch of data during each iteration. The other thing to notice is that you loop `while True` for your training; during each epoch, the iterator will consume the entire batch set and then throw a `tf.errors.OutOfRangeError` that you catch to break the `while True` loop and move on to the next epoch.

The validation batch size is the full size of the set during training. During each training epoch, you get a batch size of 128 images, which you configured in listing 15.17. The code will also handle validation every five epochs and save the model checkpoint during that time by getting a list of all the file paths and iterating over that list, removing the previous checkpoint files before saving the new model checkpoint.

Listing 15.20 Training VGG-Face Lite

Creates a saver for your model

```
with tf.Session(config=config) as sess:
    sess.run(tf.global_variables_initializer())
    saver = tf.train.Saver()                         Loops over 1,000 epochs
    for j in tqdm(range(0, epochs)):
        iter = train_ds.make_one_shot_iterator()
        val_iter = val_ds.make_one_shot_iterator()   Makes one_shot_iterators
        batch_num = 0                                 for the val and train datasets
        iter_op = iter.get_next()
        val_iter_op = val_iter.get_next()

        val_image_batch, val_label_batch = None, None

        try:
            val_image_batch, val_label_batch = sess.run(val_iter_op)
        except tf.errors.OutOfRangeError:
            pass                                       Training batch size 128
                                                       images per batch
        while True:
            try:
                image_batch, label_batch = sess.run(iter_op)
                onehot_labels = tf.one_hot(label_batch, len(label_names),
                    on_value=1., off_value=0., axis=-1).eval()
                onehot_val_labels = tf.one_hot(val_label_batch,
                    len(label_names), on_value=1., off_value=0.,
                    axis=-1).eval()
                _, accuracy_val, t_cost = sess.run([train_op, accuracy,
                    cost], feed_dict={x:image_batch, y: onehot_labels})
                batch_num += 1

            except tf.errors.OutOfRangeError:
                print("Step %d Accuracy %f Loss %f " % (j, accuracy_val,
                    t_cost))
```

Gets one-hot labels for train and validation

```
                          break
```

> Every five steps, measure validation loss and accuracy.

```
        if j != 0 and j % 5 == 0:          ◄────┘
            v_loss, v_accuracy = sess.run([cost, accuracy],
            ➥ feed_dict={x:val_image_batch, y:onehot_val_labels,
            ➥ keep_prob:1.0})
            print("Step %d Validation Accuracy %f Validation Loss %f" % (j,
            ➥ v_accuracy, v_loss))
            last_v_accuracy = v_accuracy

        if j != 0 and j % 10 == 0:
            print('Saving model progress.')
```

Save the new model checkpoint.

```
            fileList = glob.glob('vgg-face-'+str(epochs)+'epochs.ckpt*')

            for filePath in fileList:
                try:
                    os.remove(filePath)
                except:
                    print("Error while deleting file : ", filePath)

            saver.save(sess, './vgg-face-'+str(epochs)+'epochs.ckpt')
```

Next, I'll show you how to make predictions with the model and how to evaluate it.

15.5.7 *Evaluating and predicting with VGG-Face Lite*

You can take the trained output model and construct a `predict` function for input facial images (listing 15.21), reusing code from listing 15.8. You load the graph and its logits and then ensure that the input image is sized to `IMAGE_SIZE` (64 × 64 × 3) for three-channel RGB. The output class name and class number of the most confident of the four celebrities are emitted by the function, along with the softmax confidence for all predictions and their values.

Listing 15.21 Predicting with VGG-Face Lite

```
def predict(img_data, noise=False):
    class_num, class_name, confidence = None, None, 0.
    with tf.Session() as sess:
        loaded_graph = tf.Graph()
```

Loads the graph

> Reshapes the input image to 1 × 64 × 64 × 3

```
        image = img_data
        im_data = tf.reshape(image, [1, IMAGE_SIZE, IMAGE_SIZE, 3])   ◄───┘

    with tf.Session() as sess:
        im_data = im_data.eval()

    with tf.Session(graph=loaded_graph) as sess:
        loader = tf.train.import_meta_graph('vgg-face-
        ➥ '+str(epochs)+'epochs.ckpt' + '.meta')
        loader.restore(sess, 'vgg-face-'+str(epochs)+'epochs.ckpt')
```

```
                  loaded_x = loaded_graph.get_tensor_by_name('input_x:0')
                  loaded_logits = loaded_graph.get_tensor_by_name('logits:0')
                  logits_out = sess.run(tf.nn.softmax(loaded_logits),
Applies the         ➥ feed_dict={'keep_prob:0': 1.0, 'input_x:0': im_data})
logits to the     class_num = np.argmax(logits_out, axis=1)[0]
input image and   class_name = label_names[class_num]
gets the softmax   confidence = logits_out[0,class_num]          Returns the
                  all_preds = logits_out                         highest predicted
                                                                 class number,
                                                                 name, confidence,
          return (class_num, class_name, confidence, all_preds) ◁── and all the logits
```

As with CIFAR-10, you can run your `predict` function over the entire validation dataset to evaluate loss and accuracy during training. You can build a `get_test_accuracy` for VGG-Face that is also a duplicate of listing 15.8, except for the different model name used during loading. Using that function for VGG-Face shows a test accuracy of 97.37%, which is amazing across the four classes of celebrity faces.

You can use `predict` and `get_test_accuracy` to generate the ROC curve across all four celebrity classes and evaluate your model performance, using the code in listing 15.22. This listing is similar to listing 15.10 except that VGG-Face Lite has four output classes instead of ten. The output shown in figure 15.12 indicates a 98% micro-average ROC and exceptional performance for your first deep CNN for facial recognition.

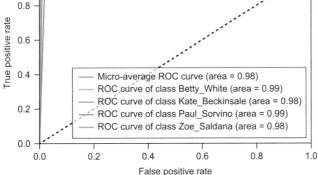

ROC curve for VGG Deep Face CNN 1000 iter TensorFlow (area = %0.98)

Figure 15.12   ROC curve for VGG-Face Lite

Listing 15.22   Generating the VGG-Face Lite ROC curve

```
outcome_test = label_binarize(test_label_batch)
predictions_test = label_binarize(predict_vals, classes=np.arange(0,
➥ len(test_names)))
n_classes = outcome_test.shape[1]

fpr = dict()          Computes ROC curve and
tpr = dict()          ROC area for each class
```

```
roc_auc = dict()
for i in range(n_classes):
    fpr[i], tpr[i], _ = roc_curve(outcome_test[:, i], predictions_test[:, i])
    roc_auc[i] = auc(fpr[i], tpr[i])

fpr["micro"], tpr["micro"], _ = roc_curve(outcome_test.ravel(),
➥ predictions_test.ravel())
roc_auc["micro"] = auc(fpr["micro"], tpr["micro"])

plt.figure()
plt.plot(fpr["micro"], tpr["micro"],
        label='micro-average ROC curve (area = {0:0.2f})'
              ''.format(roc_auc["micro"]))
for i in range(n_classes):
    plt.plot(fpr[i], tpr[i], label='ROC curve of class {0} (area = {1:0.2f})'
                              ''.format(test_names[i], roc_auc[i]))

plt.plot([0, 1], [0, 1], 'k--')
plt.xlim([0.0, 1.0])
plt.ylim([0.0, 1.05])
plt.xlabel('False Positive Rate')
plt.ylabel('True Positive Rate')
roc_mean = np.mean(np.fromiter(roc_auc.values(), dtype=float))
plt.title('ROC curve for VGG Deep Face CNN '+str(epochs)+' iter Tensorflow
➥ (area = %{0:0.2f})'.format(roc_mean))
plt.legend(loc="lower right")
plt.show()
```

Annotations:
- `fpr["micro"], tpr["micro"], _ = roc_curve(...)` — **Computes micro-average ROC curve and ROC area**
- `plt.figure()` — **Plots ROC curve**

One final function you can borrow from earlier in the chapter is the `evaluate_model()` function. For VGG-Face, the function is slightly different because you won't use data from the internet; you can use your validation dataset. But this function is valuable in that you can see how confident your model is in each class prediction. The output is generated by the function shown in listing 15.23.

Listing 15.23   Evaluating VGG-Face Lite with validation images

```
def evaluate_model(im_data, test_labels, predicted, div=False):
    n_predictions = len(predicted)
    fig, axes = plt.subplots(nrows=n_predictions, ncols=2, figsize=(24,24))
    fig.tight_layout()
    fig.suptitle('Softmax Predictions for '+str(len(predicted))+' VGG Deep
    ➥ Face CNN '+str(epochs)+' iter Test Data', fontsize=20, y=1.1)

    n_predictions = 4          ◁─── Number of output classes
    margin = 0.05
    ind = np.arange(n_predictions)
    width = (1. - 2. * margin) / n_predictions

    for i in range(0, len(im_data)):    ◁─┐  Iterates over the predictions and
        pred_names = label_names           │  shows the image on the left and the
        pred_values = predicted[i]         │  softmax predictions on the right
        correct_name = pred_names[test_labels[i]]
```

```
        if div:
            axies[i][0].imshow(im_data[i] / 255.)
        else:
            image = (1/(2*2.25)) * im_data[i] + 0.5
            axies[i][0].imshow(image)
        axies[i][0].set_title(correct_name)
        axies[i][0].set_axis_off()

        axies[i][1].barh(ind + margin, pred_values, width)
        axies[i][1].set_yticks(ind + margin)
        axies[i][1].set_yticklabels(pred_names)
        axies[i][1].set_xticks([0, 0.5, 1.0])

for i in range(1, 5):
    evaluate_model(test_data[(i-1)*10:i*10], test_labels[(i-1)*10:i*10],
    ➥ out_logits[(i-1)*10:i*10])
```

Phew! This chapter has been a lot of work. Now that you've applied CNNs to object recognition, facial recognition, and facial detection, I'm sure that you can think of other similar problems to try them on. You don't need faces or objects; there are plenty of other things to train and predict. You've got all the tools necessary!

Summary

- CNNs can be used for general image-matching problems and building facial identification systems, but unless you apply optimizations in the real world, they will not perform well.
- Training a CNN without applying optimizations such as dropout, deeper architectures, and image augmentation leads to overfitting, and models won't perform well on unseen data.
- TensorFlow provides functions for augmenting image data and for preventing memorization in CNN architectures using the dropout technique, as well as APIs for scanning datasets and preparing them for training to make creating real-world CNNs simple.

16
Recurrent neural networks

This chapter covers

- Understanding the components of a recurrent neural network
- Designing a predictive model of time-series data
- Using the time-series predictor on real-world data

Back in school, I remember my sigh of relief when one of my midterm exams consisted of only true-or-false questions. I can't be the only one who assumed that half the answers would be true and the other half would be false.

I figured out answers to most of the questions and left the rest to guessing. But that guessing was based on something clever, a strategy that you might have employed as well. After counting my number of true answers, I realized that a disproportionate number of false answers were lacking. So a majority of my guesses were false to balance the distribution.

It worked. I sure felt sly in the moment. What is this feeling of craftiness that makes us feel so confident in our decisions, and how can we give a neural network the same power?

One answer is to use context to answer questions. Contextual cues are important signals that can improve the performance of machine-learning algorithms. Suppose that you want to examine an English sentence and tag the part of speech of each word (a problem that may be more familiar to you after chapter 10).

The naïve approach is to classify each word individually as a noun, an adjective, and so on without acknowledging the neighboring words. Consider trying that technique on the words in *this* sentence. The word *trying* is used as a verb, but depending on the context, you can also use it as an adjective, making parts-of-speech tagging a *trying* problem.

A better approach considers the context. To bestow contextual cues on neural networks, you'll study an architecture called a *recurrent neural network* (RNN). Instead of natural language data, you'll be dealing with continuous time-series data, such as stock market prices. By the end of the chapter, you'll be able to model the patterns in time-series data to predict future values.

16.1 Introduction to RNNs

To understand RNNs, look at the simple architecture in figure 16.1. This architecture takes as input a vector $X(t)$ and generates as output a vector $Y(t)$ at some time (t). The circle in the middle represents the hidden layer of the network.

Figure 16.1 A neural network with the input and output layers labeled $X(t)$ and $Y(t)$, respectively

With enough input/output examples, you can learn the parameters of the network in TensorFlow. Let's refer to the input weights as a matrix W_{in} and the output weights as a matrix W_{out}. Assume that there's one hidden layer, referred to as a vector $Z(t)$.

As shown in figure 16.2, the first half of the neural network is characterized by the function $Z(t) = X(t) \times W_{in}$, and the second half of the neural network takes the form $Y(t) = Z(t) \times W_{out}$. Equivalently, if you prefer, the whole neural network is the function $Y(t) = (X(t) \times W_{in}) \times W_{out}$.

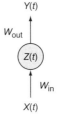

Figure 16.2 The hidden layer of a neural network can be thought of as a hidden representation of the data, which is encoded by the input weights and decoded by the output weights.

After spending nights fine-tuning the network, you probably want to start using your learned model in a real-world scenario. Typically, that process implies calling the model multiple times, as depicted in figure 16.3.

At each time t, when calling the learned model, this architecture doesn't take into account knowledge about the previous runs. This process is like predicting stock-market trends by looking only at data from the current day. A better idea is to

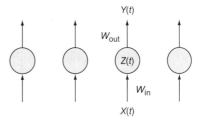

Figure 16.3 Often, you end up running the same neural network multiple times without using knowledge about the hidden states of the previous runs.

exploit overarching patterns from a week's or
month's worth of data.

A RNN is different from a traditional neural network because it introduces a transition weight W to
transfer information over time. Figure 16.4 shows
the three weight matrices that must be learned in
an RNN. The introduction of the transition weight
means that the next state is dependent on the previous model as well as the previous state, so your
model has a "memory" of what it did.

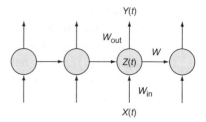

Figure 16.4   RNN architecture can use
the previous states of the network to its
advantage.

Diagrams are nice, but you're here to get your hands dirty. Let's get right to it! Section 16.2 shows how to use TensorFlow's built-in RNN models. Then you'll use an
RNN on real-world time-series data to predict the future.

16.2   *Implementing a recurrent neural network*

As you implement the RNN, you'll use TensorFlow to do much of the heavy lifting.
You won't need to build a network manually, as shown in figure 16.4, because the
TensorFlow library already supports some robust RNN models.

> **NOTE**   For TensorFlow library information on RNNs, see https://www.svds
> .com/tensorflow-rnn-tutorial.

One type of RNN model is *long short-term memory* (LSTM)—a fun name that means
exactly what it sounds like. Short-term patterns aren't forgotten in the long term.

The precise implementation details of LSTM are beyond the scope of this book.
Trust me, a thorough inspection of the LSTM model would distract from the chapter
because there's no definite standard yet. TensorFlow comes to the rescue by taking
care of how the model is defined so you can use it out of the box. And as TensorFlow
is updated, you'll be able to take advantage of improvements in the LSTM model without modifying your code.

> **TIP**   To see how to implement LSTM from scratch, I suggest the web page
> https://apaszke.github.io/lstm-explained.html. The paper that describes the
> implementation of regularization used in this chapter's listings is available at
> https://arxiv.org/abs/1409.2329. Finally, this tutorial for RNNs and LSTMs
> provides some real notebooks and code to try: https://www.svds.com/tensor-
> flow-rnn-tutorial.

Begin by writing your code in a new file called simple_regression.py. Then import the
relevant libraries, as shown in listing 16.1.

Listing 16.1   Importing relevant libraries

```
import numpy as np
import tensorflow as tf
from tensorflow.contrib import rnn
```

Next, define a class called `SeriesPredictor`. The constructor, shown in listing 16.2, will set up model hyperparameters, weights, and the `cost` function.

Listing 16.2 Defining a class and its constructor

```
class SeriesPredictor:
    def __init__(self, input_dim, seq_size, hidden_dim=10):

        self.input_dim = input_dim
        self.seq_size = seq_size                    Hyperparameters
        self.hidden_dim = hidden_dim

        self.W_out = tf.Variable(tf.random_normal([hidden_dim, 1]),
            name='W_out')
        self.b_out = tf.Variable(tf.random_normal([1]), name='b_out')
        self.x = tf.placeholder(tf.float32, [None, seq_size, input_dim])
        self.y = tf.placeholder(tf.float32, [None, seq_size])

        self.cost = tf.reduce_mean(tf.square(self.model() - self.y))
        self.train_op = tf.train.AdamOptimizer().minimize(self.cost)

        self.saver = tf.train.Saver()        ⟵──── Auxiliary ops
```

Weight variables and input placeholders

Cost optimizer

Next, use TensorFlow's built-in RNN model `BasicLSTMCell`. The hidden dimension of the cell passed into the `BasicLSTMCell` object is the dimension of the hidden state that gets passed through time. You can run this cell with data by using the `rnn.dynamic_rnn` function to retrieve the output results. Listing 16.3 details how to use TensorFlow to implement a predictive model with LSTM.

Listing 16.3 Defining the RNN model

```
def model(self):                                        Runs the cell
    """                                                 on the input
    :param x: inputs of size [T, batch_size, input_size]    to obtain
    :param W: matrix of fully-connected output layer weights   tensors for
    :param b: vector of fully-connected output layer biases    outputs and
    """                                                      states
    cell = rnn.BasicLSTMCell(self.hidden_dim)
    outputs, states = tf.nn.dynamic_rnn(cell, self.x, dtype=tf.float32) ⟵──┘
    num_examples = tf.shape(self.x)[0]
    W_repeated = tf.tile(tf.expand_dims(self.W_out, 0),
        [num_examples, 1, 1])
    out = tf.matmul(outputs, W_repeated) + self.b_out
    out = tf.squeeze(out)
    return out
```

Creates an LSTM cell

Computes the output layer as a fully connected linear function

With a model and `cost` function defined, you can implement the training function, which will learn the LSTM weights, given example input/output pairs. As listing 16.4 shows, you open a session and repeatedly run the optimizer on the training data.

NOTE   You can use cross-validation to figure out how many iterations you need to train the model. In this case, you assume a fixed number of epochs. Some good insights and answers are available at Q&A sites such as ResearchGate (http://mng.bz/lB92).

After training, save the model to a file so you can load it later.

Listing 16.4   Training the model on a dataset

```
def train(self, train_x, train_y):
    with tf.Session() as sess:
        tf.get_variable_scope().reuse_variables()
        sess.run(tf.global_variables_initializer())
        for i in range(1000):
            _, mse = sess.run([self.train_op, self.cost],
                feed_dict={self.x: train_x, self.y: train_y})
            if i % 100 == 0:
                print(i, mse)
        save_path = self.saver.save(sess, 'model.ckpt')
        print('Model saved to {}'.format(save_path))
```

Runs the train op 1,000 times — (annotation pointing to `_, mse = sess.run([self.train_op, self.cost]` / `feed_dict={self.x: train_x, self.y: train_y})`)

Let's say that all went well, and your model has learned parameters. Next, you'd like to evaluate the predictive model on other data. Listing 16.5 loads the saved model and runs the model in a session by feeding in test data. If a learned model doesn't perform well on testing data, you can try tweaking the number of hidden dimensions of the LSTM cell.

Listing 16.5   Testing the learned model

```
def test(self, test_x):
    with tf.Session() as sess:
        tf.get_variable_scope().reuse_variables()
        self.saver.restore(sess, './model.ckpt')
        output = sess.run(self.model(), feed_dict={self.x: test_x})
        print(output)
```

It's done! But to convince yourself that it works, make up some data to try to train the predictive model. In listing 16.6, you'll create input sequences (train_x) and corresponding output sequences (train_y).

Listing 16.6   Training and testing on dummy data

```
if __name__ == '__main__':
    predictor = SeriesPredictor(input_dim=1, seq_size=4, hidden_dim=10)
    train_x = [[[1], [2], [5], [6]],
               [[5], [7], [7], [8]],
               [[3], [4], [5], [7]]]
    train_y = [[1, 3, 7, 11],
               [5, 12, 14, 15],
               [3, 7, 9, 12]]
```

```
predictor.train(train_x, train_y)
test_x = [[[1], [2], [3], [4]],     ⊲──┐ Predicted result should be 1, 3, 5, 7.
          [[4], [5], [6], [7]]]     ⊲──┐
predictor.test(test_x)                 │ Predicted result should be 4, 9, 11, 13.
```

You can treat this predictive model as a black box and train it with real-world time-series data for prediction. In section 16.3, you'll get data to work with.

16.3 *Using a predictive model for time-series data*

Time-series data is abundantly available online. For this example, you'll use data about international airline passengers for a specific period. You can obtain this data from http://mng.bz/ggOV. Clicking that link takes you to a nice plot of the time-series data, shown in figure 16.5.

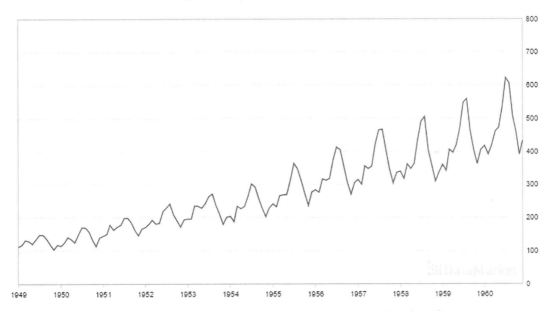

Figure 16.5 Raw data showing the number of international airline passengers throughout the years

You can download the data by clicking the Data tab and then selecting CSV. You'll have to edit the CSV file manually to remove the header line and the additional footer line.

In a file called data_loader.py, add the code in listing 16.7.

Listing 16.7 Loading data

```
import csv
import numpy as np
import matplotlib.pyplot as plt

def load_series(filename, series_idx=1):
```

```
try:
    with open(filename) as csvfile:
        csvreader = csv.reader(csvfile)

        data = [float(row[series_idx]) for row in csvreader
                                       if len(row) > 0]
        normalized_data = (data - np.mean(data)) / np.std(data)
        return normalized_data
except IOError:
    return None

def split_data(data, percent_train=0.80):
    num_rows = len(data) * percent_train
    return data[:num_rows], data[num_rows:]
```

Loops through the lines of the file and converts to a floating-point number

Calculates training data samples

Preprocesses the data by mean-centering and dividing by standard deviation

Splits the dataset into training and testing

Here, you define two functions: `load_series` and `split_data`. The first function loads the time-series file on disk and normalizes it; the other function divides the dataset into two components for training and testing.

Because you'll be evaluating the model multiple times to predict future values, let's modify the `test` function from `SeriesPredictor` to take a session as an argument instead of initializing the session on every call. See listing 16.8 for this tweak.

Listing 16.8 Modifying the `test` function to pass in the session

```
def test(self, sess, test_x):
    tf.get_variable_scope().reuse_variables()
    self.saver.restore(sess, './model.ckpt')
    output = sess.run(self.model(), feed_dict={self.x: test_x})
    return output
```

Now you can train the predictor by loading the data in the acceptable format. Listing 16.9 shows how to train the network and then use the trained model to predict future values. You'll generate the training data (`train_x` and `train_y`) to look like the data shown earlier in listing 16.6.

Listing 16.9 Generate training data

```
if __name__ == '__main__':
    seq_size = 5
    predictor = SeriesPredictor(
        input_dim=1,
        seq_size=seq_size,
        hidden_dim=100)

    data = data_loader.load_series('international-airline-passengers.csv')
    train_data, actual_vals = data_loader.split_data(data)

    train_x, train_y = [], []
    for i in range(len(train_data) - seq_size - 1):
        train_x.append(np.expand_dims(train_data[i:i+seq_size],
        ➥ axis=1).tolist())
```

The dimension of each element of the sequence is a scalar (1D).

Length of each sequence

Size of the RNN hidden dimension

Loads the data

Slides a window through the time-series data to construct the training dataset

```
                train_y.append(train_data[i+1:i+seq_size+1])

        test_x, test_y = [], []
        for i in range(len(actual_vals) - seq_size - 1):
            test_x.append(np.expand_dims(actual_vals[i:i+seq_size],
               axis=1).tolist())
            test_y.append(actual_vals[i+1:i+seq_size+1])

        predictor.train(train_x, train_y, test_x, test_y)

    with tf.Session() as sess:
        predicted_vals = predictor.test(sess, test_x)[:,0]
        print('predicted_vals', np.shape(predicted_vals))
        plot_results(train_data, predicted_vals, actual_vals,
        'predictions.png')

        prev_seq = train_x[-1]
        predicted_vals = []
        for i in range(20):
            next_seq = predictor.test(sess, [prev_seq])
            predicted_vals.append(next_seq[-1])
            prev_seq = np.vstack((prev_seq[1:], next_seq[-1]))
        plot_results(train_data, predicted_vals, actual_vals,
        'hallucinations.png')
```

Uses the same window-sliding strategy to construct the test dataset

Trains a model on the training dataset

Visualizes the model's performance

The predictor generates two graphs. The first graph is prediction results of the model, given ground-truth values (figure 16.6).

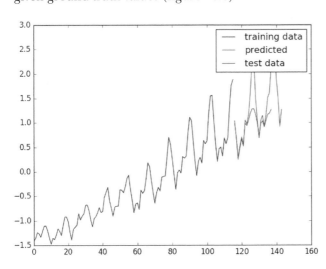

Figure 16.6 The predictions match trends fairly well when tested against ground-truth data.

The other graph shows the prediction results when only the training data is given (blue line)—nothing else (figure 16.7). This procedure has less information available, but it still does a good job of matching data trends.

You can use time-series predictors to reproduce realistic fluctuations in data. Imagine predicting market boom-and-bust cycles based on the tools you've learned so far.

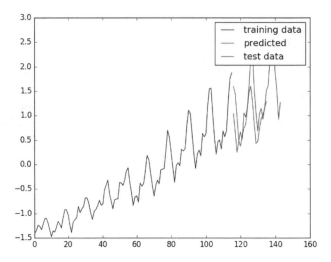

Figure 16.7   If the algorithm uses previously predicted results to make further predictions, the general trend matches well, but not specific bumps.

What are you waiting for? Grab some market data, and learn your own predictive model!

16.4 *Applying RNNs*

RNNs are meant to be used with sequential data. Because audio signals are a dimension lower than video (linear signal versus 2D pixel array), it's a lot easier to get started with audio time-series data. Consider how much speech recognition has improved over the years; it's becoming a tractable problem.

Like the audio histogram analysis on clustering audio data that you conducted in chapter 7, most speech recognition preprocessing involves representing the sound in a chromagram of sorts. A common technique is to use *mel-frequency cepstral coefficients* (MFCCs). A good introduction is outlined in this blog post: http://mng.bz/411F.

Next, you'll need a dataset to train your model. A few popular ones include the following:

- LibriSpeech (www.openslr.org/12)
- TED-LIUM (www.openslr.org/7)
- VoxForge (www.voxforge.org)

An in-depth walkthrough of a simple speech-recognition implementation in Tensor-Flow that uses these datasets is available at https://svds.com/tensorflow-rnn-tutorial.

Summary

- A recurrent neural network (RNN) uses information from the past. That way, it can make predictions by using data with high temporal dependencies.
- TensorFlow comes with RNN models out of the box.
- Time-series prediction is a useful application for RNNs because of temporal dependencies in the data.

17

LSTMs and automatic speech recognition

This chapter covers

- Preparing a dataset for automatic speech recognition using the LibriSpeech corpus
- Training a long short-term memory (LSTM) RNN for converting speech to text
- Evaluating the LSTM performance during and after training

Speaking and talking to your electronic devices is commonplace nowadays. Years ago, on an early version of my smartphone, I clicked the microphone button and used its dictation function to try to speak an email into existence. The email that my boss received at work had a whole bunch of typos and phonetic errors, though, and he wondered whether I was mixing a little too much after-work activity with my official duties!

The world has evolved, and so has the accuracy of neural networks in performing *automatic speech recognition* (ASR), which is the process of transforming spoken audio into written text. Whether you are using your phone's intelligent digital assistant to ask it to schedule a meeting for you, dictating that trusty email, or asking your smart device at home to order something, play background music, or even start your car, the tasks are powered by ASR functionality.

How did ASR become part of everyday life? Previous ASR systems relied on brittle statistical models that depended on language-specific grammars, whereas today's ASR systems are built on top of robust recurrent neural networks (RNNs) and in particular on long short-term memory (LSTM) networks, which are a specific type of RNN. Using LSTMs, you can teach a computer to hear audio in segments and to convert those segments to language characters over time. Like convolutional neural networks (CNNs) and other biologically inspired neural networks discussed in this book, LSTMs for speech recognition learn the way humans learn. Each small audio segment corresponds to a character of language, and you use as many cells as there are characters in the speech. You are trying teach the network to understand language the way a human would. As the network learns through each invocation, the network weights are updated and fed forward and backward to the LSTM cells, which learn each sound and the letters to which it corresponds. The combination of letters mapped to sound becomes language.

These approaches were made famous by the Deep Speech architecture from Baidu, used to outperform the state-of-the-art speech recognition system in 2015 and later implemented in open source by the Mozilla Foundation, using your and my favorite toolkit, TensorFlow. The original paper is at https://arxiv.org/abs/1412.5567. I'll show you how to collect and prepare the training data for the deep speech automated speech-to-text model, how to train it with TensorFlow, and how to use it to evaluate real-world sound data.

> **Hey, TensorFlow!**
> Ever wonder how your phone works when you say, "Hey, Digital Assistant"? At first, the assistant may not always get the words right, but Silicon Valley phone and computer makers say it will get better over time. Well, they are right. That's why a digital assistant asks for feedback about whether it interpreted words right. Frameworks like TensorFlow allow you to train your own model and also provide pretrained LSTM models that refine per-character and per-word ASR outputs with user feedback from millions of people around the world. In fact, recognition *does* get better over time.

One common source of training for ASR networks is audiobooks. Audiobooks are useful in that they typically have both a parallel corpus of sound and transcripts mapping to the spoken words. The LibriSpeech corpus is part of the Open Speech and Language Resources (OpenSLR) project and can be used to train the deep-speech model. As you know by now, however, you'll have to take care of some data cleaning to get the information ready for training.

17.1   Preparing the LibriSpeech corpus

Audiobooks are useful inventions that allow us to listen to our favorite books while driving and doing other activities. They typically are large sets of sounds—possibly hundreds of hours' worth—broken into smaller snippets and almost always include corresponding transcriptions in case you want to read the text you are hearing.

One set of open-source audiobooks is available from the Open Speech and Language Resources (OpenSLR) webpage and the LibriSpeech corpus. LibriSpeech is a set of short clips from audiobooks and transcripts to go with those clips. LibriSpeech includes more than 1,000 hours of recorded 16KHz English-speech audio, including metadata; original MP3 files; and a separated and an aligned training set of 100, 360, and 500 hours of speech. The dataset includes transcriptions, along with a dev dataset for per-epoch validation and a test set for post-training testing.

Unfortunately, the dataset isn't usable in the deep-speech model because the model expects the Windows Audio Video (.wav) interleaved file audio format instead of the Free Lossless Audio Codec (.flac) file format that LibriSpeech comes in. As usual, your first step for machine learning involves—you guessed it—data preparation and cleaning.

17.1.1 Downloading, cleaning, and preparing LibriSpeech OpenSLR data

First, you need to download one of the training corpora: the 100, 360, or 500 hours of training. Depending on how much memory you have, you can choose any of the three, but my recommendation is to grab the 100 hours because that's plenty to train a decent deep-speech model. There is only one dev (validation) and test set, so you don't need to choose different hours for those files.

The overall process of preparing the downloaded LibriSpeech data is fairly straightforward:

1. Download the tarballs for train-100-clean, dev-clean, and test-from http://www.openslr.org/12.
2. Unpack the tarballs into LibriSpeech/train-clean-100, LibriSpeech/dev-clean, and LibriSpeech/test-clean folders.
3. Convert the .flac audio files to .wav audio files for training, validation, and test.
4. Take the aggregated transcript files, each of which contains one line for each audio file in the chapter. Each line contains the extracted words corresponding to the referenced short sound clip. Reformat these aggregate transcripts as one .txt transcript file per .wav audio file.
5. Collect the subfolders of .wav and .txt audio/transcript tuples into one flat folder structure, and clean up the aggregated transcript and .flac files by removing them.

The process is shown from left to right in figure 17.1.

The good news is that you can build this data cleaning and preparation pipeline with some simple Python utility code. You'll start in listing 17.1 with the file downloads, using the `urllib` and `tarfile` libraries, which allow you to download remote URLs and untar the archive files.

> **WARNING** Downloading this data can take quite a while, because the training data alone is ~7 GB. Be prepared to wait for hours, depending on your bandwidth.

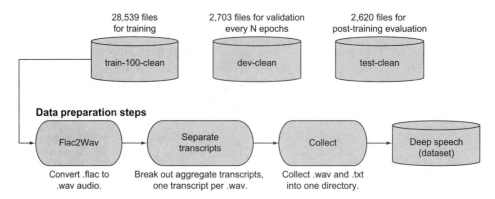

Figure 17.1   The data cleaning and preparation process that transforms the LibriSpeech OpenSLR data for the deep-speech model

---

Listing 17.1   Downloading and untarring the train, dev, and test LibriSpeech data

```
import urllib
import tarfile

def download_and_extract_tar(url):
    print("Downloading and extracting %s " % (url))
    tar_stream = urllib.request.urlopen(url)
    tar_file = tarfile.open(fileobj=tar_stream, mode="r|gz")
    tar_file.extractall()

train_url = "http://www.openslr.org/resources/12/train-clean-100.tar.gz"
dev_url = "http://www.openslr.org/resources/12/dev-clean.tar.gz"
test_url = "http://www.openslr.org/resources/12/test-clean.tar.gz"

download_and_extract_tar(train_url)
download_and_extract_tar(dev_url)
download_and_extract_tar(test_url)
```

Imports the urllib downloading library and tarfile library for extracting the archives

Creates a function to download a tarfile from a URL and extract it locally

OpenSLR 100 hours train, dev (validation), and test sets

Downloads the data and extracts the stream to its local folders

---

For the next step in the data preparation pipeline, you'll need to convert the .flac audio files to .wav files. Luckily, an easy-to-use Python library called `pydub` can perform this task, as well as other conversions and manipulations of multimedia files. Though `pydub` is robust, you are using only a subset of its features here. Play around with it to discover more.

17.1.2   Converting the audio

When the tar files are extracted, they appear locally in your LibriSpeech/<data> directory where <data> is one of train-clean-100, dev-clean, and test-clean. Below those folders are more subfolders, which correspond to different chapter numbers and even more subfolders corresponding to sections of chapters. So your code will need to traverse these subfolders and for each .flac file use pydub to create a .wav file. You'll handle the process as shown in listing 17.2. Go get a cup of coffee if you are running this code on your laptop; the conversion can take up to an hour and a half.

Listing 17.2   Converting .flac files to .wav files and traversing datasets

```
import pydub
import os
import tqdm
import glob

def flac2wav(filepath):
    base_file_path = os.path.dirname(filepath)
    filename = os.path.basename(filepath)
    filename_no_ext = os.path.splitext(filename)[0]
    audio = AudioSegment.from_file(filepath, "flac")
    wav_file_path = base_file_path + '/' + filename_no_ext +'.wav'
    audio.export(wav_file_path, format="wav")

def convert_flac_to_wav(train_path, dev_path, test_path):
    train_flac = [file for file in glob.glob(train_path + "/*/*/*.flac")]
    dev_flac = [file for file in glob.glob(dev_path + "/*/*/*.flac")]
    test_flac = [file for file in glob.glob(test_path + "/*/*/*.flac")]

    print("Converting %d train %d dev and %d test flac files into wav files"
          % (len(train_flac), len(dev_flac), len(test_flac)))

    print("Processing train")
    for f in tqdm(train_flac):
        flac2wav(f)

    print("Processing dev")
    for f in tqdm(dev_flac):
        flac2wav(f)

    print("Processing test")
    for f in tqdm(test_flac):
        flac2wav(f)
```

Given a file path such as LibriSpeech/
train-clean-100/307/127535/307-127535-
000.flac, get its directory name
(base_file_path) and filename.

Strips the extension and
gets the file base name,
such as 307-127535-000

**Reads
the FLAC
file using
Pydub**

Derives the .wav filename,
which is basename + .wav

Uses Pydub to save
the new .wav file

Uses the glob library to get
a list of all .flac files in train,
dev (validation), and test

Processes the train,
dev and test .flac
files to .wav

With the audio files in the right format, you have to handle the other parts of Libri-Speech: the transcripts from step 4 mentioned previously with one text file transcript per audio clip. As they come with the dataset, the transcripts are aggregated into subchapter collections, one transcript per subchapter, with each line in the transcript subchapter file corresponding to one audio file in that subdirectory. For deep speech, you need one text file transcript per audio file. Next, you'll generate per-audio transcripts, one per file.

17.1.3   Generating per-audio transcripts

To create per-audio transcripts, you read each subchapter directory transcript aggregation file. Break each line in that file into a separate text transcript file, one per audio file, in the subchapter folder. The simple Python in listing 17.3 handles this task for you. Note that running this code is fairly quick compared with the .flac file conversion.

Listing 17.3   Breaking the subchapter aggregations into single .wav file transcripts

Gets the subchapter prefix filename

```
def create_per_file_transcripts(file):
    file_toks = file.split('.')
    base_file_path = os.path.dirname(file)
```

For each line in the subchapter aggregation transcript, splits on whitespace, and uses the first token as the audio filename for that line's transcript

```
with open(file, 'r') as fd:
    lines = fd.readlines()
    for line in lines:
        toks = line.split(' ')
        wav_file_name = base_file_path + '/' + toks[0] + '.txt'

        with open(wav_file_name, 'w') as of:
            trans = " ".join([t.lower() for t in toks[1:]])
            of.write(trans)
            of.write('\n')
```

The rest of the tokens besides the first are the transcript words for that audio file.

```
def gen_transcripts(train_path, dev_path, test_path):
    train_transcripts = [file for file in glob.glob(train_path +
⟱  "/*/*/*.txt")]
    dev_transcripts = [file for file in glob.glob(dev_path + "/*/*/*.txt")]
    test_transcripts = [file for file in glob.glob(test_path + "/*/*/*.txt")]

    print("Converting %d train %d dev and %d test aggregate transcripts into
⟱  individual transcripts"
            % (len(train_transcripts), len(dev_transcripts),
⟱  len(test_transcripts)))
```

Gets the transcript files for all sub chapters in train, dev, and test

```
    print("Processing train")
    for f in tqdm(train_transcripts):
        create_per_file_transcripts(f)
```

Processes train, dev, and test into individual transcripts

```
    print("Processing dev")
    for f in tqdm(dev_transcripts):
        create_per_file_transcripts(f)

    print("Processing test")
    for f in tqdm(test_transcripts):
        create_per_file_transcripts(f)
```

17.1.4 Aggregating audio and transcripts

The final step in the data processing—step 5, if you are keeping score—is collecting all the audio .wav files and their associated transcripts into an aggregated top-level directory and cleaning up by removing the .flac files and the aggregated transcripts. A simple move file function and a delete function call in Python can take care of this task for you, as shown in listing 17.4. You can use the following simple paths to represent the dataset top-level paths for aggregation:

```
speech_data_path = "LibriSpeech"
train_path = speech_data_path + "/train-clean-100"
dev_path = speech_data_path + "/dev-clean"
test_path = speech_data_path + "/test-clean"

all_train_path = train_path + "-all"
all_dev_path = dev_path + "-all"
all_test_path = test_path + "-all"
```

The code in listing 17.4 ought to run fairly quickly because it's cleanup. It's important to note that you have to run the cleanup steps because you do not want to double-count transcripts or audio files.

Listing 17.4   Aggregating audio and transcripts, and cleaning up

```
def move_files(from_path, to_path):
    if not os.path.exists(to_path):
        print("Creating dir %s" % (to_path))
        os.makedirs(to_path)
    for root, _, files in os.walk(from_path):
        for file in files:
            path_to_file = os.path.join(root, file)
            base_file_path = os.path.dirname(file)
            to_path_file = to_path + '/' + file
            print("Moving file from %s to %s " % (path_to_file,
            to_path_file))
            shutil.move(path_to_file, to_path_file)

def remove_files_with_ext(directory, ext):
    for root, _, files in os.walk(directory):
        for file in files:
            if file.endswith(ext):
                path_to_file = os.path.join(root, file)
                print("Removing file %s " % (path_to_file))
                os.remove(path_to_file)

remove_files_with_ext(train_path, "flac")
remove_files_with_ext(dev_path, "flac")
remove_files_with_ext(test_path, "flac")

move_files(train_path, all_train_path)
move_files(dev_path, all_dev_path)
move_files(test_path, all_test_path)

remove_files_with_ext(all_train_path, "trans.txt")
remove_files_with_ext(all_dev_path, "trans.txt")
remove_files_with_ext(all_test_path, "trans.txt")
```

> If the target path doesn't exist, create it.

> Walks the top-level train, dev, and test directories, and for each audio and transcript file in them (assuming that you delete the .flac files first), moves them to the target path

> Crawls through a directory and removes all files with the provided extension

> Removes the .flac files

> Moves the audio .wav and associated transcripts to top-level directories

> Removes the aggregated transcripts

Armed with the prepared LibriSpeech dataset aggregations in train-clean-100-all, dev-clean-all, and test-clean-all, you're ready to start training with deep speech and TensorFlow.

17.2   Using the deep-speech model

Deep Speech is a neural network built in 2014 and 2015 by Baidu in the course of trying to make search better. Baidu is a company in China that offers internet services and products; it collects and crawls the web and uses artificial intelligence to enhance users' experience of finding what they are looking for. So it's safe to say that Baidu has a ton of data, including speech data. The need to allow for dictation to aid search on mobile devices was increasing in 2015 and is expected as a default capability today.

Baidu's paper "Deep Speech: Scaling Up End-to-End Speech Recognition" (available at https://arxiv.org/abs/1412.5567) describes a multilayered neural network that combines convolutional layers as feature extractors from input audio spectrograms that have been segmented into character level utterances. Each input audio file is segmented into an utterance corresponding to a letter in the alphabet. After feature extraction, the output features are provided to a bidirectional LSTM network that feeds forward its output weights to a backward layer, which in turn feeds its outputs as it learns. The outputs of the bidirectional backward layer are fed into an additional feature extractor and used to predict a particular character in the alphabet to which the utterance corresponds. The overall architecture is shown in figure 17.2.

1. Each audio file is broken into segments by performing an MFCC that generates 26 amplitudes to correspond to the sound at that time step. Time step n_context in the past is taken, along with n in the future to represent the current letter of text.

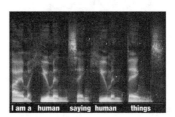

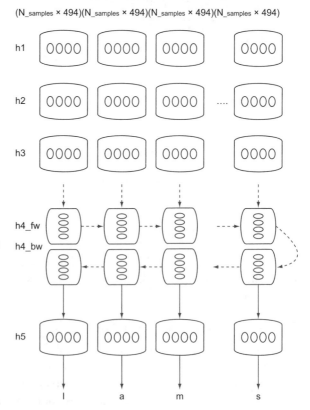

2. CNN layers are used h1-h3 to featurize the incoming N × 494 audio features, and the output of them is fed into a bidirectional LSTM (h4_fw and h4_bw).

3. The forward layer of the LSTM gets features from h3 and feeds them forward to the last cell in the sample; the output is fed into the backward layer, and then each output from h4_bw is fed into h5 for character output.

Figure 17.2   The deep-speech model. Audio is fed in and segmented into samples corresponding to character-level utterances. Those utterances are guessed by a bidirectional LSTM network (MFCC = Mel frequency cepstral coefficient).

One of the most famous implementations of the deep-speech architecture was undertaken by the Mozilla Foundation and implemented with TensorFlow; it is available at https://github.com/mozilla/DeepSpeech. Rather than reimplement all the bells and whistles of this implementation, which would require much more space and cover more than a few chapters of this book, I am going to highlight the important bits to walk you through setting up and running a simplified version of the code. Note that training a deep-speech model from scratch will take quite a few days, even with a GPU.

17.2.1 Preparing the input audio data for deep speech

In chapter 7, I showed you how to use the BregmanToolkit to convert audio files from the frequency domain to the time domain. That library isn't the only one that can perform that process, however. A similar process generates the Mel frequency cepstral coefficient (MFCC) for an audio file. This process runs a fast Fourier transformation (FFT) on the audio file and outputs the file as samples corresponding to the requested number of cepstral (or frequency bins) on which the input sound registers. The amplitude of those bins, as with the BregmanToolkit, is unique for each audio file and can be used to generate features for use in machine learning.

The BregmanToolkit generates an approximation of these bins, but now I'm going to show you a different method that uses TensorFlow native code, along with code that uses SciPy. TensorFlow ships with some handy functionality for dealing with audio files called audio_ops. The library includes code to read .wav files, to decode them into spectrograms (similar to chromagrams; chapter 7), and then run the MFCC transformation on them into the time domain. Listing 17.5 has some simple code that generates MFCC features, using TensorFlow's audio_ops from a random .wav file in the LibriSpeech corpus. Running the code generate a feature-vector sized (1, 2545, 26) or 2,545 samples of 26 cepstral amplitudes for each sample.

Listing 17.5   Generating MFCC features from wav files with TensorFlow

```
numcep=26                          ⟵——  The number of cepstral bins to use
with tf.Session() as sess:               (26, per the Deep Speech paper)
    filename =  'LibriSpeech/train-clean-100-all/3486-166424-0004.wav'
    raw_audio = tf.io.read_file(filename)        Reads the file and
    audio, fs = decode_wav(raw_audio)            interprets the .wav sound
    spectrogram = audio_ops.audio_spectrogram(
            audio, window_size=1024,stride=64)
    orig_inputs = audio_ops.mfcc(spectrogram, sample_rate=fs,    Generates the
    ⮑ dct_coefficient_count=numcep)                             corresponding
                                                                spectrogram and
    audio_mfcc = orig_inputs.eval()   Prints the               generates MFCC
    print(np.shape(audio_mfcc))    ⟵— output shape             features
```

You can look at a few of the samples from the audio file and convince yourself that there is something for the machine-learning algorithm to learn by reusing some plotting code from chapter 7 and plotting the first samples corresponding to the 26 bins. The code in listing 17.6 performs this plotting, and its output is shown in figure 17.3.

Listing 17.6   Plotting five samples from the audio file's MFCC features

```
labels=[]
for i in np.arange(26):          ←——— 26 cepstral bins
    labels.append("P"+str(i+1))

fig, ax = plt.subplots()
ind = np.arange(len(labels))
width = 0.15
colors = ['r', 'g', 'y', 'b', 'black']
plots = []
                                      ⎤ 5 samples of the 2,545 total
for i in range(0, 5):            ←———⎦
    Xs = np.asarray(np.abs(audio_mfcc[0][i])).reshape(-1)  ←⎤
    p = ax.bar(ind + i*width, Xs, width, color=colors[i])   ⎤ Takes the absolute
    plots.append(p[0])                                        ⎦ value so that there are
                                                               no negative bin sizes
xticks = ind + width / (audio_mfcc.shape[0])
print(xticks)
ax.legend(tuple(plots), ('S1', 'S2', 'S3', 'S4', 'S5'))
ax.yaxis.set_units(inch)
ax.autoscale_view()
ax.set_xticks(xticks)
ax.set_xticklabels(labels)

ax.set_ylabel('Normalized freq coumt')
ax.set_xlabel('Pitch')
ax.set_title('Normalized frequency counts for Various Sounds')  ⎤ Shows
plt.show()                                                 ←———⎦ the plot
```

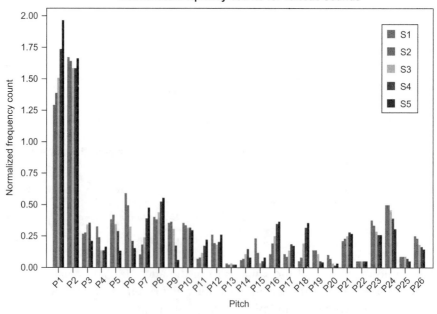

Figure 17.3   MFCC features for five samples of an audio file from the LibriSpeech corpus

There are variances among samples. The various samples correspond to different times in the sound file, and ultimately, you will want your ASR machine-learning model to predict letters for these utterances. In the Deep Speech paper, the authors define a *context,* which is a set of backward-looking samples and forward-looking samples along with the present sample. Having some overlap among samples allows for better differentiation, because word- and character-level tones tend to overlap in language. Think about saying the word *best.* The *b* and the *e* overlap in sound. This same concept applies to training a good machine-learning model because you want it to reflect the real world as much as possible.

You can set up a time window to look at several time steps—call this time window *numcontext* samples—in the past and future. Taken along with the present sample, your new feature vector becomes $N \times (2 * number\ cepstrals * numcontext + numcepstrals)$. Through some testing locally, 9 is a reasonable value for numcontext, and because you are using 26 cepstrals, you have a new feature vector of size $(N \times 2 * 26 * 9 + 26)$ or $(N \times 494)$, where N is the number of samples. You can use the code from listing 17.5 to generate this new feature vector for each sound file, and then use the code in listing 17.7 to complete the job. Another technique the authors of the Deep Speech paper used was to take only half the samples from the audio file to further reduce the sample density, especially with a forward- and backward-looking window. Listing 17.7 takes care of that job for you too.

Listing 17.7 Generating a contextual window of past, present, and future MFCC

**Takes every second sample
and subsets the data by half**

```
orig_inputs = orig_inputs[:,::2]
audio_mfcc = orig_inputs.eval()
train_inputs = np.array([], np.float32)
train_inputs.resize((audio_mfcc.shape[1], numcep + 2 * numcep *
➥ numcontext))

empty_mfcc = np.array([])
empty_mfcc.resize((numcep))
empty_mfcc = tf.convert_to_tensor(empty_mfcc, dtype=tf.float32)
empty_mfcc_ev = empty_mfcc.eval()

time_slices = range(train_inputs.shape[0])
context_past_min = time_slices[0] + numcontext
context_future_max = time_slices[-1] - numcontext

for time_slice in tqdm(time_slices):
    need_empty_past = max(0, (context_past_min - time_slice))
    empty_source_past = np.asarray([empty_mfcc_ev for empty_slots in
    ➥ range(need_empty_past)])
    data_source_past = orig_inputs[0][max(0, time_slice -
    ➥ numcontext):time_slice]
```

Generates (N × 494 samples) placeholder

Starting min point for past content; has to be at least 9 ts

Picks up to numcontext time slices in the past, and completes with empty MFCC features

Ending point max for future content; size time slices 9 ts

```
need_empty_future = max(0, (time_slice - context_future_max))
empty_source_future = np.asarray([empty_mfcc_ev for empty_slots in
    range(need_empty_future)])
data_source_future = orig_inputs[0][time_slice + 1:time_slice +
    numcontext + 1]
```

Picks up to numcontext time slices in the future, and completes with empty MFCC features

Pads if needed for the past or future, or takes past and future

```
if need_empty_past:
    past = tf.concat([tf.cast(empty_source_past, tf.float32),
        tf.cast(data_source_past, tf.float32)], 0)
else:
    past = data_source_past

if need_empty_future:
    future = tf.concat([tf.cast(data_source_future, tf.float32),
        tf.cast(empty_source_future, tf.float32)], 0)
else:
    future = data_source_future
```

Takes the mean over the standard deviation and normalizes the input values for learning

```
past = tf.reshape(past, [numcontext*numcep])
now = orig_inputs[0][time_slice]
future = tf.reshape(future, [numcontext*numcep])

train_inputs[time_slice] = np.concatenate((past.eval(), now.eval(),
    future.eval()))
train_inputs = (train_inputs - np.mean(train_inputs)) /
    np.std(train_inputs)
```

Now you've got your audio in good shape for training and can run the data preparation over the LibriSpeech audio files. Take heed: this process may take many hours for data preparation, depending on how much training data you use. There are more than 25,000 files, and my recommendation is to start small, with maybe 100 for training. This sample would yield a feature vector of $(100 \times N \times 494)$, where N is the number of samples (two per audio file).

The other data preparation you'll need to take care of involves those transcripts. The character-level data needs to be converted to numbers, which is a straightforward process that I'll show you in section 17.2.2.

17.2.2 *Preparing the text transcripts as character-level numerical data*

With the work you did to prepare the LibriSpeech corpus, for every audio data file like LibriSpeech/train-clean-100-all/3486-166424-0004.wav, you've got a corresponding LibriSpeech/train-clean-100-all/3486-166424-0004.txt file with contents like the following:

```
a hare sat upright in the middle of the ancient roadway the valley itself lay
    serenely under the ambering light smiling peaceful emptied of horror
```

To take your input feature vector sized $(1 \times N \times 494)$ and map it to the character-level output, you have to process the text output into numbers. One simple way is to use Python's ord() function, because all characters in Python are numbers represented onscreen as characters by means of a charset. A *charset* is a table that maps a particular integer value to some character in the table. Popular charsets include ASCII, UTF-8, and UTF-16 for 8-bit and 16-bit Unicode. Python's ord() function returns the integer representation of a character, which will work well for your network.

The first steps are opening the transcript file, making sure that it is ASCII-formatted, and removing any funky characters. In general, deep speech has been ported to support other character sets (language encodings) but I'll focus on ASCII and English in this chapter. (You can find other datasets at https://github.com/mozilla/DeepSpeech.) The easiest method is to use Python's codecs module to force the file to be read as UTF-8 and then force-convert it to ASCII. Listing 17.8 has the snippet that performs this task. The code also lowercases the text.

Listing 17.8 Opening the transcript, forcing it to ASCII, and normalizing the text

Opens the file as UTF-8

```
def normalize_txt_file(txt_file, remove_apostrophe=True):
    with codecs.open(txt_file, encoding="utf-8") as open_txt_file:
        return normalize_text(open_txt_file.read(),
            remove_apostrophe=remove_apostrophe)

def normalize_text(original, remove_apostrophe=True):
    result = unicodedata.normalize("NFKD", original).encode("ascii",
        "ignore").decode()
    if remove_apostrophe:
        result = result.replace("'", "")
    return re.sub("[^a-zA-Z']+", ' ', result).strip().lower()
```

The only supported characters are letters and apostrophes.

Removes apostrophes to keep contractions together

Returns lowercase alphabetic characters

Converts any Unicode characters to ASCII equivalents

When the text is normalized and clean, you can convert it to a numerical array by using the ord() function. The text_to_char_array() function converts the cleaned text to a numerical array. To do so, the function scans the string text, converts the string to an array of letters—such as ['I' '<space>' 'a' 'm'] for *I am*—and then replaces the letters with their ordinal representation—[9 0 1 13]—for the transcript *I am*. Listing 17.9 provides the function that performs the transcript-to-array conversion.

Listing 17.9 Generating a numerical array from the clean transcript

```
SPACE_TOKEN = '<space>'
SPACE_INDEX = 0
FIRST_INDEX = ord('a') - 1
def text_to_char_array(original):
    result = original.replace(' ', '  ')
    result = result.split(' ')
```

Reserves 0 for the space character

Creates list of sentence's words with spaces replaced by "

```
result = np.hstack([SPACE_TOKEN if xt == '' else list(xt) for xt in
    result])

return np.asarray([SPACE_INDEX if xt == SPACE_TOKEN else ord(xt) -
    FIRST_INDEX for xt in result])
```

Converts each word to
an array of its letters

Converts the letters to the
ordinal representation

With the audio input prepared and numerical transcripts, you have what you need to train the LSTM deep-speech model. Section 17.2.3 takes a quick look at its implementation.

17.2.3 *The deep-speech model in TensorFlow*

The TensorFlow implementation of deep speech is complex, so you have little need to jump into its depths. I prefer to use a slimmed-down version made popular by the Silicon Valley Data Science tutorial at https://www.svds.com/tensorflow-rnn-tutorial and the associated GitHub code, which has moved to https://github.com/ mrubash1/RNN-Tutorial. The tutorial defines a simpler version of the deep-speech architecture, which I'll cover in listing 17.10 and later listings.

The model takes as input training samples of shape $(M, N, 494)$, where M is the size of the training batch, N is the number of samples in a file divided in half, and 494 includes 26 cepstrals and a context of 9 steps in the past and future. The first steps of the model involve setting up the network and its initial three hidden layers to learn features from the input audio. The initial hyperparameters for the work are taken from the Deep Speech paper, including setting dropout to `0.5` in layers 1–3, `0` in the LSTM bidirectional layer, and `0.5` in the output layer.

The amount of time you'd would spend learning these hyperparameters would not an excellent use of your time, so use them as-is from the paper. The `relu_clip` is a modified ReLU activation function used by the deep-speech authors that sets any input to the following:

- Any value less than 0 to 0
- Any value X greater than 0 and less than that of the clip value (20) to X itself
- Any value greater than the clip value (20) to the clip value (20)

Activations are scaled and shifted using this activation function, also from the paper.

The network uses 1,024 hidden neurons for its initial three hidden layers and for the bidirectional LSTM cell layers, and 1,024 neurons for the last hidden layer before making character-level predictions for 29 characters a–z, including space, apostrophe, and blank. Listing 17.10 starts the model definition.

Listing 17.10 Hyperparameters and setup for deep speech

```
def BiRNN_model(batch_x, seq_length, n_input, n_context):
    dropout = [0.05, 0.05, 0.05, 0.0, 0.0, 0.05]
    relu_clip = 20
```

Dropout to use
in each layer

```
b1_stddev = 0.046875
h1_stddev = 0.046875
b2_stddev = 0.046875
h2_stddev = 0.046875
b3_stddev = 0.046875
h3_stddev = 0.046875
b5_stddev = 0.046875
h5_stddev = 0.046875
b6_stddev = 0.046875
h6_stddev = 0.046875
```
◁—— **Uses ReLU clipping as defined in the paper**

```
n_hidden_1 = 1024
n_hidden_2 = 1024
n_hidden_5 = 1024
n_cell_dim = 1024
```
◁—— **Number of hidden dimensions in each layer**

```
n_hidden_3 = 2048
n_hidden_6 = 29
n_character = 29
```
◁—— **Output probabilities for the 29 characters for each cell**   **Input shape: [batch_size, n_steps, n_input + 2*26 cepstrals*9 window backwards/forwards]**

```
batch_x_shape = tf.shape(batch_x)                    ◁——
batch_x = tf.transpose(batch_x, [1, 0, 2])
batch_x = tf.reshape(batch_x,
                     [-1, n_input + 2 * n_input * n_context])   ◁——
```
Reshapes for first-layer input (n_steps*batch_size, n_input + 2*26 cepstrals*9 window)

The next three layers of the model in listing 17.11 pass the input batches of data to learn audio features that will be used as input to the bidirectional LSTM cells (size 1,024 each). The model also stores TensorFlow summary variables that you can inspect with TensorBoard, as I showed you in earlier chapters, in case you need to inspect the variable values for debugging.

Listing 17.11   The audio feature layers of deep speech

```
with tf.name_scope('fc1'):                           ◁——  Implements
    b1 = tf.get_variable(name='b1', shape=[n_hidden_1],       the first layer
  initializer=tf.random_normal_initializer(stddev=b1_stddev))
    h1 = tf.get_variable(name='h1', shape=[n_input + 2 * n_input *
      ➥ n_context, n_hidden_1],

    initializer=tf.random_normal_initializer(stddev=h1_stddev))
    layer_1 = tf.minimum(tf.nn.relu(tf.add(tf.matmul(batch_x, h1), b1)),
      ➥ relu_clip)                                   ◁——  Uses clipped ReLU
    layer_1 = tf.nn.dropout(layer_1, (1.0 - dropout[0]))    activation

    tf.summary.histogram("weights", h1)
    tf.summary.histogram("biases", b1)
    tf.summary.histogram("activations", layer_1)
                                                      Implements the
with tf.name_scope('fc2'):                            ◁——  second layer
```

```
    b2 = tf.get_variable(name='b2', shape=[n_hidden_2],
➥       initializer=tf.random_normal_initializer(stddev=b2_stddev))
    h2 = tf.get_variable(name='h2', shape=[n_hidden_1, n_hidden_2],
➥       initializer=tf.random_normal_initializer(stddev=h2_stddev))
    layer_2 = tf.minimum(tf.nn.relu(tf.add(tf.matmul(layer_1, h2), b2)),
➥       relu_clip)                                            ◄──────  Uses clipped ReLU
    layer_2 = tf.nn.dropout(layer_2, (1.0 - dropout[1]))              activation

    tf.summary.histogram("weights", h2)
    tf.summary.histogram("biases", b2)
    tf.summary.histogram("activations", layer_2)
                                                      ┌──────  Implements the
with tf.name_scope('fc3'):                     ◄──────┘        third layer
    b3 = tf.get_variable(name='b3', shape=[n_hidden_3],
   initializer=tf.random_normal_initializer(stddev=b3_stddev))
    h3 = tf.get_variable(name='h3', shape=[n_hidden_2, n_hidden_3],
➥       initializer=tf.random_normal_initializer(stddev=h3_stddev))
    layer_3 = tf.minimum(tf.nn.relu(tf.add(tf.matmul(layer_2, h3), b3)),
➥       relu_clip)                                            ◄──────  Uses clipped ReLU
    layer_3 = tf.nn.dropout(layer_3, (1.0 - dropout[2]))              activation

    tf.summary.histogram("weights", h3)
    tf.summary.histogram("biases", b3)
    tf.summary.histogram("activations", layer_3)
```

Deep speech includes the bidirectional LSTM layers in listing 17.12 to learn the audio features and their mapping to single-character-level outputs. The initial weights (`lstm_fw_cell`) are passed to each forward cell for learning; then the backward cell weights (`lstm_bw_cell`) are used to propagate the learning for character prediction in reverse.

Listing 17.12 The bidirectional LSTM layers

```
with tf.name_scope('lstm'):
    lstm_fw_cell = tf.contrib.rnn.BasicLSTMCell(n_cell_dim,    │ Forward
➥      forget_bias=1.0, state_is_tuple=True)           ◄──────┘ direction cell
    lstm_fw_cell = tf.contrib.rnn.DropoutWrapper(lstm_fw_cell,
        input_keep_prob=1.0 - dropout[3],
        output_keep_prob=1.0 - dropout[3])

    lstm_bw_cell = tf.contrib.rnn.BasicLSTMCell(n_cell_dim,    │ Backward
➥      forget_bias=1.0, state_is_tuple=True)                    direction cell
    lstm_bw_cell = tf.contrib.rnn.DropoutWrapper(lstm_bw_cell,
        input_keep_prob=1.0 - dropout[4],
        output_keep_prob=1.0 - dropout[4])

    layer_3 = tf.reshape(layer_3, [-1, batch_x_shape[0], n_hidden_3])  ◄─┐

    outputs, output_states =                                            │
➥      tf.nn.bidirectional_dynamic_rnn(cell_fw=lstm_fw_cell,
cell_bw=lstm_bw_cell,
inputs=layer_3,
dtype=tf.float32,                                    Reshapes to [n_steps,
time_major=True,                                 batch_size, 2*n_cell_dim]
```

```
sequence_length=seq_length)
```

Reshapes to
[n_steps*batch_size,
2*n_cell_dim]

```
        tf.summary.histogram("activations", outputs)
        outputs = tf.concat(outputs, 2)
        outputs = tf.reshape(outputs, [-1, 2 * n_cell_dim])
```

The final layers featurize the LSTM output by using one more hidden layer before mapping it to a fully connected layer that corresponds to a softmax distribution over the 29 character classes (listing 17.13).

Listing 17.13 Final layers of deep speech

Fifth layer with clipped ReLU activation and dropout

```
with tf.name_scope('fc5'):
    b5 = tf.get_variable(name='b5', shape=[n_hidden_5],
  initializer=tf.random_normal_initializer(stddev=b5_stddev))
    h5 = tf.get_variable(name='h5', shape=[(2 * n_cell_dim), n_hidden_5],
      initializer=tf.random_normal_initializer(stddev=h5_stddev))
    layer_5 = tf.minimum(tf.nn.relu(tf.add(tf.matmul(outputs, h5), b5)),
      relu_clip)
    layer_5 = tf.nn.dropout(layer_5, (1.0 - dropout[5]))

    tf.summary.histogram("weights", h5)
    tf.summary.histogram("biases", b5)
    tf.summary.histogram("activations", layer_5)

with tf.name_scope('fc6'):
    b6 = tf.get_variable(name='b6', shape=[n_hidden_6],
  initializer=tf.random_normal_initializer(stddev=b6_stddev))
    h6 = tf.get_variable(name='h6', shape=[n_hidden_5, n_hidden_6],
      initializer=tf.random_normal_initializer(stddev=h6_stddev))
    layer_6 = tf.add(tf.matmul(layer_5, h6), b6)

    tf.summary.histogram("weights", h6)
    tf.summary.histogram("biases", b6)
    tf.summary.histogram("activations", layer_6)

layer_6 = tf.reshape(layer_6, [-1, batch_x_shape[0], n_hidden_6])
summary_op = tf.summary.merge_all()
return layer_6, summary_op
```

Creates output logits of 29 character classes distribution]

Reshapes to time major n_steps, batch_size, n_hidden_6 distribution

The output of deep speech is a probability distribution over the 29 character classes for each sample for each audio file in a batch. If the batch size is 50, and each file has 75 time steps or samples, the output would be at each step *N*, 50 output characters corresponding to the sound utterance at that step for each of the 50 files in the batch.

The last thing to talk about before running deep speech is how the predicted character utterances are evaluated. In section 17.2.4, I'll discuss how connectionist temporal classification (CTC) is used to discern language that overlaps among consecutive time steps.

17.2.4 *Connectionist temporal classification in TensorFlow*

The ideal situation in the deep-speech RNN would be for each utterance and time step in the audio file input to map directly to a character in the predicted output from the network. But the reality is that as you divide the input into time steps, an utterance and ultimately character-level output may overlap multiple time steps. In the audio file *I am saying human things* (figure 17.4), it's entirely possible that the predicted output at the first four time steps (t_1–t_3) will correspond to the letter *I* because the utterance occurs at each step, but a portion of that utterance also bleeds into time step t_4, which is predicted as letter *a* because that's where the *a* sound starts to occur.

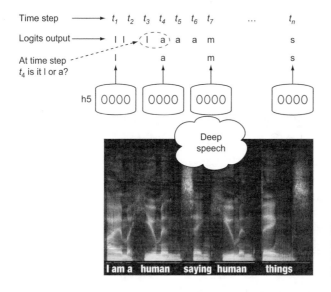

Figure 17.4   CTC and deep speech aim to generate plausible character-level outputs for overlapping possibilities at a time step (t).

In this scenario, how do you decide whether time step t_4 represents the letter *I* or *a*, given the overlap?

You can use CTC. The technique is a loss function similar to cross-entropy loss with logits (chapter 6). The loss function calculates all the possible character-level combinations for output, given the size (number of time steps) of the input and the relationship over steps of time. It defines a function to relate all the output-probability classes at each time step over time. The predictions themselves at each time step are considered not independently, but together.

TensorFlow comes with a CTC loss function called `ctc_ops` as part of the `tensorflow.python.ops` package. You provide to it the logits corresponding to the character-level time-step predictions and a placeholder (`int32`) for the predictions. You will fill the predictions during each training step with the sparse transcript conversion to numerical data, as I showed you in section 17.2.2, along with the desired output length and in each epoch. Then the CTC loss is computed and can be used to scan across the per-time step character predictions and converge toward full transcript predictions which minimize the loss or in turn have the highest likelihood over the prediction space.

In the preceding example, CTC loss would look across all possible predictions at the character level and look for minimal loss, not only for time step t_4, but also for t_3–t_5, which in turn suggests including a space before *a* and after *I*, properly delineating the words in the transcription. Because the desired sequence length is provided and is equal to the length of the converted sparse transcript, the CTC algorithm can figure out how to weight spaces and other nonletter characters to achieve the optimal transcription output. Listing 17.14 sets up the CTC loss function and prepares the model.

Listing 17.14 Setting up CTC loss and preparing to train the model

Inputs converted audio features

```
input_tensor  = tf.placeholder(tf.float32, [None, None, numcep + (2 * numcep
⇒ * numcontext)], name='input')
```

1D array of size [batch_size]

```
seq_length = tf.placeholder(tf.int32, [None], name='seq_length')
targets = tf.sparse_placeholder(tf.int32, name='targets')

logits, summary_op = BiRNN_model(input_tensor, tf.to_int64(seq_length),
⇒ numcep, numcontext)
```

Sets up the BiRNN model

Uses sparse_placeholder; will generate a SparseTensor, required by ctc_loss op

```
total_loss = ctc_ops.ctc_loss(targets, logits, seq_length)
avg_loss = tf.reduce_mean(total_loss)
```

Sets up the CTC loss function with input audio features (logits), the sparse transcript targets, and desired transcript length (seq length)

```
beta1 = 0.9
beta2 = 0.999
epsilon = 1e-8
learning_rate = 0.001
optimizer = tf.train.AdamOptimizer(learning_rate=learning_rate,
                                   beta1=beta1,
                                   beta2=beta2,
                                   epsilon=epsilon)

train_op = optimizer.minimize(avg_loss)
```

Creates the optimizer with hyperparameters from the Deep Speech paper and train operation

With the CTC loss function defined and ready, the model is ready for training, which I'll help you set up in section 17.3.

17.3 Training and evaluating deep speech

Running the deep-speech model using TensorFlow is similar to running all the other models you've created thus far. You'll set train size, which controls the number of audio files to use for training. I recommended using hundreds of them at a time on a laptop if possible, but not thousands, and with the LibriSpeech corpus, you have more than 25,000 files to use for training.

A batch size of 50, given 150 training files, creates 3 iterations per epoch. Fifty epochs can be trained in a few hours on a CPU and in minutes on a GPU. You can tweak these hyperparameters to suit your computing resources. Listing 17.15 uses the TensorFlow dataset API (chapter 15) to create the dataset as a TensorFlow operator lazily loaded in each epoch.

Listing 17.15 Setting up the training parameters and dataset for deep speech

```
num_epochs = 50
BATCH_SIZE=50              Hyperparameters, 50 epochs, with 3 batches
train_size=150            of 50 for 150 training files per epoch
train_audio_ds =
⟹ tf.data.Dataset.from_tensor_slices(train_audio_wav[0:train_size])
train_audio_ds = train_audio_ds.batch(BATCH_SIZE)
train_audio_ds = train_audio_ds.shuffle(buffer_size=train_size)
train_audio_ds = train_audio_ds.prefetch(buffer_size=AUTOTUNE)
```

**Builds a TensorFlow dataset from training files,
and sets up random shuffling and prefetching**

Listing 17.16 trains the model and outputs CTC loss per batch and average train loss per epoch by dividing the loss by number of training files. The audio input is prepared, using the techniques described earlier to create MFCC features with contextual windows of nine steps in the past and nine in the future, with padding. The transcript data is turned into integers based on ordinal values for 26 alpha characters, and also space, blank, and apostrophe, totaling 29 different character values.

Listing 17.16 Training deep speech

```
train_cost = 0.
with tf.Session() as sess:                    ←──────    Creates a new
    sess.run(tf.global_variables_initializer())          TF session

    for epoch in tqdm(range(0, num_epochs)):
        iter = train_audio_ds.make_one_shot_iterator()
        batch_num = 0
        iter_op = iter.get_next()
                                              Gets the batch of training audio
                                              filenames and then gets the
        while True:                           corresponding transcript names
            try:
                train_batch = sess.run(iter_op)
                trans_batch = [fname.decode("utf-8").split('.')[0]+'.txt' for
                ⟹ fname in train_batch]
                audio_data = [process_audio(f) for f in train_batch]
                train, t_length = pad_sequences(audio_data)

                trans_txt = [normalize_txt_file(f) for f in trans_batch]
                trans_txt = [text_to_char_array(f) for f in trans_txt]
                transcript_sparse = sparse_tuple_from(np.asarray(trans_txt))

                feed = {input_tensor: train,
                        targets: transcript_sparse,
```

Creates a new Dataset iterator operation (annotation pointing to `iter_op = iter.get_next()`)

Prepares the audio data by creating MFCC with context window and pads sequences (annotation)

Creates numerical per-character level transcripts (annotation)

```
                        seq_length: t_length}
          batch_cost, _ = sess.run([avg_loss, train_op],
              feed_dict=feed)
          train_cost += batch_cost * BATCH_SIZE
          batch_num += 1
          print('Batch cost: %.2f' % (batch_cost))
      except tf.errors.OutOfRangeError:
          train_cost /= train_size
          print('Epoch %d | Train cost: %.2f' % (epoch, train_cost))
          break
```

Prepares the input to each training step and runs the training operation

Prints per-batch loss

Prints per-epoch average loss per training sample

One of the most comprehensive toolkits and clean code bases for running deep speech is the RNN-Tutorial GitHub repo at https://github.com/mrubash1/RNN-Tutorial. It allows for the following:

- Easy tweaking of model parameters
- Use of hyperparameters
- Training, test, and development sets
- Per-epoch dev-set validations
- Final test set validation

It also prints model decodings per epoch and at the end of training so that you get output such as the following:

```
2020-07-04 17:40:02,850 [INFO] tf_train_ctc.py: Batch 0, file 35
2020-07-04 17:40:02,850 [INFO] tf_train_ctc.py: Original: he was impervious
    to reason
2020-07-04 17:40:02,850 [INFO] tf_train_ctc.py: Decoded:  he was om pervius
    trreason____

2020-07-04 17:40:02,850 [INFO] tf_train_ctc.py: Batch 0, file 36
2020-07-04 17:40:02,850 [INFO] tf_train_ctc.py: Original: which clouds seeing
    that there was no roof sometimes wept over the masterpiece of ursus
2020-07-04 17:40:02,850 [INFO] tf_train_ctc.py: Decoded:  whicht clouds saing
    the tere was no re some timns wath ofprh them master peaes eafversus

2020-07-04 19:50:36,602 [INFO] tf_train_ctc.py: Batch 0, file 45
2020-07-04 19:50:36,602 [INFO] tf_train_ctc.py: Original: the family had been
    living on corncakes and sorghum molasses for three days
2020-07-04 19:50:36,602 [INFO] tf_train_ctc.py: Decoded:  the femwigh ha been
    lentang on qarncaes and sord am maolassis fo thre bys
```

Another nifty feature automatically uses TensorFlow's Summary operations API to log events so that you can use TensorBoard to visualize the model as it's running.

Using a GPU across several days, I managed to train quite a few variations of the deep-speech model; I watched validation loss, accuracy, and train loss, and plotted them with TensorBoard. Figure 17.5 shows the first 500 epochs of deep-speech training.

The model converges quickly in the first 90 epochs, and train loss and validation loss head in the right direction. The validation label error rate, computed every two

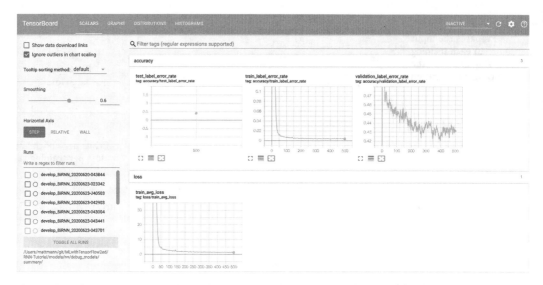

Figure 17.5   TensorBoard output for the first 500 epochs of the deep-speech model

epochs by default in the RNN-Tutorial code repo, also heads in the right direction, demonstrating the robustness of the model.

Congratulations—you have learned how to create your own ASR system! The big web companies aren't the only ones who can do this. RNNs, data, and some TensorFlow are the tools you need to get the job done.

Summary

- Intelligent digital assistants, from home devices to your phones to your TV, recognize speech and convert it to text by using RNNs and special instances of them called LSTM models. This process is called ASR.
- You can obtain open data from audiobooks such as the OpenSLR and Libri-Speech data of 100, 500, and 1000 hours of recordings, along with aligned textual transcripts of those books that you can use to train an LSTM model for ASR.
- One of the most famous models for ASR is called Deep Speech. You can re-create this model with TensorFlow and the LibriSpeech data by building the deep-speech LSTM model.
- TensorFlow and associated toolkits provide methods to featurize the audio with MFCCs, converting from the frequency domain to the time domain.
- Text transcripts can be featurized with Python's `ord()` function and utilities to convert text transcripts to numbers.
- CTC is a loss function and algorithm that allows speech input over nonuniform time steps to be aligned with uniform character-level transcripts to obtain the best transcriptions in RNNs.

18

Sequence-to-sequence models for chatbots

This chapter covers

- Examining sequence-to-sequence architecture
- Performing vector embedding of words
- Implementing a chatbot by using real-world data

Talking to customer service over the phone is a burden for both the customer and the company. Service providers pay a good chunk of money to hire customer service representatives, but what if it's possible to automate most of this effort? Can we develop software to interface with customers through natural language?

The idea isn't as far-fetched as you might think. Chatbots are getting a lot of hype because of unprecedented developments in natural language processing using deep-learning techniques. Perhaps, given enough training data, a chatbot could learn to navigate the most commonly addressed customer problems through natural conversations. If the chatbot were truly efficient, it could not only save the company money by eliminating the need to hire representatives, but also accelerate the customer's search for an answer.

In this chapter, you'll build a chatbot by feeding a neural network thousands of examples of input and output sentences. Your training dataset is a pair of English utterances. If you ask "How are you?" for example, the chatbot should respond, "Fine, thank you."

> **NOTE**   In this chapter, we're thinking of *sequences* and *sentences* as interchangeable concepts. In our implementation, a sentence will be a sequence of letters. Another common approach is to represent a sentence as a sequence of words.

In effect, the algorithm will try to produce an intelligent natural language response to each natural language query. You'll be implementing a neural network that uses two primary concepts taught in previous chapters: multiclass classification and recurrent neural networks (RNNs).

18.1 *Building on classification and RNNs*

Classification is a machine-learning approach to predict the category of an input data item. Furthermore, multiclass classification allows for more than two classes. You saw in chapter 6 how to implement such an algorithm in TensorFlow. Specifically, the cost function between the model's prediction (a sequence of numbers) and the ground truth (a one-hot vector) tries to find the distance between two sequences by using the cross-entropy loss.

> **NOTE**   A one-hot vector is like an all-zero vector, except that one of the dimensions has a value of 1.

In this case, implementing a chatbot, you'll use a variant of the cross-entropy loss to measure the difference between two sequences: the model's response (which is a sequence) against the ground truth (which is also a sequence).

Exercise 18.1

In TensorFlow, you can use the cross-entropy loss function to measure the similarity between a one-hot vector, such as (1, 0, 0), and a neural network's output, such as (2.34, 0.1, 0.3). On the other hand, English sentences aren't numeric vectors. How can you use the cross-entropy loss to measure the similarity between English sentences?

Answer

A crude approach would be to represent each sentence as a vector by counting the frequency of each word within the sentence. Then compare the vectors to see how closely they match up.

You may recall that RNNs are a neural network design for incorporating not only input from the current time step, but also state information from previous inputs. Chapters 16 and 17 covered these networks in great detail, and they'll be used again in this chapter. RNNs represent input and output as time-series data, which is exactly what you need to represent sequences.

A naïve idea is to use an out-of-the-box RNN to implement a chatbot. Let's see why this is a bad approach. The input and output of the RNN are natural language sentences, so the inputs $(x_t, x_{t-1}, x_{t-2}, …)$ and outputs $(y_t, y_{t-1}, y_{t-2}, …)$ can be sequences of words. The problem in using an RNN to model conversations is that the RNN produces an output result immediately. If your input is a sequence of words (*How, are, you*), the first output word will depend on only the first input word. The output sequence item y_t of the RNN couldn't look ahead to future parts of the input sentence to make a decision; it would be limited by knowledge of only previous input sequences $(x_t, x_{t-1}, x_{t-2}, …)$. The naïve RNN model tries to come up with a response to the user's query before they've finished asking it, which can lead to incorrect results.

Instead, you'll use two RNNs: one for the input sentence and the other for the output sequence. When the first RNN finished processing the input sequence, it'll send the hidden state to the second RNN to process the output sentence. You can see the two RNNs, labeled Encoder and Decoder, in figure 18.1.

We're bringing concepts of multiclass classification and RNNs from previous chapters into designing a neural network that learns to map an input sequence to an output sequence. The RNNs provide a way of encoding the input sentence, passing a summarized state vector to the decoder, and then decoding it to a response sentence. To measure the cost between the model's response and the ground truth, we look to the function used in multiclass classification—cross-entropy loss—for inspiration.

This architecture is called a *sequence-to-sequence* (seq2seq) neural network architecture. The training data you use will be thousands of pairs of sentences mined from movie scripts. The algorithm will observe these dialogue examples and eventually learn to form responses to arbitrary queries you might ask it.

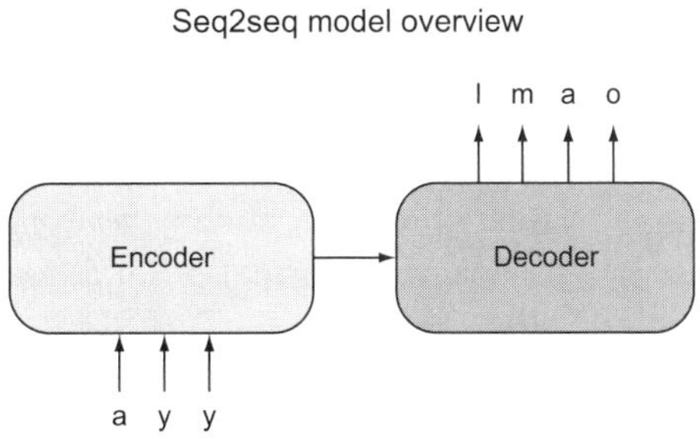

Figure 18.1 Here's a high-level view of your neural network model. The input *ayy* is passed into the encoder RNN, and the decoder RNN is expected to respond with *lmao*. These examples are toy examples for your chatbot, but you could imagine more-complicated pairs of sentences for the input and output.

Exercise 18.2
What other industries could benefit from a chatbot?

Answer
One example is a conversation partner for young students as a tool to teach subjects such as English, math, and even computer science.

By the end of the chapter, you'll have your own chatbot that can respond somewhat intelligently to your queries. It won't be perfect, because this model always responds the same way for the same input query.

Suppose that you're traveling to a foreign country without any ability to speak the language. A clever salesman hands you a book, claiming that it's all you need to respond to sentences in the foreign language. You're supposed to use the book like a dictionary. When someone says a phrase in the foreign language, you can look it up, and the book will have the response written out for you to read aloud: "If someone says *Hello*, you say *Hi*."

Sure, this book might be a practical lookup table for small talk, but can a lookup table get you the correct response for arbitrary dialogue? Of course not! Consider looking up the question "Are you hungry?" The answer is stamped in the book and will never change.

The lookup table is missing state information, which is a key component in dialogue. In your seq2seq model, you'll suffer from a similar issue, but the model is a good start. Believe it or not, at present, hierarchical state representation for intelligent dialogue still isn't the norm; many chatbots start with these seq2seq models.

18.2 *Understanding seq2seq architecture*

The seq2seq model attempts to learn a neural network that predicts an output sequence from an input sequence. Sequences are a little different from traditional vectors because a sequence implies an ordering of events.

Time is an intuitive way to order events: we usually end up alluding to words related to time, such as *temporal, time series, past,* and *future.* We like to say that RNNs propagate information to *future time* steps, for example, or that RNNs capture *temporal dependencies.*

NOTE   RNNs are covered in detail in chapter 16.

The seq2seq model is implemented with multiple RNNs. A single RNN cell is depicted in figure 18.2; it serves as the building block for the rest of the seq2seq model architecture.

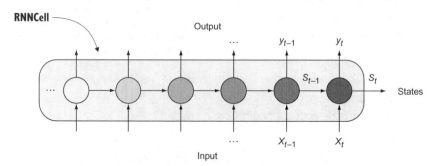

Figure 18.2   The input, output, and states of an RNN. You can ignore the intricacies of how an RNN is implemented. All that matters is the formatting of your input and output.

First, you'll learn how to stack RNNs to improve the model's complexity. Then you'll learn how to pipe the hidden state of one RNN to another RNN so that you can have an encoder and decoder network. As you'll begin to see, starting to use RNNs is fairly easy.

After that, you'll get an introduction to converting natural language sentences to a sequence of vectors. After all, RNNs understand only numeric data, so you'll absolutely need this conversion process. Because a *sequence* is another way of saying "a list of tensors," you need to make sure that you can convert your data accordingly. A sentence is a sequence of words, but words aren't tensors. The process of converting words to tensors or, more commonly, vectors is called *embedding*.

Last, you'll put all these concepts together to implement the seq2seq model on real-world data. The data will come from thousands of conversations from movie scripts.

You can hit the ground running with the code in listing 18.1. Open a new Python file, and start copying the listing code to set up constants and placeholders. You'll define the shape of the placeholder as [None, seq_size, input_dim], where None means that the size is dynamic (the batch size may change), seq_size is the length of the sequence, and input_dim is the dimension of each sequence item.

Listing 18.1 Setting up constants and placeholders

```
import tensorflow as tf      ◁──── All you need is TensorFlow.

input_dim = 1   ◁──── Dimension of each sequence element
seq_size = 6   ◁──────┐
                       └ Maximum length of sequence
input_placeholder = tf.placeholder(dtype=tf.float32,
                                   shape=[None, seq_size, input_dim])
```

To generate an RNN cell like the one in figure 18.2, TensorFlow provides a helpful LSTMCell class. Listing 18.2 shows how to use this class and extract the outputs and states from the cell. For convenience, the listing defines a helper function called make_cell to set up the LSTM RNN cell. Defining a cell isn't enough, however; you also need to call tf.nn.dynamic_rnn on it to set up the network;

Listing 18.2 Making a simple RNN cell

```
def make_cell(state_dim):                              Check out the tf.contrib.rnn
    return tf.contrib.rnn.LSTMCell(state_dim)   ◁──── documentation for other
                                                       types of cells, such as GRU.
with tf.variable_scope("first_cell") as scope:
    cell = make_cell(state_dim=10)
 ┌─▷ outputs, states = tf.nn.dynamic_rnn(cell,                          Input sequence
 │                                  input_placeholder,   ◁────────────┘ to the RNN
 │   Two results will be generated:  dtype=tf.float32)
 │   outputs and states.
```

You may remember from previous chapters that you can improve a neural network's complexity by adding hidden layers. More layers means more parameters, which likely means that the model can represent more functions because it's more flexible.

You know what? You can stack cells. Nothing is stopping you. Doing so makes the model more complex, so perhaps this two-layered RNN model will perform better because it's more expressive. Figure 18.3 shows two cells stacked.

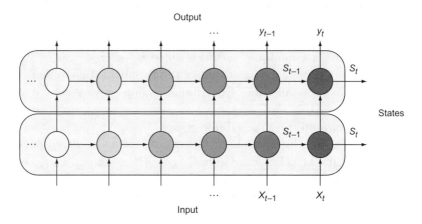

Figure 18.3   You can stack RNN cells to form a more complicated architecture.

> **WARNING**   The more flexible the model is, the more likely it'll be to overfit the training data.

In TensorFlow, you can intuitively implement this two-layered RNN network. First, you create a new variable scope for the second cell. To stack RNNs, you can pipe the output of the first cell to the input of the second cell, as shown in listing 18.3.

Listing 18.3   Stacking two RNN cells

```
with tf.variable_scope("second_cell") as scope:       Defining a variable scope helps
    cell2 = make_cell(state_dim=10)                    prevent runtime errors due to
    outputs2, states2 = tf.nn.dynamic_rnn(cell2,       variable reuse.
                            outputs,
                            dtype=tf.float32)
```

Input to this cell will be the other cell's output.

What if you want four layers of RNNs? Figure 18.4 shows four RNN cells stacked.

The TensorFlow library provides a useful shortcut for stacking cells called `MultiRNNCell`. Listing 18.4 shows how to use this helper function to build arbitrarily large RNN cells.

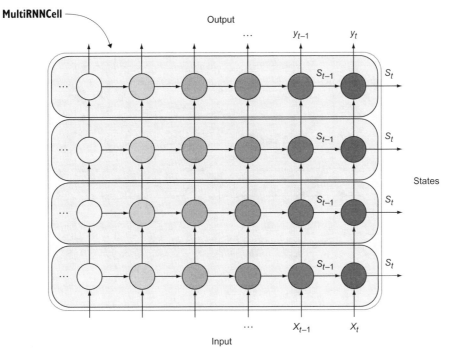

Figure 18.4 TensorFlow lets you stack as many RNN cells as you want.

Listing 18.4 Using `MultiRNNCell` to stack multiple cells

```
def make_multi_cell(state_dim, num_layers):
    cells = [make_cell(state_dim) for _ in range(num_layers)]
    return tf.contrib.rnn.MultiRNNCell(cells)

multi_cell = make_multi_cell(state_dim=10, num_layers=4)
outputs4, states4 = tf.nn.dynamic_rnn(multi_cell,
                                      input_placeholder,
                                      dtype=tf.float32)
```

> The for-loop syntax is the preferred way to construct a list of RNN cells.

So far, you've grown RNNs vertically by piping outputs of one cell to the inputs of another. In the seq2seq model, you'll want one RNN cell to process the input sentence and another RNN cell to process the output sentence. To communicate between the two cells, you can also connect RNNs horizontally by connecting states from cell to cell, as shown in figure 18.5.

You've stacked RNN cells vertically and connected them horizontally, vastly increasing the number of parameters in the network. Is what you've done utter blasphemy? Yes. You've built a monolithic architecture by composing RNNs every which way. But there's a method to this madness, because this insane neural network architecture is the backbone of the seq2seq model.

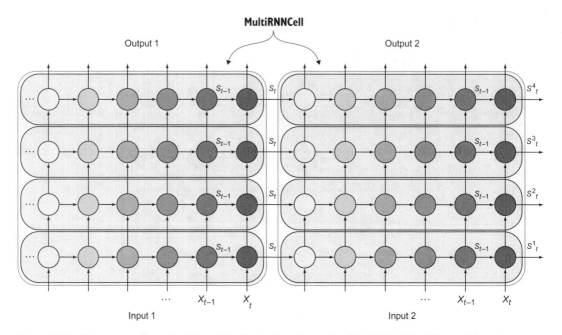

Figure 18.5   You can use the last states of the first cell as the next cell's initial state. This model can learn mapping from an input sequence to an output sequence.

As you can see in figure 18.5, the seq2seq model appears to have two input sequences and two output sequences. But only input 1 will be used for the input sentence, and only output 2 will be used for the output sentence.

You may be wondering what to do with the other two sequences. Strangely enough, the output 1 sequence is entirely unused by the seq2seq model. And as you'll see, the input 2 sequence is crafted with some output 2 data in a feedback loop.

Your training data for designing a chatbot will be pairs of input and output sentences, so you'll need to better understand how to embed words in a tensor. Section 18.3 covers how to do so in TensorFlow.

Exercise 18.3

Sentences may be represented by a sequence of characters or words, but can you think of other sequential representations of sentences?

Answer

Both phrases and grammatical information (verbs, nouns, and so forth) could be used. More frequently, real applications use *natural language processing* (NLP) lookups to standardize word forms, spellings, and meanings. One example of a library that does this translation is fastText from Facebook (https://github.com/facebookresearch/fastText).

18.3 *Vector representation of symbols*

Words and letters are symbols, and converting symbols to numeric values is easy in TensorFlow. Suppose that you have four words in your vocabulary: $word_0$: *the*; $word_1$: *fight*; $word_2$: *wind*; and $word_3$: *like*.

Now suppose that you want to find the embeddings for the sentence "Fight the wind." The symbol *fight* is located at index 1 of the lookup table, *the* at index 0, and *wind* at index 2. If you want to find the embedding of the word *fight*, you have to refer to its index, which is 1, and consult the lookup table at index 1 to identify the embedding value. In the first example, each word is associated with a number, as shown in figure 18.6.

Word	Number
the	17
fight	22
wind	35
like	51

Figure 18.6 A mapping from symbols to scalars

The following snippet shows how to define such a mapping between symbols and numeric values with TensorFlow code:

```
embeddings_0d = tf.constant([17, 22, 35, 51])
```

Or maybe the words are associated with vectors, as shown in figure 18.7. This method is often the preferred way of representing words. You can find a thorough tutorial on vector representation of words in the official TensorFlow docs: http://mng.bz/35M8.

Word	Vector
the	[1, 0, 0, 0]
fight	[0, 1, 0, 0]
wind	[0, 0, 1, 0]
like	[0, 0, 0, 1]

Figure 18.7 A mapping from symbols to vectors

You can implement the mapping between words and vectors in TensorFlow, as shown in listing 18.5.

Listing 18.5 Defining a lookup table of 4D vectors

```
embeddings_4d = tf.constant([[1, 0, 0, 0],
                             [0, 1, 0, 0],
                             [0, 0, 1, 0],
                             [0, 0, 0, 1]])
```

This may sound over the top, but you can represent a symbol by a tensor of any rank you want, not numbers (rank 0) or vectors (rank 1) alone. In figure 18.8, you're mapping symbols to tensors of rank 2.

Word	Tensor
the	[[1, 0], [0, 0]]
fight	[[0, 1], [0, 0]]
wind	[[0, 0], [1, 0]]
like	[[0, 0], [0, 1]]

Figure 18.8 A mapping from symbols to tensors

Listing 18.6 shows how to implement this mapping of words to tensors in TensorFlow.

Listing 18.6 Defining a lookup table of tensors

```
embeddings_2x2d = tf.constant([[[1, 0], [0, 0]],
                               [[0, 1], [0, 0]],
                               [[0, 0], [1, 0]],
                               [[0, 0], [0, 1]]])
```

The `embedding_lookup` function provided by TensorFlow is an optimized way to access embeddings by indices, as shown in listing 18.7.

Listing 18.7   Looking up the embeddings

Embeddings lookup corresponding to the words *fight*, *the*, and *wind*

```
ids = tf.constant([1, 0, 2])
lookup_0d = sess.run(tf.nn.embedding_lookup(embeddings_0d, ids))
print(lookup_0d)

lookup_4d = sess.run(tf.nn.embedding_lookup(embeddings_4d, ids))
print(lookup_4d)

lookup_2x2d = sess.run(tf.nn.embedding_lookup(embeddings_2x2d, ids))
print(lookup_2x2d)
```

In reality, the embedding matrix isn't something you ever have to hardcode. These listings are provided so that you can understand the ins and outs of the `embedding_lookup` function in TensorFlow, because you'll be using it heavily soon. The embedding lookup table will be learned automatically over time by training the neural network. You start by defining a random, normally distributed lookup table. Then TensorFlow's optimizer will adjust the matrix values to minimize the cost.

Exercise 18.4

Follow the official TensorFlow word2vec tutorial at www.tensorflow.org/tutorials/word2vec to get more familiar with embeddings.

Answer

This tutorial will teach you to visualize the embeddings by using TensorBoard and TensorFlow.

18.4   Putting it all together

The first step in using natural language input in a neural network is deciding on a mapping between symbols and integer indices. Two common ways to represent sentences are a sequence of *letters* and a sequence of *words*. Let's say, for simplicity, that you're dealing with sequences of letters, so you'll need to build a mapping between characters and integer indices.

> **NOTE**   The official code repository is available on the book's website (http://mng.bz/emeQ) and GitHub (http://mng.bz/pz8z). From there, you can get the code running without needing to copy and paste from the book.

Listing 18.8 shows how to build mappings between integers and characters. If you feed this function a list of strings, it'll produce two dictionaries, representing the mappings.

Listing 18.8 Extracting character vocab

```
def extract_character_vocab(data):
    special_symbols = ['<PAD>', '<UNK>', '<GO>',  '<EOS>']
    set_symbols = set([character for line in data for character in line])
    all_symbols = special_symbols + list(set_symbols)
    int_to_symbol = {word_i: word
                    for word_i, word in enumerate(all_symbols)}
    symbol_to_int = {word: word_i
                    for word_i, word in int_to_symbol.items()}

    return int_to_symbol, symbol_to_int

input_sentences = ['hello stranger', 'bye bye']        ◁───┐  List of input sentences
output_sentences = ['hiya', 'later alligator']   ◁───┐       for training

input_int_to_symbol, input_symbol_to_int =                  List of corresponding output
    extract_character_vocab(input_sentences)                sentences for training

output_int_to_symbol, output_symbol_to_int =
    extract_character_vocab(output_sentences
```

Next, you'll define all your hyperparameters and constants in listing 18.9. These elements usually are values that you can tune by hand through trial and error. Typically, greater values for the number of dimensions or layers result in a more complex model, which is rewarding if you have big data, fast processing power, and lots of time.

Listing 18.9 Defining hyperparameters

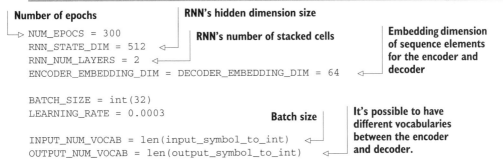

```
Number of epochs          RNN's hidden dimension size
                                                              Embedding dimension
 ╰─▷ NUM_EPOCS = 300            RNN's number of stacked cells  of sequence elements
     RNN_STATE_DIM = 512   ◁─┘                                for the encoder and
     RNN_NUM_LAYERS = 2  ◁────┘                               decoder
     ENCODER_EMBEDDING_DIM = DECODER_EMBEDDING_DIM = 64  ◁──┘

     BATCH_SIZE = int(32)
     LEARNING_RATE = 0.0003                              It's possible to have
                                     Batch size          different vocabularies
     INPUT_NUM_VOCAB = len(input_symbol_to_int)   ◁──┘   between the encoder
     OUTPUT_NUM_VOCAB = len(output_symbol_to_int) ◁──┘   and decoder.
```

Next, list all placeholders. As you can see in listing 18.10, the placeholders nicely organize the input and output sequences necessary to train the network. You'll have to track both the sequences and their lengths. For the decoder part, you'll also need to compute the maximum sequence length. The None value in the shape of these placeholders means that the tensor may take on an arbitrary size in that dimension. The batch size may vary in each run, for example. But for simplicity, you'll keep the batch size the same at all times.

Listing 18.10   Listing placeholders

```
# Encoder placeholders
encoder_input_seq = tf.placeholder(      ◁──┐ Sequence of integers for
    tf.int32,                                │ the encoder's input
    [None, None],                 ◁──┐
    name='encoder_input_seq'         │ Shape is batch-size
)                                    │ × sequence length.

encoder_seq_len = tf.placeholder(      ◁──── Lengths of sequences in a batch
    tf.int32,
    (None,),                    ◁──┐
    name='encoder_seq_len'         │ Shape is dynamic because the
)                                  │ length of a sequence can change.

# Decoder placeholders
decoder_output_seq = tf.placeholder(      ◁──┐ Sequence of integers for
    tf.int32,                                 │ the decoder's output
    [None, None],                 ◁──┐
    name='decoder_output_seq'        │ Shape is batch-size
)                                    │ × sequence length.

decoder_seq_len = tf.placeholder(      ◁──── Lengths of sequences in a batch
    tf.int32,
    (None,),                    ◁──┐
    name='decoder_seq_len'         │ Shape is dynamic because the
)                                  │ length of a sequence can change.

max_decoder_seq_len = tf.reduce_max(      ◁──┐
    decoder_seq_len,                         │ Maximum length of a decoder
    name='max_decoder_seq_len'               │ sequence in a batch
)
```

Let's define helper functions to construct RNN cells. These functions, shown in listing 18.11, should appear familiar to you from section 18.3.

Listing 18.11   Helper functions to build RNN cells

```
def make_cell(state_dim):
    lstm_initializer = tf.random_uniform_initializer(-0.1, 0.1)
    return tf.contrib.rnn.LSTMCell(state_dim, initializer=lstm_initializer)

def make_multi_cell(state_dim, num_layers):
    cells = [make_cell(state_dim) for _ in range(num_layers)]
    return tf.contrib.rnn.MultiRNNCell(cells)
```

You'll build the encoder and decoder RNN cells by using the helper functions you've defined. As a reminder, I've copied the seq2seq model for you in figure 18.9 to visualize the encoder and decoder RNNs.

Let's talk about the encoder cell part first, because in listing 18.12, you'll build the encoder cell. The produced states of the encoder RNN will be stored in a variable

Seq2seq model overview

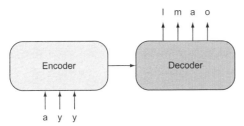

Figure 18.9 **The seq2seq model learns a transformation between an input sequence to an output sequence by using an encoder RNN and a decoder RNN.**

called encoder_state. RNNs also produce an output sequence, but you don't need access to that in a standard seq2seq model, so you can ignore or delete it.

It's also typical to convert letters or words in a vector representation, often called *embedding*. TensorFlow provides a handy function called embed_sequence that can help you embed the integer representation of symbols. Figure 18.10 shows how the encoder input accepts numeric values from a lookup table. You can see the encoder in action at the beginning of listing 18.13.

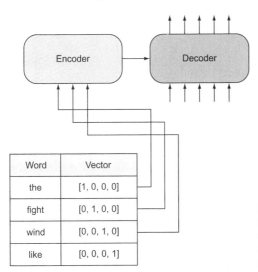

Encoder embedding matrix

Figure 18.10 **The RNNs accept only sequences of numeric values as input or output, so you'll convert your symbols to vectors. In this case, the symbols are words, such as *the*, *fight*, *wind*, and *like*. Their corresponding vectors are associated in the embedding matrix.**

Listing 18.12 **Encoder embedding and cell**

```
encoder_input_embedded = tf.contrib.layers.embed_sequence(
    encoder_input_seq,            ◁──── Input seq of numbers (row indices)
    INPUT_NUM_VOCAB,
    ENCODER_EMBEDDING_DIM         ◁──── Columns of embedding matrix
)
```

Rows of embedding matrix ▷ (points to INPUT_NUM_VOCAB)

```
# Encoder output
```

```
encoder_multi_cell = make_multi_cell(RNN_STATE_DIM, RNN_NUM_LAYERS)

encoder_output, encoder_state = tf.nn.dynamic_rnn(
    encoder_multi_cell,
    encoder_input_embedded,
    sequence_length=encoder_seq_len,
    dtype=tf.float32
)

del(encoder_output)          ◁──┐  You don't need to
                                 │  hold on to that value.
```

The decoder RNN's output is a sequence of numeric values representing a natural language sentence and a special symbol to represent that the sequence has ended. You'll label this end-of-sequence symbol as <EOS>. Figure 18.11 illustrates this process.

The input sequence to the decoder RNN will look similar to the decoder's output sequence, but instead of having the <EOS> (end of sequence) special symbol at the end of each sentence, it will have a <GO> special symbol at the front. That way, after the decoder reads its input from left to right, it starts with no extra information about the answer, making it a robust model.

Seq2seq model overview

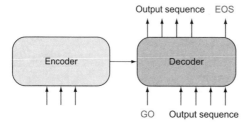

Figure 18.11 The decoder's input is prefixed with a special <GO> symbol, whereas the output is suffixed by a special <EOS> symbol.

Listing 18.13 shows how to perform these slicing and concatenating operations. The new sequence for the decoder's input will be called decoder_input_seq. You'll use TensorFlow's tf.concat operation to glue matrices together. In the listing, you define a go_prefixes matrix, which will be a column vector containing only the <GO> symbol.

Listing 18.13   Preparing input sequences to the decoder

Crops the matrix by ignoring the last column

Creates a column vector of <GO> symbols

```
decoder_raw_seq = decoder_output_seq[:, :-1]
go_prefixes = tf.fill([BATCH_SIZE, 1], output_symbol_to_int['<GO>'])   ◁──┘
decoder_input_seq = tf.concat([go_prefixes, decoder_raw_seq], 1)   ◁──
```

Concatenates the <GO> vector to the beginning of the cropped matrix

Now let's construct the decoder cell. As shown in listing 18.14, you'll first embed the decoder sequence of integers in a sequence of vectors, called `decoder_input_embedded`.

The embedded version of the input sequence will be fed to the decoder's RNN, so create the decoder RNN cell. One more thing: you'll need a layer to map the output of the decoder to a one-hot representation of the vocabulary, which you call `output_layer`. The process of setting up the decoder starts out being similar to the setup process for the encoder.

Listing 18.14 Decoder embedding and cell

```
decoder_embedding = tf.Variable(tf.random_uniform([OUTPUT_NUM_VOCAB,
                                                    DECODER_EMBEDDING_DIM]))
decoder_input_embedded = tf.nn.embedding_lookup(decoder_embedding,
                                                decoder_input_seq)

decoder_multi_cell = make_multi_cell(RNN_STATE_DIM, RNN_NUM_LAYERS)

output_layer_kernel_initializer =
    tf.truncated_normal_initializer(mean=0.0, stddev=0.1)
output_layer = Dense(
    OUTPUT_NUM_VOCAB,
    kernel_initializer = output_layer_kernel_initializer
)
```

Okay, here's where things get weird. You have two ways to retrieve the decoder's output: during training and during inference. The training decoder will be used only during training, whereas the inference decoder will be used for testing on never-before-seen data.

The reason for having two ways to obtain an output sequence is that during training, you have the ground-truth data available, so you can use information about the known output to help speed the learning process. But during inference, you have no ground-truth output labels, so you must resort to making inferences by using only the input sequence.

Listing 18.15 implements the training decoder. You'll feed `decoder_input_seq` into the decoder's input, using `TrainingHelper`. This helper op manages the input to the decoder RNN for you.

Listing 18.15 Decoder output (training)

```
with tf.variable_scope("decode"):

    training_helper = tf.contrib.seq2seq.TrainingHelper(
        inputs=decoder_input_embedded,
        sequence_length=decoder_seq_len,
        time_major=False
    )

    training_decoder = tf.contrib.seq2seq.BasicDecoder(
```

```
        decoder_multi_cell,
        training_helper,
        encoder_state,
        output_layer
    )

    training_decoder_output_seq, _, _ = tf.contrib.seq2seq.dynamic_decode(
        training_decoder,
        impute_finished=True,
        maximum_iterations=max_decoder_seq_len
    )
```

If you care to obtain output from the seq2seq model on test data, you no longer have access to decoder_input_seq. Why? Well, the decoder input sequence is derived from the decoder output sequence, which is available only with the training dataset.

Listing 18.16 implements the decoder output op for the inference case. Here again, you'll use a helper op to feed the decoder an input sequence.

Listing 18.16   Decoder output (inference)

```
with tf.variable_scope("decode", reuse=True):
    start_tokens = tf.tile(
        tf.constant([output_symbol_to_int['<GO>']],
                    dtype=tf.int32),
        [BATCH_SIZE],
        name='start_tokens')

    inference_helper = tf.contrib.seq2seq.GreedyEmbeddingHelper(
        embedding=decoder_embedding,                              Helper for
        start_tokens=start_tokens,                                the inference
        end_token=output_symbol_to_int['<EOS>']                   process
    )

    inference_decoder = tf.contrib.seq2seq.BasicDecoder(
        decoder_multi_cell,
        inference_helper,
        encoder_state,                                            Basic decoder
        output_layer
    )

    inference_decoder_output_seq, _, _ = tf.contrib.seq2seq.dynamic_decode(
        inference_decoder,                                        Performs dynamic
        impute_finished=True,                                     decoding by using
        maximum_iterations=max_decoder_seq_len                    the decoder
    )
```

Compute the cost by using TensorFlow's sequence_loss method. You'll need access to the inferred decoder output sequence and the ground-truth output sequence. Listing 18.17 defines the cost function in code.

Listing 18.17   The cost function

```
training_logits =
    tf.identity(training_decoder_output_seq.rnn_output, name='logits')
inference_logits =
    tf.identity(inference_decoder_output_seq.sample_id, name='predictions')
```
> **Renames the tensors for your convenience**

```
masks = tf.sequence_mask(
    decoder_seq_len,
    max_decoder_seq_len,
    dtype=tf.float32,
    name='masks'
)
```
> **Creates the weights for sequence_loss**

```
cost = tf.contrib.seq2seq.sequence_loss(
    training_logits,
    decoder_output_seq,
    masks
)
```
> **Uses TensorFlow's built-in sequence loss function**

Last, call an optimizer to minimize the cost. But you'll do one trick you might have never seen before. In deep networks like this one, you need to limit extreme gradient change to ensure that the gradient doesn't change too dramatically, using a technique called *gradient clipping*. Listing 18.18 shows you how.

Exercise 18.5

Try the seq2seq model without gradient clipping to experience the difference.

Answer

You'll notice that without gradient clipping, the network sometimes adjusts the gradients too much, causing numerical instabilities.

Listing 18.18   Calling an optimizer

```
optimizer = tf.train.AdamOptimizer(LEARNING_RATE)

gradients = optimizer.compute_gradients(cost)
capped_gradients = [(tf.clip_by_value(grad, -5., 5.), var)
                    for grad, var in gradients if grad is not None]
train_op = optimizer.apply_gradients(capped_gradients)
```
> **Gradient clipping**

That listing concludes the seq2seq model implementation. In general, the model is ready to be trained after you've set up the optimizer, as in listing 18.18. You can create a session and run `train_op` with batches of training data to learn the parameters of the model.

Oh, right—you need training data from someplace! How can you obtain thousands of pairs of input and output sentences? Fear not; section 18.5 covers that process.

18.5   *Gathering dialogue data*

The Cornell Movie-Dialogs Corpus (http://mng.bz/W28O) is a dataset of more than 220,000 conversations from more than 600 movies. You can download the zip file from the official web page.

> **WARNING**   Because there's a huge amount of data, you can expect the training algorithm to take a long time. If your TensorFlow library is configured to use only the CPU, it might take an entire day to train. On a GPU, training this network may take 30 minutes to an hour.

Here is an example of a small snippet of back-and-forth conversation between two people (A and B):

A: *They do not!*

B: *They do too!*

A: *Fine.*

Because the goal of the chatbot is to produce intelligent output for every possible input utterance, you'll structure your training data based on contingent pairs of conversation. In the example, the dialogue generates the following pairs of input and output sentences:

- "They do not!" → "They do too!"
- "They do too!" → "Fine."

For your convenience, we've already processed the data and made it available for you online. You can find it at http://mng.bz/OvlE. After completing the download, you can run listing 18.19, which uses the `load_sentences` helper function from the GitHub repo under the `Listing 18-eoc-assign.ipynb` Jupyter notebook.

Listing 18.19   Training the model

Loads the input sentences as a list of strings

Loads the corresponding output sentences the same way

```
input_sentences = load_sentences('data/words_input.txt')
output_sentences = load_sentences('data/words_output.txt')

input_seq = [
    [input_symbol_to_int.get(symbol, input_symbol_to_int['<UNK>'])
        for symbol in line]
    for line in input_sentences
]
output_seq = [
    [output_symbol_to_int.get(symbol, output_symbol_to_int['<UNK>'])
        for symbol in line] + [output_symbol_to_int['<EOS>']]
    for line in output_sentences
]
```

Loops through the letters

Loops through the lines of text

Appends the EOS symbol to the end of the output data

Loops through the lines

```
sess = tf.InteractiveSession()
sess.run(tf.global_variables_initializer())      It's a good idea to save
saver = tf.train.Saver()                ◀────────  the learned parameters.

for epoch in range(NUM_EPOCS + 1):  ◀──── Loops through the epochs      Loops by the
                                                                       number of
    for batch_idx in range(len(input_sentences) // BATCH_SIZE): ◀─┘   batches

──────▷     input_data, output_data = get_batches(input_sentences,
                                                  output_sentences,
Gets input and output pairs                       batch_idx)
for the current batch

            input_batch, input_lenghts = input_data[batch_idx]
            output_batch, output_lengths = output_data[batch_idx]

            _, cost_val = sess.run(  ◀───┐ Runs the optimizer
                [train_op, cost],        │ on the current batch
                feed_dict={
                    encoder_input_seq: input_batch,
                    encoder_seq_len: input_lengths,
                    decoder_output_seq: output_batch,
                    decoder_seq_len: output_lengths
                }
            )

saver.save(sess, 'model.ckpt')
sess.close()
```

Because you saved the model parameters to a file, you can easily load the model into another program and query the network for responses to new input. Run the `inference_logits` op to obtain the chatbot response.

Summary

- TensorFlow can build a seq2seq neural network, based on knowledge you've acquired from the book so far.
- You can embed natural language in TensorFlow.
- RNNs can be used as a building block for a more interesting model.
- After training the model on examples of dialogue from movie scripts, you can treat the algorithm like a chatbot, inferring natural language responses from natural input.

19

Utility landscape

This chapter covers

- Implementing a neural network for ranking
- Image embedding with VGG16
- Visualizing utility

Processing sensory input enables robots to adjust their model of the world around them. In the case of a vacuum-cleaner robot, the furniture in the room may change day to day, so the robot must be able to adapt to chaotic environments.

Let's say you own a futuristic housemaid robot, which comes with a few basic skills but also with the ability to learn new skills from human demonstrations. Maybe you'd like to teach it how to fold clothes.

Teaching a robot how to accomplish a new task is a tricky problem. Some immediate questions come to mind:

- Should the robot simply mimic a human's sequence of actions? Such a process is referred to as *imitation learning*.
- How do a robot's arms and joints match up to human poses? This dilemma is often referred to as the *correspondence problem*.

In this chapter, you're going to model a task from human demonstrations while avoiding both imitation learning and the correspondence problem. Lucky you!

Exercise 19.1

The goal of imitation learning is for the robot to reproduce the action sequences of the demonstrator. This goal sounds good on paper, but what are the limitations of such an approach?

Answer

Mimicking human actions is a naïve approach to learning from human demonstrations. Instead, the agent should identify the hidden goal behind a demonstration. When someone folds clothes, for example, the goal is to flatten and compress them, which are concepts independent of a human's hand motions. By understanding why the human is producing their action sequence, the agent is better able to generalize the skill it's being taught.

You'll achieve this task by studying a way to rank states of the world with a *utility function*, which takes a state and returns a real value representing its desirability. You'll not only steer clear of imitation as a measure of success, but also bypass the complications of mapping a robot's set of actions to that of a human (the correspondence problem).

In section 19.1, you'll learn how to implement a utility function over the states of the world obtained through videos of human demonstrations of a task. The learned utility function is a model of preferences.

You'll explore the task of teaching a robot how to fold articles of clothing. A wrinkled article of clothing is almost certainly in a configuration that has never been seen before. As shown in figure 19.1, the utility framework has no limitations on the size of the state space. The preference model is trained specifically on videos of people folding T-shirts in various ways.

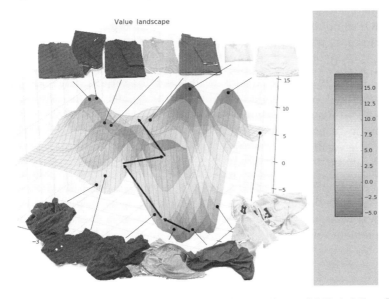

Value landscape

Figure 19.1 Wrinkled clothes in a less-favorable state than well-folded clothes. This diagram shows how you might score each state of a piece of cloth; higher scores represent a more-favorable state.

The utility function generalizes across states (wrinkled T-shirt in novel configuration versus folded T-shirt in familiar configuration) and reuses knowledge across clothes (T-shirt folding versus pants folding).

We can further illustrate the practical applications of a good utility function with the following argument: in real-world situations, not all visual observations are optimized toward learning a task. A teacher demonstrating a skill may perform irrelevant, incomplete, or even incorrect actions, yet humans are capable of ignoring the mistakes.

When a robot watches human demonstrations, you want it to understand the causal relationships that go into achieving a task. Your work enables the learning phase to be interactive, where the robot is actively skeptical of human behavior, to refine the training data.

To accomplish this goal, you first learn a utility function from a small number of videos to rank the preferences of various states. Then, when the robot is shown a new instance of a skill through human demonstration, it consults the utility function to verify that the expected utility increases over time. Finally, the robot interrupts the human demonstration to ask whether the action was essential for learning the skill.

19.1 *Preference model*

We assume that human preferences are derived from a *utilitarian* perspective, meaning that a number determines the rank of items. Suppose that you surveyed people to rank the fanciness of various foods (such as steak, hot dog, shrimp cocktail, and burger).

Ranking food by fanciness

Steak > Hotdog

Shrimp cocktail > Burger

Figure 19.2 shows a couple of possible rankings between pairs of food. As you might expect, steak is ranked higher than hot dog and shrimp cocktail higher than burger on the fanciness scale.

Figure 19.2 A possible set of pairwise rankings between objects. Specifically, you have four food items, and you want to rank them by fanciness, so you employ two pairwise ranking decisions: steak is a fancier meal than a hot dog, and shrimp cocktail is a fancier meal than a burger.

Fortunately for the individuals being surveyed, not every pair of items needs to be ranked. It might not be so obvious which is fancier between hotdog and burger or between steak and shrimp cocktail. There's a lot of room for disagreement.

If a state s_1 has a higher utility than another state s_2, the corresponding ranking is denoted $s_1 > s_2$, implying that the utility of s_1 is greater than the utility of s_2. Each video demonstration contains a sequence of n states $s_0, s_1, ..., s_n$, which offers $n(n-1)/2$ possible ordered pairs ranking constraints.

Let's implement our own neural network capable of ranking. Open a new source file, and use listing 19.1 to import the relevant libraries. You're about to create a neural network to learn a utility function based on pairs of preferences.

Listing 19.1 Importing relevant libraries

```
import tensorflow as tf
import numpy as np
import random
%matplotlib inline
import matplotlib.pyplot as plt
```

To learn a neural network for ranking states based on a utility score, you'll need training data. Let's create dummy data to begin with; you'll replace it with something more realistic later. Reproduce the 2D data in figure 19.3 by using listing 19.2.

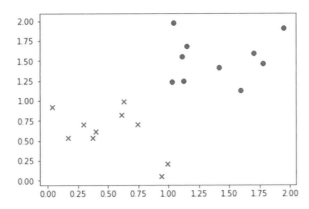

Figure 19.3 Example data that you'll work with. The circles represent more-favorable states, whereas the crosses represent less-favorable states. You have an equal number of circles and crosses because the data comes in pairs; each pair is a ranking, as in figure 19.2.

Listing 19.2 Listing 19.2 Generating dummy training data

```
n_features = 2          ◁─┐ You'll generate 2D data so that
                          │ you can visualize it easily.
def get_data():
    data_a = np.random.rand(10, n_features) + 1  ◁──┐ The set of points that
    data_b = np.random.rand(10, n_features)   ◁────── should yield higher utility

    plt.scatter(data_a[:, 0], data_a[:, 1], c='r', marker='x')
    plt.scatter(data_b[:, 0], data_b[:, 1], c='g', marker='o')
    plt.show()

    return data_a, data_b

data_a, data_b = get_data()
```

The set of points that should yield higher utility

The set of points that are less preferred

Next, you need to define hyperparameters. In this model, let's stay simple by keeping the architecture shallow. You'll create a network with one hidden layer. The corresponding hyperparameter that dictates the hidden layer's number of neurons is

```
n_hidden = 10
```

The ranking neural network will receive pairwise input, so you'll need to have two separate placeholders—one for each part of the pair. Moreover, you'll create a placeholder to hold the `dropout` parameter value. Continue by adding listing 19.3 to your script.

Listing 19.3 Placeholders

Input placeholder for preferred points

Input placeholder for nonpreferred points

```
with tf.name_scope("input"):
    x1 = tf.placeholder(tf.float32, [None, n_features], name="x1")
    x2 = tf.placeholder(tf.float32, [None, n_features], name="x2")
    dropout_keep_prob = tf.placeholder(tf.float32, name='dropout_prob')
```

The ranking neural network will contain only one hidden layer. In listing 19.4, you define the weights and biases, and then reuse these weights and biases on each of the two input placeholders.

Listing 19.4 Hidden layer

```
with tf.name_scope("hidden_layer"):
    with tf.name_scope("weights"):
        w1 = tf.Variable(tf.random_normal([n_features, n_hidden]), name="w1")
        tf.summary.histogram("w1", w1)
        b1 = tf.Variable(tf.random_normal([n_hidden]), name="b1")
        tf.summary.histogram("b1", b1)

    with tf.name_scope("output"):
        h1 = tf.nn.dropout(tf.nn.relu(tf.matmul(x1,w1) + b1),
    keep_prob=dropout_keep_prob)
        tf.summary.histogram("h1", h1)
        h2 = tf.nn.dropout(tf.nn.relu(tf.matmul(x2, w1) + b1),
    keep_prob=dropout_keep_prob)
        tf.summary.histogram("h2", h2)
```

The goal of the neural network is to calculate a score for the two inputs provided. In listing 19.5, you define the weights, biases, and fully connected architecture of the output layer of the network. You'll be left with two output vectors: s1 and s2, representing the scores for the pairwise input.

Listing 19.5 Output layer

```
with tf.name_scope("output_layer"):
    with tf.name_scope("weights"):
        w2 = tf.Variable(tf.random_normal([n_hidden, 1]), name="w2")
        tf.summary.histogram("w2", w2)
        b2 = tf.Variable(tf.random_normal([1]), name="b2")
        tf.summary.histogram("b2", b2)
```

Utility score of input x2

```
    with tf.name_scope("output"):
        s1 = tf.matmul(h1, w2) + b2      ←——— Utility score of input x1
        s2 = tf.matmul(h2, w2) + b2
```

You'll assume that when training the neural network, x1 should contain the less-favorable items. s1 should be scored lower than s2, so the difference between s1 and s2 should be negative. As listing 19.6 shows, the loss function tries to guarantee a negative difference by using the softmax cross-entropy loss. You'll define a train_op to minimize the loss function.

Listing 19.6 Loss and optimizer

```
with tf.name_scope("loss"):
    s12 = s1 - s2
    s12_flat = tf.reshape(s12, [-1])

    cross_entropy = tf.nn.softmax_cross_entropy_with_logits(
                        labels=tf.zeros_like(s12_flat),
                        logits=s12_flat + 1)

    loss = tf.reduce_mean(cross_entropy)
    tf.summary.scalar("loss", loss)

with tf.name_scope("train_op"):
    train_op = tf.train.AdamOptimizer(0.001).minimize(loss)
```

Now follow listing 19.7 to set up a TensorFlow session, which involves initializing all variables and preparing TensorBoard debugging by using a summary writer.

NOTE You used a summary writer at the end of chapter 2, when you were introduced to TensorBoard.

Listing 19.7 Preparing a session

```
sess = tf.InteractiveSession()
summary_op = tf.summary.merge_all()
writer = tf.summary.FileWriter("tb_files", sess.graph)
init = tf.global_variables_initializer()
sess.run(init)
```

You're ready to train the network! Run train_op on the dummy data you generated to learn the parameters of the model (listing 19.8).

Listing 19.8 Training the network

```
for epoch in range(0, 10000):
    loss_val, _ = sess.run([loss, train_op], feed_dict={x1:data_a, x2:data_b,
      dropout_keep_prob:0.5})
    if epoch % 100 == 0 :
        summary_result = sess.run(summary_op,
                        feed_dict={x1:data_a,
                            x2:data_b,
                            dropout_keep_prob:1})
        writer.add_summary(summary_result, epoch)
```

Training dropout keep_prob is 0.5.

Preferred points

Nonpreferred points

Testing dropout keep_prob should always be 1.

Finally, visualize the learned score function. As shown in listing 19.9, append 2D points to a list.

Listing 19.9   Preparing test data

```
grid_size = 10
data_test = []
for y in np.linspace(0., 1., num=grid_size):        Loops through the rows
    for x in np.linspace(0., 1., num=grid_size):     Loops through the columns
        data_test.append([x, y])
```

You'll run the s1 op on the test data to obtain the utility values of each state and visualize this data as shown in figure 19.4. Use listing 19.10 to generate the visualization.

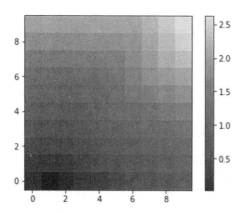

Figure 19.4   The landscape of scores learned by the ranking neural network

Listing 19.10   Visualizing results

```
def visualize_results(data_test):
    plt.figure()
    scores_test = sess.run(s1, feed_dict={x1:data_test, dropout_keep_prob:1})
    scores_img = np.reshape(scores_test, [grid_size, grid_size])
    plt.imshow(scores_img, origin='lower')
    plt.colorbar()

visualize_results(data_test)
```

Computes the utility of all the points

Reshapes the utilities to a matrix so you can visualize an image by using Matplotlib

19.2   *Image embedding*

In chapter 18, you summoned the hubris to feed a neural network some natural language sentences. You did so by converting words or letters in a sentence to numeric forms, such as vectors. Each symbol (whether it was a word or letter) was embedded in a vector by means of a lookup table.

Fortunately, images are already in numeric form, represented as a matrix of pixels. If the image is grayscale, perhaps the pixels take on scalar values indicating luminosity. For colored images, each pixel represents color intensities (usually three: red, green, and blue). Either way, an image can easily be represented by numeric data structures, such as a tensor, in TensorFlow.

Feeding a neural network a large image—say, of size 1280×720 (almost 1 million pixels)—increases the number of parameters and, consequently, escalates the risk of overfitting the model. The pixels in an image are highly redundant, so you can try to capture the essence of an image in a more-succinct representation. Figure 19.5 shows the clusters formed in a 2D embedding of images of clothes being folded.

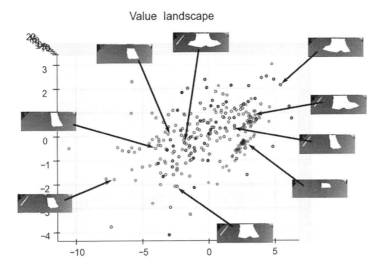

Value landscape

Figure 19.5 Images can be embedded in much lower dimensions, such as 2D (shown here). Notice that points representing similar states of a shirt occur in nearby clusters. Embedding images allows you to use the ranking neural network to learn a preference between the states of a piece of cloth.

You saw in chapters 11 and 12 how to use autoencoders to reduce the dimensionality of images. Another common way to accomplish low-dimensional embedding of images is to use the penultimate layer of a deep convolutional neural network image classifier. Let's explore the latter in more detail.

Because designing, implementing, and learning a deep image classifier isn't the primary focus of this chapter (see chapters 14 and 15 for CNNs), you'll instead use an off-the-shelf pretrained model. A common go-to image classifier that many computer-vision research papers cite is VGG16; you used it in chapter 15 to build a facial recognition system.

Many online implementations of VGG16 exist for TensorFlow. I recommend using the one by Davi Frossard (https://www.cs.toronto.edu/~frossard/post/vgg16). You can download the vgg16.py TensorFlow code and the vgg16_weights.npz pretrained model parameters from his website.

Figure 19.6 is a depiction of the VGG16 neural network from Frossard's page. As you see, it's a deep neural network, with many convolutional layers. The last few are the usual fully connected layers, and the output layer is a 1000D vector indicating the multiclass classification probabilities.

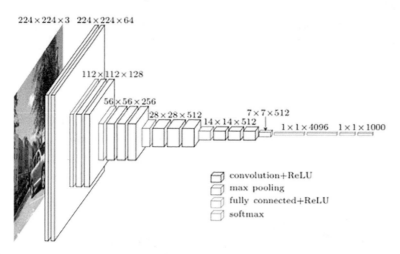

Figure 19.6   The VGG16 architecture is a deep convolutional neural network used for classifying images. This particular diagram is from https://www.cs.toronto.edu/~frossard/post/vgg16.

Learning how to navigate other people's code is an indispensable skill. First, make sure you have vgg16.py and vgg16_weights.npz downloaded, and test that you're able to run the code by using python vgg16.py my_image.png.

NOTE You may need to install SciPy and Pillow to get the VGG16 demo code to run without issues. You can download both via pip.

Let's start by adding TensorBoard integration to visualize what's going on in this code. In the main function, after creating a session variable `sess`, insert the following line of code:

```
my_writer = tf.summary.FileWriter('tb_files', sess.graph)
```

Now running the classifier once again (python vgg16.py my_image.png) will generate a directory called tb_files, to be used by TensorBoard. You can run TensorBoard to visualize the computation graph of the neural network. The following command runs TensorBoard:

```
$ tensorboard --logdir=tb_files
```

Open TensorBoard in your browser, and navigate to the Graphs tab to see the computation graph, shown in figure 19.7. At a glance, you can get an idea of the types of layers involved in the network; the last three layers are fully connected dense layers labeled fc1, fc2, and fc3.

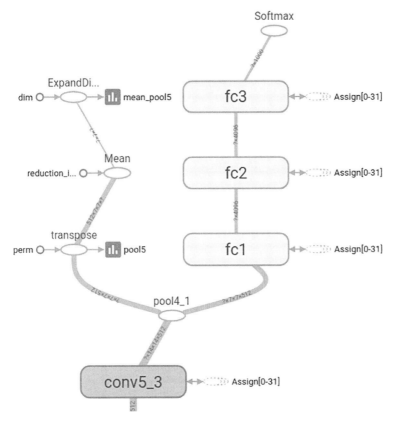

Figure 19.7   A small segment of the computation graph shown in TensorBoard for the VGG16 neural network. The topmost node is the softmax operator used for classification. The three fully connected layers are labeled fc1, fc2, and fc3.

19.3   *Ranking images*

You'll use the VGG16 code in section 19.2 to obtain a vector representation of an image. That way, you can rank two images efficiently in the ranking neural network you designed in section 12.1.

Consider videos of shirt-folding, as shown in figure 19.8. You'll process videos frame by frame to rank the states of the images. That way, in a novel situation, the algorithm can understand whether the goal of cloth-folding has been reached.

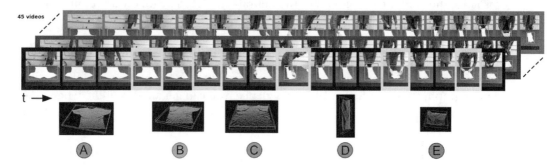

Figure 19.8   **Videos of folding a shirt reveal how the cloth changes form through time. You can extract the first state and the last state of the shirt as your training data to learn a utility function to rank states. Final states of a shirt in each video should be ranked with a higher utility than the one used for those shirts near the beginning of the video.**

First, download the cloth-folding dataset from http://mng.bz/eZsc. Extract the zip file. Keep note of where you extract file; you'll call that location DATASET_DIR in the code listings.

Open a new source file, and import the relevant libraries in Python (listing 19.11).

Listing 19.11   Importing libraries

```
import tensorflow as tf
import numpy as np
from vgg16 import vgg16
import glob, os
from scipy.misc import imread, imresize
```

For each video, you'll remember the first and last images. That way, you can train the ranking algorithm by assuming that the last image is of a higher preference than the first image. In other words, the last state of cloth-folding brings you to a higher-valued state than the first state of cloth-folding. Listing 19.12 shows how to load the data into memory.

Listing 19.12 Preparing the training data

```
DATASET_DIR = os.path.join(os.path.expanduser('~'), 'res',        Directory of
⟹ 'cloth_folding_rgb_vids')                                       downloaded files
NUM_VIDS = 45                      ⟵——— Number of videos to load
```

```
def get_img_pair(video_id):
    img_files = sorted(glob.glob(os.path.join(DATASET_DIR, video_id,
⟹ '*.png')))
    start_img = img_files[0]
    end_img = img_files[-1]
    pair = []
    for image_file in [start_img, end_img]:
        img_original = imread(image_file)
        img_resized = imresize(img_original, (224, 224))
        pair.append(img_resized)
    return tuple(pair)

start_imgs = []
end_imgs= []
for vid_id in range(1, NUM_VIDS + 1):
    start_img, end_img = get_img_pair(str(vid_id))
    start_imgs.append(start_img)
    end_imgs.append(end_img)
print('Images of starting state {}'.format(np.shape(start_imgs)))
print('Images of ending state {}'.format(np.shape(end_imgs)))
```

Gets the starting and ending image of a video

Running listing 19.12 results in the following output:

```
Images of starting state (45, 224, 224, 3)
Images of ending state (45, 224, 224, 3)
```

Use listing 19.13 to create an input placeholder for the image that you'll be embedding.

Listing 19.13 Placeholder

```
imgs_plc = tf.placeholder(tf.float32, [None, 224, 224, 3])
```

Copy over the ranking neural network code from listings 19.3–19.7; you'll reuse it to rank images. Then prepare the session in listing 19.14.

Listing 19.14 Preparing the session

```
sess = tf.InteractiveSession()
sess.run(tf.global_variables_initializer())
```

Next, you'll initialize the VGG16 model by calling the constructor. Doing so, as shown in listing 19.15, loads all the model parameters from disk to memory.

Listing 19.15   Loading the VGG16 model

```
print('Loading model...')
vgg = vgg16(imgs_plc, 'vgg16_weights.npz', sess)
print('Done loading!')
```

Next, prepare training and testing data for the ranking neural network. As shown in listing 19.16, you'll feed the VGG16 model your images; then you'll access a layer near the output (in this case, fc1) to obtain the image embedding.

In the end, you'll have a 4096D embedding of your images. Because you have a total of 45 videos, you'll split them, using some for training and some for testing:

- Train
  - Start-frame size: (33, 4096)
  - End-frame size: (33, 4096)
- Test
  - Start-frame size: (12, 4096)
  - End-frame size: (12, 4096)

Listing 19.16   Preparing data for ranking

```
start_imgs_embedded = sess.run(vgg.fc1, feed_dict={vgg.imgs: start_imgs})
end_imgs_embedded = sess.run(vgg.fc1, feed_dict={vgg.imgs: end_imgs})

idxs = np.random.choice(NUM_VIDS, NUM_VIDS, replace=False)
train_idxs = idxs[0:int(NUM_VIDS * 0.75)]
test_idxs = idxs[int(NUM_VIDS * 0.75):]

train_start_imgs = start_imgs_embedded[train_idxs]
train_end_imgs = end_imgs_embedded[train_idxs]
test_start_imgs = start_imgs_embedded[test_idxs]
test_end_imgs = end_imgs_embedded[test_idxs]

print('Train start imgs {}'.format(np.shape(train_start_imgs)))
print('Train end imgs {}'.format(np.shape(train_end_imgs)))
print('Test start imgs {}'.format(np.shape(test_start_imgs)))
print('Test end imgs {}'.format(np.shape(test_end_imgs)))
```

With your training data ready for ranking, run train_op an epoch number of times (listing 19.17). After training the network, run the model on the test data to evaluate your results.

Listing 19.17   Training the ranking network

```
train_y1 = np.expand_dims(np.zeros(np.shape(train_start_imgs)[0]), axis=1)
train_y2 = np.expand_dims(np.ones(np.shape(train_end_imgs)[0]), axis=1)
for epoch in range(100):
    for i in range(np.shape(train_start_imgs)[0]):
        _, cost_val = sess.run([train_op, loss],
```

```
                              feed_dict={x1: train_start_imgs[i:i+1,:],
                                         x2: train_end_imgs[i:i+1,:],
                                         dropout_keep_prob: 0.5})
        print('{}. {}'.format(epoch, cost_val))
        s1_val, s2_val = sess.run([s1, s2], feed_dict={x1: test_start_imgs,
                                                       x2: test_end_imgs,
                                                       dropout_keep_prob: 1})
        print('Accuracy: {}%'.format(100 * np.mean(s1_val < s2_val)))
```

Notice that accuracy approaches 100% over time. Your ranking model learns that the images that occur at the end of the video are more favorable than the images that occur near the beginning.

Out of curiosity, let's see the utility over time of a single video, frame by frame, as shown in figure 19.9. The code to reproduce figure 19.9 requires loading all the images in a video, as outlined in listing 19.18.

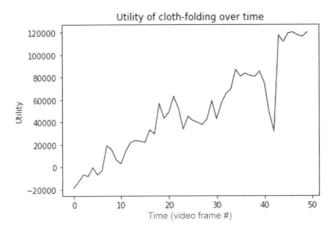

Figure 19.9 The utility increases over time, indicating that the goal is being accomplished. The utility of the cloth near the beginning of the video is near 0, but it increases dramatically—to 120,000 units—by the end.

Listing 19.18 Preparing image sequences from video

```
def get_img_seq(video_id):
    img_files = sorted(glob.glob(os.path.join(DATASET_DIR, video_id,
    ➥ '*.png')))
    imgs = []
    for image_file in img_files:
        img_original = imread(image_file)
        img_resized = imresize(img_original, (224, 224))
        imgs.append(img_resized)
    return imgs

imgs = get_img_seq('1')
```

You can use your VGG16 model to embed the images and then run the ranking network to compute the scores, as shown in listing 19.19.

Listing 19.19   Computing the utility of images

```
imgs_embedded = sess.run(vgg.fc1, feed_dict={vgg.imgs: imgs})
scores = sess.run([s1], feed_dict={x1: imgs_embedded,
                                   dropout_keep_prob: 1})
```

Visualize your results to reproduce figure 19.9 (listing 19.20).

Listing 19.20   Visualizing utility scores

```
from matplotlib import pyplot as plt
plt.figure()
plt.title('Utility of cloth-folding over time')
plt.xlabel('time (video frame #)')
plt.ylabel('Utility')
plt.plot(scores[-1])
```

Summary

- You can rank states by representing objects as vectors and learning a utility function over such vectors.
- Because images contain redundant data, you used the VGG16 neural network to reduce the dimensionality of your data so that you can use the ranking network with real-world images.
- You learned how to visualize the utility of images over time in a video to verify that the video demonstration increases the utility of the cloth.

What's next

You've finished your TensorFlow journey! The 19 chapters of this book approached machine learning from different angles, but together, they taught you the concepts required to master these skills:

- Formulating an arbitrary real-world problem into a machine-learning framework
- Understanding the basics of many machine-learning problems
- Using TensorFlow to solve these problems
- Visualizing a machine-learning algorithm and speaking the lingo
- Using real-world data and problems to show off what you learned

Because the concepts taught in this book are timeless, the code listings should be too. To ensure the most up-to-date library calls and syntax, I actively manage a GitHub repository at http://mng.bz/Yx5A. Please feel free to join the community there and file bugs or send me pull requests.

> **TIP** TensorFlow is in a state of rapid development, so more functionality will become available all the time.

appendix
Installation instructions

NOTE This book assumes that you'll be using Python 3 unless otherwise stated, as in chapter 7, where the associated dependency, BregmanToolkit, requires Python 2.7. Similarly, in chapter 19, the VGG16.py library requires Python 2.7. Code listings for Python 3 abide by TensorFlow v1.15, and the examples in chapter 7 and 19 use TensorFlow 1.14.0 because it's compatible with Python 2.7. The accompanying source code on GitHub will always be up to date with the latest version (http://mng.bz/GdKO). Additionally, **there is currently a major effort to port the examples in the book to TensorFlow 2.x, and that work is present in the tensorflow2 branch in the GitHub repo**. You can find updated listings there, so check back often.

You can install TensorFlow in a couple of ways. This appendix covers one installation method that works on all platforms, including Windows. If you're familiar with UNIX-based systems (such as Linux and macOS), feel free to use one of the installation approaches in the official documentation at http://mng.bz/zrAQ or, if you are experimenting with the TensorFlow2 code branch, at https://www.tensorflow.org/install. As Scott Penberthy, head of applied AI and TensorFlow at Google, states in the foreword for this book, the fields of AI and ML are evolving so fast that in the time it took to write this edition of the book, several versions of TensorFlow were released, including some in the 2.x series and a few in the 1.x series. The techniques for model building in all chapters will persist independently of any changes in the TensorFlow API or improvements in any individual model.

I also make note of required datasets in this appendix, as well as the libraries that are needed to run the code examples in the book. I've collected the datasets for you in a Dropbox location, so pay attention to where to place the input data, and the code examples will take care of the rest.

Finally, to give you a feel for some of the minor differences in TensorFlow 2 and TensorFlow 1, I'll walk you through a few changes you'll need to make to get the customer-call-center prediction example working with TensorFlow 2.

Without further ado, let's install TensorFlow by using a Docker container.

A.1 Installing the book's code with Docker

Docker is a system for packaging software dependencies to keep everyone's installation environment identical. This standardization helps limit inconsistencies among computers.

> **TIP** You can install TensorFlow in many ways other than using a Docker container. Visit the official documentation for more details on installing Tensor-Flow: https://www.tensorflow.org/install. Also check out the official Dockerfile for the book, which describes what software and libraries and data you will need to run through the book with ease (http://mng.bz/0ZA6).

A.1.1 Installing Docker in Windows

Docker works only on 64-bit Windows (7 or later) with virtualization enabled. Fortunately, most consumer laptops and desktops satisfy this requirement. To check whether your computer supports Docker, open Control Panel, click System and Security, and then click System. You see the details about your Windows machine, including processor and system type. If the system is 64-bit, you're almost good to go.

The next step is checking whether your processor can support virtualization. In Windows 8 or later, open the Task Manager (press Ctrl-Shift-Esc), and click the Performance tab. If Virtualization shows up as Enabled (figure A.1), you're all set. For Windows 7, you should use the Microsoft Hardware-Assisted Virtualization Detection Tool (http://mng.bz/cBlu).

A.1.2 Installing Docker in Linux

Now that you know whether your computer can support Docker, install Docker Toolbox, located at http://mng.bz/K580. Run the downloaded setup executable, and accept all the defaults by clicking Next in the dialog boxes. When the toolbox is installed, run the Docker Quickstart Terminal.

A.1.3 Installing Docker in macOS

Docker works in macOS 10.8 Mountain Lion or later. Install the Docker Toolbox from http://mng.bz/K580. After installation, open the Docker Quickstart Terminal from the Applications folder or Launchpad.

A.1.4 Using Docker

I've created a Dockerfile that builds an image containing Python 3.7 and 2.7, installs Jupyter and the required libraries with Python's `pip` installer, and then creates the necessary dependency libraries and folder structure to run the code examples from the book. You can use the `build_environment.sh` and `run_environment.sh` scripts,

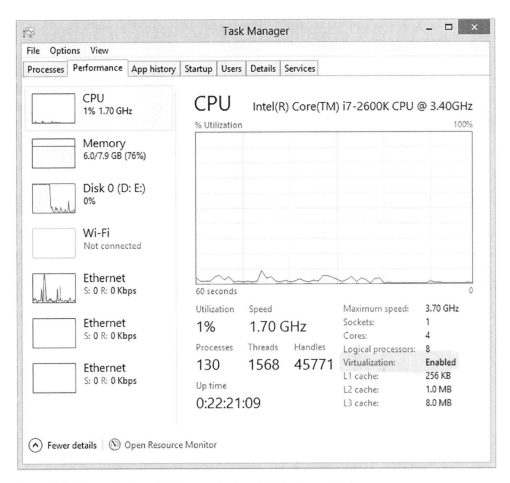

Figure A.1 Ensure that your 64-bit computer has virtualization enabled.

respectively, to build and run the Docker image if you want to build it from scratch. The Docker build also includes all necessary third-party libraries to run the notebooks and the input data needed to train models.

> **WARNING** Be careful—the container is ~40 GB when it's built, because machine learning is data- and compute-intensive. Prepare yourself for the space on your laptop and/or the time to build the Docker container.

Alternatively, you can run the following commands to execute the image I've created and pushed up to DockerHub for you:

```
docker pull chrismattmann/mltf2
./run_environment.sh
```

Think of DockerHub as being a home for prebuilt environment images. You can explore various containers that the community has published at https://hub.docker .com. The environment contains a Jupyter Notebooks hub that you can visit by entering **http://127.0.0.1:8888** in your browser. Remember to select the right kernel (Python3 or Python2), depending on the specific chapter examples.

A.2   *Getting the data and storing models*

You will generate lots of data when running the notebooks, particularly during the steps of the machine-learning process that involve building models. But to train and build those models, you also need data. I have created an Dropbox folder where you can download input data for use in training models from the book. Access the folder at http://mng.bz/9A41.

The following pointers tell you what data you need for which chapters and where to put it. Unless otherwise specified, data should be placed in the data/ folder. Note that as you are running the notebooks, the notebooks will generate TensorFlow models, writing them and checkpoint files to the models/ folder. A `download-data.sh` script is provided in the GitHub repo to automate downloading the data for each chapter and placing that data in the folder that the notebooks expect. Additionally, if you are using the Docker build, the container will automatically run the script and download the data for you.

- Chapter 4
  - data/311.csv
- Chapter 6
  - data/word2vec-nlp-tutorial/labeledTrainData.tsv
  - data/word2vec-nlp-tutorial/testData.tsv
  - data/aclImdb/test/neg
  - data/aclImdb/test/pos
- Chapter 7
  - data/audio_dataset
  - data/TalkingMachinesPodcast.wav
- Chapter 8
  - data/User Identification From Walking Activity
- Chapter 10
  - data/mobypos.txt
- Chapter 12
  - data/cifar-10-batches-py
  - data/MNIST_data (if you try the MNIST extra example)
- Chapter 14
  - data/cifar-10-batches-py

- Chapter 15
  - data/cifar-10-batches-py
  - data/vgg_face_dataset—The VGG-Face metadata, including celebrity names
  - data/vgg-face—The actual VGG-Face data
  - data/vgg_face_full_urls.csv—Metadata information about VGG-Face URLs
  - data/vgg_face_full.csv—Metadata information about all VGG-Face data
  - data/vgg-models/checkpoints-1e3x4-2e4-09202019—To run the VGG-Face Estimator additional example
- Chapter 16
  - data/international-airline-passengers.csv
- Chapter 17
  - data/LibriSpeech
  - libs/basic_units
  - libs/RNN-Tutorial
- Chapter 18
  - data/seq2seq
- Chapter 19
  - libs/vgg16/laska.png
  - data/cloth_folding_rgb_vids

A.3   *Necessary libraries*

Though the book has TensorFlow in its name, the book is as much about generalized machine learning and its theory, as well as the suites of frameworks that come in handy for dealing with machine learning. The requirements for running the notebooks are outlined in the following list; they can also be installed by hand or automatically installed by the requirements.txt and requirements-py2.txt files in Docker. Also, the GitHub repo has a `download-libs.sh` script that you can run by hand or let Docker run for you. This script grabs specialized libraries required by the notebooks that can't be installed via `pip`. You should `pip`-install the rest of them, using your favorite Python version. The examples in this book have been shown to work in Python 2.7 and Python 3.7. I didn't have time to test all of them, but I am happy to receive pull requests and code contributions for things I've missed.

- TensorFlow (book works in 1.13.1, 1.14.0, 1.15.0, and active development in tensorflow2 branch on version 2.2 and later)
- Jupyter
- Pandas (for dataframes and easy tabular data manipulation)
- NumPy and SciPy
- Matplotlib
- NLTK (for anything text or natural language processing such as sentiment analysis from chapter 6)

- TQDM (for progress bars)
- SK-learn (for various helper functions)
- BregmanToolkit (for audio examples in chapter 7)
- Tika
- Ystockquote
- Requests
- OpenCV
- Horovod (use 0.18.2 or 0.18.1 with the Maverick2 VGG-Face model)
- VGG16: vgg16.py, vgg16_weights.npz, imagenet_classes.py, and laska.png (works only with Python 2.7; place the software in libs/vgg16)
- PyDub (used in chapter 17 with LSTMs)
- Basic Units (chapter 17; place in libs/basic_units/ folder)
- RNN-Tutorial (used in chapter 17 to help implement and train the deep speech model)

A.4   *Converting the call-center example to TensorFlow2*

TensorFlow v2 (TFv2) has introduced a variety of breaking changes. Some of these changes affect workflow; others require adopting new paradigms. Eager execution, for example, requires a change from declarative to imperative programming. You no longer use TensorFlow's `Placeholders`; instead, you rely on different libraries to accomplish tasks that have been deprecated in v2. The examples, exercises, and listings in the text and on the GitHub repository page are actively being translated from TensorFlow to TensorFlow2 in the `tensorflow2` branch of the book's repository (http://mng.bz/Qmq1). I am using the following methodologies:

- I use the official TFv1-to-TFv2 migration guide wherever possible.
- When the migration guide does not suffice, I attempt to replicate results attained in the text and in the master branch of the repository.

If you're interested in how a more-elaborate project in TensorFlow would be migrated from v1 to v2, I encourage you to check out the migration guide linked at https://www.tensorflow.org/guide/migrate. Also, you can see whether the official upgrade script would work in your situation. The upgrade script is located at https://www.tensorflow.org/guide/upgrade. Note that I am not attempting to use the automatic upgrade script in this repository for two reasons:

- The conversion script automates as much as possible, but some syntactical and stylistic changes cannot be performed by the script.
- There is value in fully examining the changes from TF v1 to TF v2. Going through the process itself is a learning experience, and even I have (plenty of) things to learn!

Finally, there is a one-liner of code that allows full backward compatibility with TensorFlow 1 even while using the new TensorFlow v2 library. You place this line at the top of your code for it to behave like TFv1. Per the TensorFlow v1-to-v2 migration guide, insert the following at the beginning of the listings in the book to run unmodified TFv1 code in TFv2:

```
import tensorflow.compat.v1 as tf
tf.disable_v2_behavior()
```

That's it! Simple, right? You would also remove the `import tensorflow` declaration present in the listing and replace it with the preceding one, of course. In section A.4.1, I quickly revisit the call-center prediction example from chapter 4 to show you the crux of converting from TFv1 to TFv2.

A.4.1 The call-center example with TF2

Chapter 4 applies the machine-learning concept of regression by using real call-center data from New York City's 311 service to make a TensorFlow graph that learns the week 1–52 call-volume values and tries to predict them accurately. Because the data is continuous and not discrete, in machine learning, this problem is called *regression*, not *classification*. Figure A.2 shows the 311 call-center data.

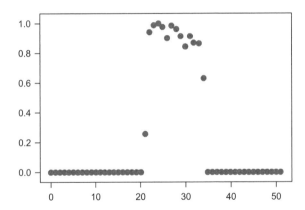

Figure A.2 A plot of call-frequency counts on the y-axis compared with weeks of the year (0–51) on the x-axis. Activity swells in the May 2014 timeframe and tapers in late August 2014.

In the original TFv1 portion of the code, I discussed in the chapter how to read the CSV New York City 311 data and parse it into a Python dictionary. Then I showed you how to convert that dictionary into X_train and Y_train variables representing the input week and call-volume data. The data is normalized by highest call volume in a 52-week span to achieve a 0-to-1 y-axis scale for Y_train. To construct the TensorFlow model graph, I use the nonlinear Gaussian model (bell-curve shape) to represent the volume. You built a TensorFlow graph training for 1,000 epochs to learn the variables mu and sigma that are input into the Gaussian model. After the model learns the parameters, I show you how to input them into a NumPy version of the model, print the learned curve, and visualize and plot error and accuracy. The original listing is shown in listing A.1 for your reference.

Listing A.1   Setting up and training the TensorFlow model for your Gaussian curve

```
learning_rate = 1.5        ◁———— Sets the learning rate for each epoch
training_epochs = 5000     ◁———┐
                               └ Trains for 5,000 epochs

X = tf.placeholder(tf.float32)    │ Sets up the input (X) and
Y = tf.placeholder(tf.float32)    │ the values to predict (Y)

def model(X, mu, sig):
    return tf.exp(tf.div(tf.negative(tf.pow(tf.subtract(X, mu), 2.)),
    ➡ tf.multiply(2., tf.pow(sig, 2.)))))

mu = tf.Variable(1., name="mu")    │ Defines the learned parameters
sig = tf.Variable(1., name="sig")  │ mu and sig for our model
y_model = model(X, mu, sig)    ◁———┐
                                   └ Creates the model based on the TensorFlow graph
cost = tf.square(Y-y_model)
train_op = tf.train.GradientDescentOptimizer(learning_rate).minimize(cost)

sess = tf.Session()                          │ Initializes the
init = tf.global_variables_initializer()     │ TensorFlow
sess.run(init)                               │ session

for epoch in range(training_epochs):
    for(x, y) in zip(X_train, nY_train):
        sess.run(train_op, feed_dict={X:x, Y:y})    ◁———┐
                                                        │ Performs the training and learns
                                                        │ the values for mu and sig
mu_val = sess.run(mu)
sig_val = sess.run(sig)
print(mu_val)      │ Prints the learned
print(sig_val)     │ values for mu and sig
sess.close()    ◁———┐
                    └ Closes the session
```

Defines the cost function as the L2 norm and sets up the training operation

What if I told you that the TensorFlow 2 version of chapter 4 reuses all the same data preparation, evaluation and plotting code, with only a slight change to listing A.1 (the model)? I hope you'd say that's believable because as I've shown you, much of the work in machine learning involves TensorFlow *and friends*—helper libraries to do data preparation such as Pandas or Tika, or data evaluation and exploratory analysis using Jupyter and Matplotlib. All that code stays the same and is independent of TensorFlow.

The TensorFlow code follows this pattern throughout the book:

1   Sets up the model hyperparameters. Sometimes, I show you how to derive hyperparameters by using the data you're using in the book. At other times, I point out that other people have spent lots of time and resources deriving them, so you should reuse them.

2   Trains the model on data that you (or someone else) gathered and that you've cleaned and prepared.

3   Evaluates the learned model and how well you did and it did,

Steps 1 and 2 are slight changes in the call-center prediction model. First, Tensor-Flow2 natively incorporates the Keras library for machine learning. This incorporation was done for reasons beyond the scope of this book, but one benefit is the use of Keras's optimizers. Instead of using optimizers from `tf.train` such as `tf.train` `.GradientDescentOptimizer`, you use `tf.keras.optimizers` such as `tf.keras` `.optimizers.SGD` instead.

Another change is that instead of running through each week in a `for` loop per epoch and injecting the week's individual call-volume value via `placeholders` in TFv1, in TFv2 the desire is to do away with them, so you use declarative programming. In other words, the `train` function should take the data stepwise or whole-cloth and train on it without per-step injection in the `feed_dict` parameter. There is no need to use data injection. You can use `tf.constant` instead, seed the constant with the 52 weeks of data per epoch, and eliminate a `for` loop in the process. Because TFv2 encourages declarative programming without injection, you can use Python's lambda inline functions to define your model, and use `cost` and `loss` as inline functions to construct the model declaratively.

That's all that changes, as you can see in listing A.2.

Listing A.2   TensorFlow 2 version of the call-center prediction model

Defines the hyperparameters (unchanged from TFv1 listing)

New hyperparameter for Keras optimizer accelerates gradients in the right direction.

Placeholders are gone, replaced by the constant whole-cloth week/call-volume data.

Defines the declarative Gaussian model using lambda functions and uses real X values, not placeholders

Learned parameters

Defines the cost by using real Y values

Uses Keras optimizers

Trains in a declarative way and removes the for loop with injection present in listing A.1

Obtains the learned parameters and prints the result

```
learning_rate = 1.5
training_epochs = 5000
momentum=0.979

X = tf.constant(X_train, dtype=tf.float32)
Y = tf.constant(nY_train, dtype=tf.float32)
mu = tf.Variable(1., name="mu")
sig = tf.Variable(1., name="sig")

model = lambda _X, _sig, _mu:
    tf.exp(tf.div(tf.negative(tf.pow(tf.subtract(tf.cast(_X,tf.float32), _mu),
    2.)), tf.multiply(2., tf.pow(_sig, 2.))))
y_model = lambda: model(X, mu, sig)
cost = lambda: tf.square(Y - y_model())

train_op = tf.keras.optimizers.SGD(learning_rate, momentum=momentum)
for epoch in tqdm(range(training_epochs)):
    train_op.minimize(cost, mu, sig)

mu_val = mu.value()
sig_val = sig.value()

print(mu_val.numpy())
print(sig_val.numpy())
```

You can examine the working TensorFlow v2 call-center listing at http://mng.bz/WqR1. The remainder of the notebook is the same as the TensorFlow v1 version, including steps that handle data reading and cleaning, preparation, and exploratory analysis.

Check back in the tensorflow2 branch of the code repository and follow along as I and others (possibly you!) convert the notebooks to TensorFlow v2. I'll be using the best practices defined in the migration guide and in this appendix. It's important to point out that most of the code and techniques will remain the same independent of the publication of this book and the future versions of TensorFlow that are released. Stick to the data preparation, cleaning, and hyperparameter selection and model-building techniques I've taught you. Regardless of the TensorFlow version, they'll last a lifetime!

index

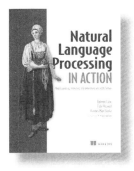

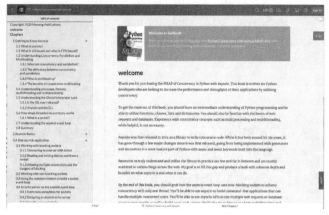

A new online reading experience

liveBook, our online reading platform, adds a new dimension to your Manning books, with features that make reading, learning, and sharing easier than ever. A liveBook version of your book is included FREE with every Manning book.

This next generation book platform is more than an online reader. It's packed with unique features to upgrade and enhance your learning experience.

- Add your own notes and bookmarks
- One-click code copy
- Learn from other readers in the discussion forum
- Audio recordings and interactive exercises
- Read all your purchased Manning content in any browser, anytime, anywhere

As an added bonus, you can search every Manning book and video in liveBook—even ones you don't yet own. Open any liveBook, and you'll be able to browse the content and read anything you like.*

Find out more at www.manning.com/livebook-program.

*Open reading is limited to 10 minutes per book daily

The Manning Early Access Program

Don't wait to start learning! In MEAP, the Manning Early Access Program, you can read books as they're being created and long before they're available in stores.

Here's how MEAP works.

- **Start now.** Buy a MEAP and you'll get all available chapters in PDF, ePub, Kindle, and liveBook formats.

- **Regular updates.** New chapters are released as soon as they're written. We'll let you know when fresh content is available.

- **Finish faster.** MEAP customers are the first to get final versions of all books! Pre-order the print book, and it'll ship as soon as it's off the press.

- **Contribute to the process.** The feedback you share with authors makes the end product better.

- **No risk.** You get a full refund or exchange if we ever have to cancel a MEAP.

Explore dozens of titles in MEAP at www.manning.com.

MANNING

Hands-on projects for learning your way

liveProjects are an exciting way to develop your skills that's just like learning on-the-job.

In a Manning liveProject you tackle a real-world IT challenge and work out your own solutions. To make sure you succeed, you'll get 90 days full and unlimited access to a hand-picked list of Manning book and video resources.

Here's how liveProject works:

- **Achievable milestones.** Each project is broken down into steps and sections so you can keep track of your progress.

- **Collaboration and advice.** Work with other liveProject participants through chat, working groups, and peer project reviews.

- **Compare your results.** See how your work shapes up against an expert implementation by the liveProject's creator.

- **Everything you need to succeed.** Datasets and carefully selected learning resources come bundled with every liveProject.

- **Build your portfolio.** All liveProjects teach skills that are in-demand from industry. When you're finished, you'll have the satisfaction that comes with success and a real project to add to your portfolio.

Explore dozens of data, development, and cloud engineering liveProjects at www.manning.com!